The Civil War in Appalachia

The Civil War in Appalachia

Collected Essays

Edited by Kenneth W. Noe
and Shannon H. Wilson

The University of Tennessee Press / Knoxville

Library of Congress Cataloging-in-Publication Data

The Civil War in Appalachia : collected essays / edited by Kenneth W. Noe and
Shannon H. Wilson.—1st ed.
     p. cm.
Includes bibliographical references and index.
ISBN 0-87049-971-8 (cloth : alk. paper)
1. United States—History—Civil War, 1861–1865—Social aspects.
2. Appalachian Region, Southern—History. 3. Mountain whites (Southern
States)—History—19th century. I. Noe, Kenneth W., 1957– . II. Wilson,
Shannon H.
E469.C583 1997
973.7'13'097509143—dc20   96-35632
                                               CIP

Contents

Illustrations

Figures

Maps

Tables

Acknowledgments

We are most grateful to the many people who helped make this volume a reality. Most obviously, we must thank our many contributors, who not only gave their time and effort, but also cheerfully tolerated our sometimes impossible demands and frantic telephone calls as deadlines approached. Meredith Morris-Babb and Jennifer M. Siler of the University of Tennessee Press were supportive of the project from the first, which helped immeasurably down the road. Mavis Bryant was a wonderful copyeditor. Durwood Dunn, Mark Franklin, William G. Piston, James Prichard, Philip Racine, Stuart Seely Sprague, Altina L. Waller, and several anonymous readers offered many useful suggestions which are incorporated here.

At Berea College, Dean Alfred Perkins assisted Wilson with a timely grant of sabbatical leave, and Gerald Roberts offered wise counsel and friendship. At West Georgia College, Steve Taylor, chair of history, helped Noe with a grant of released time. Vedat Gunay repeatedly saved the day with his ability to translate a plethora of software packages into the one Noe's Model-T computer could read, and Jason Gibson triumphed over Noe's inability to download e-mail.

Most important, we are grateful to our families: Nancy Noe, Jesse Noe, Janey Wilson, Erik Wilson, and Case Wilson.

Introduction:
Appalachia's Civil War
in Historical Perspective

Kenneth W. Noe and Shannon H. Wilson

During the Civil War Battle of Perryville, fought in Kentucky on October 8, 1862, participants experienced an unusual atmospheric phenomenon known as an "acoustic shadow." Due to a combination of wind and terrain, sound carried only a short distance, producing a "silent battle." As a result, many nearby soldiers, and even Federal commander Don Carlos Buell, never heard or took part in the fighting. The men who died at Perryville, in appalling numbers, thus seem to have done so in a vacuum.

In an analogous way, modern readers have experienced an intellectual acoustic shadow in regard to the Civil War as it occurred in an entire section of the South that began to rise just miles to the east of Perryville. This is the region now called the Southern Highlands, the Southern Mountains, or, most commonly, Appalachia. The area is here defined using John C. Campbell's familiar model of the mountain counties of Alabama, Georgia, Kentucky, Maryland, North Carolina, South Carolina, Tennessee, Virginia, and West Virginia (map 0.1).[1] During the Civil War, the Southern Mountains endured major campaigns and guerrilla bands, repression and emancipation, deprivation and desolation—in short, the southern war experience in microcosm. The valleys of Appalachia acted as a crucible where Unionism and sentiments in favor of secession mixed to create an explosive reaction.

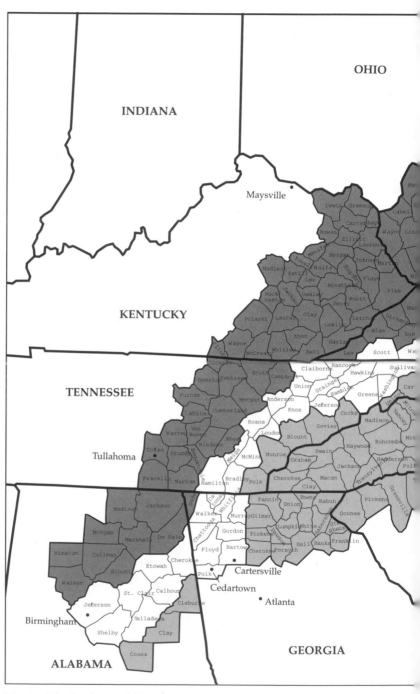

Map 0.1. The Southern Highland Region. From John C. Campbell,
The Southern Highlander and His Homeland (1921).

The Southern
Highland Region

- Blue Ridge Belt
- Greater Appalachian Valley
- Allegheny-Cumberland Belt

Nonetheless, standard histories of the war invariably give the region short shrift. They mention mountain Unionism during the secession crisis and again in the conflict's last year; reiterate Abraham Lincoln's passion to liberate East Tennessee from Confederate control; and discuss, almost out of geographical context, Appalachia's four major campaigns—Antietam, Chickamauga, Chattanooga, and the Hundred Days of the Atlanta Campaign. West Virginia secedes from the Old Dominion, to be heard from no more; Western Maryland dourly greets the Army of Northern Virginia in 1862, then fades into the background scenery; northern Alabama, East Tennessee, and North Georgia serve as brief venues for the major western armies; eastern Kentucky, western North Carolina, the most northwestern of South Carolina's districts, and southwestern Virginia hardly exist. As a result, to most general readers at least, the phrase "Appalachia's Civil War" appears almost an oxymoron, and most conclude that, beyond a very few battles, little of importance occurred there. Even modern residents of the region commonly believe that the Civil War, or at least "the important part," was something that largely took place elsewhere.[2]

Historians who are particularly interested in the Southern Mountains have done a better job of coming to grips with the region's war, but even here, the overall record is frankly spotty. To be sure, classic works such as Harry Caudill's *Night Comes to the Cumberlands* and Campbell's *The Southern Highlander and His Homeland* deal extensively, if perhaps melodramatically, with the Civil War and its aftermath. Most older works, however, do little more than perpetuate the two competing, yet paradoxically compatible, major stereotypes successfully propagated by outsiders during and immediately after the war, despite the presence of veterans and civilians who knew the truth to be otherwise.

One such stereotype, the "Myth of Unionist Appalachia," incorrectly depicted a region fervently and nobly loyal to the Union and to Lincoln, the latter after all essentially a mountaineer himself, according to certain northern-born missionary-fundraisers. Mountain people, according to this Unionist myth, were pseudonortherners, New England's "contemporary ancestors," who opposed slavery just as much as they did secession.

The other familiar image involving the legacy of the Civil War exaggerated the primitive savagery of celebrated feudists. In what one might call the "Myth of Savage Appalachia," the Civil War served to ignite passions that exploded after the war into the region's celebrated feuds. No legend exemplified this stereotype better than the archetypal mountain saga of the ex-Confederate Hatfields and the formerly Unionist McCoys, enemies since Fort Sumter but now reduced to bloodshed in a banal struggle over ownership of a hog.

Although widely dissimilar, these two interpretations surprisingly existed together in harmony for decades, as they proved to be "usable" history. Like Native Americans, mountaineers could be depicted as either "noble" or "savage," whenever it fit an author's purposes.[3]

In the late 1970s, a group of revisionist Appalachian scholars, largely natives of the region, arose to challenge the accepted wisdom on nearly every front. In the roughly twenty years that have followed, they have all but destroyed much of the mythology and slander that often passed for Appalachian history, much to the benefit of everyone interested in the region's past. These scholars' record on antebellum and Civil War Appalachia, however, frankly has been the weak link in their chain; clearly they have been less comfortable dealing with the conflict and its immediate legacy than with what came later. Indeed, with a few notable exceptions—particularly Gordon B. McKinney's *Southern Mountain Republicans* and John Alexander Williams's *West Virginia*—the revisionists have dealt with the war either gingerly or not at all. Largely social historians, the revisionists have been interested primarily in the results of the industrialization that, after 1880, served to create modern Appalachia and its ills. When the earlier period appeared at all, it usually functioned as a romanticized prologue to the machine age, as a "world we have lost" from which to survey the evils that followed. More commonly, the war has been ignored altogether. It has not been unusual to read an article containing data that jumped from the 1860 manuscript census to that of 1870, without any reference to, or apparent knowledge of, the conflagration of Civil War and Reconstruction that occurred in the interim.[4]

The problems with this sort of approach did finally become obvious to a few scholars in the late 1970s and early 1980s, however. In addition to the work of McKinney and Williams, Philip Shaw Paludan's *Victims* helped call attention to the mountain war, through a study of the Shelton Laurel Massacre in western North Carolina.[5] Then, midway through the eighties, a small avalanche of articles, books, and conference papers suddenly appeared, as historians working largely in isolation from one another began to ask similar questions and reach many of the same conclusions. The pace of this work shows no sign of slowing. Today it is hard to imagine a meeting of the Appalachian Studies Association without a panel devoted to the war; recently the topic has become respectable even at meetings of the major historical conferences.

In general, these newer scholars have eschewed the standard "American epic" approach, the "drums and trumpets" of battle narratives centered around commanders. Instead, reflecting a trend in scholarly Civil War historiography as a whole, they have embraced an approach to the war drawn from the so-called "new social history," examining such topics as the experiences and ideology of common soldiers, both individually and in groups; the Civil War home front; guerrillas and deserters; African Americans; and women. Much of the research is quantitative in emphasis. To take an example for the sake of argument, these historians generally are less concerned with what men such as the Southwest Virginians of the 54th Virginia Infantry did at Chickamauga than they are interested in why those men decided to support secession and the Confederacy in the first place; why some were still fighting and others had deserted by late 1863; how the war affected families, slaves, and dissenters back home; what happened in the area while the soldiers were elsewhere; and what occurred when the veterans came home to their mountains. What the mountaineers of the 54th Virginia did on Horseshoe Ridge is a story that deserved to be told and indeed has been told well. The other, unanswered questions are the concerns of this new historiography.[6]

The present volume marks the first attempt to bring together in one volume practitioners of the new Appalachian Civil War history. Taken as a whole, the essays provide the closest thing historians have to a comprehensive history of the Southern Mountains at war, as they follow southern mountaineers through the secession crisis, the mountain war, and into the postwar world. The editors realize, of course, that a collection of essays is no substitute for badly needed monographs. Much necessarily remains in the shadows. Rather, the editors' goals are more basic: to provide a useful introduction to the social history of Appalachia's Civil War, illustrating both the strengths and weaknesses of current historiography; to sum up where we have been and suggest where we need to go; and to point out the need to integrate Appalachian scholarship with studies of the Civil War and vice versa.

The secession crisis of 1860–61 serves as a useful starting point for examining both Appalachia's Civil War history and its current historiography. Appalachia on the eve of the Civil War clearly was not a Unionist monolith, as often has been claimed, but rather was a house divided. Indeed, there was such diversity in the behavior of the mountainous sections of the nine antebellum states of the Southern Mountain that one is reminded again how much "Appalachia" itself is a postwar concept. That model was supplied decades after the war by self-proclaimed "experts" from elsewhere; while it is a concept that we have come to regard as necessary, it is dangerously presentist. For example, the mountain districts of upcountry South Carolina—Greenville, Pickens, and Spartanburg—offered a striking contrast to the Myth of Unionist Appalachia. In those areas, support for South Carolina's secession was nearly universal.[7]

Closer to the other extreme, the Unionist-mountaineer stereotype sometimes veered toward accuracy. Unconditional Unionists were in the majority in many mountain districts, especially before Fort Sumter and Lincoln's subsequent call for volunteers. In western Maryland, Unionism was pervasive, an anchor that helped to keep the state in the Union. Similarly, in northwestern Virginia support for the Union was strong. Of that region's thirty-one delegates to the Virginia Secession Convention, only five voted for secession after Fort Sumter, and the subsequent secession ordinance lost among these delegates by a three-to-one majority. Shortly thereafter, northwestern Unionist leaders set in motion the process of creating a separate state. Unionism also was a majority doctrine in East Tennessee, where voters rejected secession two-to-one and leaders such as William G. Brownlow and Andrew Johnson longed to follow West Virginia's example. In November 1861, after Unionism metamorphosed from rhetoric to bridge burnings, the Confederacy clamped down on East Tennessee as it would have upon an occupied foe. Some Unionists were executed, others were imprisoned, and many more were forced into Confederate service, at least until they deserted. Indeed, in April 1862, the Confederate government officially designated East Tennessee enemy territory. Ultimately, the region supplied the Union with tens of thousands of troops.[8]

In those areas, Unionism was not universal, however. Minority support for secession and the Confederacy existed in both northwestern Virginia and East Tennessee. In the former, as Richard O. Curry has indicated, perhaps a third of the population, silenced and intimidated, supported the Confederacy. Both Altina L. Waller's history of the Hatfields and McCoys and Kenneth W. Noe's essay in this volume indicate that mountaineers favoring secession at least were numerous in this region and were determined enough to set in motion a vicious cycle of guerrilla warfare. In East Tennessee, meanwhile, 30 percent of East Tennesseans voted for secession; and, as W. Todd Groce relates in this volume, enough men supported the Confederacy to man eighty Confederate companies in 1861. Indeed, as Peter Wallenstein points out in his present essay, more East Tennesseans fought initially in gray than in blue, although large numbers switched sides later in the conflict.[9]

The Appalachian sections of Georgia and Alabama were more evenly divided, making it harder to gauge whether Unionism or support for the Confederacy was dominant. The governor of Georgia, ardent secessionist Joseph E. Brown, was a North Georgian who aimed his economic and racist appeals in part at the state's mountaineers, whose support for secession was the great question for Georgia Immediatists after Lincoln's election. Nonetheless, few North Georgia counties turned out a majority for secession, and the region's delegates to the subsequent state secession convention split nearly fifty-fifty, with Unionists particularly strong along the borders of North Carolina and Tennessee. Despite Brown's early solicitousness, many North Georgia mountaineers never became reconciled to the Confederacy, as Jonathan D. Sarris's present essay makes abundantly clear.

The story was the same, only writ larger, in northern Alabama. Nearly all of that region's delegates to the state secession convention supported Cooperation rather than immediate secession. While all but a few of the leaders ultimately agreed to support the new Confederacy, thousands of other mountaineers proclaimed their loyalty to the Union and in 1862 joined Federal regiments. Winston County, the "Free State of Winston," remains particularly famous for its opposition to the Confederacy, but Unionism was strong elsewhere along the southern bank of the Tennessee River. As in West Virginia and East Tennessee, many Unionist North Alabamians spoke openly of seceding from their state, and the pro-Union Peace Society eventually became active in the mountains of both Alabama and Georgia.[10]

Elsewhere, support for secession was the stronger sentiment, and only a conditional and ultimately doomed Unionism dominated debate between Lincoln's election and the firing on Fort Sumter. This Unionism was contingent upon the new administration's eschewing abolition and coercion of the new Confederacy. Unlike their northwestern brethren, half of Southwest Virginia's delegates to the Virginia Secession Convention were moderate "wait-a-bits," willing to secede as a last resort, while seven called for immediate secession and only four unconditionally supported the Union. After Fort Sumter, pro-Confederate sentiment swept the region.

Conditional Unionism likewise prevailed in western North Carolina. In February 1861, the region split on whether to call a convention, and only three of fifteen delegates selected supported immediate secession. Unionism began to wane soon after, however, and, following Fort Sumter, all fifteen counties sent representatives favoring secession to the state's May convention.

In both Southwest Virginia and western North Carolina, then, Unconditional Unionists made up only a minority in mid-April. Like members of minorities elsewhere, however, many would escape to other states—"going across the mountain" to Kentucky in the former case and to East Tennessee in the latter—to join opposing armies. Others would rise up in guerrilla warfare against their secessionist neighbors and against what was for them an oppressive government.[11]

Eastern Kentucky provides yet another case in point. The Bluegrass State as a whole stood perilously divided at every level and in every region, with a secessionist governor, a Unionist legislature, two rival state armies, and a frightened populace. Eastern Kentucky was no exception within the state; indeed, local divisions were so numerous and varied that no clear sectional pattern of Kentucky Unionism emerged at all, unlike the situations in other Appalachian states. Not surprisingly, the state's initial response was neutrality; Kentucky would stay out of the war unless one side violated its borders. Only as the summer of 1861 passed did Unionism begin to surpass support for secession. Neutrality ended finally in September, when Confederate units entered the state; but in retrospect it seems clear that invasion probably only hastened the inevitable.[12]

The question of why some white mountaineers supported the Union and others secession has intrigued observers since the time of the war itself, and it remains one of the major themes of current research. In the past, observers generally have pointed not to ideology, but rather to two factors related to class—economic standing and the relatively small number of slaveholders in the mountains. Writing from the West Virginia front in 1861, future U.S. President Rutherford B. Hayes, for example, argued that it was the aristocratic slaveholding elite and the poor, subservient, "good-for-nothing" highlanders who supported secession, while the sturdy, hardworking, antislavery middle class remained loyal to the Union.[13]

Economic class, including membership in the slaveholding elite, continues to dominate discussions of mountaineers' allegiances, but there is as yet no real agreement on the degree of its importance. Some scholars—Richard Nelson Current and William L. Barney, to point out two recent examples—have continued more or less to support the classic explanation enunciated by Hayes. Likewise, Paludan in *Victims* saw Unionism in western North Carolina as a result of "the hostility of the mountaineers toward slaveholders and a system that benefited them in no clear way, the growing isolation and poverty of the mountains, and . . . family and neighborhood traditions and personal antagonisms." Only elites and the region's poorest residents—the latter motivated by racism and the desire to please local leaders—sided with the Confederacy.[14] In this volume, Robert Tracy McKenzie and Peter Wallenstein similarly contend that East Tennessee Unionists as a rule tended to be non-elites and nonslaveholders from predominately white areas, where resentment of slaveholding elites was prevalent immediately before the war. There was a direct link between Union loyalty on the one hand and class on the other, they maintain. These authors strongly disagree with the traditional model, however, in identifying the poorest East Tennesseans as Unionists, not secessionists.[15]

Groce, in his complementary study of the region's Confederate leadership, agrees with the class-based explanation to a point, noting that secession leaders tended to be townsmen engaged in nonfarming professions, whereas

Unionist leaders were predominately farmers from outlying areas. However, he stresses additional factors as well, and indeed in some ways turns Hayes's explanation on its head. Confederate officers from East Tennessee were younger than the Unionist leaders, suggesting something of a generation gap. They tended to be prewar Democrats, less alienated from the Democratic state government in Nashville. And, finally, most lived along major transportation corridors, notably railroads. In Groce's words, Confederate leaders were not the scions of the slaveholding gentry, but rather were part of a "rising commercial-professional middle class . . . firmly integrated into the market economy" and particularly oriented toward southern markets. As in the North Georgia counties described here by Sarris, commercial ties between East Tennessee and the wider South had given rise to collateral ideological ties and a "southern" self-image.[16]

Altina Waller's recent monograph on the Hatfield-McCoy feud also focuses on the importance of commercial ties between Appalachia and the rest of the nation, but in a manner almost the opposite of Groce's approach. For the mass of mountaineers, Waller maintains, integration into the market economy was not an ideological magnet but rather a negative, repellent force that produced resistance and defense of older forms of autonomy. In North Georgia and western North Carolina, preserving the old ways meant rejecting commercial connections to the wider South, which in 1861 came to mean rejecting the Confederacy as well. In contrast, in the Tug River Valley, the most threatening outsiders wore blue; thus resistance meant embracing at least the trappings of the Confederacy.[17]

Martin Crawford, here and in other published essays on Ashe County, North Carolina, also cites class as one of many interrelated factors; yet, like Groce, he maintains that economic class cannot be considered "the key" to a region's dominant sentiment. Other factors, he contends, were equally important in Ashe County—notably, kin relationships with East Tennesseans, opportunity, religion, the stance taken by the leading family of a neighborhood, and a tradition of dissent that could be traced back to Loyalist sentiments during the American Revolution. Ultimately, Crawford's explanation is grounded as much in neighborhood as in class.[18]

Ralph Mann took this kin-neighborhood approach even further in a recently published article which informs his essay in this volume. In the Sandy Basin of Virginia, Mann maintains, class was hardly a factor at all, as both Unionists and secessionists came from very similar economic backgrounds. The answer, rather, is to be found in the kin and power relationships of family groups and local neighborhoods that originated before migration into the area and matured after settlement. Confederate family groups largely had migrated earlier from Virginia, whereas Unionists tended to be more recent arrivals from North Carolina. Both tended to settle with others of their group in distinctive neighborhoods. Religion also was a factor in the Sandy Basin, particularly as members of pacifist sects refused to serve the Confederacy.[19]

Clearly, no consensus has emerged about why mountaineers chose the Confederacy or the Union during the Civil War. Perhaps the answer ultimately will require rejecting the concept of the Appalachian monolith and accepting the idea that several different regions, each with a unique history, behaved in equally different ways, based upon one or more important local conditions.

At any rate, whatever side a mountaineer and his community, county, or region chose in 1861, and whatever the reasons, they soon had to confront both invasion from without and, especially, violence from within. Throughout the war, Confederate and Union armies periodically crisscrossed parts of Appalachia. In 1861, a Federal army commanded first by George B. McClellan and then by William S. Rosecrans crossed the Ohio River into northwestern Virginia; brushed aside weak resistance, including a Confederate force at Cheat Mountain commanded by Robert E. Lee; and by winter controlled the northern two-thirds of what was soon to become West Virginia, including all of northwestern Virginia and the northernmost counties of southwestern Virginia. There, however, they were largely stalemated for the duration of the conflict. Meanwhile, after Kentucky's neutrality ended in September, other Union forces entered eastern Kentucky from the west to confront Confederates approaching from Tennessee and Virginia. Fighting swirled particularly along the Virginia line and around the Cumberland Gap well into 1862. Further south, Don Carlos Buell's Army of the Ohio (later the Army of the Cumberland) crossed from Corinth, Mississippi, into North Alabama during the summer of 1862, in an ultimately unsuccessful attempt to seize Chattanooga.[20]

The Shenandoah Valley also was the scene of dramatic action in 1862. In May and June, Thomas J. "Stonewall" Jackson, the offspring of Northwest Virginia mountain gentry, outmarched and outfought three times as many Federals before heading eastward to join in the defense of Richmond. Later that summer, Robert E. Lee led his Army of Northern Virginia away from the Confederate capital and ultimately northward into western Maryland, in a bold but unsuccessful gamble to win the war. Along Antietam Creek, the two contending armies suffered almost twenty-three thousand casualties, making September 17, 1862, the single bloodiest day of the war.[21]

For many Federal armies east and west, the ultimate goal in 1862 remained

East Tennessee, as Lincoln ardently desired the liberation of that region's Unionists. That aim was not to be achieved, however, until late in the summer of 1863, as rugged terrain and formidable guerrilla opposition stymied the Union effort; what seemed possible on a map proved nearly impossible on muddy mountain roads. For East Tennessee's Unionists, deliverance only came when Rosecrans's Army of the Cumberland moved on Chattanooga from Middle Tennessee in his brilliant Tullahoma Campaign of June 1863; and Ambrose Burnside's Army of the Ohio occupied the Knoxville area the following September. Even then, continued control of East Tennessee was not a certainty, for Confederate armies moved quickly to crush the invaders and retake the region. The result was Chickamauga, fought in the North Georgia mountains just south of Chattanooga. Braxton Bragg's victorious Confederate Army of Tennessee failed to destroy Rosecrans at Chickamauga, but it did force the Federals back into Chattanooga, where they were besieged and nearly starved out. For internal, political reasons—he was the target of unhappy subordinates—Bragg dispatched part of his army under the command of rival James Longstreet to retake Knoxville. In the end, however, the Confederacy experienced only an Indian summer. Longstreet failed to crack Knoxville's defenses, and his presence in the region through the winter provided pro-Confederates only a brief respite. More important for the larger war effort, Federals, reinforced in part from North Alabama, fought their way out of Chattanooga at Lookout Mountain and Missionary Ridge and forced the Confederates back to Dalton, Georgia.[22]

Ulysses S. Grant, who had engineered the relief of Chattanooga, became the man of the hour and was called back to Washington to take command of all Union armies. Lincoln then handed Grant the task of winning the war before the November 1864 elections in the North. The celebrated plan that resulted included three major Appalachian components. Union forces were to march up the Valley of Virginia, while other Federals were to sweep simultaneously into Southwest Virginia and destroy the vital Virginia and Tennessee Railroad, depriving Lee's Army of Northern Virginia of desperately needed supplies produced in the mountains. Meanwhile, from Chattanooga, William Tecumseh Sherman was to lead three Union armies through northwestern Georgia to the rail and manufacturing center of Atlanta.

The Virginia and Tennessee (V&T) Railroad Raid, led by Gen. William Averell and Gen. George Crook in May 1864, only partially achieved the intended result, as damage to the railroad was soon repaired; not until December did a subsequent raid led by Gen. George Stoneman manage to close the V&T. Union forces fared even worse in the Valley of Virginia, where first Franz Sigel and then David Hunter faltered in the face of strong Confederate opposition, leaving Confederate Gen. Jubal Early free to raid as far north as Pennsylvania. Only with the appointment of Philip Sheridan in August did Grant present Early with a worthy foe. Sheridan decisively defeated Early at Cedar Creek in October and laid waste the valley as well.[23]

Sherman's successes were more spectacular. Leaving Chattanooga on May 1, Sherman by mid-July had maneuvered Gen. Joseph E. Johnston's Confederates back to Atlanta. As during the Chickamauga and Chattanooga campaigns, the mountainous terrain played a major role in dictating strategy. After briefly pursuing the Confederates back into North Georgia in September after the fall of Atlanta, Sherman turned away from Appalachia and moved eastward to the sea. By the time of Appomattox, northern Alabama, eastern Kentucky, western Maryland, East Tennessee, and most of the new state of West Virginia rested safely in Federal hands. Western North Carolina, the mountain districts of South Carolina, and Southwest Virginia remained largely under Confederate control; and North Georgia was cut almost in half.[24]

The major campaigns had devastating effects on local economies. In East Tennessee, for example, as McKenzie illustrates here, both Confederate and Union armies impressed with such zeal that the region was left in a "deplorable condition." However, major campaigns and battles were only one part of the mountaineers' Civil War, and to concentrate solely on the traditional war would be to miss the forest for a few big trees. For most mountain people, the major armies were but a passing plague, and war more often meant four years of deprivation, disruption, loneliness, loss, and terror. The region's women particularly bore the brunt of what we might call the domestic mountain war. Gordon McKinney recently pointed out, in an examination of western North Carolina, that mountain women faced a plethora of problems during wartime: separations, divided families, closed churches and schools, famine, pillaging, shortages of necessary goods, relocations, and an overall breakdown of kinship and community ties. Some still managed to surmount at least some of their trials, as John Inscoe's recent article on budding slaveowner Mary Bell indicates.[25]

Highlanders, whether men or women, certainly had less to fear from Longstreet or Sherman than they did from vengeful fellow mountaineers, armed bands of deserters and guerrillas, and occupation troops who adopted the guerrillas' tactics in an effort to defeat and destroy them. Indeed, guerrilla fighting was much more commonplace in the mountains than traditional warfare, and the most fearful enemy often was a former neighbor. From eastern Kentucky early in 1862, James A. Garfield captured the traditional view of this element of Appalachia's Civil War, writing that the conflict had turned the area "into a home of fiends, and converted this war into a black hole in which to murder any man that any soldier[,] from envy, lust, or revenge, hated."[26]

Guerrilla warfare in Appalachia has attracted a significant amount of scholarly attention recently, including the essays in this volume by Mann, Noe, and Sarris, and, to a certain extent, those of Crawford and Wallenstein. What once was called "the American Way of War" certainly was the predominant "Appalachian Way of War" between 1861 and 1865. Scholars who reject Garfield's analysis—and not all do—generally cite a combination of factors in explaining the prevalence of bushwhacking and the rising tide of violence: an escalating pattern of violence that marked the war everywhere; occupation by the enemy or, when local troops were friendly, a perceived need to enforce conformity; a need to defend one's family and community from local, readily identifiable enemies as well as threats emanating from beyond the mountains; and personal hatreds exacerbated by the nihilistic freedom of war.[27]

Mann examines the activities of a sometimes irregular Confederate unit of the Kentucky-Virginia borderland, Ezekiel Counts's company of Southwest Virginians. Counts was a contemporary of Devil Anse Hatfield, and indeed the two occasionally rode together. Mann's study, however, stresses the ideology of mountain partisans and the relationship between them and regular Confederate authorities. He demonstrates that, in the Big Sandy Basin, while the line between compliant volunteer service and irregular guerrilla activities seemed thin indeed to both the Union and the Confederate governments, guerrilla warfare made perfect sense to men whose primary fight was to defend home and community most expediently at any given moment. As far as Counts was concerned, his men—at least the willing ones—were good, loyal Confederates.

Likewise, many of the Confederates in Sarris's essay concluded that loyally serving their southern nation meant fighting a localized war at home rather than marching off with Johnston or Lee. Using the execution of three North Georgia Unionists as a springboard, he demonstrates how the so-called War Between the States became, in part of Georgia, a war between two counties, one self-consciously modern and pro-South, the other less developed and Unionist, with both fighting to preserve the stability of their local communities. Like Groce, Sarris links modernity to support for secession in the mountains.

Noe's essay focuses on how guerrilla warfare affected regular uniformed troops from outside Appalachia who were assigned to mountain posts. He maintains that Federal counterinsurgency in West Virginia deteriorated as early as late 1861 into a war of intimidation, burning, and killing unarmed civilians, as angry, frustrated Federal soldiers learned to mimic bush-whacker tactics. Thus, mountaineers were not alone responsible for turning parts of the Southern Highlands into the "black holes" Garfield described. Men like his own were equally responsible.

All of these essays demonstrate how the character of the mountain war helped shape negative perceptions of mountain people themselves, setting the stage for the negative "myth of Appalachian savagery." In many cases, because of wartime service in the mountains, both northerners and non-mountain southerners were ready to believe that mountaineers were deceitful, ignorant, primitive, savage, and violent brutes lacking in any Christian virtue, a sort of Euro-Indian who needed to be Christianized and Americanized. There was very little difference between portrayals of wartime bushwhackers and postwar feudists.[28]

Not all came away with such an impression, however. Indeed, as John C. Inscoe illustrates in his study of the popular postwar genre of prison narratives, the positive, if condescending, countermyth of mountain Unionism also had its wartime precursors. Perceptions could change quickly when Federal escapees suddenly needed help to reach friendly lines. The accounts that some later wrote offered an alternative to the savage image. Mountaineers appeared in these narratives as solid American Unionists, and African Americans and women particularly were praised for their courage and humanity. In the years that followed, as Shannon H. Wilson adds in the concluding essay, such an interpretation spread to the point where it evoked a great emotional response among many northerners and even a few southerners. Well into the twentieth century, in fact, at least two mountain institutions, Berea College and the significantly named Lincoln Memorial University, used Civil War imagery, albeit in crucially different ways, to elicit funding and extend hegemony across the Southern Mountains. In so doing, they helped perpetuate the twin myths of Appalachia.

Like Inscoe's escapees, a young escaped slave named John McCline also left the region with positive memories. As Jan Furman relates in her exploration of McCline's memoirs, the mountains of East Tennessee embodied freedom as well as beauty for the pre-teenager from Middle Tennessee. McCline's experiences in the mountains of East Tennessee and North Georgia remind us that the Civil War not only helped create a new view of mountaineers as a "strange . . . and peculiar people,"[29] whether savage or noble, but also set in motion the destruction of mountain slavery.

African-American mountaineers often have been ignored by scholars, although they comprised some 10 percent of the total mountain population. Their wartime activities particularly have remained elusive. Yet, as elsewhere in the South, mountain slaves and free blacks saw in the sectional crisis an opportunity to realize the Day of Jubilee, despite mountain masters' determination to preserve the institution. A few participated as guerrillas; more, like McCline, soldiered or toiled as laborers.[30]

Certainly the war had a dramatic effect on the postwar regional economy. Appalachia greeted the summer of 1865 not only bereft of the peculiar institution but traumatized, devastated, and impoverished as well. Yet to what degree can the war be blamed for the region's postwar economic ills? In the recent past, many historians, such as Durwood Dunn and Noe, have assigned primary blame for Appalachia's well-known economic woes to the destruction wrought by war. Dunn sees the war as a "watershed," after which the Cades Cove community of East Tennessee turned inward upon itself. Others, however, notably Paludan, Paul Salstrom, Waller, and in this volume McKenzie, have argued that, for most mountaineers, the economy had started to decline well before Fort Sumter, because of a worsening ratio of population, which was rising, to land ownership and per-capita farm production, which were declining. The result was a decline in self-sufficiency. The difficulties spawned by the conflict, they contend, only served to make an already precarious situation worse.[31]

As agriculture and living standards in Appalachia, for whatever reasons, declined, industrialization took hold. As noted above, most recent Appalachian scholarship has focused on the coming of the machine age and its destructive effects upon what scholars have viewed as a premodern society. The antebellum region thus has been depicted as a sort of Jeffersonian garden minus the Hamiltonian machines. More recently, however, historians such as Wilma Dunaway, Dunn, Inscoe, Noe, and Salstrom have stressed the importance of antebellum mountain industries, commerce, tourism, and, especially, interstate trade. Their cumulative verdict is that mountain modernization began before the Civil War, not after. If portions of Appalachia indeed had begun to modernize before the war, then what was the effect of the war upon that industrialization, particularly in light of Emory M. Thomas's contention that the war acted as a stimulus for industrial growth even in the Southern Mountains? Did the Civil War play any important role in the postwar industrialization that followed?

There is no agreement. Some see the war as a crucial step in the process of industrialization. Noe, for example, has maintained that, in Southwest Virginia, the war led to the expansion of antebellum, railroad-dependent industries, particularly the production of iron, lead, and salt, while simultaneously it drove a wedge of distrust between the minority who profited and the majority who suffered.[32]

Others see wartime mountain industrialization as less successful or important. In this collection, McKinney maintains that the Confederate Asheville Armory, one of the first attempts to build a modern mountain factory, was "a failure in virtually every conceivable way." Both managers and workers lacked the necessary skills, and, in addition, workers were unable to adjust to the discipline demanded by modern factory employment. Moreover, the introduction of African-American workers and resurgent Unionism among whites factionalized the work force. Finally, the armory suffered from inadequate transportation. Overall, McKinney asserts, the failure of the armory proved that Appalachian industrialization required "a tremendous commitment of capital and outside expertise. . . . industrialization could come to the mountain South in no other way."

In conclusion, we can say that the Civil War played a major role in shaping modern Appalachia, although the nature of that role is debated by the region's scholars. At the same time, the mountain South had an important effect upon the war as a whole. At the very least, the mountains offer a new perspective on what we know, and what we think we know, about the Civil War. Much more remains to be done, however. If this volume successfully illustrates the current state of Appalachian Civil War historiography, we still would be remiss not to note that it has exposed current gaps and weaknesses as well. One might, for example, point to geographical imbalance. As in other Appalachian subfields, most scholarship continues to focus on western North Carolina and East Tennessee. Even this collection, despite the editors' efforts, is skewed. Northern Alabama, western Maryland, and the Blue Ridge areas of South Carolina fail to appear at all as topics in this collection, as they do in Appalachian studies as a whole. As we pose new questions about the wartime mountain experience, we also must remember to ask some of the old questions about areas heretofore ignored.

As for those new questions, this collection, through its unavoidable but unfortunate gender and topical imbalances, at least reveals many possible directions. Much more needs to be done, for example, with mountain women during wartime. The same holds true for racial minorities, particularly African Americans and Native Americans. Considering the importance of modernization theory to Appalachian studies, wartime industrialization begs for more attention. There is room for new local community studies, as well as for comparative studies. One might ask, for example, how the experience of guerrilla war in a mountain community differed from that in a place such as Middle Tennessee or the Kentucky Bluegrass. Or how did an Appalachian community at war resemble one in Mississippi or Minnesota? How unique was the Appalachian experience? All in all, Appalachia's Civil War is a field ripe for further investigation. It should continue to be that for scholars who envision a role in helping to lift Appalachia's wartime acoustic shadow.

Notes

1. Definitions of Appalachia are numerous and contradictory, and none is likely to please everyone. While most authorities recognize the same core area, they differ widely on extent and boundaries. Here we have relied on perhaps the most familiar definition, that postulated by John C. Campbell in *The Southern Highlander and His Homeland* (New York: Russell Sage Foundation, 1921). Campbell took historical influences seriously into consideration in delineating the Southern Highlands. However, a survey of recent literature suggests that most practitioners of Appalachian history seem to have adopted a *de facto* definition that excludes Maryland, South Carolina, and sometimes Alabama. A promising start toward a new definition is found in John Alexander Williams, "Counting Yesterday's People: Using Aggregate Data to Address the Problem of Appalachia's Boundaries," *Journal of Appalachian Studies* 2 (Spring 1996): 3–27, which appeared too late for inclusion in this volume.

2. See, for example, the best modern history of the war, James M. McPherson's monumental *Battle Cry of Freedom: The Civil War Era* (New York: Oxford Univ. Press, 1988); Ken Burns's television series, *The Civil War* (videocassettes, 9 pts., approx. 60 min. each, Florentine Films in association with WETA-TV, Washington, D.C.,1990); or the scant attention to antebellum and Civil War Appalachia in two essays: Randolph B. Campbell, "Planters and Plain Folks: The Social Structure of the Antebellum South," in *Interpreting Southern History: Historiographical Essays in Honor of Sanford W. Higginbotham,* ed. John B. Boles and Evelyn Thomas Nolen, 48–77 (Baton Rouge: Louisiana State Univ. Press, 1988); and Joe Gray Taylor, "The White South from Secession to Redemption," in Boles and Nolen, *Interpreting Southern History,* 161–98.

3. John C. Campbell, *Southern Highlander*; Harry M. Caudill, *Night Comes to the Cumberlands: A Biography of a Depressed Area* (Boston: Atlantic Monthly, 1963). On the stereotypes, see, respectively, Kenneth W. Noe, "Toward the Myth of Unionist Appalachia, 1865–1883," *Journal of the Appalachian Studies Association* 6 (1994): 73–80; and Altina L. Waller, *Feud: Hatfields, McCoys, and Social Change in Appalachia, 1860–1900* (Chapel Hill: Univ. of North Carolina Press, 1988), esp. 1–18, 29–33. The best overall works on the Appalachian stereotype are Rodger Cunningham, *Apples on the Flood: The Southern Mountain Experience* (Knoxville: Univ. of Tennessee Press, 1987); Henry D. Shapiro, *Appalachia on Our Mind: The Southern Mountains and Mountaineers in the American Consciousness, 1870–1920* (Chapel Hill: Univ. of North Carolina Press, 1978); and Allen W. Batteau, *The Invention of Appalachia* (Tucson: Univ. of Arizona Press, 1990).

4. Gordon B. McKinney, *Southern Mountain Republicans, 1865–1900: Politics and the Appalachian Community* (Chapel Hill: Univ. of North Carolina Press, 1978); John Alexander Williams, *West Virginia: A Bicentennial History* (New York: Norton, 1976). One also should note Paul D. Escott's treatment of mountain Confederates in *After Secession: Jefferson Davis and the Failure of Confederate Nationalism* (Baton Rouge: Louisiana State Univ. Press, 1978).

5. Phillip Shaw Paludan, *Victims: A True Story of the Civil War* (Knoxville: Univ. of Tennessee Press, 1981).

6. Notable published examples that deal, at least in part, with the Civil War include Martin Crawford, "Confederate Volunteering and Enlistment in Ashe County, North Carolina," *Civil War History* 37 (Mar. 1991): 29–50; Martin Crawford, "Political Society in a Southern Mountain Community: Ashe County, North Carolina, 1850–1861," *Journal of Southern History* 55 (Aug. 1989): 373–90; Durwood Dunn, *Cades Cove: The Life and Death of a Southern Mountain Community, 1818–1937* (Knoxville: Univ. of Tennessee Press, 1988); John C. Inscoe, "Coping in Confederate Appalachia: Portrait of a Mountain Woman and Her Community at War," *North Carolina Historical Review* 69 (Oct. 1992): 388–413; John C. Inscoe, *Mountain Masters: Slavery and the Sectional Crisis in Western North Carolina* (Knoxville: Univ. of Tennessee Press, 1989); John C. Inscoe, "Mountain Unionism, Secession, and Regional Self-Image: The Contrasting Cases of Western North Carolina and East Tennessee," in *Looking South: Chapters in the Story of an American Region*, ed. Winfred B. Moore, Jr., and Joseph F. Tripp, 115–32 (Westport, Conn.: Greenwood, 1989); John C. Inscoe, "Thomas Clingman, Mountain Whiggery, and the Southern Cause," *Civil War History* 33 (Mar. 1987): 42–62; Ralph Mann, "Family Group, Family Migration, and the Civil War in the Sandy Basin of Virginia," *Appalachian Journal* 19 (Summer 1992): 374–93; Ralph Mann, "Guerrilla Warfare and Gender Roles: Sandy Basin, Virginia, as a Test Case," *Journal of the Appalachian Studies Association* 5 (1993): 59–66; Gordon B. McKinney, "Women's Role in Civil War Western North Carolina," *North Carolina Historical Review* 69 (Jan. 1992): 37–56; Kenneth W. Noe, "'Appalachia's' Civil War Genesis: Southwest Virginia as Depicted by Northern and European Writers, 1825–1865," *West Virginia History* 50 (1991): 91–108; Kenneth W. Noe, "Red String Scare: Civil War Southwest Virginia and the Heroes of America," *North Carolina Historical Review* 69 (July 1992): 301–22; Kenneth W. Noe, *Southwest Virginia's Railroad: Modernization and the Sectional Crisis* (Urbana: Univ. of Illinois Press, 1994); several essays in Mary Beth Pudup, Dwight Billings, and Altina L. Waller, eds., *Appalachia in the Making: The Mountain South in the Nineteenth Century* (Chapel Hill: Univ. of North Carolina Press, 1995); Jonathan D. Sarris, "Anatomy of an Atrocity: The Madden Branch Massacre and Guerrilla Warfare in North Georgia, 1861–1865," *Georgia Historical Quarterly* 77 (Winter 1993): 679–710; Peter Wallenstein, "South vs. South," *Now and Then: The Appalachian Magazine* 10 (Summer 1993): 5–7; Peter Wallenstein, "Which Side Are You On? The Social Origins of White Union Troops from Civil War Tennessee," *Journal of East Tennessee History* 63 (1991): 72–103; and Waller, *Feud,* esp. 2, 29–33.

The more general Civil War literature is, of course, vast. Joe Gray Taylor, "White South," 162–81, provides a good starting point, but covers only works published through 1982. A short list of the most essential works of the "new Civil War history" would include Stephen E. Ambrose, "Yeoman Discontent in the Confederacy," *Civil War History* 8 (Sept. 1962): 259–68; Stephen V. Ash, *Middle Tennessee Society Transformed, 1860–1870: War and Peace in the Upper South* (Baton Rouge: Louisiana State Univ. Press, 1988); William T. Auman and David Scarboro, "The Heroes of America in Civil War North Carolina," *North Carolina Historical Review* 58 (Oct. 1981): 327–63; Fred Arthur Bailey, *Class and Tennessee's Confederate Generation* (Chapel Hill: Univ. of North Carolina Press, 1987); Michael Barton, *Goodmen: The Character of Civil War Soldiers* (University Park, Pa.: Pennsylvania State Univ. Press, 1981); Marvin R. Cain, "A 'Face of Battle' Needed: An Assessment of Motives and Men in Civil War Historiography," *Civil War History* 28 (Mar. 1982): 5–27; Catherine Clinton and Nina Silber, eds., *Divided Houses: Gender and the Civil War* (New York: Oxford Univ. Press, 1992); Daniel W. Crofts, *Reluctant Confederates: Upper South Unionists in the Secession Crisis* (Chapel Hill: Univ. of North Carolina Press, 1989); Wayne K. Durrill, *War of Another Kind: A Southern Community in the Great Rebellion* (New York: Oxford Univ. Press, 1990); Escott, *After Secession*; Paul D. Escott, "'The Cry of the Sufferers': The Problem of Welfare in the Confederacy," *Civil War History* 23 (Sept. 1977): 228–40; Michael Fellman, *Inside War: The Guerrilla Conflict in Missouri during the American Civil War* (New York: Oxford Univ. Press, 1989); Joseph T. Glatthaar, *The March to the Sea and Beyond: Sherman's Troops in the Savannah and Carolina Campaigns* (New York: New York Univ. Press, 1985); Joseph T. Glatthaar, *Forged in Battle: The Civil War Alliance of Black Soldiers and White Officers* (New York: Free Press, 1990); Earl J. Hess, *Liberty, Virtue and Progress: Northerners and Their War for the Union* (New York: New York Univ. Press, 1988); Randall C. Jimerson, *The Private Civil War: Popular Thought during the Sectional Conflict* (Baton Rouge: Louisiana State Univ. Press, 1988); Gerald Linderman, *Embattled Courage: The Experience of Combat in the American Civil War* (New York: Free Press, 1987); Reid Mitchell, *Civil War Soldiers* (New York: Viking, 1988); Reid Mitchell, *The Vacant Chair: The Northern Soldier Leaves Home* (New York: Oxford Univ. Press, 1993); George Rable, *Civil Wars: Women and the Crisis of Southern Nationalism* (Urbana: Univ. of Illinois Press, 1989); Charles Royster, *The Destructive War: William Tecumseh Sherman, Stonewall Jackson, and the Americans* (New York: Vintage, 1991); and Maris Vinovskis, ed., *Toward a Social History of the American Civil War* (Cambridge: Cambridge Univ. Press, 1990). On the 54th Virginia Infantry, see George L. Sherwood and Jeffrey C. Weaver, *54th Virginia Infantry* (Lynchburg, Va.: H. E. Howard, 1993).

7. Lacy K. Ford, Jr., *Origins of Southern Radicalism: The South Carolina Upcountry, 1800–1860* (New York: Oxford Univ. Press, 1988), viii–ix, 369–70.

8. McPherson, *Battle Cry of Freedom*, 282–99; Crofts, *Reluctant Confederates*; Ralph A. Wooster, *The Secession Conventions of the South* (Princeton:

Princeton Univ. Press, 1962), 138–54, 173–89. On Maryland, see also Barbara J. Fields, *Slavery and Freedom on the Middle Ground: Maryland during the Nineteenth Century* (New Haven, Conn.: Yale Univ. Press, 1985). On West Virginia, see also Richard Orr Curry, *A House Divided: A Study of Statehood Politics and the Copperhead Movement in West Virginia* (Pittsburgh: Univ. of Pittsburgh Press, 1964), esp. 1–12, 28–68; Waller, *Feud,* 29–33; and John Alexander Williams, *West Virginia,* 57–86. On Tennessee, see also Charles Faulkner Bryan, Jr., "The Civil War in East Tennessee: A Social, Political, and Economic Study" (Ph.D. diss., Univ. of Tennessee, Knoxville, 1978), esp. 7–73; Mary Emily Robertson Campbell, *The Attitude of Tennesseans toward the Union, 1847–1861* (New York: Vantage, 1961); and Noel Fisher, "'The Leniency Shown Them Has Been Unavailing': The Confederate Occupation of East Tennessee," *Civil War History* 40 (Dec. 1994): 275–91.

9. Curry, *House Divided,* 1–14, 21–27, 46–54; Waller, *Feud,* 29–33.

10. Wooster, *Secession Conventions,* 62–66, 93–100. On Georgia, see T. Conn Bryan, *Confederate Georgia* (Athens: Univ. of Georgia Press, 1953), esp. 137–55; Sarris, "Anatomy of an Atrocity," 684–92; and Michael P. Johnson, *Toward a Patriarchal Republic: The Secession of Georgia* (Baton Rouge: Louisiana State Univ. Press, 1977), esp. 22–23, 49–52. Johnson's interpretation generally ignores regional differences. See Crofts's comments on Johnson's book in *Reluctant Confederates,* 379–81. Crofts maintains that Johnson's evidence suggests that Georgia Unionism was weaker and less class-based than Johnson himself implied.

The extent of Unionism in Alabama remains a controversial topic. For varying views, see Hugh Bailey, "Disloyalty in Early Confederate Alabama," *Journal of Southern History* 23 (1957): 522–28; William L. Barney, *The Secessionist Impulse: Alabama and Mississippi in 1860* (Princeton, N.J.: Princeton Univ. Press, 1974), esp. 238, 257–58, 270–74; William Stanley Hoole, *Alabama Tories: The First Alabama Cavalry, U.S.A., 1862–1865* (Tuscaloosa, Ala.: Confederate, 1960), 5–24; Durward Long, "Unanimity and Disloyalty in Secessionist Alabama," *Civil War History* 11 (Sept. 1965): 266–73; and J. Mills Thornton, III, *Politics and Power in a Slave Society: Alabama, 1800–1860* (Baton Rouge: Louisiana State Univ. Press, 1978), esp. 343–46, 409, 413, 437–39.

11. Noe, *Southwest Virginia's Railroad,* 93–108; Inscoe, *Mountain Masters,* 211–57; Inscoe, "Mountain Unionism," 115–32; Paludan, *Victims,* 56–83; Wooster, *Secession Conventions,* 190–203. The mountain Unionist song, "Going Across the Mountain," along with other war-related songs from the hills, can be found on Jim Taylor, *The Bright Sunny South,* PearlMaeMusic, audiocassette, 1994.

12. On Kentucky in general, see E. Merton Coulter, *The Civil War and Readjustment in Kentucky* (Chapel Hill: Univ. of North Carolina Press, 1926); Lowell H. Harrison, *The Civil War in Kentucky* (Lexington: Univ. Press of Kentucky, 1975), 1–16; William H. Townshend, *Lincoln and the Bluegrass: Slavery and Civil War in Kentucky* (Lexington: Univ. Press of Kentucky, 1955), 254–55, 279–82, 284–85; and Wooster, *Secession Conventions,* 207–22.

13. Rutherford B. Hayes, diary, Jan. 15, 1862, in *Diary and Letters of Rutherford Birchard Hayes, Nineteenth President of the United States,* ed. Charles Richard Williams (Columbus: Ohio Archaeological and Historical Society, 1922), 1:187. Curiously missing, of course, are the ideological arguments relating to the Union and emancipation stressed for other regions of the divided nation. For Appalachia, there is nothing comparable to, for example, James M. McPherson, *What They Fought For, 1861–1865* (Baton Rouge: Louisiana State Univ. Press, 1994).

14. Barney, *Secessionist Impulse,* 270–72, 274; Richard Nelson Current, *Lincoln's Loyalists: Union Soldiers from the Confederacy* (Boston: Northeastern Univ. Press, 1992), esp. 133–38; Paludan, *Victims,* 62, 64.

15. See also Wallenstein, "Which Side Are You On?"

16. For similar explanations, see Bryan, "Civil War in East Tennessee," 25–33; Inscoe, "Mountain Unionism," 121–35; and Noe, *Southwest Virginia's Railroad.*

17. Waller, *Feud,* 31.

18. See also Crawford, "Confederate Volunteering."

19. Mann, "Family Group," esp. 379–80. While conceding that secessionists were "superficially" wealthier, Mann adds that, in reality, the differences were quite small.

20. On West Virginia, in addition to works listed above, see George Ellis Moore, *A Banner in the Hills: West Virginia's Statehood* (New York: Appleton-Century-Crofts, 1963); and T. Harry Williams, *Hayes of the Twenty-Third: The Civil War Volunteer Officer* (New York: Alfred A. Knopf, 1965). On Kentucky, see also Frederick D. Williams, ed., *The Wild Life of the Army: Civil War Letters of James A. Garfield* (Lansing: Michigan State Univ. Press, 1964), 49–70; and Allan Peskin, *Garfield* (Kent, Ohio: Kent State Univ. Press, 1978), 101–31.

21. Military-oriented accounts of both the Valley Campaign and the Antietam Campaign are numerous. Two good places to start are Robert G. Tanner, *Stonewall in the Valley: Thomas J. "Stonewall" Jackson's Shenandoah Valley Campaign, Spring, 1862* (Garden City, N.Y.: Doubleday, 1976); and Stephen W. Sears, *A Landscape Turned Red: The Battle of Antietam* (New York: Ticknor and Fields, 1983).

22. The best discussion of the underappreciated Tullahoma Campaign is in Herman Hattaway and Archer Jones, *How the North Won: A Military History of the Civil War* (Urbana: Univ. of Illinois Press, 1983), 402–5, 446. On Chickamauga, see Peter Cozzens, *This Terrible Sound: The Battle of Chickamauga* (Urbana: Univ. of Illinois Press, 1992). On Chattanooga, see James Lee McDonough, *Chattanooga: A Death Grip on the Confederacy* (Knoxville: Univ. of Tennessee Press, 1984).

23. Two excellent studies of the fighting in Southwest Virginia are William Marvel, *Southwest Virginia in the Civil War: The Battles for Saltville* (Lynchburg, Va.: H. E. Howard, 1992); and Howard Rollins McManus, *The Battle of Cloyd's Mountain: The Virginia and Tennessee Railroad Raid, April 29–May 19, 1864* (Lynchburg, Va.: H. E. Howard, 1989). On the Valley of Virginia, see William C. Davis, *The Battle of New Market* (Garden City, N.Y.: Doubleday, 1975); Frank Vandiver, *Jubal's Raid: General Early's Famous Attack on Washington in 1864* (New York: McGraw-Hill, 1960); and Edward J. Stackpole, *Sheridan in the Shenandoah: Jubal Early's Nemesis* (Harrisburg, Pa.: Stackpole, 1961).

24. Albert Castel, *Decision in the West: The Atlanta Campaign of 1864* (Lawrence: Univ. Press of Kansas, 1992).

25. McKinney, "Women's Role"; Inscoe, "Coping in Confederate Appalachia."

26. Frederick D. Williams, *Wild Life of the Army*, 65–66.

27. In addition to the essays in this volume, see Bryan, "Civil War in East Tennessee," 86–95, 113, 119–59; Willene B. Clark, ed., *Valleys of the Shadow: The Memoir of Confederate Captain Reuben G. Clark* (Knoxville: Univ. of Tennessee Press, 1994); Dunn, *Cades Cove*; Mann, "Family Group," 374–75, 381–87; Mann, "Guerrilla Warfare"; James B. Martin, "Black Flag over the Bluegrass: Guerrilla Warfare in Kentucky, 1863–1865," *Register of the Kentucky Historical Society* 86 (Autumn 1986): 352–75; Noe, *Southwest Virginia's Railroad*, 115–20, 124–30, 133–38; Paludan, *Victims*; Sarris, "Anatomy of an Atrocity"; Waller, *Feud*, 31–33.

28. See also Noe, "'Appalachia's' Civil War Genesis," 102–5.

29. This frequently quoted phrase is from Will Wallace Harney, "A Strange Land and a Peculiar People," *Lippincott's Magazine* 12 (Oct. 1873): 429–38, one of the earliest attempts to deal with Appalachia's Civil War.

30. Far too little attention has been given to African-American mountaineers, but see Richard B. Drake, "Slavery and Antislavery in Appalachia," *Appalachian Heritage* 14 (Winter 1986): 25–33; Inscoe, *Mountain Masters*; Noe, *Southwest Virginia's Railroad*, 67–84; James B. Murphy, "Slavery and Freedom in Appalachia: Kentucky as a Demographic Case Study," *Register of the Kentucky Historical Society* 80 (Spring 1982): 151–69; Stuart Seely Sprague, "From Slavery to Freedom: African-Americans in Eastern Kentucky, 1860–1884," *Journal of the Appalachian Studies Association* 5 (1993): 67–74; Stuart Seely Sprague, "Slavery's Death Knell: Mourners and Revelers," *Filson Club History Quarterly* 65 (Oct. 1991): 441–73; Robert P. Stuckert, "Black Populations of the Southern Appalachian Mountains," *Phylon* 48 (June 1987): 141–51; and finally, Carter G. Woodson's classic "Slavery and Freedom in Appalachian America," *Journal of Negro History* 1 (Apr. 1916): 132–50.

31. Wilma A. Dunaway, *The First American Frontier: Transition to Capitalism in Southern Appalachia, 1700–1860* (Chapel Hill: Univ. of North Carolina Press, 1996); Dunn, *Cades Cove*, 123–41; Noe, *Southwest Virginia's Railroad*, esp. 138–43; Paludan, *Victims*, 8–30; Paul Salstrom, *Appalachia's Path to Dependency: Rethinking a Region's Economic History, 1730–1940* (Lexington: Univ. Press of Kentucky, 1994), xv, xvii, 1–22, 44; Waller, *Feud*, 32, 38–40.

32. Dunn, *Cades Cove*, 63–89; Inscoe, *Mountain Masters*; Noe, *Southwest Virginia's Railroad*, 31–66, 111–12; Salstrom, *Appalachia's Path to Dependency*; Emory M. Thomas, *The Confederacy as a Revolutionary Experience* (Englewood Cliffs, N.J.: Prentice-Hall, 1971), 87–99; Emory M. Thomas, *The Confederate Nation: 1861–1865* (New York: Harper and Row, 1979), 134–35, 206–14.

Chronology of Major Events
in Appalachia's Civil War

December 20, 1860	South Carolina secedes.
January 11, 1861	Alabama secedes.
January 19, 1861	Georgia secedes.
February 9, 1861	Jefferson Davis chosen provisional president of the Confederacy.
March 4, 1861	Abraham Lincoln inaugurated president of the United States.
April 12, 1861	Confederates fire on Fort Sumter, South Carolina.
April 17, 1861	Virginia Secession Convention approves a secession ordinance.
April 18, 1861	Virginia forces occupy Harper's Ferry, Virginia.
May 6, 1861	Tennessee Secession Convention endorses secession.
May 20, 1861	North Carolina secedes.
May 20–21, 1861	East Tennessee Unionist convention in Knoxville.
May 23, 1861	Virginia's official vote to secede.
May 26, 1861	Federals under the command of Gen. George B. McClellan cross Ohio River into West Virginia.
June 3, 1861	Battle of Philippi, West Virginia.
June 8, 1861	Tennessee votes to secede.

June 11, 1861	Battle of Rich Mountain, West Virginia.
June 11, 1861	Second Wheeling Convention convenes.
June 13, 1861	Unionists sweep congressional elections in Maryland.
June 17–20, 1861	Greeneville Convention of East Tennessee Unionists.
June 20, 1861	Francis Pierpont appointed governor of the "restored" government of Virginia.
September 3, 1861	Confederate forces enter Kentucky, ending that state's neutrality.
September 10–15, 1861	Battle of Carnifex Ferry, West Virginia.
September 11, 1861	Battle of Cheat Mountain, West Virginia.
October 24, 1861	West Virginia voters approve separate statehood.
November 1–3, 1861	Battle of Gauley Bridge, West Virginia.
November 8–9, 1861	Unionist bridge burnings in East Tennessee.
January 10, 1862	Battle of Middle Creek, Kentucky.
January 18, 1862	Battle of Logan's Cross Roads, Kentucky.
March 23, 1862	Battle of Kernstown, Virginia.
April 3, 1862	West Virginia's new constitution ratified.
April 12–August. 10, 1862	Gen. Don Carlos Buell's Chattanooga campaign across northern Alabama.
April 30–June 17, 1862	Gen. Thomas J. "Stonewall" Jackson's Shenandoah Valley campaign.
May 23, 1862	Battle of Lewisburg, West Virginia.
May 25, 1862	First Battle of Winchester, Virginia.
June 18, 1862	Union forces commanded by Gen. G. W. Morgan occupy Cumberland Gap.
Aug. 14, 1862	Gen. Edmund Kirby Smith's Confederates leave Knoxville for eastern Kentucky.
Aug. 28, 1862	Gen. Braxton Bragg's forces march from Chattanooga to begin invasion of Kentucky.
Aug. 30, 1862	Battle of Richmond, Kentucky.
September 6–16, 1862	Confederate Kanawha campaign, West Virginia.
September 6, 1862	Gen. Robert E. Lee's Army of Northern Virginia enters western Maryland.
September 14, 1862	Battle of South Mountain, Maryland.
September 15, 1862	Jackson seizes Harper's Ferry, Virginia.
September 17, 1862	Battle of Antietam, Maryland.
September 17, 1862	Union forces abandon Cumberland Gap.
September 22, 1862	Lincoln issues preliminary Emancipation Proclamation.
October 22, 1862	Confederate forces under Bragg reclaim Cumberland Gap.
January 1, 1863	Lincoln signs the Emancipation Proclamation.

Chronology

January 18, 1863	Shelton Laurel Massacre, North Carolina.
April 20–May 14, 1863	Gen. William E. Jones and Gen. John Imboden's joint raid into West Virginia.
June 20, 1863	West Virginia enters the Union.
July 13–25, 1863	Col. John T. Toland's Wytheville Raid, Virginia.
September 2, 1863	Gen. Ambrose Burnside's Federals occupy Knoxville.
September 8–10, 1863	Burnside reclaims Cumberland Gap.
September 9, 1863	Gen. William Rosecrans's Federals occupy Chattanooga, Tennessee.
September 19–20, 1863	Battle of Chickamauga, Tennessee.
November 1–8, 1863	Gen. William W. Averell's Lewisburg Raid, West Virginia.
November 6, 1863	Battle of Droop Mountain, West Virginia.
November 17, 1863	Gen. James A. Longstreet's siege of Knoxville begins.
November 24, 1863	Battle of Lookout Mountain, Tennessee.
November 25, 1863	Battle of Missionary Ridge, Tennessee.
November 29, 1863	Longstreet repulsed at Fort Sanders.
December 3, 1863	Longstreet ends siege of Knoxville and moves deeper into East Tennessee.
April 29–May 11, 1864	Gen. George Crook and Averell's joint raid against the Virginia and Tennessee Railroad.
May 7, 1864	Gen. William T. Sherman opens the Atlanta Campaign by moving on Dalton, Georgia.
May 9, 1864	Battle of Cloyd's Mountain, Virginia.
May 14–15, 1864	Battle of Resaca, Georgia.
May 15, 1864	Battle of New Market, Virginia.
May 24–27, 1864	Sherman attacks Gen. Joseph E. Johnston along the Dallas–New Hope Church line.
July 5, 1864	Jubal Early crosses the Potomac River into Maryland.
Aug. 6. 1864	Gen. Philip Sheridan assumes command of Federal forces in the Shenandoah Valley.
September 19, 1864	Third Battle of Winchester, Virginia.
September 22, 1864	Battle of Fisher's Hill, Virginia.
October 2, 1864	Battle of Saltville, Virginia.
October 19, 1864	Battle of Cedar Creek, Virginia.
December 1, 1864–January 1, 1865	Gen. George Stoneman's raid in Southwest Virginia.
March 23–April 26, 1865	Stoneman's Raid in North Carolina and Virginia.
April 9, 1865	Lee surrenders to Gen. U. S. Grant at Appomattox.
April 26, 1865	Final surrender agreement between Johnston and Sherman at Durham Station, North Carolina.

Abbreviations

BCA	Berea College Archives, Berea College, Berea, Kentucky
EC-GDAH	Executive Correspondence, Georgia Department of Archives and History, Atlanta
EJS Papers	Elihu J. Sutherland Papers, Wyllie Library, Clinch Valley College of the Univ. of Virginia, Wise, Virginia
LMU	Lincoln Memorial University, Harrogate, Tennessee
MAC-LCPL	Madeleine Anthony Collection, Lumpkin County Public Library, Dahlonega, Georgia
NA	National Archives and Records Administration, Washington, D.C.
OHS	Ohio Historical Society, Columbus, Ohio
OIR-BCA	Office of Information Records, Berea College Archives, Berea College, Berea, Kentucky
OR	U.S. Dept. of War, *The War of Rebellion: A Compilation of the Official Records of the Union and Confederate Armies* (Washington, D.C.: U.S. Government Printing Office, 1880–1901)
RG	Record Group
SAA	Southern Appalachian Archives, Berea College, Berea, Kentucky
UA-LMU	University Archives, Lincoln Memorial University, Harrogate, Tennessee

Abbreviations

USAMHI   U.S. Army Military History Institute, Carlisle Barracks, Pennsylvania

WVU   West Virginia and Regional History Archives, University Libraries, West Virginia University, Morgantown, West Virginia

1

"Helping to Save the Union": The Social Origins, Wartime Experiences, and Military Impact of White Union Troops from East Tennessee

Peter Wallenstein

Leaders of the United States and the Confederate States alike viewed the Appalachian South as a wild card in the Civil War. On the eve of the war, southern leaders feared three threats to their economic and political control; when the war began, those threats intensified. The most obvious danger came from the North, with its public opinion, its political power, and now its military might. Within the South, two groups—African American slaves and mountain whites—were ominous presences. As the war approached, and when it came, the possibility emerged that linkages might develop between external enemies and internal ones.[1] As the war continued, Confederate authorities did what they could to manage loyalty. Employing the proverbial carrot, they tried to retain the support of nonslaveholding whites by providing food and other supplies to the families of Confederate soldiers.[2] Resorting to the stick, certainly in East Tennessee, appeared vital as well.

On the other side, President Abraham Lincoln viewed East Tennessee as critical in the Union's effort to put down the Rebellion. He saw the area as vital from a strategic standpoint, and he saw it as a major potential recruiting ground for Union soldiers. As early as the summer of 1861, he directed General-in-Chief Winfield Scott to "send an officer to Tennessee to muster into the service of the United States 10,000 men." Some military leaders shared the president's view of the region's crucial importance for recruiting an army for the Union as well as for deploying it against the Confederacy. That fall George B. McClellan, commander of the Army of the Potomac, wrote Brig. Gen. Don Carlos Buell, urging that he focus on Knoxville, not Nashville: "It so happens that a large majority of the inhabitants of eastern Tennessee are in favor of the Union." Moving on Knoxville, rather than on some point farther west, would "enable the loyal citizens of Eastern Tennessee to rise, while you at the same time cut off the railway communication between Eastern Virginia and the Mississippi."[3]

Knoxville went untended. Efforts to reach the area, in hopes of liberating it, failed.[4] In early 1862, the president again urged military action to gain control of East Tennessee as a higher priority than Nashville—"first, because it cuts a great artery of the enemies' communication, which Nashville does not, and secondly because it is in the midst of loyal people, who would rally around it, while Nashville is not." He continued, "But my distress is that our friends in East Tennessee are being hanged and driven to despair, and even now I fear, are thinking of taking rebel arms for the sake of personal protection. In this we lose the most valuable stake we have in the South."[5]

Nashville fell to Union troops in February 1862, and although Nashville was not Knoxville, its capture facilitated a move to the east. Lincoln appointed Andrew Johnson military governor; Johnson's new responsibilities included supervising recruitment of Union troops in Tennessee. In the summer of 1862, Lincoln wrote to Johnson: "You are aware we have called for a big levy of new troops. If we can get a fair share of them in Tennessee I shall value it more highly than a like number most anywhere else," partly for symbolic significance and partly "because they will be at the very place that needs protection. Please do what you can, and do it quickly. Time is everything."[6]

Progress in liberating the area proved desperately slow. A full year later, responding to a petition from East Tennesseans, Lincoln wrote, "I do as much for East Tennessee as I would, or could, if my own home, and family were in Knoxville." But he pointed out "the difficulties of getting a Union army into that region, and of keeping it there. . . . Start by whatever route they may, their lines of supply are broken before they get half way."[7]

The Lincoln administration during the Civil War, like British leaders during the American Revolution, looked to a great mass of Tories to help put down rebellion. In Lincoln's case, his sense of the situation in East Tennessee proved to have been more or less on target. He was right about how much a Union victory depended upon large-scale recruitment of Union soldiers from the area. He was correct, too, in his sense that large numbers of men there would fight for the Union if they could. By the thousands, they did. By no means did all southern troops fight for the Confederacy. One simple way to suggest the significance of Union soldiers from the Appalachian South is to note that, whereas England failed to find its Tories and put down the American Revolution, Lincoln found his, and the Confederate independence movement was turned back.

Getting into a Federal unit was no easy matter for a resident of East Tennessee. Early in the war, Gov. Isham G. Harris vowed that no Tennessean would reach Union lines to become a Federal soldier, and he did what he could to see that none did. But the effort itself required substantial Confederate manpower. The governor wrote to Confederate Secretary of War Leroy P. Walker, "I am satisfied from the movements of the Union men of East Tennessee that more troops should be stationed in that division of the State. . . . The rebellious spirit of that people," in keeping Confederate leaders from assuming solidarity at home, prevented full focus on a foreign foe. Many men were needed to keep Tennesseans from fleeing to Kentucky to join Union units there.[8] Thousands of Union men did leave the state to join such units. After the Union army began to wrest control of East Tennessee, many more thousands formed units of their own.

A half-century after the Civil War, two spokesmen from East Tennessee—white veterans of the Union army—reflected upon the events of the 1860s and their parts in them. Roane County's Wiley M. Christian, who fought in the First Tennessee Infantry, remembered seeking "only to uphold and preserve the union of states and we did it." And Greene County's Charles Lafayette Broyles, who had fought in the First Tennessee Cavalry, asserted, "I am thankful that I am still alive and had the experience of helping to save the Union."[9]

Southern Unionism:
Historiographical Problem and Opportunity

The history of the Civil War continues to be told largely in terms of "North" versus "South." Such abbreviated notation suggests—indeed, exemplifies—the premise that all southern troops wore Confederate gray. Masking a more complex reality, it ignores the many tens of thousands of southerners, both white and black, who wore Union blue. To find white southern troops in blue, one might look to Tennessee, which had the largest white population in the Confederacy. In fact, the white population of East Tennessee—numbering 380,292—itself outranked that of Louisiana, Mississippi, Arkansas, South Carolina, or Florida.[10]

A minor theme in the historiography of the Civil War South recognizes the existence of widespread Unionist sentiment among white southerners. It recognizes that Union forces sought to recruit soldiers among nonelite white men, particularly in the upcountry, and that some pro-Union whites converted attitudes into actions.[11]

But how many? Sources exist that might permit quantitative answers to questions of class, region, and loyalty. This essay proposes, in a series of steps, to assess attitudes and behavior and to project absolute as well as proportional numbers for Tennessee Unionists. In the absence of such analysis, it is possible to exaggerate the magnitude of East Tennessee's contribution to the Union army, just as it often has proven easy to deny or overlook the presence of those Unionists or the critical role they played in defeating the separatists' bid for independence. Although East Tennesseans who wore gray outnumbered those who wore blue, so many men joined the ranks of the Union army that the area's net contribution to the Confederate forces turned out to be—from a Confederate perspective—disastrously small.

Two sources, combined, permit a tentative reconstruction of Tennesseans' attitudes and behavior regarding slavery, secession, and Civil War. One source, *Tennesseans in the Civil War,* lists the names and military units of Tennessee men who fought on each side.[12] The other, *The Tennessee Civil War Veterans Questionnaires,* offers the recollections of Civil War veterans long after the event. Employed in tandem, these sources suggest some conclusions about the connections among class, region, and political loyalty in the crucible of Civil War.

Only in recent years have the questionnaires become widely known and readily available.[13] More than sixteen hundred of them exist, some of them created in 1915 but the majority in 1922. Two directors of the Tennessee Department of Archives and History, Gustavus W. Dyer and John Trotwood Moore, distributed them to Civil War veterans living at the time in Tennessee.[14] The veterans' questionnaires permit a reconsideration of social relations among white southerners in the 1850s and 1860s.

A large majority of the completed questionnaires came from Confederate veterans, but some came from Union soldiers.[15] The compilers of *The Tennessee Civil War Veterans Questionnaires* classed as Union veterans 121 of the 1,648 total respondents. Of those 121 men, 14 are dropped here who had no connection with Tennessee except for having been engaged in battle there, or who settled there only after the war.[16] Because this essay focuses on white members of white units, it also excludes a former slave, Peter Collman. Several respondents, listed as Unionists, in fact fought first for the Confederacy and then for the Union.[17] All six are treated as Union soldiers. Thus, 106 men appear below in the quantitative work, and many of them appear in the narrative.

The Union respondents were not many, but their questionnaires supply a basis for suggestive findings. These men were old when they labored to fill out the questionnaires, but they offered rich detail in some cases, though apologies for forgetfulness in others.[18] Although most of the events they were describing had taken place half a century earlier, they recognized them as central to their personal lives as well as to the life of their country; and, prompted by an inquiry from the state capital, they did what they could to set their thoughts on paper. Although the interviews, such as they were, took place on paper, what resulted was oral history of a sort, oral history from a time before the tape recorder.[19]

Both groups of questionnaires, Union and Confederate, permit an analysis of attitudes, of perceptions of opportunity—or at least of reports of recollections of perceptions. And they offer a window through which to view a society in which men had to make ultimate decisions about war and political allegiance.

In *Class and Tennessee's Confederate Generation*, Fred Arthur Bailey has analyzed the Confederate questionnaires. On the basis of those questionnaires, Bailey concludes that tensions characterized prewar white society, that nonslaveholders resented the structure of opportunity that left most of southern society's advantages in the hands of slaveowning families. And he shows that the men of slaveholding families continued to benefit from their wealth and educational opportunities long after the end of the war and slavery.

An analysis of the Union veterans' responses can provide a complementary perspective on prewar southern white society. And a comparison of Union with Confederate veterans provides a basis for reconsidering the reasons for the choices that free men made when the war came. Some readers who find the approach in this essay generally plausible may wish to revise some definition, assumption, or method. To facilitate further work and any such revisions, the text and notes provide the data and specify the procedures used. Table 1.1 supplies data on the 106 free Federal troops from Tennessee whose stories are analyzed here.

Table 1.1

Data on 106 Union Troops from Tennessee

REGION[1] 1: SOUTHWEST TENNESSEE

7 counties. <70 percent white: none

REGION 2: NORTHWEST TENNESSEE

20 counties; >70 percent white: 21

Name	Birth Year[2]	Slaves[3]	Land[3]	County[4]	Form[5]	Class[6]	Rank	Unit
Adair, George W.	1846	0	130	Decatur	2	3	Private	Co. C, 2nd Tenn. Mounted Infantry
Adair, James David	1844	0	128	Decatur	2	3	Private	Co. C, 2nd Tenn. Mounted Infantry
Birdwell, Albert	[1838][7]	0	150	Carroll	1*	3	Private	Co. D, 7th Tenn. Cavalry
Blair, William C.	1825	3	200	Carroll	1	2	Private	Co. G, 2nd Tenn. Mounted Infantry
Brown, Samuel Arthur	1842	0	600	Carroll	1*	3		Co. F, 52nd INDIANA Infantry
Carter, John Wesley	1843	0	200	Carroll	1*	3	Private	Co. F, 7th Tenn. Cavalry
Giles, Cyrus G.	1841	0	120	Carroll	1*	3		52nd INDIANA Infantry
Hampton, Irvin	1845	0	100	Carroll	1*	3	Private	Co. G, 7th Tenn. Cavalry
Hickerson, William J.	[1843]	0	100	Perry	2	3	Private	Co. E, 2nd Tenn. Mounted Infantry
King, William Pressly	1849	4	160	Carroll	1*	2	Private	Co. I, 7th Tenn. Cavalry
Parker, William N.	1844	0	150	Gibson	1*	3	Private	Co. M, 6th Tenn. Cavalry
Pinkley, Richard K.	1841	0	[0]	Carroll	1*	[4]	Corporal	Co. B, 7th Tenn. Cavalry
Pitts, John***[8]	1841	3	600	Hardin	1*	2		46th OHIO
Robinson, William	[1832/39]	0	240	Carroll	1**	3		7th Tenn. Cavalry
Shelton, George W.	1843	18	250	Perry	2	2	Private	Co. G, 2nd Tenn. Mounted Infantry
Smith, James M	1842	0	400	Carroll	1*	3	Private	Co. E, 7th Tenn. Infantry
Starbuck, William	1848	0	1200	Perry	2	3	Private	Co. E, 2nd Tenn. Mounted Infantry
Taylor, James	1844	0	lot	Carroll	1*	3		7th Tenn. Cavalry
Tucker, John Wesley	1843	0	yes	Carroll	1*	[4]		7th Tenn. Cavalry
Wilkins, William Alexander	1842	1	309	Decatur	1*	2	Corporal	Co. C, 2nd Tenn. Mounted Infantry
Wolverton, James T.	1845	0	lot	[McNairy]	2	3	Corporal	Co. G, 6th Tenn. Cavalry

Continued on next page

Table 1.1—*Continued*

12 counties; <70 percent white): 5

Name	Birth Year	Slaves	Land	County	Form	Class	Rank	Unit
George, S[amuel]	[1836]	0	0	Wilson	1*	4	Private	Co. B, 5th Tenn. Cavalry
Holmes, [Albert F.]	1831	0	100	Sumner	2	3	Private	Co. A, 43rd MISSOURI
Ke[a]lton, James	1846	0	0	[Wilson]	2	4	[Private]	Co. E, 4th Tenn. Mounted Infantry
Norwood, George W.	1836	0	200	Giles	2	3	Corporal	Co. H, 13th INDIANA Cavalry
Wi[ks], Mar[t]	[1841]	0	0	Sumner	1**	4	Private	Co. D, 8th Mounted Infantry

REGION 4: EAST TENNESSEE
45 counties; >70 percent white): 80

Name	Birth Year	Slaves	Land	County	Form	Class	Rank	Unit
Acuff, Joel A.	1846	0	150	Grainger	1*	4	Sergeant	Co. A, 2nd Tenn. Cavalry
Allison, Uriah S.	1839	0	yes	Roane	2	[4]	Private	1st Tenn. Infantry
Anderson, John Fain	1844	1	yes	Sullivan	1*	2	[]	
Atchly, William D.	1841	0	140	Sevier	2	3	2nd Lt.	Co. B, 6th Tenn. Infantry
Babb, William Landon	1846	0	300	Greene	2	3	Private	Batt. E, 1st Tenn. Light Artillery
Bales, Harry	1824	0	100	[Jefferson]	2	3	Private	Co. M, 1st Tenn. Cavalry
Barnett, John Wilson	1847	0	160	[Bradley]	2	3	Private	Co. H, 12th Tenn. Cavalry
Bennett, Benjamin F.	1848	0	55	DeKalb	1*	4	Private	Co. L, 5th Tenn. Cavalry
Bewley, Josiah B.	1846	2	500	Greene	2	2	Private	Co. A, 2nd Tenn. Cavalry
Blankenship, Samuel S. M.	1842	0	300	Macon	2	3	Private	Co. I, 9th KENTUCKY
Boyer, Creed Fulton	1846	7	1000	Cocke	2	2	Private	Co. A, 3rd Tenn. Mounted Infantry
Bozarth, Joseph	1845	0	300	DeKalb	1*	3	Corporal	Co. C, 1st Tenn. Mounted Infantry
Brewer, William	1847	0	0	Marion	2	4	Private	Co. D, 7th Tenn. Cavalry
Brimer, John	1846	0	0	Jefferson	2	4	Private	Co. F, 9th Tenn. Cavalry

Continued on next page

Table 1.1—Continued

Name	Birth Year	Slaves	Land	County	Form	Class	Rank	Unit
Broyles, Charles LaFayette	1844	0	155	Greene	2	3	Sergeant	Co. M, 1st Tenn. Cavalry
Bullington, Marvin	1848	0	300	Putnam	1**	3		1st Tenn. Mounted Infantry
Chambers, Oliver P.	[1845]	0	lot	Cocke/Knox	2	3	Private	Co. A, 11th Tenn. Cavalry
Chatman, Isaac***	[1833/40]	0	0	Smith	1**	4	[]	
Christian, Wiley M.	1837	0	0	Roane	2	4	1st Lt.	Co. B, 1st Tenn. Infantry
Cogdell, Joseph	1842	0	0	Cocke	2	4	Sergeant	Tenn. Cavalry
Cox, Leroy Pate	1842	0	100	Macon	2	3	Private	Co. I, 9th KENTUCKY Infantry
Davis, Tom	[1842]	0	0	DeKalb	1*	4		4th Tenn. Mounted Infantry
DeLaVergne, George	1840	0	300	Cumberland	2	3	Lt. Col.	Co. I, 8th Tenn. Mounted Infantry
DEPEW, Robert E.[9]	1842	0	0	Sullivan	2	4	Private	Batt. E, 1st KENTUCKY Lt. Artillery
Dickson, William	[1822]	0	0	Cocke	2	4	Private	Co. I, 1st Tenn. Cavalry
Dinsmore, John W.	1847	0	0	Hawkins	2	4	Private	Co. F, 1st Tenn. Light Artillery
Dotson, Wiley	1847	[0]	120	Macon	2	3		Co. D, 8th Tenn. Mounted Infantry
Douglas, William A.	1843	15	400	Henderson	1*	2	Private	Co. A, 7th Tenn. Cavalry
Duncan, William Franklin	1842	0	100	Washington	2	3		Co. M, 4th Tenn. Cavalry
Finger, Marion	1844	0	0	Blount	2	4	Private	Co. H, 5th Tenn. Infantry
Fox, Gilbert	1845	0	222	Sevier	2	3	Private	Co. A, 9th Tenn. Cavalry
Frank, George W.	1845	0	0	[McMinn]	2	4	Private	Co. C, 11th Tenn. Cavalry
George, William [H.]	[1840]	0	800	DeKalb	1*	3	Corporal	5th Tenn. Cavalry
Gore, Overton	1847	0	300	Overton	1*	3		8th Tenn. Mounted Infantry
GRAY, John[9]	1848	0	150	Greene	2	3	Private	Co. H, 13th Tenn. Cavalry
Grindstaff, Isaac	[1842]	0	30	Carter	2	4	Private	Co. G, 13th Tenn. Cavalry
Hannah, Isaac Addison	1843	0	150	Blount	2	3	Private	Co. H, 2nd Tenn. Cavalry
H[arra]d, William	1844	0	80	McMinn	2	3	Private	Co. B, 7th Tenn. Mounted Infantry
Hawkins, Carry N.	1846	0	75	Jackson	2	4	Private	Co. B, 8th Tenn. Infantry
Headrick, John W.	1844	0	lot	Carter	2	3	Private	Co. A, 13th Tenn. Cavalry

Continued on next page

Table 1.1—*Continued*

Name	Birth Year	Slaves	Land	County	Form	Class	Rank	Unit
Helton, Joab	1847	2	200	Grainger	1*	2		Co. M, 9th Tenn. Cavalry
Hoback, John	1845	0	320	McMinn	2	3	Private	Co. C, 3rd Tenn. Cavalry
Hol[ck]er, Alfred Meigs	1846	0	yes	McMinn	2	[4]		[Co. H, 5th Tenn.]
Johnston, William J.	1842	0	yes	Marion	2	2	Private	Co. E, 6th Tenn. Mounted Infantry
Jones, Frederick J.***	1844	0	150	Sequatchie	2	[3]	Sergeant	Co. E, 6th Tenn. Mounted Infantry
Jones, Henry H.	[1846]	2	200	Smith	1*	3	Corporal	Co. G, 4th Tenn. Mounted Infantry
Knowles, John Fletcher	1842	0	150	White	2	2	Private	Co. F, 3rd ILLINOIS
Krantz, Mike	1845	0	[0]	[Smith]	2	3	Private	Co. D, 8th Tenn. Mounted Infantry
Lane, Moses E.	1838	0	500	Cocke	2	[4]	Private	Co. B, 3rd Tenn. Infantry
Layman, Asa	1840	2	175	Sevier	2	3	Private	Co. M, 2nd Tenn. Cavalry
Layne, Charles	[1842]	0	200	Marion	2	2	Private	Co. D, 1st Videt Cavalry
Lowry, William	1843	0	160	McMinn	2	3	Private	Co. D, 5th Tenn. Mounted Infantry
McCloud, Joseph	1840	0	50	Johnson	2	3	2nd Sgt.	Co. G, 13th Tenn. Cavalry
McCollum, William Smith***	1829	0	300	Greene	2	4	Bugler	Co. F, 3rd Tenn. Mounted Infantry
Mason, Thomas	1847	3	342	DeKalb	1*	3	Private	Co. K, 4th Tenn. Mounted Infantry
Miles, Samuel D.[10]	1838	0	0	Rhea	2	2	Private	Co. E, 2nd Tenn. Cavalry
Miller, Moses	1844	0	80	Jefferson	2	4	Private	Co. F, 9th Tenn. Cavalry
Mills, Benjamin	1838	0	0	[Henderson]	2	3	Corporal	Co. A, 48th ILLINOIS Infantry
Mitchell, William T.	1845	0	lot	Greene	1*	4	Private	Co. E, 4th Tenn. Infantry
Mooney, John	1842	0	160	Henderson	2	3	Private	Co. C, 6th Tenn. Cavalry
Moore, John L.	1843	0	184	Greene	2	3	Private	Co. E, 4th Tenn. Infantry
Naugher, Jackson L.	1841	0	yes	Sevier	2	3	Private	Batt. E, 1st Tenn. Light Artillery
Patton, D. T.	1846	0	0	[Putnam]	2	4	Private	Co. E, 9th Tenn. Cavalry
Pierce, James W.	1846	0	0	Greene	1*	4		Co. A, 13th Tenn. Cavalry
Prince, Martin V.	1837	0	100	[Bradley]	2	3	Sergeant	Co. K, 12th Tenn. Cavalry
Roach, Anderson J.	1847	0	35	Grainge=	1*	4	Private	Co. F, 8th Tenn. Cavalry
Roberts, William	[1837]	0	150	Greene	1*	3	Private	Co. D, 6th INDIANA

Continued on next page

Table 1.1—Continued

Name	Birth Year	Slaves	Land	County	Form	Class	Rank	Unit
Shelton, Mark	1841	0	22	Claiborne	1*	4	Private	Co. H, 1st Tenn. Cavalry
Shrader, Samuel	1844	0	75	Sevier	1*	4	Private	Co. F, 9th Tenn. Cavalry
Smel[c]er, Newton	1842	0	3	Greene	1*	4	Private	Co. E, 1st Tenn. Cavalry
Spickard, Jacob	1831	0	0	Jefferson	2	4		Co. A, 9th Tenn. Cavalry
Warren, Lot	1847	5	1800	[Marion]	2	2	Private	Co. C, 1st Videt Cavalry
Whitaker, Timothy	1840	0	200	Claiborne	1*	3		Co. I, 3rd Tenn. Infantry
Whitaker, William***	1837	0	100	[Jackson]	2	3	Private	Co. C, 9th KANSAS
White, James Lawson	1841	0	200	Carter	2	3	Private	Co. G, 13th Tenn. Cavalry
White, Stephen Logan	1845	0	0	Macon	2	4	Private	Co. D, 8th Tenn. Mounted Infantry
Williams, Ezekiel Harrison	1841	0	0	Jefferson	1*	4	Private	Co. E, 8th Tenn. Infantry
Wilson, James	[1830]	0	0	[Hawkins]	2	4	Private	Co. G, 13th Cavalry
Wilson, Jefferson	1846	0	yes	Jackson	2	4	Private	Co. B, 8th Tenn. Mtd. Infantry
Wood, William T.	1844	0	0	Henderson	1*	4	Private	Co. A, 7th Tenn. Cavalry

NOTES:

This table employs the information that the veterans themselves supplied, supplemented with detail from *Tennesseans in the Civil War: A Military History of U.S. Confederate and Union Units, with Available Rosters of Personnel* (Nashville, Tenn.: Civil War Centennial Commission, 1964), vol. 2, and from Byron Sistler and Barbara Sistler, comps., *1890 Civil War Veterans Census—Tennessee* (Evanston, Ill.: Byron Sistler and Associates, 1978). See n. 26, this essay.

[1] The regions are defined in terms of map 1.1.

[2] Regarding year of birth, see n. 18, this essay.

[3] *Slaves* and *Land* indicate ownership either by the respondent (if living on his own place in 1860–61) or by his father. See n. 21, this essay.

[4] *County* indicates county of residence in 1860–61. See n. 21, this essay.

[5] *Form* indicated is either Form 1 (distributed in 1915) or Form 2 (distributed in 1922). See n. 24, this essay. Form 1 is designated *Form 1** where the evidence (internal or in the census) suggests that it was filled out several years after 1915 (in most cases in 1922), and *Form 1*** in those cases where I have not determined whether the form was filled out in 1915 or 1922.

[6] *Class* is indicated as "1" for planter (owner of at least 20 slaves); "2" for small slaveholder (1–19 slaves); "3" for nonslaveholding yeoman (a town lot or at least 80 acres of farm land); or "4" for poor family (no slaves and less than 80 acres of land). See n. 33, this essay.

[7] Brackets signify considerable uncertainty about the spelling of a man's name, the year of his birth, his (or his father's) ownership of slaves or land, or his county of residence in 1860–61.

[8] If a name is followed by three asterisks, that man appears to have fought first for the Confederacy and then for the Union. I have indicated six such cases. See n. 17, this essay.

[9] The corrected spellings of the names of Robert E. Depew and John Gray are given in capital letters.

[10] Samuel D. Miles joined a "white" Federal company of free Tennesseans, but he and his parents and siblings are listed as mulatoes in the 1850 and 1860 Free Population census schedules. According to the man who assisted Miles in filling out his questionnaire, "Mr. Miles is what we call here a Mohegeon."

What did Unionist veterans recollect? And how did Unionists compare with the Confederates? Did Union and Confederate veterans come from similar social backgrounds and geographical areas, or did they tend to come from quite different families and regions? One can readily hypothesize that Union troops from Tennessee, much more than their Confederate counterparts, came from nonslaveholding families in the upcountry. But, if so, to what degree was that the case?

Tennessee's political geography tended to follow its social geography. Tennessee in 1860 can be divided into two predominantly white areas encompassing a combined total of sixty-five counties, with populations at least 70 percent white, and two Black-Belt areas encompassing a combined total of nineteen counties more than 30 percent black (see map 1.1). As might be expected, the questionnaires show that most of Tennessee's white Union troops hailed from the two predominantly white sections of the state.[20] East Tennessee supplied 75 percent of the entire state's Union veterans but only 36 percent of Tennessee's Confederate soldiers. The white counties of West Tennessee, though fewer in number and smaller in total white population than East Tennessee, also supplied substantial numbers of Union soldiers; that area furnished 20 percent of Tennessee's Unionists and 19 percent of its Confederate troops. In contrast, the two Black-Belt areas together generated 45 percent of the Confederate troops but only 5 percent of the white Union forces from Tennessee.[21]

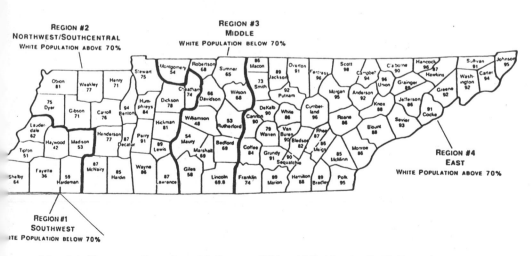

Map 1.1. Tennessee Counties with Percent White, 1860. Map by R. B. Rosenburg. Adapted from Fred Arthur Bailey, *Class and Tennessee's Confederate Generation* (Chapel Hill: University of North Carolina Press, 1987), with permission of University of North Carolina Press.

This essay emphasizes East Tennessee. That region supplied three-fourths of Tennessee's white Union soldiers. Moreover, its ratio of men in blue was roughly twice that of the other predominantly white region. This essay defines East Tennessee, much as Bailey did, as a block of forty-five counties among the eighty-four in Tennessee in 1860. The region stretched west from Johnson County (in northeastern Tennessee) to Macon County (on the Kentucky border) and Franklin County (on the Alabama border). These forty-five counties had white percentages ranging from 73 to 98, and all but five of them had populations at least 85 percent white. East Tennessee contained 46 percent of the white residents of Tennessee but only 17 percent of the slaves.[22]

Prewar Tennessee: Attitudes and Social Relations

The two men who gathered all the questionnaire information, Dyer and Moore, hoped to demonstrate that prewar Tennessee society had been characterized by white solidarity, that a democratic social ethos had enveloped slaveholding and nonslaveholding whites alike.[23] Thus they asked such questions as: Were the two groups "friendly" or "antagonistic" toward each other? Did the two groups "mingle freely" and "on a footing of equality?" Did some white men lead "lives of idleness" and "let others do their work for them?"[24] These questions were asked with optimism, not apprehension. The results are mixed, even among Confederate respondents, as Bailey has made clear. If anything, Union veterans proved less cooperative.

Dyer and Moore had in mind a prewar world characterized by white solidarity. They also conceived a world in which slaves, slaveholders, and nonslaveholding yeomen families lived more or less together. East Tennesseans, however, recollected a very different social world. Jefferson County's John Brimer, for one, reported "no slaves in my community." Most respondents recalled that the wealthy owned slaves, regardless of whether they also worked whites. William Dickson, who had owned neither land nor slaves in 1860, recalled about slaveowners that "they felt biggety and above poor folk who did not have slaves" and that "they would not mingle togather at all." William Roberts, who "was a bound boy had no chance for school," reported that "the white men that owned slaves did not do much work[,] them that had no slaves did honest work," and that "the men that owned slaves felt themselves better than the non slave holder[,] never had no dealings with them only on business."

Throwing back the language of the question, Anderson J. Roach, from a family that had owned only thirty-five acres and a one-room log house in Grainger County, said about slaveowners and nonelite whites that "they

seemed to be on friendly terms but there was no perticular association between them[,] and when a slave holder hired a non slave holder he was principally looked on as being no better than a slave and was treated as one."

Other respondents gave no indication of class conflict or at least couched
their perceptions in softer terms. DeKalb County's William H. George, for
example, recalled a world in which the two groups were generally "friendly,"
but "the slave holding people mixed together and the non slaving people
together." Wiley M. Christian, whose folks in Roane County had owned
neither land nor slaves, wrote that slaveholders were "very few" and must
have "had to associate with non slave holders or be quite lonesome."

On this question of the texture of social relations between slaveholding
and white nonslaveholding families, some respondents displayed a sense
of change over time. Tensions, previously latent, surfaced in the crisis of
secession and war. William Franklin Duncan reported that, in Washington
County, the two groups "did associate together as friend and citizens"
"without Fricsun up to 1860," being "naborly and friends up [to] 1860."
Similarly, Joab Helton of Grainger County remembered that "after the war
opened[,] faction of differences became so great that they did not [ease]
until the war was over." William T. Wood wrote that "just as the war was
coming up there seemed to be a little coolness between them." George
DeLaVergne recalled that "not many owned slaves in our section & those
were good friendly neighbors, until the war came on, then some estrangement." In fact, he allowed, he "cast my first ballot for the State to remain in
the Union; after this I was treated as an outlaw & was obliged to go north."
After enlisting in New York as a Federal soldier, "at Parson Brownlows
solictation" he went to Kentucky and "drilled & organized refugees."

The questionnaires comprise a valuable means to get at the values and
attitudes of nineteenth-century Tennesseans. But they offer a surer guide
to behavior. They permit a means of measuring the probability that men of
various social groups would choose to wear the blue or the gray when civil
war came. They enable observers long afterwards to reconstruct the behavior of a critical group of white southerners who, when they were
asked—or asked themselves—"Which side are you on?" responded, by
their public actions, that they could be counted on the side that was trying,
as Charles Lafayette Broyles put it, "to save the Union."

Wartime Experience

John W. Headrick wrote that "my experinge was a bout like all solders of
the war." Perhaps so, but his statement emphasizes, rather than reduces,

the importance that his and other questionnaires have in depicting Tennessee men's wartime experiences.[25] Along the way, some told how various other members of their families had fought, too. Headrick himself reported that "my father Charles Headrick was a soldier in the federal army"—in Company A, 13th Tennessee Cavalry, the same unit as the son.[26]

But this was a civil war within Appalachia in general and in East Tennessee in particular.[27] Respondents reported divergent loyalties, divided families, and men who found themselves changing sides. Alfred Meigs Hocker, Union veteran, said of his father: "He was a Confederate Soldier." Among men who wore the gray and then switched to blue, William Smith McCollum confessed that he had been "conscriped about May 1862 in Confederate and was in that for five months. I left and scouted a while and then enlisted in the federal army." He fought for the Confederacy when he had to and then for the Union when he could.

Any number of respondents recounted military experience against irregular forces. William W. Lowry's first fight was against "Confederate deserters and out laws"; Tom Davis's "last fite was with the Bush wackers." John Wilson Barnett reported that "we went to scouting over the country fighting guerillas," and Joseph Bozarth recalled being "in a continuel giriler fit all of the time in the comberland mountain contry."

The veterans were asked, too, about camp life. William Dickson was unusual among Union veterans in complaining that, as a soldier, he had "starved most of the time." By contrast, William T. Mitchell said, "We was well taken care of." Wiley Dotson spoke for most Federal veterans, as to quantity, quality, and menu, when he wrote that he had had "plenty to eat such as it was, fat meat and hard tack was the fare had good coffie and sugar." Wiley M. Christian remembered that he had generally been "well fed, . . . but I know what it is to be on half rations and what it is to be entirely out"; the food was "not always the most palatable but nutritious." Anderson J. Roach wrote, "While in regular camps we had plenty to eat plenty to wear and good treatment, but when we were on raids, as we were most of the time, we suffered untold agony from cold and exposure."[28]

Whatever life may have been like as a soldier, respondents who had been captured by Confederate forces wrote with horror about prison camps. Samuel D. Miles, for example, recalled having spent time "in prison Richmond Bells Island . . . no food to be gotten. Most of them died—disease. [T]hen taken to Andersonville—the awfullest place was built for men to live in—Torment on earth." William A. Douglas remembered being "clothed pretty well until I got in prison" at Andersonville.

Who Chose the Union Side?

These and other vignettes of the lives of Union veterans from Tennessee offer fascinating glimpses of social tensions and economic opportunities in antebellum Tennessee, just as they recount political loyalties and the experiences of war. But the questionnaires also can be used, in conjunction with another source, to reconstruct the numbers of Tennesseans of various social groups from each region of the state who joined each side in the war.

The compilation *Tennesseans in the Civil War* supplies 608 pages of names of soldiers, together with their military units. Calculating at 300 names per page, with 452 pages for Confederate troops and 156 pages for Union soldiers, we come up with totals of about 135,600 Confederates (74 percent of the total) and 46,800 Unionists (the other 26 percent), an aggregate of 182,400. A significant minority (roughly 22 percent, or 10,300) of the Union soldiers in the compilation were black troops in "colored" units,[29] with the other 36,500 (78 percent) white.

Among the 172,100 white Tennesseans who fought in the Civil War, then, we have 135,600 Confederates (79 percent of the total) and 36,500 Unionists (21 percent). How many of each group came from East Tennessee? The 1,250 white Confederate Tennessee veterans who responded to the questionnaires of 1915 and 1922 included 449 from East Tennessee (36 percent of all Confederates). The 106 Tennessee Unionists who also filled out questionnaires included 80 East Tennesseans (75 percent of all Unionists).[30]

Given that Dyer and Moore wanted Confederate respondents, not Federal veterans, Unionists were greatly underrepresented in the source, and thus we cannot simply assume ratios on the order of 80 Unionists and 449 Confederates from the area.[31] But we can reconstruct likely numbers if we go back to *Tennesseans in the Civil War.* From that compilation, we estimated 36,500 white Unionists. If we apply the regional figures that we find among the 106 Unionist respondents, 75 percent of 36,500 amounts to 27,400 East Tennessean Unionists.

If we perform the same operation using the figures on Confederate troops, and apply the 36 percent figure (from Bailey's work with Confederate respondents) to the total, 135,600, we come up with an estimate of 48,800 Confederate troops from East Tennessee. Thus East Tennessee supplied 27,400 white men to the U.S. Army and 48,800 to the Confederacy. These figures accounted for 36 percent of Confederate troop strength and 75 percent of Union troops among white Tennesseans, compared with 46 percent of Tennessee's whites who lived in the area.

We can go further and ask about the class backgrounds of East Tennessee's white soldiers on each side.[32] If we borrow Bailey's categories, we may directly compare the two groups.[33] But here we shall reconstruct numbers that should approximate the actual figures among Tennessee's soldiers, not just the numbers among those few who filled out questionnaires long after the event. We shall apply, to the totals for each group (the Confederates and the Unionists among whites from East Tennessee), the percentages to be found among the respondents.

Table 1.2 displays the results. Among East Tennessee Confederates, the group with the largest representation (35 percent) is nonslaveholding yeomen, but nearly half (44 percent) came from families that owned slaves, and the families of one in six Bailey classified as "wealthy," in most cases owning at least twenty slaves. Among East Tennessee Unionists, by contrast, only 11 percent owned any slaves, and none owned as many as twenty.[34]

We can see that, in fact, not only did men from slaveowning families overwhelmingly choose to join the Confederate forces, but an absolute majority of white soldiers from poor families in East Tennessee joined the Union side. As table 1.3 shows, according to these reconstructed figures, 100 percent of all soldiers from planters' families in the region joined the Confederacy. The figure drops to 81 percent among smaller slaveholders, 57 percent among families owning no slaves but at least eighty acres of land (or a house and lot in town), and only 48 percent among owners of no land at all or, in any case, less than eighty acres.

The two sources, taken together, permit another procedure. The compilation *Tennesseans in the Civil War* understates the number of Union soldiers, in that it lists only the men who fought in Tennessee units, while many

Table 1.2
Number and Percentage of East Tennessee Soldiers, by Army and Class

Class	Confederate		Union		Totals	
	(#)	(%)	(#)	(%)	(#)	(%)
Planters	8,150	16.7	—	—	8,150	10.7
Yeomen/SO	13,180	27.0	3,080	11.25	16,260	21.3
Yeomen/NSO	16,930	34.7	13,020	47.50	29,950	39.3
Poor	10,540	21.6	11,300	41.25	21,840	28.7
Total	48,800	100.0	27,400	100.0	76,200	100.0

NOTES: SO = Slaveowners; NSO = Nonslaveholders. The Federal figures result from taking the distribution of the 80 East Tennessee respondents summarized in table 1.1—9 slaveholders, 38 nonslaveholding yeomen, and 33 "poor" families—and applying it to the total 27,400 Federal troops from the region. Similarly, the Confederate figures result from applying the distribution among Rebel respondents from East Tennessee (in Fred Arthur Bailey, *Class and Tennessee's Confederate Generation* [Chapel Hill: Univ. of North Carolina Press, 1987], 147) to the estimated total number of Confederate troops from the region.

Table 1.3

Percentage of East Tennessee Soldiers, by Army and Class

Army	Planters		YSO		YNSO		Poor		Total	
	(#)	(%)	(#)	(%)	(#)	(%)	(#)	(%)	(#)	(%)
CSA	8,150	100.0	13,180	81.1	16,930	56.5	10,540	48.3	48,800	64.0
Union	—	—	3,080	18.9	13,020	43.5	11,300	51.7	27,400	36.0
Total No.	8,150	100.0	16,260	100.0	29,950	100.0	21,840	100.0	76,200	100.0

NOTE: YNSO = Nonslaveholding yeomen; YSO = Holders of 1–19 slaves.

Unionists fled Tennessee and fought in units organized in other states. To judge from the questionnaires, at least one in ten white Federal soldiers from Tennessee enlisted in a unit from another state. George DeLaVergne's enlistment in New York offers just one example. We shall assume that the missing Tennessee men were distributed by region—and also by class—in the same proportions as the respondents who appear in the compilation. Thus it is likely that, instead of 27,400 white Federal troops from East Tennessee, there were more than 30,000. The new numbers—new absolute numbers and, hence, new proportions—appear in table 1.4.[35]

According to these adjusted figures, men from slaveholding families in East Tennessee tended to go Confederate by a margin of 86 to 14, as planters went Confederate by 100 percent and smaller slaveholders by 79 percent. By contrast, men from nonslaveholding families—a combined group that, in East Tennessee, was more than twice as numerous—divided evenly at 50 percent. The nonslaveholding yeomen gave a majority (54 percent) to the Confederacy, but men from poor families gave a similar majority (54 percent) to the Union.[36]

In sum, then, across the eastern half of the Confederate state with the largest white population, the lower third—or half, or even two-thirds—of the social order may have supplied more manpower for the Federal army than for the Confederate.

Table 1.4

Adjusted Percentage of East Tennessee Soldiers, by Army and Class

Army	Planters		YSO		YNSO		Poor		Totals	
	(#)	(%)	(#)	(%)	(#)	(%)	(#)	(%)	(#)	(%)
CSA	8,150	100.0	13,180	79.4	16,930	54.0	10,540	45.7	48,800	61.6
Union	—	—	3,420	20.6	14,450	46.0	12,540	54.3	30,400	38.4
Total No.	8,150	100.0	16,260	100.0	29,950	100.0	21,840	100.0	76,200	100.0

NOTES: YNSO = Nonslaveholding yeomen; YSO = Holders of 1–19 slaves. The data is derived from table 1.3, with the figures for each category of Federal troops multiplied by 1.11 to account for those Tennessee men who enlisted in non-Tennessee units.

Regardless of precise numbers, two conclusions are evident from this analysis of the questionnaires. Among white Tennesseans, Union soldiers overwhelmingly came from the nonplantation counties. And, in stepwise fashion, the lower their economic standing, the more likely men were to fight for the Union.[37] Slaveholding families in the Tennessee Black Belt provided men for the Confederacy. The men from nonslaveholding families in the Tennessee upcountry, who were far, far more numerous, could not be counted upon to aid the rebellion. Rather, they played a crucial role in suppressing it.

To be sure, a majority of East Tennessee's soldiers fought for the Confederacy. But if only one-third fought for the Union, that reduced the region's contribution to Confederate manpower by a third. Moreover, those men offset—neutralized—another third. That is, every additional Union soldier from East Tennessee, in effect, reduced the effective level of Confederate forces by two men, not just one.[38] In fact, the Union share appears to have been larger than one-third. A fraction of three-eighths—reducing the number of Confederate soldiers from East Tennessee by three-eighths and offsetting another three-eighths—would mean that the area's net contribution to the Confederate military forces was only one-fourth what the size of its white population would have suggested.

Thus, although the eastern half of Tennessee had a larger white population (380,292) than did all of South Carolina (291,300), its net contribution to Confederate manpower may have been less than one-third as large. The Confederacy could hardly afford such losses in manpower.

In McMinn County, East Tennessee, a monument to Union soldiers from the town of Athens, dating from 1925, states in part: "Blest be the memory of the grand army boys,/through danger and conflict they purchase our joys./Though Kingdoms shall crumble like rocks into sand,/this union of states shall eternally stand." Whether the "union of states" would "eternally stand" was, of course, by no means certain in the early 1860s. That the Confederacy died—that it died at all, that it died when and how it did—can be explained, in large part, in terms of the Appalachian South. Although West Virginia contributed a great many men to the cause, East Tennessee supplied even more. Wiley M. Christian, like a great number of his comrades from Appalachia, could report not only that he had gone off to war hoping "to uphold and preserve the union of states" but also that "we did it." Charles Lafayette Broyles was far from alone among East Tennesseans in having had "the experience of helping to save the Union."

Appalachia could not escape the war.[39] But the Confederacy could not escape Appalachia.

After the War

Union respondents generally had little or nothing to say about the politics of Reconstruction and its aftermath. That should not surprise us, given that the questionnaires focused on prewar and wartime matters. What some men offered nonetheless conveys to late-twentieth-century readers some idea of the soldiers' transition to a postwar world, and some idea, too, of how those who put away blue uniforms differed from those who had fought for the Confederacy.

Union veteran John Gray remembered, about the last six months of the war, that "I was on the go all the time after the Bulls Gap Stampeed went to Knoxville drew new equip[m]ents horses & co went on by rail to Virginia. Destroyed the salt works burnt the bridge to cross new river had several scurmeshes. then back to Knoxvill then joined the Stonman Raid south." In 1865, he was all of seventeen years old when he returned to Greene County: "Happy to get home. Went at once to farming on my fathers farm went to school for some time."

Some reported trying times at the end of the war. Newton Smelcer tried "farming as best I could being wounden and broken down in health." William T. Wood wrote that, after his return home, "Didnt do anything for some time, because I was not able, owning to exposure and starvation in Andersonville prison."

For most respondents, the trek home was memorable primarily in that the war was over and they were, as William M. Harrad wrote, "free to return home once moor as a citizen of this our America country." At the close of the war, Samuel Arthur Brown was "the happiest boy you ever saw when I met my loved ones." George W. Norwood was reunited with "my dear wife and my little boy." John W. Headrick recalled returning "to our homes and dear ones that we had left 2 year be four. I went to work at any thing that I cold get to doo to get miney to pay yp detes that my mother had mad to live."

Again and again, we find that the respondents, most of them still young men in 1865, returned home to pick up their work where they had left off, and to marry and start a family. John W. Headrick, for example, "maid [married] Mis Cordela Fletcher" six months after his return home to Carter County; they raised six children and "we live hapy to gather" until her death in 1910. Joel A. Acuff, after his discharge from the Union army in May 1865, made his way home to Grainger County and "went to work on the farm again just as I had dun before the war. In Nov. '65 I maried and settled down to farming and after a hard strugle I finaly suceeded in buying a farm and raised my family on it."

Aware of how the Civil War had been a war among Tennesseans as well as a war between Union and Confederacy, some respondents offered observations about the maintenance or retrieval of community in their localities. Despite all the tensions and changes, Oliver P. Chambers exhibited a steadfastness in one friendship; hiking home from the war, he "met one of my friends of befor the war who was a confederate soldier . . . and we were friends till his death."

Looking Back

In contrast to their Confederate counterparts, these Union veterans were likely to identify as Republicans and to receive federal pensions.[40] John W. Headrick wrote, "I ame now car[ed for] by the government I spent 2 years of my young manhood to save." William M. Harrad, raised an orphan in McMinn County, said, "I have bin a true republican true to my country," and, now a widower, he alternated between living with his grandchildren and "at the soldiers home." William Brewer, son of a propertyless farmer from Marion County, finished his questionnaire on a quiet note: Having grown "disable" and no longer able to continue "shoe coblin," he wrote, "I am living on my pencion me and my wife wee have no children." David Moss, a resident of Cherokee County in far western North Carolina before the war, joined the 13th Tennessee Cavalry and resided after the war in Greene County, Tennessee. Defiant and proud, he declared, "I am a Baptis and a Republican." Whatever John Trotwood Moore may have been expecting to hear, Moss continued: "I fought for my govmnt and I vote the way I shot."

The Tennessee questionnaires of Union veterans permit a hundred men or so, inhabitants of a significant part of the mountain South, to tell their stories of the Civil War era. They remind us of another South, different from the plantation South. Planters set the agenda in the late antebellum era and led eleven states out of the Union and into the Confederacy. But the South had another voice, a voice from the upcountry, where slaves and slaveholders alike were far less prevalent. Within the Appalachian South, particularly in families that owned neither land nor slaves, tens of thousands of citizens resisted planter control and planter initiatives. That resistance helped to bring down the Confederate experiment.

Tens of thousands of white southerners joined with, and threw their support behind, the Federal army. In 1861 and 1862, their opposition to the Confederacy meant that thousands of soldiers in gray were tied down controlling the home front rather than being free to battle the North. But if the Confederacy could not defeat the Union during those years, neither could the Union defeat the Confederacy. The stalemate began to break in 1863, and by late 1864 a powerful current had begun to sweep away the Confederacy. Like black Unionists from both the North and the South, white Unionists from the mountain South contributed mightily to breaking the logjam of 1863 and redirecting the course of nineteenth-century American history. Planters did not speak for all southerners, black or white, and thus the revolution failed.

Notes

1. Peter Wallenstein, *From Slave South to New South: Public Policy in Nineteenth-Century Georgia* (Chapel Hill: Univ. of North Carolina Press, 1987), 99–120.

2. Peter Wallenstein, "Incendiaries All: Southern Politics and the Harpers Ferry Raid," in *His Soul Goes Marching On: Responses to John Brown and the Harpers Ferry Raid,* ed. Paul Finkelman, 149–73 (Charlottesville: Univ. Press of Virginia, 1995).

3. Quoted in Richard Nelson Current, *Lincoln's Loyalists: Union Soldiers from the Confederacy* (Boston: Northeastern Univ. Press, 1992), 29, 36. Current's focus is on white, not black, Union troops. In contrast, other recent work on southern Unionists has emphasized black troops; see Joseph T. Glatthaar's exemplary "Black Glory: The African-American Role in Union Victory," in *Why the Confederacy Lost,* ed. Gabor S. Boritt, 135–62 (New York: Oxford Univ. Press, 1992). It better might be argued, of course, that it was precisely the combination of those two groups—black Union soldiers from the plantation South (as well as black soldiers from the North) and white Union soldiers from the Appalachian South—that tipped the balance and led to Union victory. See the discussion in David Osher and Peter Wallenstein, "Why the Confederacy Lost: An Essay Review," *Maryland Historical Magazine* 88 (Spring 1993): 95–108.

The author wishes to acknowledge the assistance of R. B. Rosenburg in preparing this essay's map, which is adapted from a map in Fred Arthur Bailey, *Class and Tennessee's Confederate Generation* (Chapel Hill: Univ. of North Carolina Press, 1987), 2. I am grateful for helpful comments on Peter Wallenstein, "Civil War and Appalachia: Union Troops from East Tennessee" (paper presented at Appalachian Studies Conference, Radford, Virginia, 1988). Portions of this essay previously appeared in Peter Wallenstein, "Which Side Are You On? The Social Origins of White Union Troops from Civil War Tennessee," *Journal of East Tennessee History* 63 (1991): 72–103, an article that received the East Tennessee Historical Association's McClung Award.

4. For a brief discussion, see Kenneth W. Noe, *Southwest Virginia's Railroad: Modernization and the Sectional Crisis* (Urbana: Univ. of Illinois Press, 1994), 112–13.

5. Abraham Lincoln to Don Carlos Buell, Jan. 6, 1862, in Abraham Lincoln, *Collected Works,* ed. Roy P. Basler (New Brunswick, N.J.: Rutgers Univ. Press, 1953–55), 5:191.

6. Abraham Lincoln to Andrew Johnson, July 3, 1862, in Lincoln, *Collected Works,* 5:302–3.

7. Abraham Lincoln to John M. Fleming and Robert Morrow, Aug. 9, 1863, in Lincoln, *Collected Works,* 6:373.

8. Current, *Lincoln's Loyalists,* 37–40. In a related incident—the Madden Branch Massacre, which took place in East Tennessee's Polk County—six men were executed who had been on their way from North Georgia to East Tennessee to join the Union army; see Jonathan D. Sarris, "Anatomy of an Atrocity: The Madden Branch Massacre and Guerrilla Warfare in North Georgia, 1861–1865," *Georgia Historical Quarterly* 77 (Winter 1993): 679–710.

9. Colleen Morse Elliott and Louise Armstrong Moxley, comps., *The Tennessee Civil War Veterans Questionnaires* (Easley, S.C.: Southern Historical Press, 1985), 1:36, 1:29.

10. Virginia's white population, according to the 1860 census, was more than a million, but a third of that figure lived in what soon became West Virginia. Virginia's revised figure, 691,773, proved a distant second to Tennessee's 826,722. Following in order among the Confederate states were North Carolina (629,942), Georgia (591,550), Alabama (526,271), and Texas (420,891). U.S. Bureau of the Census, *Population of the United States in 1860* (Washington, D.C.: U.S. Government Printing Office, 1864), 598. East Tennessee is defined here as the eastern 45 counties; see map 1.1. The rationale is explained below in n. 22.

11. Charles C. Anderson, *Fighting by Southern Federals* (New York: Neale, 1912), was an early statement regarding the enormous numbers of native southerners—some of them still residents of Kentucky or a Confederate state, others living in the North—who wore the blue. A more recent work, Carl N. Degler, *The Other South: Southern Dissenters in the Nineteenth Century* (New York: Harper and Row, 1974), 169–75, emphasizes the Civil War Unionism of mountain southerners, as does Current, *Lincoln's Loyalists.* Two more geographically focused studies are Charles Faulkner Bryan, Jr., "The Civil War in East Tennessee: A Social, Political, and Economic Study" (Ph.D. diss., Univ. of Tennessee, Knoxville, 1978); and Donald Bradford Dodd, "Unionism in Confederate Alabama" (Ph.D. diss., Univ. of Georgia, 1969).

12. *Tennesseans in the Civil War: A Military History of Confederate and Union Units, with Available Rosters of Personnel,* 2 pts. (Nashville, Tenn.: Civil War Centennial Commission, 1964). Part 1 supplies a history of the units; part 2 lists the men.

13. The Elliott and Moxley compilation appeared in five volumes in 1985. The original manuscripts of the veterans' questionnaires are filed in folders at the Tennessee State Library and Archives, Nashville. A microfilm copy is available, but it excludes some materials—photographs, for example—that respondents sent in with their questionnaires. Elliott and Moxley, *Tennessee Civil War Veterans Questionnaires,* in compiling the transcriptions, used the microfilm copy; 1:v, 1:112.

The Tennessee State Library and Archives earlier had sought to call researchers' attention to those questionnaires with *Index to Questionnaires of Civil War Veterans* (Nashville: Tennessee State Library and Archives, 1962). Already, Blanche Henry Clark (Weaver) had drawn on them for *The Tennessee Yeomen, 1840–1860* (Nashville: Vanderbilt Univ. Press, 1942). Subsequently putting them to effective use were Bryan, "Civil War in East Tennessee," and Stephen V. Ash, *Middle Tennessee Society Transformed, 1860–1870: War and Peace in the Upper South* (Baton Rouge: Louisiana State Univ. Press, 1988). But only Fred Arthur Bailey has focused on them as a major tool, first in his "Class and Tennessee's Confederate Generation," *Journal of Southern History* 51 (Feb. 1985): 31–60, and then in more detail in *Class and Tennessee's Confederate Generation*.

14. Bailey, *Class and Tennessee's Confederate Generation*, 4–11.

15. The Union veterans' questionnaires appear, in alphabetical order, in Elliott and Moxley, *Tennessee Civil War Veterans Questionnaires*, 1:1–156. The compilers' list (vol. 1, p. xx) has only 120 names but excludes William D. Atchly.

16. I excluded as non-Tennesseans: Moses S. Carlisle, Surbetus Gerard, George W. Loutham, Cyrus Miranda, Courtland Latimore Morris, David Moss, Isaac R. Sherwood, Charles Henry Smart, Edwin A. Sprague, Joseph A. Stamps, Eli T. Walters, David U. Weagley, George Washington Westgate, and Francis Marion Wofford. For the same reason, Fred Arthur Bailey, *Class and Tennessee's Confederate Generation*, 5, eliminated approximately one in six Confederate respondents from his analysis.

17. Frederick J. Jones, John Pitts, and William Smith McCollum all clearly served in both armies. Three other men appear to have been Confederates for a time: John Fain Anderson, Isaac Chatman, and William Whitaker. Anderson insisted that, although affiliated with the Confederate military and then with the Union, he "was never a soldier in either Confederate or US Army."

18. The birth dates listed in table 1.1 make it appear that the Civil War was a young man's war. Such was not the case. Rather, among the soldiers who survived the war, a much larger fraction of the older ones—those in their thirties and forties during the war—had died before the questionnaires went out. Moreover, the years of birth listed in table 1.1 are by no means accurate. I have determined the approximate years of birth from respondents' information, supplemented with data from the Free Population schedules of 1850 and 1860 (which give each person's age in years) and the Soundex (a guide to the U.S. Census population schedules) of 1900, which gives month as well as year of birth.

Respondents were asked to state their age, but Form 1 respondents cannot be assumed to have given their ages as of 1915. Internal evidence makes it evident that some turned in their questionnaires later, and the census confirms that many more did so. In fact, of the 40 Form 1 questionnaires returned among the 106 analyzed here, no more than five—and perhaps only one—came back in 1915. A large majority were returned only in 1922, at about the same time the Form 2 answers came in. It is a telling fact that, according to the dates listed in table 1.1, the Form 1 respondents had a median birth year of 1843, the same year as the Form 2 people.

19. The Tennessee veterans questionnaires of the early 1920s can be compared with the WPA slave narratives of the late 1930s. Relatively few old-timers survived to tell their stories, and the events had occurred long before. But, just as former slaves typically had graphic memories of emancipation, the old soldiers could talk with authority of their wartime experiences. Much as the WPA narratives have supplied compelling materials for various historians of the African-American experience during and after slavery, the questionnaires supply material for the reconstruction of white southerners' experiences during the war years.

20. To judge from the questionnaires, at least, some counties in the predominantly white areas were much more likely than others to produce men who wore blue. In East Tennessee, Greene County had the most recruits who, five or six decades later, became respondents. Ahead of Greene's ten, however, was Carroll County, in West Tennessee, with twelve. These were counties with substantial white populations, but only one respondent came from Knox County, the county with the largest white population in East Tennessee, and only one from Gibson, the largest in the northwest. *Population of the United States in 1860,* 466–67.

21. The figures for Confederate soldiers are derived from Bailey, *Class and Tennessee's Confederate Generation,* 147. Those for Federal troops are explained in the section titled "Who Chose the Union Side?"

This essay's approach depends upon an ability to locate each respondent's county of residence on the eve of the Civil War. Not all respondents supplied such information. The 1915 questionnaire asked veterans what county they had been living in at the time they enlisted, but the 1922 version asked no such question. Not all respondents to Form 2 were as helpful to later historians for this purpose as William Landon Babb, who related that, in 1865, he had made his way "home to Greenville"; or Creed Fulton Boyer, who wrote, "I have lived all my life in Cocke County." I have checked the prewar censuses in an effort to gather the necessary information. This task has been greatly facilitated by two works, Byron Sistler and Barbara Sistler, comps., *1850 Census—Tennessee,* 8 vols. (Evanston, Ill.: Byron Sistler and Associates, 1974–76); and Byron Sistler and Barbara Sistler, comps., *1860 Census—Tennessee,* 5 vols. (Nashville: Byron Sistler and Associates, 1981–82).

22. *Population of the United States in 1860,* 466–67. It is to be noted that the definition adopted here, and in Fred Arthur Bailey's work, differs from the conventional use of three "grand divisions" in Tennessee—West, Middle, and East. To compare the two definitions, see, e.g., Daniel W. Crofts, *Reluctant Confederates: Upper South Unionists in the Secession Crisis* (Chapel Hill: Univ. of North Carolina Press, 1989), 42, map 2-5. As part of his careful analysis of the secession crisis in Tennessee (and in North Carolina and Virginia), Crofts supplies other maps— one showing slaveholding (43, map 2-6) and one displaying the vote on secession (343, map 13-1)—that show a four-region division of Tennessee. One might argue that at least some of the counties that I have included in my definition of East Tennessee—Cannon, Coffee, and Franklin, for example—ought not to be there. Nonetheless, I have chosen to include them for two reasons. First, necessity compels it,

if I am to do the quantitative work that is central to this essay; I must use Fred Arthur Bailey's definition if I am to compare my Unionists with his Confederates. Second, these regional definitions are consistent with a demographic definition of the boundaries (in Bailey's case, the percent slave and free; in my case, the percent black or white). For what it is worth, none of the Union respondents came from any of those three problematical counties or from Warren, though a number came from DeKalb, Jackson, Macon, Smith, and other border counties; thus, by a small amount, my definition of East Tennessee actually may result in an undercounting of the representation of Unionist sentiment and recruitment among the counties more universally defined as falling in East Tennessee.

23. Bailey, *Class and Tennessee's Confederate Generation*, 6–14. The question of social structure in antebellum Tennessee has received considerable attention from historians. Like John Trotwood Moore, some sought to dispel the notion that great class differences characterized the white South. A good introduction is Frank L. Owsley and Harriet C. Owsley, "The Economic Structure of Rural Tennessee, 1850–1860," *Journal of Southern History* 8 (May 1942): 161–82, much of which reappears in Frank L. Owsley, *Plain Folk of the Old South* (Baton Rouge: Louisiana State Univ. Press, 1949), 209–29. A fuller statement can be found in a published dissertation done under Frank Owsley's direction, Blanche Clark's *Tennessee Yeomen.* While the Owsley school emphasized the middling group of landowners, including small slaveholders, Clark conceded that a large minority (more than 40 percent) of rural white families who owned no slaves also owned no land (ibid., 45). For a careful study of Georgia that emphasizes the large group of free families holding neither land nor slaves, see Frederick A. Bode and Donald E. Ginter, *Farm Tenancy and the Census in Antebellum Georgia* (Athens: Univ. of Georgia Press, 1986). For a reminder that even large slaveholders could be found in the Appalachian South, see John C. Inscoe, *Mountain Masters: Slavery and the Sectional Crisis in Western North Carolina* (Knoxville: Univ. of Tennessee Press, 1989).

24. As noted above, one batch of questionnaires was distributed in 1915 and a second series in 1922. The questionnaire forms—similar but not identical—can be consulted in either Bailey, *Class and Tennessee's Confederate Generation*, 137–46; or Elliott and Moxley, *Tennessee's Civil War Veterans Questionnaires*, 1:xi–xviii. It is evident from Bailey's version that Elliott and Moxley might better have differentiated their "Form 2" (the 1922 solicitation) into what could be called Forms 2a and 2b. Yet every single Union veteran who responded to Form 2 used Form 2a. Bailey gives all 46 questions for Form 2a but only the first 41 of the 46 questions on Form 1.

25. For a sketch of military developments, see Thomas L. Connelly, *Civil War Tennessee: Battles and Leaders* (Knoxville: Univ. of Tennessee Press, 1979). Several of the respondents were members of the 13th Tennessee Cavalry; some mention each other in their questionnaires. For their story through the war and after, see Samuel W. Scott and Samuel P. Angel, *History of the Thirteenth Regiment, Tennessee Volunteer Cavalry, U.S.A.* (Philadelphia: P. W. Ziegler, 1903; reprinted Overmountain Press, 1987).

26. To supplement the information contained in the questionnaires regarding military service, I made use of Byron Sistler and Barbara Sistler, comps., *1890 Civil War Veterans Census—Tennessee* (Evanston, Ill.: Byron Sistler and Associates, 1978). The 1890 veterans census was intended to pick up only Union veterans, but Confederate veterans comprised roughly 10 percent of the Tennessee respondents. The census gathered information on about 26,000 men who resided in Tennessee in 1890. Allowing 25 percent for men who had been Confederates or had been living outside Tennessee at the start of the Civil War leaves roughly 20,000 Union veterans, white or black, who had been living in Tennessee at the time of the war. About one hundred of these survived for another third of a century and turned in questionnaires. The special census schedule, taken by county along with the population schedule, supplies information on each man's military unit and term of service and his injuries and disabilities. The Sistler index, which specifies at which page of which county's census each entry can be found, includes that information.

27. See James Welch Patton, *Unionism and Reconstruction in Tennessee, 1860–1869* (Chapel Hill: Univ. of North Carolina Press, 1934), ch. 3; Todd Groce, "Mountain Rebels: East Tennessee Confederates and the Civil War, 1860–1870" (Ph.D. diss., Univ. of Tennessee, Knoxville, 1993); and Noel C. Fisher, "'War at Every Man's Door': The Struggle for East Tennessee, 1860–1869" (Ph.D. diss., Ohio State Univ., 1993). For a vivid recreation of one incident, at Shelton Laurel in the North Carolina upcountry, see Phillip Shaw Paludan, *Victims: A True Story of the Civil War* (Knoxville: Univ. of Tennessee Press, 1981); for another see Sarris, "Anatomy of an Atrocity."

28. Bailey, *Class and Tennessee's Confederate Generation*, 80–86, discusses the food, clothing, and health of yeomen and elite Confederates. In a comparison of the reported experiences of Confederate veterans with those of their Union counterparts, two variables are at work. Given that Union troops were more likely to come from poor families, it may be that the food and clothing actually were better than some were accustomed to. It is likely that, as a rule, bad as Union troops' food often was, it was more and better than Confederate troops typically encountered, and surely Union troops were better supplied with uniforms.

29. For more detail on the black units, see John Cimprich, *Slavery's End in Tennessee, 1861–1865* (University: Univ. of Alabama Press, 1985), ch. 6. One of the Unionist respondents to the Tennessee questionnaires was a former slave, Peter Collman.

30. The figures for Confederate respondents come from Bailey, *Class and Tennessee's Confederate Generation*, 147.

31. See, for example, ibid., 11.

32. The data on ownership of land and slaves comes from the respondents, except when respondents gave too little information, as in the case of Uriah S. Allison. I then consulted the census. In some cases, the data in table 1.1 on ownership of land and slaves relates to the respondent himself, but in most cases it relates to his father. Creed Fulton Boyer made the point when he stated that he was only a "miner" during the war and "was mustered out of service at 18th birthday."

Some men had reached adulthood and headed their own families by the time the war came. Newton Spencer had managed eventually to buy a farm: "I was about as poor as any of them and saved up enough to buy three hundred acres of land." William Dickson, however, the oldest respondent, aged 100 in 1922, had, like his father before him, been only a renter; thus he was a good example of intergenerational upward immobility.

33. Definitions of social class are central to my essay. In two ways, my categories may not be identical to those described by Fred Arthur Bailey in *Class and Tennessee's Confederate Generation*, 5. First, I have placed in the "yeoman nonslaveholding" category respondents whose parents owned a town lot; Bailey does not specify how he handled that group. Second, in addition to planters (owners of at least 20 slaves), Bailey includes among "the wealthy" members of "the professional class—merchants, attorneys, physicians, academy teachers, and ministers." However, there are four people who might have been included under these categories but whom I have classified according to ownership of land and slaves rather than occupation: William C. Blair, "farming and teaching," 200 acres and three slaves; John L. Moore, "farmer and school teacher," 184 acres, no slaves; Joel A. Acuff, "farming and preaching," 150 acres, no slaves; and William D. Atchly, "Minister of the Gospel" and "musical teacher," 140 acres, no slaves, property worth $750, and thus the smallest amount among the four.

I offer two additional observations about Bailey's categories and my use of them. First, for some purposes at least, it makes sense to divide Fred Arthur Bailey's category of "the poor" into those who owned neither land nor slaves, and those who owned 1–79 acres. Alternatively, for purposes of classification, I would distinguish yeomen as those who owned any land at all, whether rural or town.

Second, Bailey indicates that both categories of yeomen owned at least eighty acres of land, and that what distinguished them was slaveownership. It seems to me that the two groups instead should be described as nonslaveowners who owned at least eighty acres, and owners of from one to nineteen slaves, regardless of land ownership. Except in the four cases cited above, however, I have used Bailey's definitions here, so as to compare his data with mine.

Since the analysis requires reasonable reliability for the information about respondents' economic backgrounds, it would be helpful to compare their testimony against another source. Did the respondents give reliable information regarding their families' holdings? A survey of the 1860 census schedules confirms that they did. Most indicated nonslaveownership, a status consistent with the census. Among the few who reported slaveholding status, Josiah B. Bewley recalled that his father had owned two slaves, and the 1860 Slave Schedule shows a figure (for Philip "Buly") of three. Thomas Mason reported three slaves, on the other hand, and the census showed his father, Thomas T. Mason, as owning two. In some cases, the Free Population schedules showed ownership of a significant amount of personal property, consistent with the ownership of a number of slaves, and yet, when the respondents denied such ownership, the Slave Population schedules support their testimony.

34. Bryan, "Civil War in East Tennessee," 26–29 (using the questionnaires) and Dodd, "Unionism in Confederate Alabama," 96–98 and 136–51 (working from the census schedules), have demonstrated that Federal troops from the upcountry typically had less land and fewer slaves than did upcountry Confederates. A study of one regiment of East Tennessee Unionists concludes that the "average" member of the unit "possessed less than the average amount" of property, real or personal, in their region: Walter Lynn Bates, "Southern Unionists: A Socio-Economic Examination of the Third East Tennessee Volunteer Infantry Regiment, U.S.A., 1862–1865," *Tennessee Historical Quarterly* 50 (Winter 1991): 226–39, quotation at 232. Todd Groce, in "Mountain Rebels," goes farther in delineating the social status and economic ties that led many people in East Tennessee to side with the Confederacy.

35. Among the 106 Federal respondents analyzed here, twelve enlisted in units from states other than Tennessee—four in Indiana, three in Kentucky, two in Illinois, and one each in Ohio, Missouri, and Kansas. David Moss, however, offsets one of those men, for he was a North Carolinian in a Tennessee unit. Thus the 106 figure is missing a net figure of eleven Tennesseans, so only 89.6 percent appear in the compilation. Projecting such figures onto the entire compilation, we can produce a revised aggregate for white Union troops from Tennessee. The procedure calls for multiplying all Federal figures by the inverse of nine-tenths (ten-ninths, or 111 percent). The new figures are, to be sure, one remove farther from the original data. But it is probable that those figures are that much closer to historical reality.

36. A similar procedure for the Northwest region shows the Federal army enlisting one in four of the soldiers there—13 percent among slaveholders (none among the "wealthy") and 34 percent among nonslaveholders.

37. One recent work on white Union troops asks the question, "What manner of men" chose blue over gray? The author's own inconclusive answer—after surveying prominent Unionists—is such that a reviewer reports the finding in these bald terms: "Southern loyalists differed little economically or socially from their Confederate [opponents] except that they were somewhat less likely to own slaves." Current, *Lincoln's Loyalists*, ch. 6; William T. Auman, review of Current, *Lincoln's Loyalists*, in *Journal of Southern History* 60 (May 1994): 409.

38. Current adopts this approach, applies it to the entire Confederacy, and explains its rationale, in *Lincoln's Loyalists*, 196–98, 218.

39. For more detail on the ways in which the war reached into Appalachia (these being variations on the general theme of the war's impact throughout both North and South), see Peter Wallenstein, "South vs. South," *Now and Then: The Appalachian Magazine* 10 (Summer 1993): 6, and Wallenstein, *From Slave South to New South*, 99–127.

40. Regarding federal pensions for Civil War veterans, see William H. Glasson, *Federal Military Pensions in the United States* (New York: Oxford Univ. Press, 1918), pt. 2; and Theda Skocpol, *Protecting Soldiers and Mothers: The Political Origins of Social Policy in the United States* (Cambridge, Mass.: Belknap Press of Harvard Univ. Press, 1992). Some respondents, or members of their families, ap-

pear to have sought compensation from the federal government in the 1870s for damages they incurred as a consequence of their loyalty to the Union. Materials from their applications, not used in this study, might prove of considerable interest. For an index to the Tennessee claimants, see Gary B. Mills, comp., *Civil War Claims in the South: An Index of Civil War Damage Claims Filed before the Southern Claims Commission, 1871–1880* (Laguna Hills, Calif.: Aegean Park, 1980), 94–119.

2

The Social Origins of East Tennessee's Confederate Leadership

W. Todd Groce

More than fifty years ago, Samuel Cole Williams, a distinguished attorney and amateur historian, wrote that "the leaders in favor of the Confederacy in East Tennessee anterior to and during the war have been neglected—in sharp contrast with those who favored the Union cause." He encouraged historians to investigate the region's Rebel leadership, indicating that "the field is one of promise to the researcher."[1] Despite Williams's urging, no one ever truly has accepted the challenge.[2] As a consequence, East Tennessee's Civil War experience continues to be interpreted in terms of the region's Unionists and their stand against the wave of secessionist sentiment that swept across the South in 1861. In the work of most historians, East Tennessee typically is portrayed as a land of small, independent subsistence farmers, as rugged as the mountains in which they lived, who stubbornly and courageously resisted all attempts to drag them into a southern Confederacy dominated by aristocratic, slaveholding cotton planters. Secessionists, when mentioned at all, are perceived as differing little in background and motivation from their "fellow travelers" in the Deep South, and generally are cast as insignificant players who operated on the periphery, rather than at the center of events, so weak and so few that they exerted little or no control over the destiny of their region.[3]

But the saga of East Tennessee's Unionists, no matter how intriguing it may be, is only half the story. The long obsession with southerners who spurned secession has caused most writers to ignore certain important trends and people in the antebellum history of East Tennessee. In the process there has developed a myopic, if not a distorted, view of the region. By attempting to explode the old myths of solidarity in southern society on the eve of the Civil War, historians have created new myths of Unionist solidarity in Appalachia. Indeed, among historians, interest in Unionists has been so pervasive that the general public has little, if any, notion that East Tennessee possessed a large, vocal, and determined Confederate minority in 1861.[4] If ever there is to be a broader understanding of the forces which gave rise to the internecine struggle which erupted in East Tennessee during the summer of 1861, the gauntlet which Williams flung down must be taken up, and the inquiry expanded to include all segments of the region's population, including those who adhered to the Confederate cause.

What, then, were the roots of secessionist sympathy in East Tennessee? First of all, contemporaries argued that anti-Unionism in the region was an urban/town phenomenon. They recognized that such sentiment emanated from the cities and villages that dotted the Tennessee Valley floor. "Outside the towns and railroad lines," observed Oliver P. Temple, a leading East Tennessee Unionist, "with the exception of two or three counties, the country became a unit, a solid compact body, in favor of the Union."[5] Prior to the February 1861 vote calling a convention to consider secession in Tennessee, the *Knoxville Whig* asserted, "When we go out of the town [Knoxville] into the country, Secessionists are as scarce as *hen's teeth*. The honest yeomanry of the country hate secessionists, hate their doctrines, and will tell them at the ballot box . . . what they think of them."[6] Later, reporting the returns from the June 8 secession referendum in Tennessee, the *Whig* noted, "We have only partial returns from the election and these are along railroad and wires, where there has been a stream of secession fire for months. When the mountain counties come in, the returns will be more favorable to the Union ticket."[7] The *Whig's* fiery editor, William G. "Parson" Brownlow, considered the connection between businessmen and separation "the secret spring" of secession. "Merchants, Railroads and others largely indebted to the North are the most clamorous for Secession," he observed shortly after Sumter. "Wherever a merchant is found largely indebted to the North . . . they are throwing up their hats for Jeff Davis."[8] Historian James B. Campbell echoed these early observations, declaring that "supporters of the Confederacy in East Tennessee were . . . living in or near the towns."[9] Voting returns confirm that nearly every town along major transportation routes—rivers, roads, and railroads—favored separation from the Union.[10]

East Tennessee Confederate sympathizers also have been characterized as men and women of wealth and station, the largest of slaveholders, who easily found common cause with planters outside the region. "As a rule," asserted Thomas W. Humes, a prominent Knoxville Unionist, "secessionists and the disaffected toward the newly chosen government in Washington were more numerous in East Tennessee among the rich and persons of best social position, and were greatly outnumbered among the middle and poorer classes."[11]

James Campbell agreed with Humes's evaluation, noting that secessionists "were of the wealthy and aristocratic classes," while Unionists "came from the yeomanry of the rural and mountain regions." In fact, Campbell boldly asserted, "The war in East Tennessee assumed the character of a class struggle between smallholders and the plantation owners in the towns."[12] More recently, Willene B. Clark, in a similar vein, claims that "the larger landowners—the gentry—were the most likely to side with the Confederacy, for they felt more akin to the plantation South than did the subsistence farmers."[13]

Are these traditional assumptions about East Tennessee secessionists valid? Were those who assumed Confederate leadership in the region during the early months of the war indeed "aristocratic" townsmen? Unfortunately, research on Rebel leadership in the region to a large extent has been hampered by the lack of readily accessible biographical data from which to create an appropriate group profile. Unlike Unionists, who met in conventions at Knoxville and Greeneville in the summer of 1861, Confederate sympathizers held no mass meetings during the course of the secession crisis. So, while it has been possible in the past to identify and examine the backgrounds of those leaders who supported the Union by studying the delegates to the various antiseparation gatherings, it has been much more difficult to make a similar analysis of secessionists.[14]

For example, in his study of the Civil War in East Tennessee, Charles Bryan examined the delegates to the Union convention held in Knoxville in May 1861. Out of the nearly five hundred men in attendance at this meeting, Bryan selected a random sample of forty-six (10 percent of the convention) and then used the 1860 manuscript census to gather evidence concerning the characteristics of these delegates. His study revealed that a solid majority (65 percent) was involved in agriculture as an occupation. These forty-six individuals generally were older men; thirty-four (73 percent) were forty years of age or older. In addition, Bryan discovered that, although most of the convention's leadership consisted of relatively prosperous men, such as Connally F. Trigg, O. P. Temple, and John Baxter, most of the participants were by no means wealthy—over 60 percent held real and personal property valued at less than five thousand dollars. Bryan's investigation also revealed that nineteen (41 percent) of the sampled delegates were slaveholders, but the vast majority of these were small holders. Of those who owned slaves, 83 percent owned fewer than ten, and 61 percent fewer than five. Overall, the convention was made up of old Whigs, although several prominent Democrats attended, including the former governor, U.S. Senator Andrew Johnson.

Bryan argued that Unionists were strongly influenced by their age and background. Most of the delegates, he declared, had "witnessed the gradual decline of their section in state affairs during the past two or three decades." They had developed a distinct distrust of Middle and West Tennessee, regions they perceived as being dominated by men of wealth, large slaveholdings, and the Democratic party. They also nourished a growing sense of resentment toward Nashville, which they believed had fallen under the control of the plantation districts. Bryan argued that this sense of isolation and loss of influence greatly accounted for East Tennessee's stand against the secessionist wave that swept across the rest of the state after President Lincoln's call for troops to suppress the "rebellion."[15]

While the secessionists held no conventions, a comparative analysis of East Tennessee's "separationist" leadership is possible by examining the military men who served as either field or line officers in the Confederate army during the early months of the conflict.[16] As a number of recent studies have demonstrated, Civil War units, particularly those from the South, tended to replicate local personal loyalties and to reflect in their command structure local political and social relationships. For example, in his analysis of wartime Orange County, North Carolina, Robert Kenzer found that Confederate enlistment was based on "neighborhood patterns," meaning that the members of each company usually were residents of the same community. Volunteers selected for command men to whom they normally looked for leadership, because they were determined "to reproduce existing local loyalties as a means of accommodating themselves to the uncertain experiences ahead." Similarly, Martin Crawford contends that in Ashe County, North Carolina (just across the mountains from East Tennessee), there was an insistence by volunteers upon "familiar authority" when it came to selecting leaders. As in Orange County, the volunteer companies raised in Ashe were composed of members from the same neighborhoods and were "direct extensions of the community itself, communities away from home." As a consequence, volunteers recreated local allegiances "through the jealously guarded prerogative of choosing company officers."[17]

The sample upon which this study is based, therefore, consists of those officers—colonels, majors, and captains—who commanded the volunteer regiments, battalions, and companies which were tendered to the Confederate government from East Tennessee during the first year of the war. Since they were elected by the troops they commanded, rather than appointed by the authorities in Richmond, these officers, it safely may be argued, occupied positions of leadership in their towns or communities—roles that made them the logical and natural choices to command their fellow citizens in the field. This was even more the case when, as will be shown, few of these men possessed previous military experience and none could be classified as "professional" soldiers. All of this strongly suggests that their selection for command stemmed from their having exercised varying degrees of leadership as civilians, making them more comparable to the Union political leaders than one initially might suspect. It should be added that, because they were the very first to enlist for the war, these officers likely were those most enthusiastic to embrace the southern effort for independence and, therefore, truly represent the secessionist element in East Tennessee society.

During 1861, eighty Confederate cavalry, infantry, and artillery companies were raised in East Tennessee. Assuming that each company matched the roughly one hundred men required for acceptance into Confederate service, then approximately eight thousand troops volunteered from the region during the first year of the war. These units hailed from twenty-three different counties, nineteen of which are located in what is known as the Great, or Tennessee, Valley. Bounded on the east by the Smoky Mountains and on the west by the Cumberland range, the Great Valley is in fact a series of ridges and small valleys which traverse the entire length of the region on roughly a northeast-southwest axis from the Virginia border to the Georgia state line. One company was formed on the Cumberland Plateau, and the remaining three companies were organized in nearby Sequatchie Valley, a parallel geographical formation separated from the larger Tennessee Valley by a high, craggy wall known as Walden's Ridge. Only one strictly mountain county, Polk, supplied company-sized units during the initial wave of volunteering prior to the first conscription act of April 1862.[18]

Of the 108 officers who commanded East Tennessee Confederate military units during 1861, one hundred could be located in the 1860 manuscript census. Of that number, 79 percent dwelled in a town or city. Moreover, 93 percent lived on or near a major transportation route. A majority (56 percent) lived along either the East Tennessee and Georgia or the East

Tennessee and Virginia railroads. About a fifth (20 percent) resided along a major road, turnpike, or stage route, while another 14 percent lived in proximity to a navigable river.[19] These statistics confirm the strong urban/ town connection detected by other historians. They also suggest the important role that communication and trade connections to areas outside East Tennessee may have played in influencing secessionist sympathy. Particularly significant is the fact that more than half of East Tennessee's volunteer officers lived close to the railroad, which, more than any other internal improvement of the antebellum period, linked the region with markets in both the Lower South and Virginia.[20]

That commercial ties to areas outside the Great Valley may have been an important factor in the decision to support secession also is suggested by an examination of the occupations of the Confederate military leaders. As table 2.1 indicates, while the livelihood most commonly named by these men in the 1860 census was farming (38 percent), a majority (62 percent) came from commercial and professional ranks, with a quarter (25 percent) directly engaged in mercantile or related businesses as their primary source of income.[21] In this manner, secessionists markedly differed from their Unionist counterparts, of whom, according to Bryan's study, only about one-third (35 percent) appear to have been associated with business and the professions. As secessionists vied with each other for rank and prestige in the newly formed Rebel army, town-based merchants and lawyers quickly emerged as the region's most ardent Confederates. Indeed, the two men who became the only Confederate generals from East Tennessee, Alfred E. Jackson of Jonesboro and John C. Vaughn of Sweetwater, in 1860 were prosperous merchants.[22]

Table 2.1
Prewar Occupations of Selected East Tennessee Confederate Leaders

Occupation	Number
Business	
Merchants	25
Railroad-Related	2
Professional	
Lawyers	22
Doctors	5
Law students	4
Civil Servants	2
Teachers	1
Engineers	1
Farmers	38
TOTAL	100

Even those southern commanders who gave farming as their occupation often pursued several business ventures in addition to working the land. It was not uncommon for entrepreneurs to invest in a variety of money-making projects, but few were as candid as Dandridge resident William D. Fain, who gave as his occupation "farmer, merchant, & manufacturer." Such also was true of William T. Gass of Rhea County. Although listed as a farmer, Gass owned a carding factory and a grist and saw mill, practiced law, and even dabbled in iron and coal mining prior to the war. Similarly, Sterling T. Turner farmed near the Roane County town of Wrightsville, but he also found time among his many chores to serve as director of the Athens branch of the Bank of Tennessee. "Farmer" Jacob Hamilton of Hawkins County failed to mention to the census taker that he also was a merchant and hotel owner.[23] Other notable examples are Benjamin Welcker of Roane County and James W. Gillespie of Rhea County. Although he listed himself as a farmer, Welcker's family ran an extensive merchandising operation in North Alabama; while Gillespie, who referred to himself as a physician, apparently was a shrewd businessman who operated a very lucrative mercantile establishment in the county seat of Washington and on the side traded in livestock.[24]

Why so many of the sample would have been hesitant to consider themselves as merchants or businessmen is not easy to discern. Certainly the prevailing republican ideology of the mid-nineteenth century, which prized the sturdy, independent yeoman farmer, may have led many to value their agricultural pursuits above all others. It is also true that, in a society that subscribed to what Clement Eaton refers to as "the ideal of the country gentleman," southern merchants lacked prestige, ranking far below agriculturalists and professionals in the estimation of the community. Perhaps, too, a greater proportion of their income was derived from farming, which caused them to classify themselves as farmers. John Inscoe found that, across the mountains in western North Carolina, landholding and farming alone were not "viable options for accruing wealth," so most affluent western Carolinians were merchants, bankers, lawyers, doctors, or some combination, just like their neighbors in East Tennessee. Furthermore, as historian Lewis Atherton notes, it was not uncommon for farmers to move in and out of merchandising throughout the antebellum period. The changes in the Great Valley's economy during the decade prior to 1860 may have prompted some to open a mercantile operation as a second source of income. Not only did these so-called "farmers" begin to move away from diversified agriculture and into the raising of more grain crops, but also many may have sought to take advantage of the increased wealth that the railroad was bringing to the region by expanding into new areas of enterprise. Overall, they may have considered themselves still farmers, while in reality they had become much more.[25]

One might add that a careful comparison of the military and census records reveals that many of the junior officers, first and second lieutenants, who often superseded in command those in the sample, also were recruited from town-based business and professional classes. Although not included in the sample, they, too, provided leadership, frequently assisted captains in raising companies for Confederate service, and were elected to their posts by the men they commanded. Such was true of 2d Lt. Jacob Alexander, 43rd Tennessee Infantry, a twenty-one-year-old merchant from Dandridge, who later raised and commanded a company in the 62nd Regiment Infantry; 1st Lt. Chesley Jarnigan, 37th Tennessee Infantry, a twenty-eight-year-old merchant from Rutledge who rose to company command before his death at Chickamauga in September 1863; 1st Lt. Samuel Toole, 3rd Tennessee Infantry, a twenty-one-year-old law student from Maryville, scion of one of the oldest and largest mercantile and railroad-boosting families in the region, who was quickly promoted to the rank of lieutenant colonel; 1st Lt. David K. Byers, 19th Tennessee Infantry, a twenty-year-old merchant's clerk from Jonesboro; and 1st Lt. Simeon D. Reynolds, adjutant of the 29th Tennessee Infantry, a thirty-five-year-old hotel keeper from the railroad and river port town of Loudon, later major of the 62nd Regiment.[26]

Another point is clear. Despite the traditional assertion that East Tennessee's Confederate leaders were drawn from the planter class, none of the officers in this study can be classified as "planters." As the leaders of a revolutionary movement committed to preserving the slave system, they were an unusually slave-poor lot. Among the group, the average number of slaves owned was about three per officer. A majority (57 percent) did not own any slaves at all. This figure is close to the 59 percent of Unionists in Bryan's sample who held no slaves. Among those Confederates who owned slaves, 79 percent held fewer than ten, nearly matching the 83 percent of Unionists in the same category. Even the largest slaveowner, Chattanooga resident C. C. Spiller, who held fifteen slaves, does not qualify as a planter by most accepted standards. Nonslaveholders predominated among central East Tennesseans, where twenty-one of the thirty-one officers (68 percent) owned no slaves; in upper and lower East Tennessee, slaveholders and nonslaveholders were almost evenly divided, with nonslaveholders in a slight majority. Clearly, based upon an analysis of Confederate officers, in East Tennessee there seems to have been little or no correlation between slaveholding and secessionist sympathy.[27]

An examination of slaveholding patterns in East Tennessee in 1860 sheds additional light on the social origins of the region's Rebel military leadership. In all, seventeen counties were represented by the forty-three officers who owned slaves; some were the larger slaveholding counties in the region, including Bledsoe, Roane, and Jefferson. The mean average holding among slave owners in these seventeen counties was 5.5 slaves per owner, while the mean holding among those officers owning slaves was 5.6. These figures suggest that slaveholding among the sample was fairly typical of that found throughout the Great Valley. They also indicate that, of those members of the sample who held slaves, most came from the ranks of the middling, rather than from the larger, slaveholding class.[28]

In fact, a number of East Tennessee's planters took an active role in opposing the state's separation from the Union. For instance, W. C. Kyle, one of the leaders of the Knoxville convention, held fifty-two slaves, making him the largest planter in Hawkins County and one of the twelve largest in the valley.[29] Apparently, in East Tennessee, Unionism found favor not only with the poorer and nonslaveholding classes, as traditionally has been asserted, but also among the wealthiest of planters. O. P. Temple admitted as much when he wrote that "the largest as well as the third largest slaveholders in Knox County were Union men." He explained that this was not unusual, because "there were many of that class who never yielded to that delusion [secession]."[30]

Of course, economics was not the only reason for favoring secession. Another significant characteristic of East Tennessee's Confederate leaders that would have tilted them toward separation was their relative youth. In 1860, the average age of those included in the sample was 35.2 years. Seventy-four members of the group were between twenty and forty years of age, while only six were above the age of fifty. The oldest officer was Robert W. McClary of Polk County, who went into the field at sixty-seven years of age. The youngest was A. Kyle Blevins of Hawkins County, who was elected captain at the tender age of nineteen. In contrast to the Union delegates in Bryan's study, 73 percent of whom were forty years of age or older, only 28 percent of the Confederates fell into this category.[31]

Of course, a major problem when dealing with age is the fact that one would expect soldiers to be younger than political leaders. This would be especially true if the sample included officers from later in the war, once battlefield attrition, the rigors of campaigning, and incompetence all had taken their toll on the early-war commanders. By 1863, captains and field officers usually were men who had come up through the ranks and had superseded their considerably older 1861 counterparts. It is precisely for this reason that, in the hope of achieving a more accurate comparison, the sample was limited to military leaders commissioned during the first year of the war, rather than including the entire wartime officer corps.

Comparing Union and Confederate officers does not overcome the problem. Indeed, any comparative analysis of military leaders presents difficulties of its own. Most Union regiments from East Tennessee were not raised until the years 1862–64, at a time in the war when younger men were selected for command; and those few raised in 1861 were organized outside Confederate lines in Kentucky by men who would have needed youth to withstand the arduous journey over the mountains. Any attempt, then, to compare mid- to late-war Federal officers with early-war Confederates would produce questionable results. Only a comparison of 1861 Confederate leaders with 1861 Union leaders, even if one is military and the other political, can yield useful data.

Notwithstanding these difficulties, it appears that East Tennessee's Rebel leaders were younger than their Unionist counterparts. This raises the possibility of a generational difference or "gap," whereby attitudes toward separation were influenced by age and the time period during which these men reached maturity, not to mention the natural rebelliousness of youth. Indeed, the plausibility of a generational theory is even more likely given the fact that many of the leaders of the Knoxville convention, including such luminaries as T. A. R. Nelson, Thomas Arnold, W. C. Kyle, Seth J. W. Lucky, and Frederick Heiskell, had sons who served in the Confederate army or government.[32]

Further evidence suggesting a generational gap can be found in the fact that sometimes fathers and sons even faced each other on the battlefield. For example, James M. Henry, a captain in the Federal army and a Unionist from Blount County, had a son who also was a captain, but in the Rebel army.[33] The most celebrated incident in which father and son were under arms but on opposing sides was that of the Clift clan of Hamilton County. The elder Clift, a wealthy and prominent Unionist, rose to the rank of colonel in the Federal cavalry. No doubt to the old man's consternation, both his sons fought as southern officers.[34]

Rebel leaders appear to have been wealthier than their antisecessionist neighbors. While over 60 percent of the delegates to the Knoxville convention sampled by Bryan held real and personal property valued at less than five thousand dollars, only 40 percent of the separationists fell into this category. These figures seem even more remarkable when it is remembered that many of the Confederates, because of their relative youth, still were living at home when the war began or were just launching their careers and consequently had only begun to accumulate wealth. The fact that secessionists were younger and controlled more property than their Unionist counterparts is significant, since in other parts of the country and the South, wealthier men also tended to be older men.[35]

Eight officers in the sample possessed wealth in real and personal property valued at over $30,000. Leading the pack was merchant-farmer Benjamin F. Welcker of Kingston, the richest man in the sample, whose net worth was valued by the census taker at $57,000. Welcker's personal property amounted to $25,000 but included only eleven slaves. At thirty years of age, James C. Bradford of Jefferson County held $19,000 in real and $17,000 in personal property; but, surprisingly, none of it was invested in slaves. Similarly, thirty-eight-year-old Cleveland resident William L. Brown claimed $14,000 in real and $18,000 in personal property but owned no slaves, although he named farming as his occupation. Rhea County merchant Warner E. Colville was worth $36,000, of which $29,000 was in personal property. Yet Colville owned only five slaves, the total value of which, even if they all were prime field hands, would have been no more than $5,000.[36]

Total real property held by the one hundred Confederates in the sample was approximately $475,000, while total personal property amounted to roughly $510,000. While it is likely that those engaged in farming purchased more slaves in response to the boom in wheat trade, individual holdings still were small. Since most officers had little money tied up in slaves, this disparity between real and personal property, while not great, probably resulted from the emphasis on investment in store stock, such as clothing, dry goods, hardware, and groceries. A larger sum of personal property also indicates something about secessionists' attitudes toward wealth. Given their small average slaveholdings, it is possible that greater levels of personal property reflect a conscious effort on the part of these townsfolk to acquire life's "creature comforts"—larger homes, elegant furniture, fine clothes, jewelry, and carriages, perhaps even railroad stocks and bonds— rather than land and slaves, the twin investments usually associated with the planter class. Inasmuch as East Tennessee was not a significant slaveholding region (slaves composed only about 10 percent of the total population in 1860), these professionals and businessmen invested in tangible goods rather than in slaves. While it cannot be determined with any certitude, it does appear that this "conspicuous consumption" on the part of secessionists indicates an effort to use their wealth in a way that would reflect their rising status in an Appalachian society that placed limited emphasis on slaveholding as an economic system or as a symbol of affluence.

The statistical evidence gleaned from the 1860 manuscript census suggests that Confederate military leadership in East Tennessee came not from the old elite families, as earlier writers have intimated, but instead sprang from a rising commercial-professional middle class that was emerging as the region became even more firmly integrated into the market economy. Of course, a few of these men were descended from the region's gentry, for a quick glance at the roster will disclose names such as McClung, Powel, Cocke, and Brazelton, all associated with the early settlers of East Tennessee. However, an examination of the list also will show many more families—such as Brock, Holland, Hankins, Coulter, Legg, Lynch, Turner, and Dill—who were outside the traditional mainstream of power. The decade of the 1850s was a period of change in the economy of East Tennessee. Farmers continued to raise their traditional commercial products of hogs and corn but also began to shift dramatically toward the production of wheat for markets outside the Great Valley. The railroad facilitated this trade, and continued a trend already established through land and river communication, by linking even more strongly the region's towns and cities to markets in such places as Georgia, eastern Virginia, and South Carolina (states which either took an early lead in breaking up the Union or later were solidly Confederate), bringing a new era of prosperity to the region.

Apart from the planter class itself, Rebel leaders in the Tennessee highlands were primarily young farmers, merchants, and lawyers who resided in towns and villages along major transportation and communication routes. The evidence strongly suggests that economic interdependency forged closer ties between East Tennessee townsfolk, especially merchants and lawyers, and their clients and business partners in the Deep South and Virginia, and as a consequence, oriented them toward the Confederacy. By actively participating in and directing the new trade in wheat, as well as the long-established trade in grain and hogs, they may have forged strong economic and even social ties with commission agents and merchants in other parts of the South. With East Tennessee firmly integrated within the southern economy, the beneficiaries of the wheat boom and railroad lines took up the sword to sustain the prosperity that access to southern markets had brought to their region.[37]

Contact of East Tennessee merchants and businessmen with other southerners also would have contributed to anti-Unionist attitudes. Periodically, merchants were forced to take extended trips outside East Tennessee, either to sell produce obtained from farmers or to purchase the supplies needed to restock their depleted store shelves. Usually their travels took them to such places as Atlanta, Augusta, Savannah, and Charleston. There, frequent personal interaction with southern businessmen and planters would have offered East Tennessee entrepreneurs an opportunity to see and understand the world beyond their own borders. Discussing the issues of the day, sharing common concerns and fears, walking the streets of these cities all would have exposed Great Valley merchants to the South and its people and perhaps would have oriented these East Tennesseans toward a more "southern" perspective.[38]

Of course, a few exceptions to these generalizations existed. Several prominent Knoxville merchants, such as James Hervey Cowan, David Deaderick, and Perez Dickinson, remained loyal to the Union throughout the secession crisis. Significantly, however, all three men were over fifty years of age and had established their businesses over thirty to forty years prior to the war. In the case of Dickinson, his Massachusetts origins probably influenced his sympathies. But Deaderick and Cowan had younger relatives who sided with the South. Deaderick's four sons enlisted in the Confederate army over their father's objections, while Cowan's son-in-law, Charles McClung Alexander, served as major of the 59th Tennessee Infantry until his death in December 1862.[39]

Yet another factor that may have shaped the attitudes and allegiances of Great Valley secessionists toward their fellow southerners were ties to the Democratic Party. Of the thirty-five members included in the sample who held political office or gained some political experience prior to 1861, thirty were identified with a party organization. As can be seen in table 2.2, of that group, the overwhelming majority (80 percent) were Democrats, while the rest were associated with the Whig or Opposition parties. This breakdown presents a reverse image of the political affiliations of Bryan's Unionists, among whom old Whigs far outnumbered Democrats. Unlike Unionists, separationists would have felt less resentment toward a Tennessee state capital dominated by Democrats; nor would they have experienced alienation from the states of a Deep South controlled by them. Moreover, several East Tennessee Democrats who turned secessionist had held important positions within the state party organization. This was true of Samuel Powel, a thirty-eight-year-old attorney from Rogersville, who held the prestigious office of attorney general when the war began; and of thirty-six-year-old Sweetwater merchant John C. Vaughn, who was a delegate to the Democratic National Convention in Charleston in 1860. Considering the intensity of party loyalty in Jacksonian America, East Tennessee Democrats could be expected to identify with others of their own political persuasion. It should be no surprise, then, that, with a few notable exceptions, such as Andrew Johnson, they closed ranks behind Democratic Gov. Isham G. Harris after Lincoln's call for troops.[40]

Table 2.2
Prewar Party Affiliation of Selected East Tennessee Confederate Leaders

Democrat	Whig	Undetermined
24	6	5

NOTE: N = 35

Given their position, occupations, party affiliation, and relative youth, it is very likely that these officers held a view of their region which differed significantly from that held by Unionists. Profitable and stable commercial and political ties to areas beyond the mountains seem to have translated into an optimistic view of East Tennessee as a region "on the rise" economically, if not politically, and increasingly integrated with the rest of the South. Unlike Unionists, whom both Charles Bryan and John Inscoe have suggested saw the Great Valley as a region in decline, many secessionists viewed southern independence not only as a way to defend the South's racial and economic system, but also as a way to continue their efforts to bring economic prosperity to their region. Pleased with the progress that improved transportation routes had brought to East Tennessee and faced with the possibility that their Deep South and Virginia markets might be closed off if their area remained in the Union, secessionists believed that separation was a gamble worth taking. As part of a new generation of emerging wealth, secessionists represented a small but powerful minority who resented the drag which the older men, with their grudge against Nashville and the more prosperous sections of Tennessee, had placed, like a great albatross, around the neck of the economic and political fortunes or their region. Secession and war gave them the opportunity to wrest control of the valley's future away from their less forward-looking elders. Thus, while Unionists talked of preserving the nation or of forming an association of Upper South and mountain states, free from the tyranny of the planter class, secessionists set their sights upon economic and political unification with the Confederacy.[41]

This optimistic view of East Tennessee was best articulated by J. Austin Sperry, editor of the *Knoxville Register* and a rabid disunionist. In an editorial penned over a year after the war began, Sperry presented the secessionists' grievances against the Union leaders, while offering the hope that separation would translate into economic prosperity for the Great Valley. Sperry blamed the Unionists—men like Andrew Johnson, Parson Brownlow, and Horace Maynard—who had been the leaders of East Tennessee prior to the war, for using the media to attack one another for mere political gain, rather than using it as a means of attracting investment capital to the region.

"It is not strange that the attractive scenery of our mountains was neglected by southern tourists, nor that southern enterprise made no investment in our mining districts," he lamented. "The press, and thence the politics, and the character of the leading men of East Tennessee have materially affected the fortunes of the country and retarded its advancement in all the elements of wealth, intelligence, and prosperity." But now that the Great Valley was united with the Confederacy and "freed from the presence of these dangerous men," Sperry predicted that mines, schools, and resorts would spring up across the country. "Our people shall be envied," he boasted, ". . . and East Tennessee shall become the Paradise of the South."[42]

Socioeconomic and political bonds with other southerners helped to shape regional self-image in another way, too. The evidence suggests that Rebel military leaders saw East Tennessee as more "southern" and themselves more as "southerners" than did their opponents, who tended to perceive southern society and its institutions as brutish and corrupt.[43] Whereas Unionists rarely, if ever, referred to themselves as southerners or to East Tennessee as a part of the South, Confederates frequently applied those cultural and geographical terms in describing themselves and their region. In the process of becoming a part of the southern community, young merchants and professionals came to identify more with Georgians, South Carolinians, and Virginians who held similar goals and aspirations than they did with their fellow highlanders. When Confederate treasury agent J. G. M. Ramsey declared that antebellum East Tennessee "was essentially an Atlantic country"—by which he meant South Carolina and Georgia—he betrayed a perception of himself and his region as a part of the culture and economy of the Deep South.[44] Seeing himself as a southerner and deploring his native state's slowness in responding to Lincoln's election, Ramsey's friend William Gibbs McAdoo removed himself and his family to Georgia in early 1861, declaring that "if they [the cotton states] will go . . . I go with them, make common cause with them, fight for them to the last drop of my blood."[45] Similarly, Sam Houston Hynds, an officer in the 3rd Tennessee Infantry, perceived himself first as a southerner and only secondly as an East Tennessean. "I see it stated that E. Tenn is trying to disconnect herself from the middle and west, if she does, then Farewell to E. Tennessee," he declared. "I love her people and her mountains, but if her people can be lead off by such unprincipaled men as Johnson and Co. I can no longer look upon her soil as a fit place for me to stand."[46] Such language would have sounded strange coming from the mouth of Parson Brownlow, or Andrew Johnson, or Horace Maynard.

A closer examination of the personal life of one member of the sample, John M. Lillard, sheds additional light on the "making" of a Great Valley secessionist. One month shy of his thirty-fourth birthday when Fort Sumter was fired upon, Lillard, known to contemporaries as "a leader of east Tennessee Confederates," was born in that part of Rhea County which later became Meigs. After having seen action in the Mexican War as a non-commissioned officer, he returned home determined to make his fortune. He began to invest heavily in copper mining in Polk County and to acquire small tracts of real estate, a trend which he continued throughout the 1850s. A dual practice in law and medicine, coupled with a keen interest in politics, led in 1853 to his election as a Democrat to the lower house of the Tennessee General Assembly, where he served one term. During his tenure, Lillard focused most of his energy on projects which would enhance his own farming, mining, and other business interests, such as the East Tennessee and Georgia Railroad. He tried, for example, to obtain state funding for a branch line to connect Meigs County with Chattanooga, a growing city which he hoped eventually would become the hub of a major transportation network connecting river and rail traffic in the lower valley.

Along with his younger brother, Newton, a merchant through whom much of Meigs County's wheat crop found its way to Georgia and himself a future Confederate officer, John Lillard became a leading citizen of Decatur, the county seat of Meigs. His 1858 tax evaluation reflects his rising economic status: seventy acres of land ($800 value), four town lots ($100 value), copper shares ($625 value), one slave ($800 value), and one piano ($300 value), for a total value of $2,625. When war came, there was little doubt in his mind which way he would go. His reflections on secession to a friend in North Carolina betrayed his perception of himself not as an East Tennessean, but as a southerner. "I think," he declared, "that if the whole south had done so [secede] at first, war would have been avoided." But with Lincoln's call for troops, that now was an impossibility, he lamented; "it is fight or submit," he insisted, "and we know what all true southerners will do in that event." Lillard organized one of the first companies raised in Meigs County and quickly was elected colonel of the 26th Tennessee Infantry.[47]

What factors led to the selection of men such as Lillard for command? One obvious qualification, military experience, seems to have played only a minor role in the decision. As table 2.3 illustrates, only twenty-one of the sample were found to have possessed any prewar knowledge of the art of warfare. Of that figure, combat experience in Mexico predominated, with twelve having served in one of several regiments raised in East Tennessee during that conflict. Three were graduates of, or had attended, military academies (Virginia Military Institute or West Point), while an additional five had seen service as militia officers. One member's sole military qualification was that he was a veteran of the Cherokee War (of removal) of the 1830s.[48]

A more important factor was prewar government service. As noted earlier, approximately one-third (35 percent) had held public office prior to 1861 and were able to parlay their political experience into a commission in the army. Table 2.4 shows that nearly an equal number had served on both the state and county levels. Fourteen had served at least one term in the state legislature, while about as many had held some county office, such as a sheriff or court clerk. Two members of the sample had held a federal office or appointment—John H. Hannah, who was postmaster of Benton; and William M. Churchwell, who was in the U.S. House of Representatives when the war began.[49]

Given the fact that nine of the fifty-two men who possessed some military or political background could lay claim to both, only 43 percent of the sample had some recognizable prewar leadership experience. Why the remaining 57 percent were selected to command is not clear from their collective resume. Only wealth and their professional occupations—factors which Martin Crawford argues were prerequisites for leadership among the volunteer companies raised in the North Carolina mountains[50]—set them apart from the average East Tennessean and could have influenced their fellow citizens to elevate them to positions of leadership in the army. The average property holding among the sample was far greater than the regional average; and the fact that many of them owned any slaves at all placed them in a higher social and economic position than most East Tennesseans.

But if the reasons for their selection to command are uncertain, one thing is quite clear: the majority of East Tennessee's leading secessionists

Table 2.3

Prewar Military Experience of Selected East Tennessee Confederate Leaders

Type of Experience	Number
Mexican War	12
Military Academy	3*
Militia Officers	5**
Cherokee War (1830s)	1
TOTAL LEADERS	21

NOTES: *Includes one cadet who resigned prior to graduation. **Does not include those officers appointed after Apr. 1861 but prior to the June secession referendum.

Table 2.4
Prewar Political Experience of Selected East Tennessee Confederate Leaders

Type of Experience	Number
State Legislature	14
County Office	
Sheriff	5
County Clerk	4
Trustee	2
Clerk and Master	1
Judge	1
Justice of the Peace	1
Register	1
Other	
U.S. Congress	1
Postmaster	1
Presidential Elector	1
City Council	1
Census Enumerator	1
Attorney-General	1
TOTAL	35

were men who, despite their wealth, lacked either the power or the talent to control political affairs on either the state or local level. Only in the four counties of Polk (where all six company commanders were involved in politics), Sullivan (where half of the six line and field officers were political figures), Meigs (where three out of five of the sample held office), and Rhea (where half of the six military leaders also were prewar politicos) does it appear that secessionists even approached anything akin to real political power at the grassroots level. Not surprisingly, these four counties reported the largest secession majorities of any in the region: 72, 70, 64.3, and 64.1 percent, respectively.[51] Indeed, nearly half of those in the sample who held office (sixteen out of thirty-five) were politicians from five counties favoring secession. In stark contrast, none of the three officers from heavily Unionist Greene County (which included the two sons of Union leader Thomas Arnold) and none of the six from staunchly loyal Bradley County appear to have held any position of authority. Stated in another way, outside of a few counties, secessionists did not control the reins of political power in June 1861, as the vote on separation so vividly attests, and they were able to persuade only a minority of their fellow citizens to follow them into war.

Of course, there were those who possessed political power in counties where Unionists predominated. Samuel Powel, for instance, both served in the legislature as a Democrat and, as previously mentioned, was state attorney general when the war began. Powel was from Hawkins County, one of several where, even though they lost, secessionists made a good showing. Likewise, James G. Rose, a twenty-five-year-old merchant from Sneedville who represented Hancock County as a Democrat in the General Assembly, also hailed from a county with a large minority favoring separation.[52]

But such were the exceptions. In general, although they occupied an economically powerful position, the influence of secessionists was less outside the cities and towns that dotted the valley floor. Outside of a few counties, they were unable to control most of the rural voters of the region and were incapable of translating their growing economic power into any real political muscle. As table 2.5 illustrates, secessionist leaders were mirror opposites of their Unionist opponents in nearly every attribute, with the significant exception of slaveholding. In terms of occupation, wealth, political party affiliation, and age, disunionists did not fit the profile of the traditional East Tennessee leader. Deriving their strength from their commercial and business ventures rather than from agriculture and Whiggery, this young, rising middle class was unable to command the allegiance of a majority of East Tennessee's yeomanry. This failure exposed a rift between the cosmopolitan advocates of change and the defenders of the old local order—a rift which, in many ways, portended the savagery and bitterness to come.

Table 2.5

Comparison of Selected East Tennessee Unionist and Secessionist Leaders, in Various Categories

Category	Secessionists (%)	Unionists (%)
Occupation		
Agriculture	38	65
Merchant-Professional	62	35
Wealth		
Estates more than $5,000	60	40
Age		
Forty years of age or more	28	73
Slaveholding		
Slaveholders	43	41
Holdings of less than ten	79	83

NOTE: N = 146.

Notes

1. Samuel C. Williams, "John Mitchel, The Irish Patriot, Resident of Tennessee," *East Tennessee Historical Society's Publications* 10 (1938): 47. The following essay is part of a larger study of East Tennessee Confederates. For a fuller examination of southern sympathizers in East Tennessee, see W. Todd Groce, "Mountain Rebels: East Tennessee Confederates and the Civil War, 1860–1870" (Ph.D. diss., Univ. of Tennessee, 1992).

2. Fred Arthur Bailey came close, but still missed the mark. His *Class and Tennessee's Confederate Generation* (Chapel Hill: Univ. of North Carolina Press, 1987) does not deal with leadership as defined in this essay. Of the 770 respondents to the Tennessee Veterans Questionnaires, only 30 held the rank of captain or above. This is not surprising, since the questionnaires were completed fifty years after Appomattox; most respondents, therefore, had been too young during the war to have held positions of leadership. See ibid., 147, 160; and Colleen Morse Elliott and Louise Armstrong Moxley, comps., *The Tennessee Civil War Veterans Questionnaires* (Easley, S.C.: Southern Historical Press, 1985).

3. Among the most recent in a long list of studies dealing with East Tennessee Unionism is Charles Faulkner Bryan, Jr., "The Civil War in East Tennessee: A Social, Political, and Economic Study" (Ph.D. diss., Univ. of Tennessee, Knoxville, 1978); Daniel W. Crofts, *Reluctant Confederates: Upper South Unionists in the Secession Crisis* (Chapel Hill: Univ. of North Carolina Press, 1989); John C. Inscoe, "Mountain Unionism, Secession, and Regional Self Image: The Contrasting Cases of Western North Carolina and East Tennessee," in *Looking South: Chapters in the Story of an American Region,* ed. Winfred B. Moore, Jr., and Joseph F. Tripp, 115–32 (Westport, Conn.: Greenwood, 1989); Peter Wallenstein, "Which Side Are You On? The Social Origins of White Union Troops from Civil War Tennessee," *Journal of East Tennessee History* 63 (1991): 72–103; Walter Lynn Bates, "Southern Unionists: A Socio-Economic Examination of the 3rd East Tennessee Volunteer Infantry Regiment, U.S.A.," *Tennessee Historical Quarterly* 50 (1991): 226–39; and Richard N. Current, *Lincoln's Loyalists: Union Soldiers from the Confederacy* (Boston: Northwestern Univ. Press, 1992).

4. For more on the myth of mountain Unionism, see Kenneth W. Noe, "Toward the Myth of Unionist Appalachia, 1865–1883," *Journal of the Appalachian Studies Association* 6 (1994): 73–80. While Current observes that Union soldiers from the South generally have received little scholarly attention, Unionism itself has not been ignored. This is especially true for East Tennessee, as the work of Bates, Bryan, Crofts, Inscoe, and Wallenstein makes clear. Current, *Lincoln's Loyalists,* ix.

5. Oliver P. Temple, *East Tennessee and the Civil War* (Cincinnati, Ohio, 1899; reprinted Freeport, N.Y.: Books for Libraries Press, 1971), 200. For a fuller analysis of the secession vote in East Tennessee, see Groce, "Mountain Rebels," 53–89.

6. *Knoxville Whig,* Feb. 9, 1861.

7. *Knoxville Whig,* June 15, 1861.

8. *Knoxville Whig,* May 4, 1861. While Brownlow was correct in ascribing secessionist sympathies to merchants and railroad men, his observation about indebtedness to the North is less accurate. His was an assumption commonly held by many in the South about planters and others who, it was reasoned, favored separation as a means of breaking the cycle of debt to northern money houses, accumulated as part of the cotton trade. For further discussion of the link between southern debt and secession, see C. Stuart McGehee, "Wake of the Flood: A Southern City in the Civil War: Chattanooga, 1838–1878" (Ph.D. diss., Univ. of Virginia, 1985).

9. James B. Campbell, "East Tennessee during Federal Occupation, 1863–1865," *East Tennessee Historical Society's Publications* 19 (1947): 65.

10. *Nashville Banner,* June 11, 1861.

11. Thomas W. Humes, *The Loyal Mountaineers of Tennessee* (Knoxville: Ogden Bros., 1888), 91.

12. James B. Campbell, "East Tennessee during Federal Occupation," 65.

13. Willene B. Clark, ed., *Valleys of the Shadow: The Memoir of Captain Reuben G. Clark* (Knoxville: Univ. of Tennessee Press, 1994), xvii.

14. For a study of the Knoxville Convention, see Bryan, "Civil War in East Tennessee," 43–48.

15. Ibid., 48.

16. The names of these officers and the units they commanded were selected from *Tennesseans in the Civil War: A Military History of Confederate and Union Units, with Available Rosters of Personnel* (Nashville, Tenn.: Civil War Centennial Commission, 1964), pt. 1. Additional information was gleaned from Compiled Service Records of Confederate Soldiers Who Served from the State of Tennessee, RG 109, NA. While the term *separationists* is borrowed from Crofts, *Reluctant Confederates,* it was frequently employed in Tennessee in 1861 to describe secessionists.

17. Robert C. Kenzer, *Kinship and Neighborhood in a Southern Community: Orange County, North Carolina, 1849–1881* (Knoxville, Tenn.: Univ. of Tennessee Press, 1987), 71–74; Martin Crawford, "Volunteering and Enlistment in Ashe County, North Carolina, 1861–1862," *Civil War History* 37 (1991): 37–39. See also Bell I. Wiley, *The Life of Johnny Reb: The Common Soldier of the Confederacy* (New York: Charter, 1943), 18–20. There is a degree of inexactitude in comparing military with political leaders, even if those military men are drawn from the ranks of civilian leadership. However, it would be a mistake to characterize doing so as nothing more than comparing the proverbial apples and oranges. Maybe it is more like comparing oranges and tangerines.

18. The units were selected from *Tennesseans in the Civil War,* pt. 1, where they are listed by numerical designation and by county. While I have distinguished the Tennessee Valley proper from the Sequatchie Valley, for the sake of convenience I shall refer to the whole region as the Tennessee, or Great, Valley. The counties represented in the sample of officers are: Bledsoe, Blount, Bradley, Claiborne, Cocke, Cumberland, Grainger, Greene, Hamilton, Hancock, Hawkins, Jefferson, Knox, McMinn, Marion, Meigs, Monroe, Polk, Rhea, Roane, Sequatchie, Sullivan, and Washington.

19. Computed from U.S. Bureau of the Census, *8th Census of Tennessee: 1860,* Population Schedules, for various counties. Information about location of rail lines, major roads, turnpikes, and rivers, as well as about community location, size, and other determinants of whether a community qualified as a town in 1861, was obtained from a variety of sources. These include: John L. Mitchell, *Tennessee State Gazetteer and Business Directory for 1860–61* (Nashville, 1860); *Atlas to Accompany the Official Records of the Union and Confederate Armies* (Washington, D.C., 1891–95), 25, pl. 3, 142, 149; and the following maps: Thomas Cowperthwait, "New Map of Tennessee...." (N.p., 1850); J. Johnson, "Johnson's Kentucky and Tennessee" (New York, ca. 1860); and E. Mendenhall, "Railway and County Map of Tennessee...." (Cincinnati, 1864).

20. For more on internal improvements and the coming of the railroad to East Tennessee, see Groce, "Mountain Rebels," 8–26. Although the terms "urban" and "city" are employed here, probably only Knoxville qualified as a "city" by northeastern U.S. standards. Most East Tennessee towns were mere villages in 1860. Nevertheless, they were the region's main centers of transportation, communication, government, and commerce. For a similar argument about towns in other sections of antebellum Appalachia, see John C. Inscoe, *Mountain Masters: Slavery and the Sectional Crisis in Western North Carolina* (Knoxville: Univ. of Tennessee Press, 1989), 27–37; and Kenneth W. Noe, *Southwest Virginia's Railroad: Modernization and the Sectional Crisis* (Urbana: Univ. of Illinois Press, 1994), 53–66.

21. U.S. Bureau of the Census, *8th Census of Tennessee: 1860,* Population Schedules, various counties.

22. Clement A. Evans, ed., *Confederate Military History, Extended Edition* (Atlanta, 1899), 8:315, 8:339.

23. Robert M. McBride et al., comps., *Biographical Directory of the Tennessee General Assembly* (Nashville, Tennessee Historical Commission, 1975–), 1:324–25, 1:742–43, 2:329.

24. Charles Freeling Welker Papers, Calvin M. McClung Historical Collection, Knox County Public Library, Knoxville, Tenn.; T. J. Campbell, *Records of Rhea: A Condensed County History* (Dayton, Tenn.: Rhea Publishing Co., 1940), 132.

25. For an examination of the prevailing anti-aristocratic, republican ideology prevalent in East Tennessee and the Upper South in general during the antebellum period, see Crofts, *Reluctant Confederates,* 158–59; and J. Mills Thornton, III, "The Ethic of Subsistence and the Origins of Southern Secession," *Tennessee Historical Quarterly* 48 (1989): 67–85. See also Clement Eaton, *The Growth of Southern Civilization, 1790–1860* (New York: Harper and Row, 1961), 1–3, 221–22. On highland farmers with additional occupations, see Inscoe, *Mountain Masters,* 7–8, 37–39. On storekeepers moving in and out of merchandising, see Lewis C. Atherton, *The Southern Country Store, 1800–1860* (Baton Rouge: Louisiana State Univ. Press, 1949), 98.

26. U.S. Bureau of the Census, *8th Census of Tennessee: 1860,* Population Schedules, for various counties; Compiled Service Records of Confederate Soldiers Who Served from the State of Tennessee, RG 109, NA.

27. U.S. Bureau of the Census, *8th Census of Tennessee: 1860,* Population Schedules, for various counties.

28. Ibid.

29. U.S. Bureau of the Census, *8th Census of Tennessee: 1860,* Population Schedules, Hawkins County.

30. Temple, *East Tennesseans in the Civil War,* 542.

31. U.S. Bureau of the Census, *8th Census of Tennessee: 1860,* Population Schedules, for various counties.

32. In his unpublished memoirs, H. M. Doak of the 19th Tennessee Infantry mentions serving with the younger Nelson and Arnold. See Henry Melville Doak Memoirs, unpublished typescript, Tennessee State Library and Archives, Nashville. Biographies of Heiskell's sons, Carrick W. and Joseph B., both of whom were prominent Rebels, can be found in Evans, *Confederate Military History,* 8:532–35. Kyle's sons, Robert and William, served in cavalry companies raised in Hawkins County, Tenn. Details of Judge Lucky's unsuccessful attempt to keep his son from enlisting in the Confederate army are given in *Confederate Veteran* 30 (1922): 347. Knoxvillian David A. Deaderick had four sons who served in the southern ranks, three of whom joined up prior to their eighteenth birthdays, despite their father's strong Unionist proclivities. See "Register of Events," Deaderick Papers, Special Collections Library, Univ. of Tennessee, Knoxville.

33. Evans, *Confederate Military History,* 8:535–36.

34. William S. Speer, *Sketches of Prominent Tennesseans* (Nashville, 1888), 189.

35. For a study of the connection between age and wealth, see Lee Soltow, *Men and Wealth in the United States, 1850–1870* (New Haven, Conn.: Yale Univ. Press, 1975), 69–74; and Randolph B. Campbell and Richard G. Lowe, *Wealth and Power in Antebellum Texas* (College Station: Texas A&M Press, 1977), 57–60, 65, 135.

36. U.S. Bureau of the Census, *8th Census of Tennessee: 1860,* Population Schedules and Slave Schedules, various counties.

37. For a more detailed examination of the role of the merchant in East Tennessee's economic and social development, see Groce, "Mountain Rebels," 20–26.

38. A good example of a highland merchant who established numerous contacts and ties while purchasing inventory in the Deep South is William H. Thomas. Although a western North Carolinian, Thomas's experiences were not unlike those of East Tennessee businessmen. See E. Stanley Godbold, Jr., and Mattie U. Russell, *Confederate Colonel and Cherokee Chief: The Life of William Holland Thomas* (Knoxville: Univ. of Tennessee Press, 1990), 17–35. Inscoe, *Mountain Masters,* 37, 40–44, also explores this contact between highland merchants and southern coastal cities.

39. Biographies of Cowan, Deaderick, and Dickinson can be found in Mary U. Rothrock, ed., *The French Broad–Holston Country: A History of Knox County, Tennessee* (Knoxville: East Tennessee Historical Society, 1946), 401–2, 409–12.

40. Party affiliation was gleaned from biographical sketches in McBride, *Biographical Directory of the Tennessee General Assembly*; various county histories;

and Evans, *Confederate Military History.* Unfortunately, the relative obscurity of most of those in the sample prevented me from positively linking all 35 officeholders to a political organization. In some cases, party affiliation was attributed to members of the sample who hailed from counties with strongly traditional Democratic or Whig voting patterns. Information on Powel and Vaughn was obtained from the 1860 census and from McBride, *Biographical Directory of the Tennessee General Assembly,* 1:598; 2:934. For a discussion of party loyalty and organization in prewar Tennessee, see Paul H. Bergeron, *Antebellum Politics in Tennessee* (Lexington: Univ. Press of Kentucky, 1982), 64–102.

41. A closer look at the psychology of mountain Unionism can be found in Bryan, "Civil War in East Tennessee," 48; and Inscoe, "Mountain Unionism, Secession and Regional Self-Image," 123–28. An argument similar to mine about the youthfulness and radicalism of secessionists is offered in William L. Barney, *The Secessionist Impulse: Alabama and Mississippi in 1860* (Princeton, N.J.: Princeton Univ. Press, 1974), 267–316; and William L. Barney, "Towards the Civil War: The Dynamics of Change in a Black Belt Community," in *Class, Conflict, and Consensus: Antebellum Southern Community Studies,* ed. Orville Vernon Burton and Robert C. McMath, 146–72 (Westport, Conn.: Greenwood, 1982). In these studies, Barney found, for Alabama and Mississippi, evidence of correlation among Democratic (Breckinridge) party affiliation, rising levels of wealth, youth, and secessionist sympathy.

42. *Knoxville Register,* Dec. 12, 1862. During the height of the railroad craze, the *Register* attacked Andrew Johnson as an opponent of railroads, claiming that he repeatedly had voted and spoken against them as a member of the legislature and as governor. "Who ever thinks of the word 'Railroad' in connection with Andrew Johnson?" the editor asked his readers. "The idea is most ridiculous." *Knoxville Register,* July 26, 1855.

43. For an examination of the prevailing sense of moral superiority among East Tennessee Unionists, see Inscoe, "Mountain Unionism, Secession, and Regional Self-Image," 123–24.

44. William B. Hesseltine, ed., *Dr. J. G. M. Ramsey: Autobiography and Letters* (Nashville: Tennessee Historical Commission, 1954), 18.

45. William Gibbs McAdoo Diary, Dec. 12, 1860, Special Collections Library, Univ. of Tennessee, Knoxville.

46. Sam Houston Hynds to Ann Hynds, June 23, 1861, in *Civil War Records of Tennessee* (Nashville: Tennessee Historical Records Survey, 1939), 1:88.

47. Evans, *Confederate Military History,* 8:577–78; Stewart Lillard, *Meigs County, Tennessee* (Sewanee, Tenn.: Southern Historical Press, 1975), 68–104; Lillard Family Papers, Tennessee State Library and Archives, Nashville.

48. Military backgrounds were gleaned from biographical material in McBride, *Biographical Directory of the Tennessee General Assembly;* various county histories; and the Tennessee State Militia Officer Commission Books, Tennessee State Library and Archives, Nashville.

49. Data on political experience were more readily available than on military. Sources used include McBride, *Biographical Directory of the Tennessee General Assembly*; Goodspeed, *History of Tennessee: East Tennessee Edition* (Nashville, 1887); John L. Mitchell, *Tennessee State Gazetteer*; and various county histories. Goodspeed is particularly useful, since he lists all local officeholders by county, beginning with the formation of the county through the Civil War.

50. Crawford, "Volunteering and Enlistment in Ashe County," 39.

51. Anne H. Hopkins and William Lyons, *Tennessee Votes: 1799–1976* (Knoxville: Bureau of Public Administration, Univ. of Tennessee, 1978), 43.

52. McBride, *Biographical Directory of the Tennessee General Assembly*, 1:598, 1:638–39. The vote in Hawkins County was 38 percent in favor of secession; in Hancock it was 31 percent.

3

The Dynamics of Mountain Unionism: Federal Volunteers of Ashe County, North Carolina

Martin Crawford

Alfred Sutherland and Wesley Cornutt were neighbors, conceivably also friends. They may even have been related, although it is unclear how close any kin connection between their two households may have been. But Alfred's mother Diadema, widowed in 1858, was a Cornutt; two of his aunts also married into the same family. On the eve of the Civil War, the Sutherlands and the Cornutts both farmed tracts of mixed agricultural and forest land in the North Fork district of Ashe County, North Carolina, situated in the state's mountainous northwestern alcove. Although Sutherland's holdings were considerably larger than Cornutt's, in most respects the domestic preoccupations and economic priorities of the two households appeared virtually identical.[1]

Following North Carolina's secession in May 1861, the Sutherlands, in company with the majority of Ashe County's farm families, threw their support behind the Confederacy. Alfred himself was too old for military service, but in 1862 two of his sons, Harrison and Andrew, both enlisted in the North Carolina cavalry; a third son, Joseph, barely fifteen at the outbreak of hostilities, joined up in August 1864. Alfred's younger brother, Thomas Sutherland, whom a family memoir termed a "strong believer" in the Confederate cause, also joined the cavalry, although, unlike his nephews, he sought military honors under the Virginia flag. Sadly, both Harrison and Joseph Sutherland failed to survive the conflict. The former perished from the effects of anemia in a Delaware prison in August 1864, and the latter died of typhoid fever less than a month before Gen. Robert E. Lee's surrender.[2]

From the Cornutts, however, secession provoked a different response. In September 1863, forty-four-year-old Wesley Cornutt left his wife and family and, together with his teenage son David, crossed the state line to enlist in the 13th Tennessee Cavalry, a Union regiment. Unlike the Sutherlands, the Cornutts apparently saw little to applaud in the Confederate bid for independent nationality. Yet they too were prepared to risk life and limb in support of a political ideal—albeit one radically different from that of their neighbors—and, like them, the Cornutts were willing to pay the ultimate price. Young David Cornutt survived the war; his father did not. Captured at Bull's Gap, Tennessee, in November 1864, Wesley Cornutt was paroled in February of the following year, only to die of "chronic diarrhea" a few days later at Annapolis, Maryland.[3]

What prompted local households to diverge so fundamentally at this critical juncture? In particular, how should we explain the actions of men such as Wesley Cornutt and his son, whose opposition to Confederate authority led them to embark upon what Carl Degler has called "the severest test" of southern Unionism: service in the Federal armed forces?[4]

Prying open the lid of southern Unionism in a Blue Ridge mountain community allows us to reappraise the Civil War's underlying character, dimensions, and impact, by usefully suspending our preoccupation with the conflict's large-scale political and military choreography. Secession and civil war initiated many transformations in American life, but nowhere was their impact more devastating than in those border areas where divided or contested allegiances posed a severe challenge to the stability and welfare of individual communities. The Civil War was predominantly a domestic struggle, after all, and in the southern uplands it proved an unusually severe experience. The war crucially tested, if it did not in many cases fracture, the socioeconomic, kinship, and religious bonds upon which the local community, both as a system of interdependent relationships and as a social idiom, was constructed.

Focusing on a small population yields particular advantages in the study of southern Unionism, which by its very nature failed to generate the large-scale public commitment and ritual participation associated with community involvement in the Civil War. In Ashe County, as in most parts of the upland and lowland South, Unionists remained a determined minority, albeit one whose importance increased as Confederate civil and military authority evaporated during the conflict's later stages. Here there were no formalized enlistment procedures, no exhortatory speeches, no ceremonial presentation of company flags. As a consequence, one might infer, there was precious little sustaining identification with the local or wider state community. Unlike their Confederate neighbors, whose company volunteering largely reproduced local residential, kinship, and militia patterns to become, in essence, communities away from home, the overwhelming majority of Ashe County's Federal volunteers served in non–North Carolina units, principally from Tennessee. As the memoir of the southern conscript turned Federal volunteer, W. H. ("Buck") Younce, confirms, to be a Unionist was not only to set oneself against Confederate authority, but also to risk the opprobrium—even the violent hostility—of one's friends and neighbors (not to mention, in his case, the love of a good woman).

On the other hand, it would be wrong to suggest that, even when its numbers were limited, southern mountain Unionism was not grounded in the same neighborhood and kinship dynamics that sustained its prosecession counterpart. Ashe County's Unionists were not a disembodied minority; however differentiated from their neighbors by their commitment to the Federal cause, they as individuals were in most respects barely distinguishable from the dozens of other small landowners, tenant farmers, and laborers who constituted the bulk of the area's Confederate volunteers. And, like them, Unionists experienced most of the same traumas generated by the war, either as a result of physical injury and death or through material and psychological deprivation. Finding oneself ultimately on the winning side would prove scant consolation in such circumstances, moreover; and, long after the South's capitulation, strong feelings between Confederate and Unionist supporters continued to shape local behavior patterns and institutional loyalties. Tensions were especially acute in the county's church congregations, and in 1867 they led directly to the formation of the Mountain Union Baptist Association.[5] According to oral tradition, postwar relationships within Ashe County were also strained by the fact that Union veterans alone were eligible for pensions.[6]

At the outset of the disunion crisis, the ultimate preponderance of Confederate and Unionist loyalties in Ashe County would have been difficult to predict. During the late antebellum period, political allegiances in the county were divided roughly evenly between the two major party alignments: of the seven presidential and gubernatorial elections held in Ashe in the 1850s, the Democrats were successful in four and the Whigs or Opposition party in three.[7] However, in 1859, Ashe's Democratic-inclined eastern section was organized as Alleghany County, thus potentially shifting the partisan balance in its remaining districts. By 1860, moreover, a Whig revival was well under way in North Carolina. In local and state elections in August, Ashe County's voters went solidly for so-called Unionist candidates; and, following a well-attended antisecessionist rally in the county seat of Jefferson at the end of October, they gave a clear majority to the Constitutional Union ticket in the subsequent presidential election.

Opposition to the newly formed Confederacy remained strong in the county during early 1861, but as the attempts at sectional compromise failed, and particularly after Lincoln's call for seventy-five thousand volunteers following the assault upon Fort Sumter, opinion rapidly reversed, as it did elsewhere in North Carolina and the Upper South.[8] Even before North Carolina's own secession on May 21, Confederate volunteering in Ashe County was well under way. One observer, James M. Gentry, a Jefferson merchant and hotelier, reported on May 6 that such an intense unanimity of prosouthern feeling now existed in the county that "a man is in great danger to express northern prefferences [*sic*] here now." Identified by Gentry as daring to stand against this powerful local tide were three farmers: Henry Hudgens, William Blevins, and, most conspicuously, a sixty-six-year-old slaveholder, Matthew Carson, whose opinion that the county's proud new southern flag should immediately be cut down he mostly (and wisely) kept to himself. Aside from their politics and their undoubted cour-

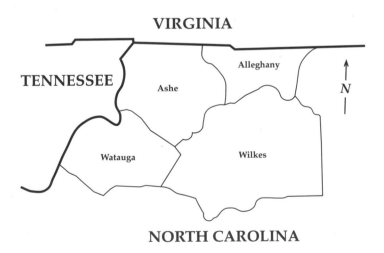

Map 3.1. Ashe County, North Carolina, 1861. Map by The University of Tennessee Cartography Lab.

age, what further distinguished Hudgens and Carson at least was their country of origin. Hudgens, a weaver by trade, had been born in England; while Matthew Carson had emigrated in 1819 from Ireland, a place to which, according to Gentry at least, it would come as no surprise if he were soon sent back.[9]

Enthusiasm for the southern cause after May 1861 soon translated into action; by August, local leaders such as Thomas N. Crumpler (formerly the county's elected representative in the state legislature and initially strongly hostile to secession), John Hartzog, and Dr. Aras B. Cox had helped organize four companies of volunteers who rapidly were mustered into North Carolina and subsequently Confederate service. The next year, 1862, following the introduction of Confederate conscription, two more companies were raised, consisting predominantly of Ashe residents. In total, perhaps over half of the county's appropriate age cohorts enlisted in the Confederacy's armed forces during the first two years of the conflict.[10] In contrast, the number of Federal volunteers was much smaller, probably no more than one hundred, a figure that nonetheless represents a significant dissenting element within Civil War Ashe County. As Richard Current has described, sizable recruitment of Unionists from the far western counties into North Carolina military organizations did not occur until 1863, by which time the activities of William W. Holden, the Heroes of America, and other "peace" dissidents had helped erode confidence in the state's Confederate authority.[11]

Given the county's location and the distortions in geopolitical and other relationships occasioned by the war, the more obvious outlet for Ashe County's Unionist energies was not downstate North Carolina but neighboring East Tennessee. Here southern Unionism achieved its most militant expression during the war; within the main body of the Confederacy, it was the only area where opposition took on the character of a mass movement. Historians have estimated that well over thirty thousand East Tennessee residents enlisted in the Federal armed forces, a figure that represents perhaps a third of all white southerners who fought against the Confederacy.[12] From the beginning of the conflict, the eastern upland counties adamantly opposed the strongly prosecessionist inclinations of middle and western Tennessee; and in June 1861, as they had in the 1780s and again in the 1840s, they attempted political separation from the parent state. Although that movement failed, as it had on the two earlier occasions, there could be no disguising the distinctive identity that East Tennessee's mountain inhabitants now claimed. Moreover, it was an identity that potentially admitted of no artificial boundaries. Invoking John Sevier's dream of uniting the mountain counties of three states into the new state of Franklin, former members of the 13th Tennessee Cavalry paid tribute to the large numbers of men from Ashe and other northwestern North Carolina counties who had joined their regiment. "Ours is virtually the same climate, the same habits of life, the same love of liberty, and we worship the same God. We are separated only by an imaginary line," they proudly insisted.[13]

The dangerous proximity of East Tennessee Unionism clearly was recognized by Ashe County's anxious residents, as they awaited a civil war with divided loyalties now all too visible. "We are only six miles from the Tennessee line here consequently close to the Tory hot bed," reported Jennie Lillard from the North Fork in August 1861.[14] With much of western North Carolina, including Ashe County, initially strongly supportive of the South's cause, it was predictable that violent clashes between pro- and anti-Confederate sympathizers would occur at a very early stage in the mountainous border region. In September 1861, James M. Gentry thanked Gov. Henry T. Clark of North Carolina for his assistance in establishing a "camp of instruction" in Ashe—a move that, he indicated, would have a salutary effect upon "the disaffected part of this county."[15] The following month, however, Gentry was complaining bitterly of the effect of Unionist "outrages" being committed in adjacent Johnson County, Tennessee, concerns the governor soon communicated to Confederate Secretary of War Judah P. Benjamin.[16] By the beginning of 1862, the area's vulnerability to Unionist incursions elicited a petition to the North Carolina governor from a group of prominent Ashe County citizens, headed by the Jefferson merchant Quincy F. Neal, requesting a military appointment to help protect against "disaffected and dangerous persons on the border."[17]

For the rest of the war, tensions remained high along the border, punctuated by innumerable incidents of violence and counterviolence, of "outrage" and revenge, the details of which are barely discernible amid the contending discourses of Confederate and Unionist partisans. Nowhere is the rhetorically irreconcilable, yet culturally universal, nature of this border conflict better illustrated than in the various accounts describing what perhaps is its most infamous incident, the hanging of James Price and his sons Hiram and Moses and nephew Solomon in the spring of 1863. For W. H. Younce, who claims to have been in the vicinity at the time, the episode was indicative of "the horrors and the sufferings" that Unionists experienced as former friends and neighbors, now Rebels, were transformed into "demons, murderers and savages." According to this version, James Price was a staunch patriot whose refusal to bow before "mob" tyranny marked him for martyrdom; Younce even reports the old man's final words, defiantly delivered after the execution of his sons to a local physician and Methodist preacher, Dr. James Wagg: "Doctor, I have done nothing to be hanged for. I am old—not even subject to military duty. I have committed no crime. I have only been loyal to my country, and if it is for this you intend to murder me, I will go into eternity as I am. I want no rebel to pray for me."[18]

Confederate sympathizers predictably sketched the event in different colors. In a letter to the *Raleigh Register*, a correspondent described Price as "a notorious tory . . . who had caused a great deal of trouble in the Western part of Ashe County." In contrast to Unionist accounts, which had the family detained and lynched by Home Guard vigilantes, this version claims that a modicum of legality, if not of due process, prevailed. The Prices were arrested, the *Register* reported, by Capt. John Hartzog, who was passing through Jefferson with a small company of men in pursuit of deserters. After ordering the elder Price to be hanged, Hartzog, of the 37th North Carolina regiment and in peacetime a prominent Ashe County farmer and slaveowner, decided to spare the family's younger members, dispatching them instead to the Jefferson jail. That afternoon, however, both soldiers and civilians became "so much exasperated at the recital of depredations committed by the ruthless gang that are lurking in the mountains" that they proceeded to remove two of the remaining Prices from their confinement and hanged them.[19] No indication is given of the fate of the other young man, to whom Unionist narratives grant a miraculous post-gallows resuscitation, forced conscription into the southern military, and, following an escape through the enemy's lines, valiant service under the Union flag.[20]

In his acclaimed recent study, Charles Royster has defined the "vicarious war" that in popular minds invested even the most brutal behavior with purpose and dignity.[21] Ashe County Unionism, whatever its socioeconomic, ideological, or cultural underpinnings, was nurtured in a violent, sectarian environment in which patterns of behavior were progressively shaped by the demands of retaliatory action. The mounting stories of cross-border vengeance, of heroic sacrifice, of daring evasion and counterattack proved fertile ground for the maturation of Unionist sympathies, particularly for young men, whose passage to adulthood after 1861 coincided with Confederate conscription, severe economic dislocation, and the fragmentation of community loyalties and values. By 1863, when Unionist volunteering began in earnest, Confederate civil and military administration had all but collapsed in many areas of the mountain region, unable either to guarantee the security or satisfy the material needs of large sections of the western North Carolina population.

Essentially an outreach of East Tennessee Unionism, active opposition to the Confederacy in Ashe County was concentrated overwhelmingly in its border North Fork district—the "disaffected part," in James M. Gentry's 1861 characterization. By late summer of 1863, following the occupation of Knoxville and Chattanooga, Union sympathizers from Ashe and neighboring communities were making their way across the Tennessee line to Federal enrollment camps in Greeneville, Taylorsville, and elsewhere. The majority of the county's Federal volunteers were mustered into the 13th Tennessee Cavalry, with much lesser numbers enlisting in North Carolina regiments, principally the 3rd Mounted Infantry. An undetermined number also joined Federal regiments much farther afield. At least three Ashe volunteers were recruited into the 2nd West Virginia Cavalry; others became members of Kentucky, Pennsylvania, Missouri, and Indiana units. Far more surprising is the appearance in the 1890 veterans' census of two Ashe County farmers, Felix Sluder and Wyatt Rose, who served in the Federal navy: Sluder on the *U.S.S. Ticonderoga* and Rose on the *James Adger.* Finally, mention should be made of the fact that least five Ashe County residents became so-called "Galvanized Yankees," ex-Confederate prisoners who were paroled on condition that they join the Union army. Among them was John Eastridge, a married man with six children who was captured at Gettysburg while fighting with the 26th North Carolina Regiment. Assigned to the 1st Regiment, U.S. Volunteer Infantry, this thirty-nine-year-old carpenter of "good character" died of scurvy on May 6, 1865, at Fort Rice, Dakota Territory, over a thousand miles from his home and family on the North Fork. In October 1864, John Eastridge's eighteen-year-old son William enlisted in Company E of the 13th Tennessee Cavalry, serving with it until his discharge at the end of the war.[22]

Perhaps unlike John Eastridge, who may have calculated that patrolling the frontier was, on balance, preferable to continued occupation of a Maryland prison cell, the vast majority of Ashe County's Union soldiers went willingly into the service of the United States. But what manner of men were they, and what distinguished them from their Confederate friends and neighbors? From Federal troop rosters and other records, a sample group of sixty-two Ashe County volunteers has been constructed and their identities verified in the 1860 population census. The majority of the group (forty-eight) served in the 13th Tennessee Cavalry, but evidence from the 1890 veterans' census and elsewhere suggests this as roughly typical of county enlistment patterns, although probably underrepresenting those who served in distant state units.

Predictably, the heaviest concentration of Union volunteering activity was in the North Fork district, where nearly two-thirds (64.5 percent) of the sample group resided in 1860. In contrast, only two volunteers came from the Town district and none from the Village of Jefferson, and the remainder were scattered fairly evenly throughout the rest of the county. In comparing this distribution to an earlier, larger sample of Confederate recruiting, it seems apparent that there existed in Ashe County a palpable division in political sentiment between the wealthier, more commercially oriented neighborhoods that embraced or were close to the county seat and outlying districts such as the North Fork, where property values were significantly lower and where subsistence production was most prevalent.[23] What further differentiated the North Fork was its extremely modest involvement in slaveowning. Only 3.1 percent (7 out of 228) of North Fork households held slaves on the eve of the Civil War, compared with 14.4 percent (23 out of 160) in the Town district and 34.6 percent (9 out of 26) in the small but highly prosperous Village of Jefferson.

The evidence from Ashe County, North Carolina, therefore, confirms and extends the belief—long a staple of southern historiography—that Civil War Unionism was strongest in nonslaveholding areas. In fact, none of the sixty-two Union volunteers in the sample group came from slaveowning households. Whatever the precise texture of political loyalties in Ashe County, Unionist activity clearly thrived in those neighborhoods and families least implicated in the slaveholding economy. Furthermore, confining the comparison solely to the North Fork district and again using enlistment samples, we find a measurable distinction in level of wealth generally between Union and Confederate households. Average real and personal property values in 1860 of those households sending volunteers into the Federal armed forces was less than half those of their equally militant Confederate neighbors. Of North Fork Unionist households, 45.7 percent (sixteen out of thirty-five) owned no real property at all in 1860, compared with only 26.2 percent (eleven out of forty-two) of those who supported the South.[24] These figures confirm the findings of other recent investigations into the relationship between mountain Unionism and low economic status. As Peter Wallenstein has concluded after analyzing Tennessee veterans' questionnaires, Unionists "overwhelmingly" came from nonplantation counties, and "in stepwise fashion, the lower their economic standing, the more likely men were to fight for the Union."[25]

That Unionism penetrated deeper than its Confederate counterpart into the poorer strata of mountain society seems well established. That social class or economic status provides the key to explaining militant opposition to the Confederate cause in Ashe and similar communities, however, is a more demanding proposition. It is important to note the heavy concentration of Unionist support in the North Fork, a district whose socioeconomic profile was broadly replicated in other parts of Ashe County where such support was not manifested to anything like the same degree. The first explanation for this disparity, of course, lies in the district's geographical location—the North Fork adjoined a strongly Unionist area, which helped to shape its political character and provided sympathizers with both the motive and the opportunity to take an active part in resistance to the Confederacy. Cross-border kin relationships doubtless exerted an influence; a number of the North Fork volunteers, including Jesse Snyder and the three Wilson brothers, either were born in Tennessee or had parents born there, while other district families—such as the Greers, who provided five members of the Ashe County sample—had strong kin connections to the neighboring state. Conversely, the pro-Confederate Sutherlands were of Virginia origin, the family having migrated across the state line in the first decade of the nineteenth century.[26]

Equally important, though more difficult to verify, was the role played by local elites in determining the direction of political support during the war. Unlike districts where sympathy for the Confederate cause was more pronounced, the North Fork's leading family group seems to have adopted an ambiguous stance in relation to the contending parties. David Worth; his father-in-law and partner, Stephen Thomas; and his brother-in-law Wiley Thomas—who all lived in adjacent households—owned almost a quarter (23.4 percent) of the North Fork district's real and personal property in 1860, including nearly two-thirds (64.8 percent) of its slaves. They also were vital to the North Fork community in other ways. Stephen Thomas was the district's first postmaster; in 1835, he was succeeded by his son-in-law, who held the position through the Civil War. Even more important was the mercantile, clothing, and tanning business the men established during the 1830s and which, by the 1850s, as the Dun Credit reports routinely indicate, was a stable, highly profitable enterprise, around which most significant commercial activity in the North Fork revolved. Last but not insignificant is the fact that the Worth-Thomas family also ran the only tavern between Jefferson and the Tennessee line.[27]

According to a modern family memoir, David Worth remained "neutral" during the Civil War. What that stance involved is not explained, but, in a letter to his cousin in December 1865, Worth revealed clearly the "awkward situation" in which his residence "about the line of the two contending partys" had placed him during the conflict. "I could not agree with either party in all things contended for by them," he admitted, "so that I was blamed by both partys to some extent." In fact, Federal enlistment records reveal a heavy concentration of volunteers from adjoining Unionist households, most if not all of whose members—including Wesley Cornutt and his family—presumably were clients of the Worth-Thomas store and tannery.[28] During the war, as he himself revealed, Worth suffered heavy financial losses; but in the longer term, his political fence-sitting proved financially astute. Anticipating an early resumption of business, he was among the first (at Taylorsville, Tennessee, on April 17, 1865) to take the oath of allegiance to the United States.[29] "I still think we can live here and do well enough provided we manage well," the pragmatic Worth noted in the late 1860s. "The people here appear quite friendly with me now and I think they will remain so if I do my duty."[30] In fact, he was being unduly pessimistic about his domestic prospects; as the Dun reports confirm, the family's business interests quickly revived after the war, and, by December 1872, the local agent could accurately describe David Worth as "one of the wealthiest men in Ashe County."[31]

The Worths' situation undeniably was awkward; the family had close kin involved with both sides in the conflict. Their eldest daughter was married to a Tennessee Unionist, and two brothers-in-law, including Wiley Thomas, served as officers in the Confederate army.[32] David Worth's neutrality, however, also may have been grounded in private conviction. Worth was a Quaker and a cousin of the North Carolina Unionist and future governor, Jonathan Worth. A native of Guilford County, David had settled on the North Fork following a visit in 1830 to purchase roots and herbs for a Greensboro company.[33] As William T. Auman and David D. Scarboro, in particular, have described, Guilford County was part of a culturally distinctive area of the North Carolina Piedmont. Often termed the "Quaker Belt," the area's development had been strongly influenced by Quaker and Moravian settlers whose pacifist and antislavery beliefs helped stimulate unusually active resistance to the Confederacy during the Civil War.[34]

David Worth was not a Unionist; his neutrality would have enraged Gen. William T. Sherman, who often condemned such passive acquiescence in Confederate rule in even harsher terms than those he reserved for its militant supporters.[35] But Worth's role in shaping local Unionism should not be discounted. By standing aloof from the conflict, Worth allowed—even encouraged—active opposition to local Confederate rule to develop unchecked. By the end of 1863, if household enlistment data is anything to go by, Worth's neighborhood on the North Fork had solidified into a strong Unionist enclave. Ironically, political "dissent" in the vicinity of the Worth store now arguably would come from families such as the Sutherlands, who, bucking local opinion, remained committed to the secessionist cause. As for David Worth's kin and business partners, the pro-Confederate Thomases, their neighborhood influence was reduced by advancing age (Stephen Thomas would die in May 1864, a few days short of his sixty-ninth birthday) and by Wiley Thomas's incarceration in an Ohio prison following his capture in October 1863.[36]

No simple formula adequately can embrace the innumerable factors that produced Ashe County Unionism, or indeed its pro-Confederate counterpart. Geopolitics, kinship, class, and ideology combined with a host of individual and family circumstances to shape political allegiances in the divided communities of the Blue Ridge, as they did elsewhere in southern Appalachia and beyond. But certain social patterns do emerge. The typical Unionist came from a poor, nonslaveholding tenant or small landowning household, located away from the county's main commercial and political centers. During the antebellum decade, economic prospects for many Ashe County families had narrowed as a consequence of diminishing land resources; and, while specific class grievances are difficult to verify, the latent frustrations of men such as Felix Sluder, still a tenant farmer at the age of thirty-seven, were bound to intensify as domestic conditions deteriorated.[37]

Yet explanations derived from a model of economic resentment need to be advanced with caution. Wesley Cornutt and his family, for example, made steady progress up the yeoman farm ladder during the 1850s, as an increase from fifteen to fifty acres lifted them into the top one-third of Ashe County's improved landholders by the end of the decade. Moreover, only in the border North Fork district did the conjunction of socioeconomic, political, and opportunistic factors manifest itself in formal opposition to the Confederacy. Most of Ashe County's poorer, nonslaveholding households—large numbers of which continued to be represented in North Carolina regiments—remained nominally loyal to the Confederate cause during the war, even though many, possibly even a majority, had by 1864 become plainly disillusioned with a conflict whose favorable outcome looked increasingly problematical.[38] Elsewhere in southern Appalachia, complex local circumstances functioned in tandem with, and sometimes contrary to, underlying socioeconomic and other influences. For example, in his study of Sandy Basin, Virginia, a frontier region with no identifiable elites, Ralph Mann, while acknowledging that Unionists were in general less wealthy and less well established than their Confederate neighbors, finds political allegiances shaped by a variety of distinctly local factors, including family migration patterns.[39]

What role, if any, did hostility to slavery play in shaping anti-Confederate resistance? It is difficult to imagine that the neutral stance of David Worth, a wealthy landowner and merchant whose economic progress had depended upon the labor of black slaves, was to any significant degree shaped by abolitionist principles. On the other hand, if W. H. Younce's memoir is to be credited, antislavery influences were present in this part of the North Carolina mountains. Younce, according to his own testimony "a close student and an earnest seeker after knowledge," made no bones about what prompted his dissent from the secessionist cause. "In politics I had been trained in the old Whig school," he recalled, "and although, on account of my youth, I had taken but little interest in the affairs of Government, living in the midst of slavery, and daily observing the evils of the whole system, I had become thoroughly imbued with the antislavery doctrine, and every day was more and more convinced in my own mind that it was wrong."[40] After conscription into the Confederate army at the age of eighteen, Younce escaped, was captured, escaped a second time, was recaptured, and, following his final escape, made his way to Franklin, Indiana, where he joined a Federal regiment.[41]

How might we explain Younce's antislavery predilections? The family lived in Ashe County's Northeastern district, which bordered on Grayson County, Virginia, where Unionist dissent also was evident.[42] In 1851, this particular stretch of border had been the scene of a violent incident involving slaves allegedly acting under the influence of an Ohio abolitionist, Jarvis Bacon, who had been operating in the area after earlier being driven out of the Quaker Belt. (Also charged with, and openly admitting, abolitionist activity was a local man, John Cornutt. Wesley Cornutt's parents, it should be recalled, originally came from Grayson County.)[43] During the early decades of the nineteenth century, abolitionists also had been active in East Tennessee. However, as John C. Inscoe has noted, there is little evidence that hostility to slavery—as opposed to resentment of slaveholders—helped shape Civil War Unionism to any marked degree in that region. Notwithstanding individual acts of conscience such as that professed by W. H. Younce, a similar conclusion seems justified for Ashe County.[44]

On the other hand, we should not discount the possibility that mountain Unionism may have been shaped by traditions of political and cultural dissent and that, in some cases, including that of Wesley Cornutt, these emanated from, or embraced, abolitionist convictions. As Paul D. Escott and Jeffrey J. Crow have pointed out, the dynamics of conflict in North Carolina during the Revolution and the Civil War were remarkably similar. In both crises, the havoc wrought by war caused the legitimacy of elite authority to be challenged by dissenting groups who drew much of their sustenance from the strength of local kinship ties. It may be no coincidence that both the mothers of W. H. Younce and another Federal volunteer, Marion Goss, were members of the Perkins family, which, during the Revolutionary War, had provided two of the area's leading Loyalists. Moreover, in 1862, one of these mothers, Rachel Goss, was arrested for trading with one of David Worth's slaves.[45] Most intriguingly, such dissenting strands may help to explain Confederate loyalties on the North Fork. In the Revolutionary War, Alfred and Thomas Sutherland's father Alexander was a British soldier who switched sides to fight for the Americans.[46] Further research may reveal similar linkages at the regional, class, and family levels.

We should be careful not to overschematize political loyalties during the Civil War (or to ignore the unknown but potentially large numbers who failed to support either side). For most southern mountaineers, the war did not resolve itself into a neat argument between divergent political ideals or social allegiances. By the spring of 1865, when many of Ashe County's Federal volunteers returned to the Blue Ridge as members of Gen. George Stoneman's unit,[47] the conflict in the mountains long since had devolved into a brutal and dehumanizing struggle for neighborhood and family supremacy that seemingly bore little relation to the grand confrontations of the major military theaters.

An incident from the North Fork provides a fitting coda to this discussion, pointing up the extent to which, by the third and fourth years of the war, Union and Confederate partisanship in Ashe County and other mountain areas had metamorphosed into the politics of vengeance.[48] In June 1864, forty-one-year-old Isaac Wilson, a Confederate officer home on furlough, was shot and killed as he attended to last-minute plowing before returning to his regiment. At one level, the shooting was part of a continuing struggle for local supremacy in the border region, between the Confederate Home Guard and so-called "scouter" groups, pro-Union irregulars whom their enemies condemned as "bushwhackers." The murder followed a number of other attacks, including one a few days earlier at Mountain City, Tennessee, in which David Worth's son-in-law, Ticy Wagner, was killed. However, the incident also exemplifies the vital role played by family group solidarity in the persisting conflict.[49]

Lieutenant Wilson's assassination seems to have occurred as a consequence of mistaken identity—involving his cousin "Big" Ike Wilson, himself later the object of attack. It was assumed that Ike had played a role in a recent affray between pro- and anti-Confederate bands that had resulted in the death of one Jack Potter. The Potters and the Wilsons were connected through marriage, Jack's father Andy having married Isaac Wilson's first cousin Sarah. The marriage had been vehemently opposed by the bride's parents, however; so relations between the Wilsons and the Potters were far from cordial. Since a number of Wilsons had been members of the Ashe County Home Guard, which was presumed responsible for Jack Potter's death, the latter's family were quick to plot revenge.

The convoluted circumstances of Isaac Wilson's murder exemplify the localized nature of the Civil War in Appalachia, where local neighborhood and even kinship ties increasingly were subordinated to a spiraling logic of violence and retaliatory counterviolence. Moreover, this was a conflict from which few could remain immune. Most of Wilson's neighbors and family on the North Fork were caught up in the incident in one way or another. (They included Alfred Sutherland, whose property was close to the Wilson farm. It was to the Sutherlands that Isaac Wilson's sister-in-law ran with news of the killing.) Among those implicated was Tennessee-born Thomas Stout, who farmed more than five hundred acres just downstream from the Wilson homestead, and who, according to one source, was a known Union partisan.[50] On the day before the killing, Stout had brought Isaac Wilson a message from his cousin Sarah Potter, requesting that he go to see her before returning to the army. Sensing a trap, Isaac did not act upon the message, but whether Stout himself was suspected at this point is not known. What seems to have to tipped the scales against him was the combined effect of local opinion, the failure of the Stouts to pay a neighborly visit to the Wilson home on the day of the murder, and, finally, the reactions of Thomas's wife Lizzie, who reportedly muttered the words "Thank God" upon learning of the shooting. Soon afterward, Mrs. Stout was identified as a lookout for the Potters' suspected guide, a man called Silvers Arnold. (Arnold was shot to death as he made his way back into Tennessee.) Tom Stout, meanwhile, confined at the Wilson house on the evening of the murder, now was accused of having played a leading role in its planning and execution. The following day, after the funeral was over, he was spirited away from the North Fork by a group of Wilson's friends, who summarily hanged him in a remote spot along Rich Mountain.[51]

Whether Thomas Stout himself was responsible for Isaac Wilson's murder cannot be determined, although one set of local sources strongly implicates the Stout sons in the attack.[52] But, by the summer of 1864, the war's violent momentum in this and other border communities had rendered such questions all but irrelevant. Like countless others in the southern uplands who suffered similar fates at the hands of local partisans, Tom Stout was the victim of—and more than likely a willing protagonist in—a vengeful, ill-defined conflict whose day-to-day outcome was difficult to predict and, even more crucial for the community's survival, almost impossible to control.

Clearly, Ashe County Unionism, like its pro-Confederate counterpart, derived much of its motivating energy from the neighborhood and kinship dynamics of mountain community life. The fragile, often conflictual, but undeniably persistent character of these dynamics historians only now are beginning to explore.[53] Yet, for all its localized intensity, the conflict in Ashe County cannot be isolated from the war's larger design nor abstracted from the shared moral, behavioral, and institutional imperatives that characterized American society as a whole in the middle decades of the nineteenth century.[54] The Sutherland brothers, Wesley and David Cornutt, the Wilsons, and the Stouts all fought—and in many cases died—as a consequence of their involvement in a conflict whose translocal character was self-evident and indeed formative. In this respect, at least, the civil war in the Blue Ridge was no different from that waged elsewhere in the Upper South and beyond, notwithstanding the distinctive flavor imparted by the partisan struggle for local supremacy in the upland border region.

Notes

1. Information on the Sutherland and Cornutt families is derived from the following sources: U.S. Bureau of the Census, *8th Census of North Carolina: 1860*, Population and Agricultural Schedules, Ashe County; and Ruth W. Shepherd, ed., *The Heritage of Ashe County, North Carolina Volume I, 1984* (Winston-Salem, N.C.: Hunter Publishing Co., 1984), 470–71. The exact proximity of the two households cannot be determined; in the 1860 census taker's listing, the Cornutts occupied household no. 338 and the Sutherlands no. 348.

2. The military records of the Sutherland family are derived from the following sources: Louis H. Manarin and Weymouth T. Jordan, comps. and eds., *North Carolina Troops, 1861–1865: A Roster*, 13 vols. to date (Raleigh: North Carolina Division of Archives and History, 1966–), 2:18, 504; Shepherd, *Heritage of Ashe County*, 471.

3. The Cornutts' military records are derived from Compiled Service Records, M395 (13th Tennessee Cavalry), RG 94, NA. David's brother Isaac (not listed in the 1860 census of Ashe County) joined the same regiment in Jan. 1864.

4. Carl N. Degler, *The Other South: Southern Dissenters in the Nineteenth Century* (New York: Harper and Row, 1974), 174.

5. Religious conflict during and after the war is recounted briefly in J. F. Fletcher, *A History of the Ashe County, North Carolina, and New River, Virginia, Baptist Associations* (Raleigh, N.C.: Commercial Printing Co., 1935), 30–55. Fletcher, an Ashe native, was ordained a Baptist minister in the county in 1876, at

the age of 18. "The Civil War dragged its bloody and soul-trying way to a close in 1865," he writes, "and in its wake came hatred and jealousies that were still flaming in our mountain country for a generation after the war" (52). The Union Baptist movement apparently was linked to the local activities of the Union League. On the relationship between mountain Unionism and postwar political alignments, see Gordon B. McKinney, *Southern Mountain Republicans, 1865–1900: Politics and the Appalachian Community* (Chapel Hill: Univ. of North Carolina Press, 1978), 30–61. The identification of Unionist loyalties with Republican partisanship is reflected in modern electoral support for the party in the North Fork district. In contrast, the county's eastern districts, where Confederate loyalties were strongest, remain predominantly Democratic. See Patricia Duane Beaver, *Rural Community in the Appalachian South* (Lexington: Univ. Press of Kentucky, 1986), 20.

6. Boyd Barlow interview, Jan. 8, 1981, p. 13, Ashe County Oral History Project, Ashe County Public Library, West Jefferson, N.C.

7. John L. Cheney, Jr., ed., *North Carolina Government, 1585–1979* (Raleigh: North Carolina Dept. of Secretary of State, 1981), 1330, 1398–1400. This remarkably balanced pattern of two-party support continued in the postwar period. In nine gubernatorial elections in Ashe County between 1865 and 1892, Democrats and Republicans were separated by only 185 votes, out of a total participation of 16,353 (ibid., 1402–4).

8. For a more detailed account of these developments, see Martin Crawford, "Political Society in a Southern Mountain Community: Ashe County, North Carolina, 1850–1861," *Journal of Southern History* 55 (Aug. 1989): 386–88. The county's political experience during the period of secession is set in broader regional context in John C. Inscoe, *Mountain Masters: Slavery and the Sectional Crisis in Western North Carolina* (Knoxville: Univ. of Tennessee Press, 1989), 211–57; William D. Cotton, "Appalachian North Carolina: A Political Study, 1860–1869" (Ph.D. diss., Univ. of North Carolina, Chapel Hill, 1954), 71–166; Marc W. Kruman, *Parties and Politics in North Carolina, 1836–1865* (Baton Rouge: Louisiana State Univ. Press, 1983), 180–221; Thomas E. Jeffrey, *State Parties and National Politics: North Carolina, 1815–1861* (Athens: Univ. of Georgia Press, 1989), 281–312; and Daniel W. Crofts, *Reluctant Confederates: Upper South Unionists in the Secession Crisis* (Chapel Hill: Univ. of North Carolina Press, 1989).

9. James M. Gentry to Jonathan Faw, May 6, 1861, in Walter Wagner Faw Papers, Tennessee State Library and Archives, Nashville. Places of birth are identified in U.S. Bureau of the Census, *8th Census of North Carolina: 1860,* Population Schedule, Ashe County. Information on Carson's slaveholding comes from U.S. Bureau of the Census, *8th Census of North Carolina: 1860,* Slave Schedule, Ashe County. The date of emigration (from Belfast) was found in Wade Edward Eller, "Collection of History and Genealogy of Ashe County," North Carolina Dept. of Archives and History, Raleigh (microfilm).

10. Martin Crawford, "Confederate Volunteering and Enlistment in Ashe County, North Carolina, 1861–1862," *Civil War History* 37 (Mar. 1991): 29–50.

11. Richard Nelson Current, *Lincoln's Loyalists: Union Soldiers from the Confederacy* (Boston: Northeastern Univ. Press, 1992), 70–73. On conflict within North Carolina during the Civil War, see Paul D. Escott, *Many Excellent People: Power and Privilege in North Carolina, 1850–1900* (Chapel Hill: Univ. of North Carolina Press, 1985), 32–84.

12. See Current, *Lincoln's Loyalists*, 213–18, for a recent estimate of southern Unionist military contributions.

13. Samuel W. Scott and Samuel P. Angel, *History of the Thirteenth Tennessee Volunteer Cavalry, U.S.A.* (Philadelphia: Ziegler and Co., n.d.), 260–61. See also the similar argument advanced by the Knoxville lawyer and historian Oliver P. Temple, in his *East Tennessee and the Civil War* (Cincinnati, Ohio, 1899; reprinted Freeport, N.Y.: Books for Libraries Press, 1971), 563–64.

14. Jennie Thomas Lillard to Dr. John M. Lillard, Aug. 8, 1861, Box 1, Folder 16, Lillard Family Papers, Tennessee State Library and Archives, Nashville.

15. James M. Gentry to Gov. Henry T. Clark, Sept. 25, 1861, Governor's Papers (Clark), vol. 154, North Carolina Division of Archives and History, Raleigh.

16. James M. Gentry to Jonathan Faw, Oct. 6, 1861, in Walter Wagner Faw Papers, Tennessee State Library and Archives, Nashville. Gov. Henry T. Clark to Judah P. Benjamin, Nov. 16, 1861, in U.S. Dept. of War, *The War of the Rebellion: A Compilation of the Official Records of the Union and Confederate Armies* (Washington, D.C.: U.S. Government Printing Office, 1880–1901; hereafter cited as *OR*), ser. 1, vol. 52, pt. 2, p. 209. See also James Wagg to Gov. Henry T. Clark, Aug. 31, 1861, Governor's Papers (Clark), vol. 153, North Carolina Division of Archives and History, Raleigh: "I take the liberty to trouble you with this to request you to issue a proclamation commanding all citizens of Ashe Co. who have been aiding or abeting the said Tennesseans by talking in their favor, joining their companies for the Northern army or in any other way encouraging the rebellion shall come forward in open court and publicly recant their former principles by taking the oath of Allegiance to the Southern Confederacy." Wagg was a Jefferson doctor. His son was killed at Gettysburg.

17. Quincy Neal et al., of Jefferson, to Gov. Henry T. Clark, Jan. 14, 1862, in Governor's Papers (Clark), vol. 157.1, North Carolina Division of Archives and History, Raleigh.

18. W. H. Younce, *The Adventures of a Conscript* (Cincinnati, Ohio: Editor Publishing Co., 1901), 58–62.

19. *Raleigh Weekly Register*, Apr. 29, 1863. The same report also appeared in the *Salem People's Press*, May 1, 1863. In the Salem report, however, the designation "notorious tory" had been changed to that of "notorious man," possibly as a concession to local "Quaker Belt" sensibilities.

20. See Younce, *Adventures of a Conscript*, 62; and Scott and Angel, *History of the 13th Regiment*, 355–56. The story does appear to be substantially true. Moses Price was revived, escaped, and served in the 21st West Virginia Cavalry. See Clarice B. Weaver, ed., *The Heritage of Ashe County, North Carolina Volume II, 1994* (West Jefferson, N.C.: Ashe County Historical Society, 1994), 246.

21. Charles Royster, *The Destructive War: William Tecumseh Sherman, Stone-*

wall Jackson, and the Americans (New York: Vintage Books, 1991), ch. 6. See also Michael Fellman, *Inside War: The Guerrilla Conflict in Missouri during the American Civil War* (New York: Oxford Univ. Press, 1989), esp. ch. 2.

22. Service information on Ashe County's Federal volunteers is derived from the following sources: *Compiled Service Records*, M395 (13th Tenn. Cavalry), M401 (3rd N.C. Mtd. Infantry), M1017 (1st U.S. Volunteers), RG 94, NA; and Special Schedule of 11th Census (1890), Union Veterans and Widows of Veterans, M123 (North Carolina), RG 94, NA. Identification has been established further in U.S. Bureau of the Census, *8th Census of North Carolina: 1860,* Population Schedule, Ashe County; Shepherd, *Heritage of Ashe County*; and Wade Edward Eller, "Collection of History and Genealogy."

Recent genealogical research has uncovered the intriguing case of Adam Roberts, a young Ashe County free black who served in the 119th U.S. Colored Infantry during the last few months of the war. Roberts's mother was white, and he was raised in the household of Mary Milam, the widow of a minister. After the war, Adam Roberts established a blacksmith shop in Jefferson and later ran a grist mill. He died in Veterans Hospital, Johnson City, Tenn., in Dec. 1913. See Weaver, *Heritage of Ashe County Volume II,* 261–62, 398.

23. Average household real property values for the North Fork in 1860 were $472.88; for the Town district, $904.25; for the Village of Jefferson, $1867.68.

24. The sample of North Fork volunteers is made up of 35 Union and 42 Confederate households. In 1860, the two groups compared as follows. In terms of average value of real property, Union volunteers had $319.29, while Confederates had $644.88. Median value of real property was $75.00 for Union partisans and $300.00 for Confederates. Average combined value of real and personal property was $579.31 for Unionists and $1,173.45 for Confederates. Sixteen Union households (45.7 percent) and 11 Confederate households (26.2 percent) had no real property at all.

25. Peter Wallenstein, "Which Side Are You On? The Social Origins of White Union Troops from Civil War Tennessee," *Journal of East Tennessee History* 63 (1991): 72–103. See also Walter Lynn Bates, "Southern Unionists: A Socio-Economic Examination of the 3rd Tennessee Volunteer Infantry Regiment, U.S.A., 1862–1865," *Tennessee Historical Quarterly* 50 (Winter 1991): 226–39; and Phillip Shaw Paludan, *Victims: A True Story of the Civil War* (Knoxville: Univ. of Tennessee Press, 1981), 59–64.

26. Sutherland's Unionist neighbor, Wesley Cornutt, had kinship ties to both Virginia and Tennessee. His parents, William and Mary Hatfield Cornutt, who both were deceased by the time of his enlistment, had migrated to Ashe from Grayson County, Va. His elder brother Billy, meanwhile, lived on Ackerson Creek in neighboring Johnson County, Tenn., a Unionist hotbed during the Civil War. See Freddie C. Morley, comp., *History of Johnson County, 1986* (Marceline, Mo.: Walsworth Press, for Johnson County [Tenn.] Historical Society, 1986), 225–26. The functional centrality of kinship to Ashe County society, past and present, is examined in two important works: Beaver, *Rural Community in the Appalachian South*; and Stephen William Foster, *The Past Is Another Country: Representation, Historical Consciousness, and Resistance in the Blue Ridge* (Berkeley: Univ. of California Press, 1988), esp. 62–93.

27. Information on the Worth-Thomas family is derived from the following sources: U.S. Bureau of the Census, *8th Census of North Carolina: 1860*, Population, Agricultural, and Slave Schedules, Ashe County; Shepherd, *Heritage of Ashe County Volume I*, 47–48, 473–74, 511–12; R. G. Dun and Co. Credit Reporting Ledgers, North Carolina, 2:25, in Baker Library, Harvard School of Business Administration, Cambridge, Mass.

28. David Worth to Jonathan Worth, Dec. 15, 1863, Jonathan Worth Papers, North Carolina Division of Archives and History. The Worth-Thomases lived in households numbered 340-42, in the 1860 U.S. Census. U.S. Bureau of the Census, *8th Census of North Carolina: 1860*, Population Schedules, Ashe County. Union volunteers have been identified in the following households: 326 (Osborn), 331 (Goss), 332 (Greer), 333 (Greer), 338 (Cornutt), 339 (Price), 350 (Vanover), 352 (Wilson), 353 (Potter), 359 (Wilson), 364 (Martin), 365 (Snider), 373 (Osborn), 374 (Roark), 379 (Osborn), 381 (Osborn).

29. David Worth certificate, Box 1, Folder 8, Lillard Family Papers, Tennessee State Library and Archives, Nashville.

30. Shepherd, *Heritage of Ashe County Volume I*, 47.

31. Dun Credit Reporting Ledgers, North Carolina, 2:25.

32. Shepherd, *Heritage of Ashe County Volume I*, 473–74, 502. The Worths' Unionist son-in-law, Ticy Wagner, died during the war, as did the Thomas's daughter Jennie, wife of Col. John Lillard of the 26th Tennessee (C.S.A.). Col. Lillard was killed at Chickamauga in Sept. 1863. Two of David Worth's younger daughters subsequently married former Confederate officers. On Wiley Thomas's participation in fights with marauding East Tennessee Unionists, see Stephen Thomas to Dr. John M. Lillard, Feb. 6, 1863, Box 1, Folder 16, Lillard Family Papers, Tennessee State Library and Archives, Nashville.

33. Shepherd, *Heritage of Ashe County Volume I*, 47, 511. He also was related to Daniel Worth, the Wesleyan Methodist missionary convicted in North Carolina in 1860 of selling Hinton Rowan Helper's *The Impending Crisis of the South*. See Noble J. Tolbert, "Daniel Worth: Tar Heel Abolitionist," *North Carolina Historical Review* 39 (July 1962): 284–304.

34. See William T. Auman and David D. Scarboro, "The Heroes of America in Civil War North Carolina," *North Carolina Historical Review* 58 (Oct. 1981): 327–63; and William T. Auman, "Neighbor Against Neighbor: The Inner Civil War in the Randolph County Area of Confederate North Carolina," *North Carolina Historical Review* 61 (Jan. 1984): 59–92. It should also be noted that both David Worth and Stephen Thomas were Whigs. The absence of detailed records renders impossible precise judgments about antebellum voting behavior in Ashe, but Whig support does seem to have been strongest in the western and southwestern part of the county, adjacent to the Watauga County and Johnson County, Tennessee lines. Both of these counties were strongly Whig in the 1850s. The question of the relationship between antebellum political allegiances and Civil War Unionism needs further investigation.

35. Royster, *Destructive War*, 118.

36. Stephen Thomas's wife Rebecca also had died in July 1861. Significantly, Wiley

Thomas had been commissioned in Oct. 1862 in the 7th Battalion, North Carolina Cavalry, whose ranks contained few Ashe County residents. His company transferred in Aug. 1863 to the 6th Regiment, North Carolina Cavalry. Following his capture, Thomas remained confined at Johnson's Island until released after taking the Oath of Allegiance on June 12, 1865. Manarin and Jordan, *North Carolina Troops*, 2:458, 2:552.

37. See Martin Crawford, "Mountain Farmers and the Market Economy: Ashe County during the 1850s," *North Carolina Historical Review* 72 (Oct. 1994): 430–50. On class resentments during the war, see esp. Escott, *Many Excellent People*, 59–84; and Bill Cecil-Fronsman, *Common Whites: Class and Culture in Antebellum North Carolina* (Lexington: Univ. Press of Kentucky, 1992), 203–18.

38. It is impossible to provide an accurate estimate of the extent and depth of Unionist allegiance in Ashe County, or indeed to separate it from the broader disillusionment with the war that affected most neighborhoods and households at one time or another. No Ashe County claims were made to the Southern Claims Commission, while evidence of widespread support for the "Heroes of America"—the clandestine Unionist organization in North Carolina, complete with secret signs and passwords—is difficult to substantiate. In a 1934 study, one historian used the evidence of Linville Price, a Confederate deserter, to assert that "the order was extensive" in Ashe. Close scrutiny of the original source, a detectives' report of Nov. 1864, shows that to be a misreading: the quoted words derive from the testimony of Price's companion, a native of Forsyth County in the "Quaker Belt," where, according to modern authority, the order probably was founded in 1861. However, Price, a landless farmer from Ashe's southeastern district, clearly is identified in the report as a member of the Heroes of America. See Georgia Lee Tatum, *Disloyalty in the Confederacy* (Chapel Hill: Univ. of North Carolina Press, 1934), 135. The detectives' report can be found in *OR*, ser. 4, vol. 3, p. 816, and their activities in the region are carefully evaluated in Kenneth W. Noe, "Red String Scare: Civil War Southwest Virginia and the Heroes of America," *North Carolina Historical Review* 69 (July 1992): 301–22, which concludes that organized opposition to the Confederacy in the region to the north of Ashe County has been exaggerated. Noe's study persuasively differentiates Unionist activity in southwestern Virginia from the more widespread fatigue and disillusionment with the Confederate cause.

39. Ralph Mann, "Family Group, Family Migration, and the Civil War in the Sandy Basin of Virginia," *Appalachian Journal* 19 (Summer 1992): 374–93. One should not assume that mountain Unionists invariably represented the poorer or more isolated elements. In the Tug Valley region on the Kentucky–West Virginia border, the opposite may have been the case. See Altina L. Waller, *Feud: Hatfields, McCoys, and Social Change in Appalachia, 1860–1900* (Chapel Hill: Univ. of North Carolina Press, 1988), 30.

40. Younce, *Adventures of a Conscript*, 2.

41. Shepherd, *Heritage of Ashe County Volume I*, 515–16. Younce's own memoir does not pursue his career into the Federal army.

42. See Betty-Lou Fields, comp. and ed., *Grayson County: A History in Words and Pictures* (Independence, Va.: Grayson County Historical Society), 83, 88.

43. *Raleigh Weekly Register,* Sept. 3 and Oct. 1 and 8, 1851; *Raleigh Weekly Standard,* Oct. 3, 1851. Bacon was a Wesleyan Methodist preacher. See Guion Griffis Johnson, *Antebellum North Carolina: A Social History* (Chapel Hill: Univ. of North Carolina Press, 1937), 575–77. His earlier activities in the Guilford County area are noted in Gail Williams O'Brien, *The Legal Fraternity and the Making of a New South Community, 1848–1882* (Athens: Univ. of Georgia Press, 1986), 38–42.

44. John C. Inscoe, "Mountain Unionism, Secession, and Regional Self-Image: The Contrasting Cases of Western North Carolina and East Tennessee," in *Looking South: Chapters in the Story of an American Region,* ed. Winfred B. Moore, Jr., and Joseph F. Tripp (Westport, Conn.: Greenwood, 1989), 124.

45. Paul D. Escott and Jeffrey J. Crow, "The Social Order and Violent Disorder: An Analysis of North Carolina in the Revolution and the Civil War," *Journal of Southern History* 52 (Aug. 1986): 373–402; Shepherd, *Heritage of Ashe County Volume I,* 258, 393, 515. The Ashe County Perkins were descendants of 17th-century immigrants to New Haven, Conn. Rachel Goss's case is revealed in "Criminal Action Concerning Slaves, 1862," Miscellaneous Records, Ashe County, North Carolina Division of Archives and History, Raleigh. On poor white–slave interaction, see Charles C. Bolton, *Poor Whites of the Antebellum South: Tenants and Laborers in Central North Carolina and Northeast Mississippi* (Durham, N.C.: Duke Univ. Press, 1994), 43–52.

46. Shepherd, *Heritage of Ashe County Volume I,* 470–71. According to this family memoir, Alexander Sutherland "went over the mountains to reach freedom and settled in Elk Creek, Va., after the war."

47. See Ina W. Van Noppen, "The Significance of Stoneman's Last Raid," *North Carolina Historical Review* 38 (Jan. 1961): 39–40.

48. The story of Isaac Wilson's killing and related incidents is narrated in a letter written by his son, William Albert Wilson, to his brother Robert on Feb. 27, 1941. The letter is read and discussed in Boyd Barlow interview, 3–12. On the conflict elsewhere in the mountains, see esp. Paludan, *Victims*; Mann, "Family Group"; Jonathan D. Sarris, "Anatomy of an Atrocity: The Madden Branch Massacre and Guerrilla Warfare in North Georgia, 1861–1865," *Georgia Historical Quarterly* 77 (Winter 1993): 679–710; and Kenneth W. Noe, *Southwest Virginia's Railroad: Modernization and the Sectional Crisis* (Urbana: Univ. of Illinois Press, 1994), 109–38.

49. Mann, "Family Group," provides an outstanding discussion of the relationship between family and neighborhood allegiances during the war.

50. John Preston Arthur, *A History of Watauga County with Sketches of Prominent Families* (1915; reprinted Johnson City, Tenn.: Overmountain Press, 1992), 169–72. Arthur's account of Isaac Wilson's killing contains interesting detail not present in the Barlow narrative but is less certain on dating and chronology and links the attack to another set of border "depredations." The Isaac Wilson family history is detailed in Weaver, *Heritage of Ashe County Volume II,* 307.

51. The interviewee, Boyd Barlow, notes that local people remembered Lizzie Stout's discovering her husband's remains later that year on Rich Mountain, to-

gether with the noose that had been used to hang him. She supposedly carried these remains back home in an apron and buried them. Stout's killers reportedly were taking him to the Confederate prison in Morganton but "didn't get that far" (Boyd Barlow interview, 9). The story of Lizzie Stout's ghastly discovery is confirmed and elaborated by direct testimony reported in Arthur, *History of Watauga County*, 171. The date of her discovery is given there as Apr. 10, 1865.

52. Arthur, *History of Watauga County*, 171, talks about "Old Man Thomas Stout, father of the Stout boy or boys charged with having been concerned in the killing of Isaac Wilson." Stout's guilt is less clearly established in the account of William Albert Wilson (contained in Boyd Barlow interview, 3–12), who makes no mention of Stout's sons, identified by Arthur as allegedly responsible for earlier attacks in the border region. Arthur's history was constructed largely from interviews gathered in the second decade of this century.

53. See esp. Paludan, *Victims*; Ronald D Eller, *Miners, Millhands, and Mountaineers: Industrialization in the Appalachian South, 1880–1930* (Knoxville: Univ. of Tennessee Press, 1982); Waller, *Feud*; Durwood Dunn, *Cades Cove: The Life and Death of a Southern Appalachian Community, 1818–1937* (Knoxville: Univ. of Tennessee Press, 1988); and Ralph Mann, "Mountain, Land, and Kin Networks: Burkes Garden, Virginia, in the 1840s and 1850s," *Journal of Southern History* 58 (Aug. 1992): 411–34; Mann, "Family Group"; Gordon B. McKinney, "Economy and Community in Western Carolina, 1860–1865," in Mary Beth Pudup, Dwight B. Billings, Altina L. Waller, eds., *Appalachia in the Making: The Mountain South in the Nineteenth Century* (Chapel Hill: Univ. of North Carolina Press, 1995), 163–84.

54. See esp. Robert H. Wiebe, *The Opening of American Society: From the Adoption of the Constitution to the Eve of Disunion* (New York: Vintage Books, 1985), esp. 255–384.

4

Ezekiel Counts's Sand Lick Company: Civil War and Localism in the Mountain South

Ralph Mann

In early spring of 1864, Company E of the 21st Virginia Regiment of Cavalry officially ceased to exist as a unit in the Confederate Department of Southwestern Virginia. It had been recruited a year earlier, during late March, May, and early June 1863, along Sand Lick, McClure River, and Fryingpan Creek—all tributaries of the Russell Fork of the Big Sandy River, in an area of Appalachian Virginia known as the Sandy Basin—and on Dumps Creek, a branch of the Clinch River. Reporting for service in July 1863, Company E first had been posted to protect the salines at Saltville, southwestern Virginia's most vital contribution to the salt-starved Confederacy. That fall and winter, from September into January, Company E took part in its one campaign—the failed effort to dislodge Ambrose Burnside's Army of the Ohio from East Tennessee.[1]

The company evidently saw little action, as only one man was reported killed. Not death but desertion thinned its ranks. In Company E's one appearance in the Combined Service Records of Virginia units in the Confederate Army, dated August 31, 1863, just before the trip to Tennessee, one-third of its men already were listed as away without leave or as having deserted. In November, as the East Tennessee campaign continued, Company E's captain, Ezekiel K. Counts, deserted; the following February, his indignant commanding officer, David Edmundson, reported that Counts was living behind Federal lines. Counts's replacement, Jasper Colley, deserted in December; by February, as the exasperated Edmundson reported, he already had joined another Confederate regiment and had deserted from that one, too. *His* replacement, William Lockhart, may have been killed in January; he makes only three appearances in the Combined Service records as acting company commander, and family tradition in Sand Lick relates that he was killed in Tennessee. During all this time, the men of Company E, like their commanders, streamed home.

When campaigning resumed the following spring, Counts and Colley were dropped from Confederate service, and a new Company E was organized from men of Smyth and Wythe counties. The vast majority of the original Company E's 101 men disappeared from the record without a trace, the one extant piece of official evidence of their Confederate service being the company roll of August 31, 1863. By the laws of the Confederate Congress, they were deserters.[2]

Confederate officials took desertion and disaffection in mountain Virginia very seriously. Southwest Virginia supplied irreplaceable—and militarily vulnerable— natural resources: Wythe County's lead and Smyth County's salt were the largest deposits in the South. The southern extension of the Valley of Virginia was an important exporter of foodstuffs. The railroad that traversed the region, the Virginia and Tennessee, was the most convenient link between Virginia and the southwestern Confederacy; freeing it from Burnside's control was a primary goal of the advance on Knoxville. Mountain gaps exposed southwestern Virginia to Union raiders and even offered the North alternate invasion routes into the Shenandoah and eastern Virginia. Clearly the Confederate government and army had much at stake here. Just as clearly, the men of Company E had other interests.[3]

Historians attempting to explain Confederate desertion and disloyalty focus on this disjunction. Some find the key in regional diversity: portions of the Confederacy not economically rooted in slavery and staple crops—the Appalachian South especially—were less committed to the defense of the slave system. Other arguments stress class and community: the soldiers of kin-based yeoman neighborhoods deserted *en masse* once they realized that the wealthy were sacrificing less to the cause. Still others stress the expectations of equality and autonomy held by the common soldiers: desertion was caused by the coupling of an unaccustomed discipline with unacceptable privileges of rank.

All these arguments obviously overlap, especially in emphasizing forces that alienated certain soldiers and communities from the Confederate army.

And all these arguments help explain the behavior of the men in Company E. This essay, however, argues that the pull of Russell Fork was more important than any push away from the Confederacy. The fierce local loyalty held by all Civil War soldiers is widely recognized by historians but not often stressed. The Sand Lick men—and many others—stayed in or left the army primarily according to local conditions, and a threat to home would cause mass desertions.

Three basic facts about the military careers of Zeke Counts's Sand Lick soldiers suggest that their actions cannot be explained simply as expressing alienation from the Confederacy. First, many of these men had served before, under Counts and under the same colonel, William E. Peters, as members of a different unit, John B. Floyd's Virginia State Line. What is more, led by Counts, they had deserted from Floyd's command and indeed were being recruited as a unit into the 21st Cavalry even as the State Line was being officially disbanded.

Second, despite what officers like Floyd and Edmundson would see as a record of recidivist desertion, in their own minds they remained loyal Confederate soldiers. They passed on to their children proud identities as Rebels, sharply distinct from the Unionist neighbors they termed Yankees, and especially distinct from the "scouters" who hid out and avoided service altogether. They had been, they sometimes said, "on furlough"; and their tie to Company E remained, so that when they—Counts and Colley included—applied to take loyalty oaths at war's end, they designated their unit as Company E, 21st Virginia Cavalry.

Third, this identity with the Confederate army was not a mere cloak to cover cowardice or crimes against civilians. During the first days of October 1864, while Peters's command was taking a beating with Jubal Early in the Valley of Virginia and while agents of the Bureau of Conscription were searching for them, the men of the officially defunct Sand Lick company rallied once more. Led by Zeke Counts, they hiked over the mountains between Russell Fork and Levisa Fork, the branch of the Big Sandy immediately to the east, and attacked Stephen Burbridge's small Federal force as it retreated down the Levisa back into Kentucky after a failed raid on the salt works.

To Burbridge, they were simply bushwhackers; to Peters, Edmundson, Floyd, and the Confederate hierarchy, they were simply deserters; to themselves, they were Confederate soldiers defending their homes. To piece together the several identities of Company E, to find out who these men were, why they were in Counts's company, and why they deserted, this essay relies on three main sources, two official and one unofficial. The officers' reports in

The War of the Rebellion: A Compilation of the Official Records of the Union and Confederate Armies tend to dismiss Company E's men as disloyal and disorderly soldiers. The Combined Service Records allow us to sort out who served, when they joined, and, for some, when they departed. Finally, their own staunchly pro-Rebel memories of their wartime experiences, especially those of the Counts, Kiser, and Sutherland families, collected in the second and third decades of the twentieth century by their immediate descendant, Elihu Sutherland, allow us to analyze these men's actions in their own terms. Selective in what they chose to recount and tending to laugh off dangerous confrontations, Noah Sutherland, his first cousin Jasper Sutherland, and their neighbor Andy Edwards, especially, produced high-spirited accounts that still offer insight into the values of these sometime soldiers and those of their leader and the hero of their tales, Zeke Counts.[4]

The Sandy Basin of Appalachian Virginia lies on the Kentucky border, between the edge of the Cumberland Plateau and Sandy Ridge, and is drained by tributaries of the Big Sandy. At the time of the Civil War, the neighborhoods along Russell Fork were barely a generation old. Settled by migrations of siblings and in-laws moving across Sandy Ridge from the Clinch Valley, especially from the Dumps Creek area, the Sand Lick section in 1858 had been included in newly formed Buchanan County. Although many of its families lived scattered on land claims of doubtful legality, raising small corn crops and ranging cattle and hogs in the surrounding mountains for their livings, they had established an active trade with the Clinch Valley, in hides and cattle. Centered on a small store at Sand Lick run by the Colley family and dominated by Jim Colley's and Andy Owens's large herds, this trade both brought necessities into the Sandy Basin and reinforced the kinship ties that linked the Russell Fork settlements with the Valley of Virginia. Cattleman Jim Colley emerged as the section's leading figure; and Colleys, Countses, and Sutherlands held most of the offices that loosely extended Buchanan County government into the regions around Sand Lick.[5]

"People here [were] not in favor of war when Civil War came. There was a right smart of scouting," remembered Company E veteran Andy Edwards. While several men, Andy among them, hid in the mountains to avoid rumored conscription efforts, Andy's younger brother Ben, with a handful of Rebel enthusiasts, members of the Sutherland, Colley, Owens, and Fuller families, journeyed to Tazewell Court House to join the Confederate Army. When it became clear that the Tazewell company would fail to get weapons and supplies distributed before the volunteers' three-month enlistments ran out, the Sand Lick men returned home—with the permission of the

Map 4.1. Area of Operations, Company E, 21st Virginia Cavalry, 1861–1865. Map by The University of Tennessee Cartography Lab.

colonel in charge. But while some scouted and a few volunteered for the Confederate Army, many others responded to the crisis by drilling at Sand Lick with the local militia, willing to defend their homes, if not to march away to defend Richmond. Among the militiamen were several who later would resist Confederate enlistment. The few Unionists kept their opinions within their own families.[6]

The uncertainty was resolved in the summer of 1862, when Ezekiel Counts came to Sand Lick recruiting for a company to serve in John B. Floyd's Virginia State Line. Floyd, a major contributor to the Confederacy's loss of West Virginia and Kentucky, was in near disgrace after the disaster at Fort Donelson. He was organizing a Virginia—not Confederate—army pledged to protect the borderland's resources, its railroad, and its loyal citizens by fortifying the mountain passes, raiding into Kentucky, and reinvading northwestern (West) Virginia. Virginia Gov. John Letcher hoped that Floyd, an ex-governor and southwestern Virginia native, retained enough political popularity in the southwest to rally men to the cause in a region that hitherto had been very lukewarm about secession and war. Further, Letcher wanted an army that would contest all of Virginia, regardless of the strategic foci of the Confederate high command.[7]

From the beginning, Floyd's recruiting tactics brought him into bitter controversy with the regular Confederate commanders in the region—Humphrey Marshall, W. W. Loring, and especially Henry Heth. Heth, trying to defend his own recruiting area, claimed that Floyd intended to "break down" the Confederate army in southwestern Virginia and build his own on its ruins, by telling potential recruits that the conscription law passed that April was merely optional, by offering twelve-month enlistments instead of the regular Confederate enlistments of three years or the duration of the war, and by implicitly assuring the locals that his soldiers would stay in the mountains, operating only to defend the Appalachian border. Heth concluded that Floyd's State Line would be manned mostly by deserters and conscripts. Floyd defended himself to Letcher by claiming that Marshall's agents were undermining *his* command, by insisting on the importance of holding the Virginia mountains and especially by arguing that the "arrogant way" in which conscription had been carried out made it "ineffectual," even "repulsive to the community," and that the men he raised were "not likely to be gotten into the ranks at all except by the means [unspecified] that I use."[8]

For the Sandy Basin, and for Sand Lick in particular, Floyd's reasoning was sound. Zeke Counts was kin; he had been a constable at Sand Lick and now lived in the Dumps Creek section of the Clinch Valley, the family home of many Sand Lick men; and he recruited among his connections along the Clinch River and along Russell Fork. His local reputation as "brainy and resolute," plus his adherence to Floyd's doctrine of mountain defense, allowed him to attract not only his kin and men who already had sought Confederate service, but also other connections who, for their Rebel sentiments, had been violently evicted from Unionist areas of eastern Kentucky and from Roane and Logan counties of (West) Virginia. More importantly, Counts was able to sign on men like Andy Edwards, who previously had hidden out to avoid conscription. Henry Heth was right; of the twenty-one Sandy Basin enlistees traceable by age, nineteen were liable to the draft—between eighteen and thirty-five—in June and July 1862, when the Sand Lick company was organized. But Floyd also was right; the majority of these men would not have served under other circumstances. The war had been on for over a year, and only six Sand Lick men had volunteered before Counts arrived to recruit for the State Line.[9]

By August 1862, Counts's Sand Lick company had become Company B, 2d Regiment of the Virginia State Line, under the command of a former professor of Latin and Greek at Emory and Henry College, William Elisha Peters. Along with four other Sandy Basin companies, Counts's men moved up the Big Sandy to Logan Court House and established control. By mid-August, they had driven out the local Unionist military elements and adopted a policy of living off the production of Union sympathizers.

In the process, they had revenged themselves on those who earlier had driven their kin from these areas. Next, Floyd's men moved up the Guyandotte, dispersing Union Home Guards in Wayne and Cabell counties, and then struck up the Big Sandy beyond Louisa, to drive the Yankees away from the Floyd family saltworks at Warfield, Kentucky. Counts's men, returning from the Warfield raid, stopped briefly at Logan, before being ordered, in early October, back across the mountains to the more securely Confederate sections of Tazewell and New Garden. In November, the company had returned to Logan Court House.[10]

During their stay at Tazewell, several of Counts's men visited their families and helped with late harvest. They also found growing opposition to the war and, by threats and violence, squelched some vocal Unionists. They briefly arrested one woman who had made several trips across the mountains to Pike County, alleging that she was a spy who might tell the enemy "something she should not"; they held her until a junior officer in their State Line company made them let her go. Obviously nervous about opposition at home, the men on furlough were ready to believe rumors that small parties of Yankees had passed through Sand Lick on the way to the Clinch Valley. While Noah Sutherland was visiting his Uncle Johnnie Kiser's cabin, in company with his father Jim, brother Zeke, and Uncle Billy Sutherland, word came that a party of Yankees was coming up Fryingpan Creek. ("Yankees" referred, in local parlance, to Unionist neighbors and Federal soldiers alike.) "Us soldiers," Zeke, Billy, and Noah, as Noah joyfully told the story, "potter[ed] down" the creek to look into the matter. When no Yankees appeared, the boys returned; idly, as they approached within a quarter-mile of Uncle Johnnie's place, they decided to fire off a volley just to see what their father and uncle would do. Their kin, terrified, took to the woods, "storming a big brush pile" as they did, and leaving Aunt Sibbie to explain that Jim and Johnnie had "stepped out, when they heard the Yankees shoot." To Noah Sutherland, telling this story to Elihu, Billy's grandson, sixty years later, this simply was a very successful practical joke on his father and uncle. But Noah and his companions took for granted that it was their prerogative *as soldiers* to maintain order, by force, in their neighborhood. They had gone armed to visit their uncle. And their relatives' reaction reflected a growing and real fear of disorder around Sand Lick.[11]

In December 1862, according to Floyd, the State Line recorded its most brilliant military exploit. Learning of boats on the Levisa Fork of the Sandy, loaded with supplies for the Union forces at Pikeville, Floyd sent his "mountain men" to capture them and in the process routed the Yankees and briefly occupied Pikeville itself. But the Civil War memories of the veterans of Counts's company are silent about the glorious Pikeville campaign. For good reason—Counts's men had already gone home.[12]

Floyd called their departure desertion and claimed that Vincent A. Witcher, a partisan ranger from northwestern (West) Virginia, "a person of the most depraved and infamous character," had lured Counts's company off to join Humphrey Marshall's regular Confederate army in southwestern Virginia. There is no evidence that Counts's men either joined Marshall or served under Witcher, although they well may have started in that direction; Marshall, operating out of Abingdon and Saltville, was a lot closer to their homes than Floyd was. They simply may have decided to winter over at home. Noah Sutherland, whose reminiscences are the best surviving source on the Sand Lick men's experiences in the State Line, does not comment on their departure, other than to say that, after returning to Logan from New Castle, they went home. However, his account of their service under Floyd, together with the accounts of Jasper Sutherland and Andy Edwards, contains clues to the company's attitudes.[13]

Sutherland's story, quite naturally, weighed the whole war experience in terms of his home and its values. He was impressed by fine farms in areas more developed than his Fryingpan Creek home. And he judged his officers on the basis of their courage and their democracy—how courteous and obliging they were to the ranks. His uncle Zeke Counts rated high—"a true man though plain and rough," thoroughly in tune with the views of his men. He demanded none of the privileges of rank, he took part in elaborate practical jokes, and, when he was away from camp, he left Billy Sutherland, well respected in the Sand Lick section, in charge—even though Sutherland, as orderly sergeant, was outranked by others present. Other officers were measured the same way. Colonel Peters was "quiet and kind" and did not attempt to enforce much discipline or order in camp. "Everyone liked" Maj. Martin Ball. But Col. Joe Harris was "rough and disagreeable" and, as a result, had failed to raise a regiment in the mountains.[14]

But another theme dominated Noah's, Jasper's, and Andy's memories of State Line service. This was a growing awareness of the bitter personal divisions the war had created at Warfield and Logan Court House, and the destruction and violence these neighborhood rifts had caused. Their kinsman, civilian Abednego Kiser, had been shot from ambush and badly wounded near Logan by a Yankee sympathizer. That man, in turn, had been murdered in the same manner. Also near Logan, "the finest farm [Noah] ever saw" was burned out by the Unionist neighbors of its Rebel owner. In a running skirmish near the Guyandotte, after Floyd's men had overwhelmed a band of Yankee Home Guards, Jasper's commander, Bill Smith, kept shouting the name of Smith's Union counterpart and neighbor, Morgan Garrett, demanding that Garrett stop and fight. The pursuit swept past the houses of both Smith and Garrett. And at Warfield, Counts's men learned another basic lesson. The Union men made only token resistance and disappeared, leaving a town populated mostly by women. Some of the women shouted for Jeff Davis and some for Abe Lincoln, and, much to Noah's surprise, some of them fired on Counts's company. John Floyd's policy around Logan was intended "to root out the Union element among the people." He did this, in part, by feeding his troops on the wheat and cattle of Unionists. As part of this program, Andy Edwards drove a produce wagon on raids that stripped Yankee farms; Noah Sutherland later acknowledged how dangerous that duty had been. On this trip to Logan and Warfield, the Sand Lick men had seen just how vulnerable all the members of a divided society at war could be. Meanwhile, their own families were at risk. They knew, by name, the Unionists who lived on the waters of Russell Fork, as well as the neutrals who were living off the land, hiding in the mountains surrounding the Sandy Basin, supported by many people in the section. Noah Sutherland's compeers had good reason to follow Zeke Counts back to Sand Lick, as the advance guard of a migration back home that effectively would destroy Floyd's command that winter.[15]

At the end of February 1863, the Virginia legislature transferred the State Line to the Confederate army, specifying that the officers of the new regiments were to be elected from among officers of the right rank in the old State Line regiments and that those (few) in the State Line not subject to conscription could leave the service when their current enlistment was up. The State Line would cease to exist on April 1. In part, this transfer went as planned. In the Sutherland accounts, desertion or no desertion, all that seemed to change was a unit designation. William Peters, the colonel whom the Russell Fork men had admired and served under at Logan, commanded the new regiment, the 21st Virginia Cavalry. Peters seemed to hold no grudges concerning their early departure the preceding winter. Zeke Counts still would lead the men from Sand Lick, McClure, and Dumps Creek. But now Confederate rules concerning enlistment would apply. Noah Sutherland was detailed to stay home as community blacksmith. And a second Zeke Counts, who on the past campaign had proven "far too old" to serve, this time was left behind.[16]

Not everyone accepted the transfer. John S. Williams, commanding the brigade to which the former State Line troops had been assigned, complained that it "took an incredible amount of labor" to organize them into three regiments and one battalion, including the one headed by Peters. Williams did not even include the other four Sandy Basin companies of the State Line in his count. They balked at being assigned to the 7th Battalion of Confederate Cavalry, a composite unit being made up of refugee pro-South Kentuckians and mountain Virginians. Much to Williams's displeasure, they had extracted a promise that they would not have to leave the mountains, and they made it stand up. They stayed on patrol, commanded by Kentuckian Clarence J. Prentice, near the Kentucky border.[17]

In the same spirit, several of the Sand Lick men refused to join the 21st Virginia Cavalry, and Counts had to cajole and finally to coerce men into his new Company E. Reenlistment stretched out from late March to mid-July. The dates of enlistment in company records clustered on March 28, May 1, and June 1, with scatterings of individual men coming in later, some when E had already been posted for duty. In part, this delayed reorganization simply reflected the fact that Counts's company had dispersed and gone home the previous November; planting and spring hunting on the scattered homesteads along Russell Fork and Dumps Creek meant that not everybody was immediately available when Counts and Colley attempted to reorganize. But the later enlistment dates also reflect resistance. Clearly a new and bitter tone had come to war service.[18]

Scouting from the Confederate army had, at first, a humorous element. Some men openly joked about their intentions, saying that they planned to hide out in Tory Camp Hollow, a place named from its use as refuge by men avoiding the War of 1812. But all humor disappeared in the spring and summer of 1863, as Counts endeavored to fill his ranks. To the families of resisters, Ezekiel Counts became "Devil Zeke." Ike Blair had enlisted, argued with Counts, and deserted. Counts arrested him and his brother and put them on a train for prison. The Blairs escaped by jumping from the moving train. In a second attempt to arrest Ike, David Smith, an enthusiastic Rebel with a taste for fighting, shot and seriously wounded him. According to Hale family tradition (hotly denied by Counts's partisans), Jim and Isaac Hale were held for three days in a log pen by Counts and fed only parched corn until they agreed to join Company E. Jim Hale had been in the State Line and had seen enough. Elijah Counts refused to fight for religious reasons, but, despite his standing in the neighborhood and his kinship with Captain Zeke, Rebel soldiers fired on him, narrowly missing, as he stood at his cabin door. His fellow pacifist Brum McCoy escaped soldiers coming to take him into the Confederate army only by donning a girl's dress and sneaking past them in the darkness.

Looking back after the war on these events, the participants and their children could, at times, find elements of humor in them. Malissa Sutherland, whose father, Mayfield Kiser, and uncles were neutrals, recounted one war-time episode as a funny story at the expense of her younger sister, Patsy. "One day during the war," a strange man called at the gate and asked Sister Pats, "Is May here?" Pats said no.

"Where's Noah and Abe?"

"I don't know."

"Didn't they stay here last night?"

"I don't know."

"You don't know me, do you?"

"No."

"This is Jackie Kiser."

"Well, if it's Jackie Kiser, Uncle Noah and Uncle Abe are in that field over there hoeing corn. If it isn't Jackie Kiser, I don't know where they are." As in Noah Sutherland's joke on his kin, humor cloaked fear of violence. Malissa's and Patsy's father and uncles were in real danger. Shootings and beatings were becoming common, and most stemmed from forced enlistment.[19]

While Counts himself had been notoriously casual about when and where he had served under Floyd, he offered no such latitude to those he coerced into his company. Young Harman Mullins was absent without leave on August 31. His father and Jasper Colley exchanged shots when Colley came to search the Mullins cabin. There were no clashes between armed partisan bands near Sand Lick. The handful of overt Unionists early had been hounded to Kentucky. A few joined the Union army, but none had returned to contest control of the section. The families of neutrals, however, commonly told stories of bands of soldiers appearing in the night, seizing men for the army, especially men who had briefly joined Company E and then deserted. Zeke Counts was on detached service at least twice during July and August 1863, probably rounding up men for his company. Earlier, on May 30, he had been detailed to take prisoners to Richmond. There is no record of these prisoners' names, but the Blairs escaped while being sent to prison, and another of Counts's Unionist neighbors, Buck Jim Kiser, did end up in Richmond, in Castle Thunder.[20]

In the end, 101 men signed up for Company E. Although Zeke Counts and Jasper Colley dated their election as captain and first lieutenant from April 1, only thirty-two men had enlisted by that date. Many of these men were their neighbors and relations at Sand Lick, men openly identified with the Confederacy. Counts and Colley continued their efforts; by mid-May they had added twenty more. But the largest block of enlistees, forty, did not sign up until June 1. And nine more men joined the ranks in July. Some of these June and July enlistees were known Confederates who had served in the State Line, but many were new to Confederate service and came from families known as Unionist or neutral. Some obviously had been coerced. On August 31, 1863, the sole company muster of Company E took place at Saltville. Forty-seven men were present; thirteen were absent, sick; eight, including Zeke Counts and Noah Sutherland, were on detached service or detailed at home. One had died. That is, only two-thirds of the company strength was accounted for. And there is a clear correlation between enlistment date and status as of August 31. Twenty-eight were absent without leave, and nine already had deserted. All but two of the April 1 enlistees were present or on detached service (one was AWOL, and one had deserted). But only 60 percent of the May 1 enlistees, and only slightly over half of the June 1 and later enlistees, were present or excused. Seven of the nine deserters had come in on June 1 or later, probably under duress. Seventeen of the twenty-three men away without leave were June and July recruits; again, many obviously had been reluctant enlistees. Some may never have shown up at all. On five occasions in July, August, and early September, Counts and Colley requisitioned clothing—shirts, pants, jackets, drawers, and shoes—for men "nearly destitute" of these articles. In total, they outfitted sixty-four men. Most of those forced to enlist, then, probably never appeared to serve.[21]

The presumption of coercion is supported by an examination of the family loyalties of Company E's men and their records of other military service. Official records of Counts's Company B, 2d Regiment, Virginia State Line seem to be nonexistent; the thirty-eight available names of its members are drawn from Noah Sutherland's memory. Some names obviously were lost, but several points can be established with some certainty. A great majority of these men, excluding those too old for regular Confederate service in 1863, also served in Company E. Of the State Line men who did join Company E, only one was absent without leave on August 31; another would desert later. But many, perhaps half, of the nominal members of Company E had declined to serve in 1862. Deserters and absentees, almost without exception, were numbered among these new men. All identifiable deserters either had scouted before enlistment or were members of Unionist families. Half of the men AWOL were from Unionist families, had hidden out for a time, or had openly expressed Unionist sentiments. And while several absentees would return to Confederate service, the Unionists did not.[22]

Other Confederate authorities did not intervene in Counts's activities. In May 1863, Capt. Rufus Woolwine of the 51st Virginia Infantry was named enrollment officer for Wise, Russell, and Buchanan counties. He was detailed sixteen men and was instructed to round up conscripts and search out deserters. Woolwine took his duties seriously, constantly traveling the mountain counties and sending back small parties of draftees and deserters, until called back to his regiment for the campaign in East Tennessee. However, being a sane man, he rarely strayed away from the main roads and larger settlements, and he never crossed into Sandy Basin. There, recruitment to the Confederate army was in the hands of Zeke Counts and Jasper Colley, officers in the State Line and in the new Company E, and of men like David Smith, who had served under them in both companies. The fact that they all had deserted the Virginia State Line did not come into it.[23]

Indeed, the reason Counts and his men deserted the State Line, the reason they joined the 21st Virginia Cavalry, and the reason they pressured their reluctant neighbors into Company E were the same: their desire to protect their homes by controlling the Sand Lick area. Scouters, they knew, stole from the unprotected, sometimes terrorizing women and children. One very effective way to prevent this was to get as many of these men as possible into Counts's company, where they were under direct command of the area's pro-Confederate leadership. Service in the Confederate army could enforce one kind of neighborhood unity. Sam Sutherland had been tied and severely beaten for his Yankee views before he joined. He was still in camp on August 31. And even those who could not be kept in the army could be removed as immediate threats to the neighborhood. Mayfield Kiser twice was taken from his cabin by Confederate soldiers, only to flee camp; the second time he fled all the way to Ohio. Waitstill and Jasper Wright deserted before August 31; they ended in the Union army, in the 39th Kentucky Mounted Infantry, pursuing Rebel guerrillas in the Kentucky mountains, far from Sand Lick. So did Harman Mullins. Jim Hale was still in camp on August 31, but according to his family he left as soon as he could, also to join the 39th Kentucky.[24]

Service in the army for the larger purposes of the Confederacy was not on Counts's agenda. So, once Company E was organized and sent into action, a very different attitude toward desertion prevailed. When Peters's regiment was ordered to East Tennessee, Harrison Sutherland refused to go, arguing that he had enlisted to fight in Virginia, not another state. Still pro-South, he next appears as a junior officer in Prentice's 7th Confederate Battalion, patrolling the mountains between Virginia and Kentucky as his State Line company had done. Several others would follow the same course. Jasper Sutherland simply stated that he did not go with his company to Tennessee. And Andy Edwards, reluctant enlistee in the State Line, wagoner in Logan, also came home before the trip to Tennessee. His wife was expecting a baby, and a sympathetic Zeke Counts gave Andy a furlough. But Captain Counts must have been more sympathetic than the Confederate command, for, in Edwards's words, he had to "surround the guard" before he could leave camp. Once he was out of camp, however, none of the fifty-odd soldiers he met on the road asked to see his pass. After his child was born, as Andy remembered it, the war was over, so he did not have to return to the army. (In fact, the Civil War ended approximately twenty months after Andy had "surround[ed] the guard.")[25]

The 21st Virginia Cavalry that rode into East Tennessee was, by normal military standards, a notably casual outfit. Its commander, William E. Peters, certainly was brave enough, but the best that Confederate military inspector Archer Anderson could say of him was that he was "a gentleman but ignorant of military duty." A classics professor, Peters had learned what he knew of the military trade on the staff of another amateur, John B. Floyd, during the disastrous 1862 campaign in West Virginia. He had been removed from another regimental command before being restored by Floyd to lead the 2d Regiment of the State Line. Frequently absent from his regiment, twice because of wounds but once to serve a term in the Virginia Senate and on another occasion to fight a duel, Peters missed most of the campaign in East Tennessee. The Sand Lick men could appreciate a man who fought on his own terms. When Peters was away, David Edmundson commanded; in his also frequent absences, Stephen Halsey was in charge.[26]

Peters's command, and the cavalry brigade of John S. Williams to which it first belonged, gave Confederate authorities problems from the date of its organization. Believing, almost certainly correctly, that the 21st was harboring deserters from the Army of Northern Virginia, Confederate officials despairingly admitted that a search of its ranks would be fruitless, as Peters himself would have no idea how many of his men were deserters. On the march, the 21st aroused complaints—alike in largely Confederate Washington County, Virginia, and in Unionist East Tennessee—for its habit of simply taking from civilians what supplies it needed, ignoring orders to leave them survival rations. In Virginia, the problem was caused by stragglers and bands of deserters who robbed citizens; but in Tennessee, Williams evidently allowed his cavalrymen to make up shortages of mounts and forage by seizing indiscriminately what they needed. And Company E had its needs; it could muster only forty-five horses at most, and that soon after it had arrived in Tennessee. As Maj. Gen. Sam Jones, commanding in western Virginia and eastern Tennessee in October 1863, reported to Robert E. Lee, the 21st had given him and other officers "great trouble."[27]

91

During the fall and winter of 1863–64, the 21st Virginia Cavalry engaged in several skirmishes and small battles as part of the attempt to eject Ambrose Burnside's army. There were weeks when movement across rough terrain was almost constant, and weather conditions often were bitter. Many soldiers were without shoes and overcoats, and food shortages were common. But the regiment never was seriously engaged in battle. Battle losses totaled only a handful killed, wounded, and captured. Loss by desertion and sickness was another thing entirely. Despite the public execution of deserters from other regiments, by the end of the campaign Peters's 460 effectives had been reduced to 280, and most of Company E was among the missing. The company had suffered only two deaths, and one of these was by accident. But, in no particular relation to the dates of battles and hard marches, its officers and men had departed for home.[28]

Given the paucity of records, it is almost impossible to trace the fortunes of Company E; none of our principal memorialists accompanied the 21st on this campaign. Zeke Counts, as before, often was away from his men. Jasper Colley and the third in command, William Lockhart, signed the majority of the surviving requisitions and orders. The last record signed by Counts was at the end of October, "in the field" in Tennessee. David Edmundson later reported that Counts had deserted, from Rogersville, Tennessee, about November 4—that is, on the eve of a major successful assault. On November 14, as Burnside began to retreat to Knoxville in the face of Longstreet's advance from Chattanooga, Lockhart was acting in command of Company E, as he was on November 30, near Knoxville. On December 1, according to Edmundson, Jasper Colley deserted; there is no record that he had been with the company during November. In December, after the siege was lifted, and while Longstreet tarried in East Tennessee mostly to keep the Army of the Ohio occupied, Lockhart still commanded. Meanwhile, the men followed the example of their officers. At the end of November, Lockhart was drawing forage for thirty horses. At the end of December, a month mainly spent at Bean's Station watching the road from Cumberland Gap, he drew forage for twelve. Shortly afterward, Lockhart was killed; there is no record how. Richard Smith was next in line for command, but no official records exist of his having acted in that capacity. After March 10, when he was sent after deserters, he drops from sight. On March 29, the acting commander of the 21st, David Edmundson, wrote Richmond asking that Colley and Counts be dropped from the ranks of officers for reason of desertion; that was done on April 17. The remainder of the company was disbanded sometime in April, as part of a general reorganization of the 21st Virginia Cavalry. In early May, the former Company I became the second company E, and new officers were elected.[29]

Only a few of the men can be traced further in the Combined Service Records. Six continued to serve in the 21st Virginia, having been assigned to new companies. A few more, including hard-line Rebels David Smith and his brothers, moved on to the 7th Confederate under Clarence Prentice. In two cases during 1864, orders that men of Company E be returned, as deserters, to the 21st were reported as unenforceable, because they now were on the roster in the 7th. Edmundson's statement that Colley had already joined and deserted another command may also refer to a stint in Prentice's outfit. But his statement that Zeke Counts was behind enemy lines almost certainly refers simply to Zeke's having returned to the Sandy Basin. For, as Counts's men disappear from official Confederate records, they reappear in the family traditions of the Sand Lick section, endeavoring as before to quiet local opposition. Edmundson was a strict disciplinarian who admitted that his men disliked him, and conditions were harsh in East Tennessee. But Counts and company were more concerned with conditions at home than they were rebellious against conditions in the Confederate army.[30]

The attempt to control the Russell Fork by forced enlistment had exacerbated conflict, and many of those who had fled were still in the section, hiding out. The families of absent soldiers were as vulnerable to theft and robbery during the winter of 1863 as they had been in the winter of 1862, but now they believed that they were being specifically targeted. In particular, Ike Blair's younger brothers John and Andy, and their near kin Harrison Bowman and Barney Bowman, were scouting—killing sheep, stealing whatever else they needed, and planning revenge. Not really Unionist, they stole equally from both sides, but they hated and stalked the pro-Confederate neighborhood leaders. Confederate policy of enlisting Union deserters into the Rebel army and sending them to fight in southwestern Virginia added other alienated, desperate men to an increasingly violent situation. Many of these "Yankee jumpers" quickly deserted again and, now outlawed by both armies, tried to find their way through the mountains to their homes in the North. Several of these men found their way into Sandy Basin; at least two allied with the Blairs for mutual protection.[31]

Matters came to a head when Harrison Bowman shot down and seriously wounded Dave Smith, because, as Dave's daughter remembered, Smith had "tried to get men into the war." Bill Counts, Zeke's cousin, "a peaceable citizen," narrowly escaped murder by his near neighbors, the Blairs, when a tree branch deflected a bullet. In response, Jasper Colley, directed by Jasper Sutherland, led a squad of men from the Sand Lick company on a search for the Blairs, Hare Bowman, and their deserter allies. A raid on the Blair cabin turned up no males. Old Jakey Johnson, closely connected by marriage to the Blairs and Bowmans, was taken at night from his cabin by unidentified Confederates and would have been shot in the back but for the intervention of one of the Smiths. An elderly kinsman of Hare Bowman was killed by men of the 7th Confederate when he could not or would not reveal where the boys were hid. Flushed out of the Sand Lick district by Colley's searchers, the Blairs, Bowman, and a "Yankee Jumper" finally were run to earth the following spring by a squad drawn from the 7th and were massacred at a place later called Deadman's Hollow. The same day, one of the Yankee deserters appeared at the Smiths' cabin. Taking for granted that he was there to commit murder, Dave Smith's father shot him down.[32]

These deaths ended resistance on the waters of Russell Fork; the pro-Confederates once again were secure in their domination of the section. They were also secure in their identity as Confederates, for, even before the massacre at Deadman's Hollow, several members of Counts's company had fought again, this time against real Yankees. In late September 1864, Stephen Burbridge, the Union commander of the Military District of Kentucky, led a small army composed in large part of freedmen and Kentucky mountain Unionists up the Levisa Fork, across the Cumberland front, then down the Clinch Valley, in an attempt to destroy the salt works. Badly beaten outside Saltville on October 2, so that they had to abandon their wounded, Burbridge's men retraced their steps toward Kentucky. By the time the Union column had reached the Levisa again, the Buchanan County militia had been called up to oppose them. The men of Company E responded, sixty strong, according to Jasper Sutherland (their numbers probably augmented by men from outside Sand Lick). Once again they were commanded by Zeke Counts and Jasper Colley. They would stage a very irregular defense.[33]

Unable to challenge Burbridge directly, the Confederates split into small bands that scattered along the Levisa, instructed to attack the Federals any chance they had. Jasper Sutherland's band, led by Counts, felled trees across the road to create an ambush and spent the night beside this log blockade. Counts's men had brought no provisions, so the next morning they abandoned their position to search the neighborhood for breakfast. Returning, they stumbled onto Burbridge's men crossing the logs. "We darted back into the woods," said Jasper, barely escaping capture. Then followed a potentially deadly game of chase and ambush, Counts's men dodging flank patrols, stopping to fire from behind trees and rocks, and fleeing again when the return fire "got too hot" for them. To a man like Stephen Burbridge, a veteran of vicious guerrilla war in Kentucky and a man given to harsh retaliation, his opponents were mere bushwhackers. In Kentucky, Burbridge had ordered that no guerrilla prisoners be taken. So when Elijah Rasnick was captured resting with his boots off, he was extremely lucky that he was not shot out of hand. According to Sand Lick tradition, Lige, unwilling to abandon his only pair of shoes and in his haste putting them on the wrong feet, was easily run down and caught. But again, the humor common to these war stories masked a grim reality. Rasnick was questioned about the ambushers and told that he would be killed immediately if the Federals were shot at again. Operating under no command, his friends soon recommenced firing, while Rasnick sprinted for the river, shot at by the entire Federal force. Swimming the Levisa and running through an old field on the other side, Lige survived the last Civil War action of the Sand Lick Company without a scratch. So did everybody else; the rest of Counts's men also got away, claiming, in turn, no Yankee deaths.[34]

The Sand Lick men had done well just to survive the war. To the Confederate command, the men of Company E were two-time deserters, while to Burbridge they were savage guerrillas. From both perspectives, they were liable to execution if captured. To themselves, they were the legitimate Confederate presence along the Russell Fork. At home, they were as impervious to Confederate officials as they were to Federal armies; neither ever came to Sand Lick. Rufus Woolwine was given sixteen men to search three mountain counties for evaders and deserters; but the best the Confederacy could do, in its orders to return some of Company E's men to the 21st Virginia Cavalry, was to report vaguely that they had been seen in Russell County. Indeed, they had been quite visible along the Russell and Levisa forks, dogging the Blairs and sniping at Burbridge. Counts, Colley, and the Sutherlands had, of course, nothing to fear from local authorities. They *were* the local authorities, and they fought a local war, successfully.

After the war was over, Company E's men retained their collective identity and their violent habits. Never having formally surrendered, they had to take loyalty oaths on an individual basis, as Confederate prisoners or as, in the words of United States officers, "Rebel deserters." A few, picked up on unspecified business in West Virginia just before Lee's surrender, were sent as prisoners of war to Camp Chase, Ohio. Zeke Counts and Jasper Colley took the oath at Cumberland, Maryland, in May 1865, and were "sent North." In all the six cases where records are extant, the men took the oath as soldiers in Company E, 21st Virginia Cavalry, although "their" Company E had been disbanded over a year before. Both Counts and Colley claimed to be its captain.[35]

Back home, the Unionist minority of the Sutherland family gave a barbecue, with the stated intention of healing old wounds. But when the Unionists lorded it over their Rebel relatives by raising an American flag on a peeled poplar, the Rebels cut down the flagpole and beat up their noisiest family antagonist. And Zeke Counts may well have had a good reason for wanting to be sent north. Shortly after the war, he encountered Ike Blair once again. This time he stabbed Blair to death. Counts was, according to Noah Sutherland, "never the same after this trouble." He wandered from Minnesota to Kansas to Texas, changing the spelling of his name, and never came back to Virginia. Jasper Colley and his family followed Counts to Kansas. Colley, however, returned to Sand Lick to play—along with Billy Sutherland, Dave Smith, and other veterans of Counts's company—a major role in its politics.[36]

During the course of the war, Zeke Counts's Sand Lick company had evolved from a state militia to a unit in the regular Confederate Army to a guerrilla outfit outlawed by both sides, without weakening its members' sense of loyalty to the Confederacy and to their home section. And their pro-South neighbors, at least, accepted their behavior. Desertion and disloyalty did not enter into their self-image; they were loyal Confederates "on furlough."

According to the older accounts of disloyalty and desertion in the Confederacy, the disappearance of the men of Company E should come as no shock; they were mountaineers and therefore prime candidates for desertion. According to Ella Lonn, "illiterate backwoodsmen," cracker and hillbilly alike, "cut off from the mass" of their fellows, had no reason to support the Confederacy, because they had "no interest in the economic aspect of the war" and even hated slavery as the economic "foundation of their proud lowland neighbors," while a few "cherished a real love for the old Union." Georgia Lee Tatum agreed, stressing that most "mountaineers had no interest in the questions of the day and wished to be left alone," while Albert Barton Moore added that the mountain yeomen whom he rated as chief among the deserters had not learned to "relish the mandates of distant governments" and had "an innate distaste for a war for slavery." These explanations draw heavily on stereotypes concerning the nonplantation South, and the Mountain South in particular. Recent scholarship has undermined the notion of Appalachian isolation, disclosing strong and constant trade currents between the mountains and the plantation regions, and a lively interest in the political issues of the day. Nevertheless, Lonn's, Tatum's, and Moore's arguments, when applied to the Sand Lick and McClure regions of Sandy Basin, contain partial truths. Illiteracy was high, and, while trade in hides, ginseng, and cattle tied the Basin to Baltimore markets, most products of farming and hunting went to family subsistence and local exchange. There was "no particular excitement" over the election of 1860 along Russell Fork, and while only a few outspoken Unionists emerged, many locals ignored the call to arms for southern rights. As for slavery, the slaves who lived near Sand Lick in 1860 stood out to such a degree that, two generations later, local residents could still identify them by name. No one there rallied to the defense of slavery, and the central concerns of secession seemed distant.[37]

More recent analyses of disloyalty and desertion, more tolerant of mountain otherness and more sympathetic to desertion, put heavy stress on class issues. Historians like Paul Escott and Malcolm McMillan emphasize the poverty and vulnerability of yeoman mountain families whose male work-force was away in the army. Problems rooted in missing farm labor were worsened by the social chaos common to regions where Unionists, deserters of all kinds, and outlaws vied for control, and by the failure of the Confederate elite to respond to these real needs. Escott ties yeoman disaffection to a collapse of interclass unity, as the upper-class local leadership proved un-willing to support the poor, while denying yeomen their culturally vital sense of independence. McMillan demonstrates how even well-disposed Alabama governors were unable to solve the problems of the poor.

Again, these arguments apply in part to Counts's company. The Russell Fork sections suffered shortages of basic commodities, including—a bitter irony for a region whose soldiers spent much of their time guarding salt works—an almost complete lack of salt. The fear of renegades and of sol-diers on both sides was a constant in wartime Sandy Basin. But a class-based model does not explain much about Sand Lick. There was little class differentiation there, and, to the extent that a local elite existed, it bore the same relationship to the Confederacy as did everyone else; captains and pri-vates deserted together. Outsiders were largely ignored, regardless of rank.[38]

A convincing variation on this class theme emphasizes a strong bond among yeomen deserters who had joined the army as members of specific kin groups and neighborhoods. Richard Reid's quantitative study of de-sertion among North Carolina troops finds that class resentment probably contributed to desertion, as did resistance to a system of conscription im-posed by outside elites. But he finds even more evidence that desertion was fueled by loyalty to kin groups and home, especially when home and kin were threatened by occupation or civil collapse. He finds little evidence that Appalachian origin influenced decisions to desert. Other recent explana-tions for desertion and disaffection by historians such as Gerald Linderman and James I. Robertson reinforce this point of view by stressing factors com-mon to all of rural America: a lack of deference to "betters," an unwillingness to accept discipline, and a sense that each man was his own commander. These values were based not so much on class resentments as on a strong sense of self, expressed in egalitarian terms. This sense, coupled with a deeply localist outlook, established certain conditions for service, including the men's right to choose their own officers and a primary concern with local defense.

Three complementary studies of Civil War Texas amplify this point of view. Thomas W. Cutrer emphasizes a tradition of volunteer frontier officers, "chosen by their fellow citizens for the qualities they had displayed in everyday life," regardless of formal military training. David Paul Smith notes the predominance of local concerns, especially the threatening presence of Comanches, in the behavior of local militias. Richard B. McCaslin shows how the fear of chaos on a vulnerable frontier led local Confederate elites to hang forty-one members of a secret Unionist organization in Gainesville, Texas—themselves mutually allied to resist the disorder loosed by secession. Conditions on the Texas frontier are analogous to, if much more violent than, conditions in the Mountain South, and an explanation of wartime behavior based in egalitarianism and localism is very appropriate for Sand Lick. Loyalty to Ezekiel Counts was basic for the local Rebels, as was disdain for any outside officer who did not meet their cultural expectations. The officers and men of Company E had no qualms at all about putting local and personal concerns first. The Confederacy and its military affairs, and the fate of Virginia, ranked in importance below affairs around Sand Lick.[39]

So a complex set of interrelated factors—geography, class identity, and, above all, an intense localism—accounts for the behavior of the Sand Lick company. The physical setting of the remote mountain neighborhoods along Russell Fork, the subsistence economy, and the near absence of slavery largely exempted residents from involvement with the issues of secession. Mountain topography also made desertion easy and exacerbated the failure of the Confederate leadership to deal with the social problems created by the war. There was no official Confederate presence in Sandy Basin. A sense of class identity did not divide the roughly egalitarian sections around Sand Lick, but it did sharpen the division between Counts's men and the Confederate officers they encountered outside Sandy Basin. Mutual contempt best describes the contacts between the traditional military and the Russell Fork men. The Sand Lick soldiers accepted leadership only on their own terms. They represented the majority among their kin-based neighborhoods; Counts and Colley were chosen community leaders, now engaged in protecting the community from conditions created by civil war. They were accustomed to taking care of their own, and their service in the State Line, the recruitment of Company E, and the guerrilla attacks on Burbridge all revolved around the desire to protect and control their home areas. The national and professional orientations of Confederate officers, reinforced by class and cultural biases, precluded their understanding these men, and so they lost them—just as, on a larger scale, a failure to understand the power of localism was fatal to the Confederacy. The men of Company E were loyal Confederates, but their Confederacy was Sand Lick.

Notes

1. John E. Olson, *21st Virginia Cavalry* (Lynchburg, Va.: H. E. Howard, 1989), 5–15; Lee A. Wallace, *A Guide to Virginia Military Organizations, 1861–1865* (1964; reprinted Lynchburg, Va.: H. E. Howard, 1986), 61–62; *Combined Service Records: Confederate States of America—Virginia,* National Archives Microfilm Publications, Microcopy 324, Rolls 166–69; William Marvel, *Burnside* (Chapel Hill: Univ. of North Carolina Press, 1991), 291–96, 303–29; Ella Lonn, *Salt as a Factor in the Confederacy* (1933; reprinted University: Univ. of Alabama Press, 1965), 138–39. This research was furthered by grants from the Committee on Research and Creative Work and the Graduate Council on the Arts and Humanities, Univ. of Colorado, and a Mellon Fellowship from the Virginia Historical Society. I am very grateful for the support.

2. *Combined Service Records,* Rolls 166–69, esp. Ezekiel K. Counts and Jasper Colley.

3. The best succinct statement of the importance of Southwest Virginia to the Confederacy is in William C. Davis, *Breckinridge: Statesman, Soldier, Symbol* (Baton Rouge: Louisiana State Univ. Press, 1974), 408.

4. U.S. Dept. of War, *The War of Rebellion: A Compilation of the Official Records of the Union and Confederate Armies* (Washington, D.C.: U.S. Government Printing Office, 1880–1901; hereafter cited as *OR*). *Combined Service Records,* Rolls 166–69. Elihu J. Sutherland Papers (hereafter cited as EJS Papers), Wyllie Library, Clinch Valley College of the Univ. of Virginia, Wise, Va.

5. For a survey of early life along the Russell Fork, see Elihu J. Sutherland, *Meet Virginia's Baby* (Clintwood, Va.: Privately printed, 1955); and Elihu J. Sutherland, *Some Sandy Basin Characters* (Clintwood, Va.: Privately printed, 1962). On family migration and trade, also see Ralph Mann, "Family Group, Family Migration, and the Civil War in the Sandy Basin of Virginia," *Appalachian Journal* 19 (Summer 1992): 374–93.

6. Andrew J. Edwards, Nov. 1, 1924; Noah B. Sutherland, Jan. 27, 1927; both in EJS Papers.

7. Wallace, *Guide to Virginia Military,* 212–14; Opha Mason Short, "General John B. Floyd in the Civil War" (Master's thesis, West Virginia Univ., 1947), 24, 50, 62–64, 72–73; Randall Osborne and Jeffrey C. Weaver, *The Virginia State Rangers and State Line* (Lynchburg, Va.: H. E. Howard, 1994), 23–28; F. N. Boney, *John Letcher of Virginia: The Story of Virginia's Civil War Governor* (University: Univ. of Alabama Press, 1966), 157–64.

8. W. W. Loring to Hon. George W. Randolph, Aug. 22, 1862, *OR*, ser. 1, vol. 12, pt. 3, p. 939; Henry Heth to Col. G. W. C. Lee, July 4, 1862, *OR*, ser. 1, vol. 52, pt. 2, p. 327; Humphrey Marshall to Hon. George W. Randolph, Aug. 19, 1862, *OR*, ser. 1, vol. 16, pt. 1, p. 765; John B. Floyd to Hon. George W. Randolph, Nov. 19, 1862, *OR*, ser. 1, vol. 21, p. 1023; John B. Floyd to Gov. John Letcher, Nov. 24, 1862, *OR*, ser. 1, vol. 51, pt. 1, p. 657.

9. Andrew J. Edwards, Nov. 1, 1924; Ephraim Dunbar, May 20, 1923; Noah B. Sutherland, Dec. 29, 1925; Charles B. Anderson, Dec. 10, 1932; all in EJS Papers. The list of Sand Lick men in the Virginia State Line came from Noah Sutherland, May 10, 1926; I correlated it with U.S. Bureau of the Census, *8th Census of Virginia, 1860*, Population Schedules, Buchanan County, to find the ages of enlistees.

10. Noah B. Sutherland, Dec. 29, 1925, and Jan. 27, 1927; Jasper Sutherland, Jan. 15, 1930; Capt. James W. Bausell, May 7, 1931; all in EJS Papers. Short, "John B. Floyd," 64–66. Wallace, *Guide to Virginia Military*, 215. H. G. Wright to Col. Jonathan Cranor, Oct. 19, 1862, *OR*, ser. 1, vol. 16, pt. 2, p. 632. John Dils, Jr., to Maj. Gen. Horatio Wright, Oct. 25, 1862, *OR*, ser. 1, vol. 16, pt. 2, p. 644. Col. E. Siber to Captain (Bascom?), Aug. 3, 1862, *OR*, ser. 1, vol. 12, pt. 2, p. 116.

11. Noah B. Sutherland, Aug. 13, 1920, and Dec. 29, 1925, both in EJS Papers.

12. John B. Floyd to Gov. John Letcher, Dec. 17, 1862, *OR*, ser. 1, vol. 21, p. 1066. Report of Col. John N. Clarkson, Dec. 7, 1862, *OR*, ser. 1, vol. 20, pt. 1, pp. 32–33. Henry B. Scalf, *Kentucky's Last Frontier* (Pikeville, Ky.: Pikeville College Press of the Appalachian Studies Center, 1972), 316–17.

13. John B. Floyd, Nov. 24, 1862, to Gov. Letcher, *OR*, ser. 1, vol. 51, pt. 2, p. 656. Noah B. Sutherland, Dec. 29, 1925, and Jan. 27, 1927, both in EJS Papers.

14. Noah B. Sutherland, Dec. 29, 1925, EJS Papers. Harris's correct name was Harrison.

15. John B. Floyd to Gov. John Letcher, Nov. 24, 1862, *OR*, ser. 1, vol. 51, pt. 1, p. 656. Noah Sutherland, Dec. 29, 1925, and Jan. 27, 1927, in EJS Papers. John Letcher to Hon. J. A. Seddon, Mar. 19, 1863, *OR*, ser. 1, vol. 51, pt. 2, p. 686. Jasper Sutherland, Oct. 15, 1921, and Andrew J. Edwards, Nov. 1, 1924; both in EJS Papers.

16. Wallace, *Guide to Virginia Military*, 214; William F. Gordon, *An Act to Transfer the State Troops and Rangers to the Confederate Government*, passed Feb. 28, 1863, *OR*, ser. 1, vol. 51, pt. 2, p. 687. Noah B. Sutherland, Dec. 29, 1925, EJS Papers. Weaver, *State Line*, 115–19.

17. H. L. Giltner to (Williams), Aug. 25, 1863, *OR*, ser. 1, vol. 30, pt. 4, p. 606. John S. Williams to (Giltner), Aug. 30, 1863, *OR*, ser. 1, vol. 30, pt. 4, p. 605. Williams, Feb. 25, 1864, to Sam Jones, *OR*, ser. 1, vol. 27, pt. 2, p. 955; W. H. C. Whiting to Gen. Braxton Bragg, May 14, 1864, *OR*, ser. 1, vol. 51, pt. 2, p. 931; Richard M. Hagar, May 5, 1925, EJS Papers.

18. *Combined Service Records*, Rolls 166–69.

19. Margaret Yates Hale, June 14, 1925; Malvia Blair Fleming, Feb. 28, 1963; Patsy Keel Boggs, Sept. 28, 1941; Newton Sutherland, Dec. 27, 1924; Thomas A.

Colley, Nov. 2, 1924; Noah Sutherland, Dec. 29, 1925, and Jan. 27, 1927; Malissa Kiser Sutherland, Aug. 11, 1939; all in EJS papers.

20. Peg Colley, Jan. 25, 1925; Polly Taylor Yates, Jan. 15, 1928; Margaret Yates Hale, June 16, 1925. all in EJS Papers. I traced Counts's movements from his entries in the *Combined Service Records.*

21. These conclusions are drawn from the *Combined Service Records,* 21st Virginia Cavalry, esp. those of Jasper Colley and Zeke Counts.

22. Noah B. Sutherland, May 10, 1926, EJS Papers. I compared his list with a list compiled from the *Combined Service Records.* My record of Union sympathizers came from Jasper Sutherland, Jan. 15, 1930; Peg Colley, Jan. 25, 1925; Thomas A. Colley, Nov. 2, 1924; Polly Taylor Yates, Jan. 15, 1928; and Margaret Yates Hale, June 14, 1925; all in EJS Papers.

23. Rufus James Woolwine, "Memoirs of a Confederate Soldier," in Virginia Historical Society, Richmond; entries for May 12, May 26, June 12, June 14, and July 10, 1863.

24. Malissa Sutherland, Aug. 11, 1939; Polly Taylor Yates, Jan. 15, 1928; Noah B. Sutherland, Dec. 29, 1925, and Jan. 27, 1927; Margaret Yates Hale, June 14, 1925; all in EJS Papers. J. S. Butler to Col. George W. Gallop, Nov. 16, 1864, *OR,* ser. 1, vol. 45, pt. 1, pp. 918, 929–31.

25. Noah B. Sutherland, Jan. 27, 1927; Jasper Sutherland, Jan. 15, 1930; Andrew J. Edwards, Nov. 1, 1924; all in EJS Papers.

26. Archer Anderson to Headquarters, Armies of the Confederate States, May 6, 1864, *OR,* ser. 1, vol. 32, pt. 3, p. 845; Olson, *21st Virginia,* 1, 7, 11, 31; Evans, *Confederate Military History,* 3:1109–10; Robert K. Krick, *Lee's Colonels, Lieutenant Colonels, and Majors in the Army of Northern Virginia, Virginia, Confederate Army* (Dayton, Ohio: Press of Morningside Bookshop, 1979), 279; Affidavit of L. D. Q. Washington, Oct. 7, 1863, and Nov. 10, 1863, in Littleton D. Q. Washington Papers, Virginia Historical Society, Richmond.

27. William Preston Johnston to His Excellency Jefferson Davis, Sept. 5, 1863, *OR,* ser. 1, vol. 30, pt. 4, p. 602; Archer Anderson to Col. George W. Brent, Apr. 29, 1864, *OR,* ser. 1, vol. 32, pt. 3, p. 847; Sam Jones to Gen. Robert E. Lee, Oct. 9, 1863, *OR,* ser. 1, vol. 29, pt. 2, p. 781; Olson, *21st Virginia,* 8.

28. Olson, *21st Virginia,* 9–16. Marvel, *Burnside,* 281–334. "Organization of Troops in East Tennessee under Command of Lt. Gen. James Longstreet," Nov. 30, 1863, *OR,* ser. 1, vol. 31, pt. 1, p. 454. George Dallas Mosgrove, *Kentucky Cavaliers in Dixie: Reminiscences of a Confederate Cavalryman,* ed. Bell I. Wiley (Jackson, Tenn.: McCourt-Mercer Press, 1957), 68–69. Woolwine, "Memoirs of a Confederate Soldier," Nov. 10, 1863, and Jan. 1, 1864. William Jones to David Edmundson, Oct. 29, 1863, Edmundson Family Papers, Virginia Historical Society, Richmond. John T. Cooley to Julia A. Cooley, Nov. 14, 1863, Cooley Family Papers, Virginia Historical Society, Richmond. Giles B. Cooke Diary, Sept. 20 and Oct. 3, 1863, Virginia Historical Society, Richmond. John S. Deyerle to Col. Wm. E. Peters, Dec. 17, 1863, Thomas Bentley Mott Papers, Virginia Historical Society, Richmond.

29. This record of service is drawn from the *Combined Service Records,* Rolls 166–69, esp. those of Jasper Colley, Ezekiel K. Counts, William Lockhart, and Richard Smith; Marvel. *Burnside,* 295–304. Olson, *21st Virginia,* 11–12.

30. *Combined Service Records,* esp. for Abel Smith, David Smith, Jeremiah Couch, and Wilson Kiser. Patsy Keel Boggs, Sept. 28, 1941, EJS Papers. David Edmundson to Hallie, n.d., in Edmundson Family Papers, Virginia Historical Society, Richmond.

31. Jasper Sutherland, Oct. 15, 1921; Isabelle Sutherland, Dec. 26, 1921; both in EJS Papers. On Union deserters being assigned to Confederate units in southwestern Virginia and deserting again, see John McEntee to Bvt. Maj. Gen. Terry, Nov. 12, 1864, *OR,* ser. 1, vol. 42, pt. 3, pp. 608–9. For a very different reading of the activities of Counts's men, see Jeffrey C. Weaver, *The Civil War in Buchanan and Wise Counties: Bushwhackers' Paradise* (Lynchburg, Va.: H. E. Howard, 1994), 147.

32. Patsy Keel Boggs, Sept. 28, 1941; Jasper Sutherland, Oct. 15, 1921; John T. Powers, June 26, 1930; Malvia Blair Fleming, Feb. 28, 1963; Margaret Yates Hale, June 15, 1926; all in EJS Papers. Again, see Jeffrey C. Weaver, *Civil War in Buchanan and Wise,* 179.

33. Mahala Kiser Sutherland, Nov. 20, 1924; Rebecca Kilgore Willis, Mar. 20, 1932; Jasper Sutherland, Jan. 15, 1930; Noah B. Sutherland, Oct. 13, 1920, and Jan. 27, 1927; all in EJS Papers. Mosgrove, *Kentucky Cavaliers,* 199–210. Report of Stephen Burbridge, Oct. 7, 1864, *OR,* ser. 1, vol. 39, pt. 1, p. 552. Davis, *Breckinridge,* 457–60. William Marvel, *Southwest Virginia in the Civil War: The Battles for Saltville* (Lynchburg, Va.: H. E. Howard, 1992), 99–123. See Jeffrey C. Weaver, *Civil War in Buchanan and Wise,* 200–203.

34. Jasper Sutherland, Jan. 15, 1930; Noah B. Sutherland, Aug. 13, 1920; Peg Colley, Jan. 25, 1925; all in EJS Papers. James Brent Martin, "'Have Them Shot at Once . . .': Guerrilla Warfare in Kentucky, 1863–1865" (Master's thesis, Univ. of Texas, Austin, 1986), 120–25. Lowell H. Harrison, *The Civil War in Kentucky* (Lexington: Univ. Press of Kentucky, 1975), 77–78.

35. *Combined Service Records.*

36. Noah B. Sutherland, 1919; Peg Colley, Jan. 16, 1938; both in EJS Papers. Elihu J. and Hetty S. Sutherland, *Some Descendants of John Counts of Glade Hollow* (Clintwood, Va.: Privately printed, 1978), 132.

37. Ella Lonn, *Desertion during the Civil War* (1928; reprinted Gloucester, Mass.: Peter Smith, 1966), 3–4. Georgia Lee Tatum, *Disloyalty in the Confederacy* (Chapel Hill: Univ. of North Carolina Press, 1934; reprinted New York: AMS Press, 1970), 4–9. Albert Burton Moore, *Conscription and Conflict in the Confederacy* (New York: Macmillan, 1924), 18–19, 129. Ephraim Dunbar, Mar. 12, 1923, EJS Papers. For a brief overview of some of the recent literature challenging older views of an isolated, subsistence-oriented Appalachian South, see Ralph Mann, "Mountains, Land, and Kin Networks: Burkes Garden, Virginia, in the 1840s and 1850s," *Journal of Southern History* 58 (Aug. 1992): 431–44.

38. Paul Escott, *Many Excellent People: Power and Privilege in North Carolina, 1850–1900* (Chapel Hill: Univ. of North Carolina Press, 1985), 74–84; Malcolm C. McMillan, *The Disintegration of a Confederate State* (Macon, Ga.: Mercer Univ. Press, 1986), 43, 60–61, 91, 127–28.

39. Richard Reid, "A Test Case of the 'Crying Evil': Desertion among North Carolina Troops during the Civil War," *North Carolina Historical Review* 58 (July 1981): 241, 243, 247, 249, 251; Gerald Linderman, *Embattled Courage: The Experience of Combat in the American Civil War* (New York: Free Press, 1987), 36, 174; James I. Robertson, Jr., *Soldiers Blue and Gray* (Columbia: Univ. of South Carolina Press, 1988), 135–36; Thomas W. Cutrer, *Ben McCulloch and the Frontier Military Tradition* (Chapel Hill: Univ. of North Carolina Press, 1993), 3–4; David Paul Smith, *Frontier Defense in the Civil War: Texas Rangers and Rebels* (College Station: Texas A&M Univ. Press, 1992), 49–51, 63–68; Richard B. McCaslin, *Tainted Breeze: The Great Hanging at Gainesville, Texas, 1862* (Baton Rouge: Louisiana State Univ. Press, 1994), 1–4, 55–60, 89–94. See William Harris Bragg, *Joe Brown's Army: The Georgia State Line, 1862–1865* (Macon, Ga.: Mercer Univ. Press, 1987), 27–34, 63.

5

Exterminating Savages:
The Union Army and Mountain Guerrillas
in Southern West Virginia, 1861–1862

Kenneth W. Noe

In July 1861, as his army consolidated its hold on northwestern Virginia, Union Gen. George B. McClellan assured·Confederate leaders of his hope for a limited war. McClellan promised "to confine [the war's] effects to those who constitute the organized armies and meet in battle. It is my intention to cause the persons and property of private citizens to be respected, and to render the condition of prisoners and wounded as little oppressive . . . as possible." In such a manner, assuming the South followed suit, the war in Western Virginia would "remain free from the usual horrible features of civil war."[1]

Nine months later, John C. Frémont, one of McClellan's successors in western Virginia, gave his official approval to warfare of a different sort. Noting the threat created by irregular Confederate guerrillas throughout the occupied portions of the future state of West Virginia, Frémont sanctioned his men "to fight them in their own style, and by rapid marches, vigorous attacks and severe measures, annihilate them."[2] To the Union soldiers of the Mountain Department, "severe measures" had come to mean arresting and imprisoning civilians, seizing or destroying property, burning homes and even entire towns, and killing prisoners—the "horrible features of civil war" McClellan dreaded. Only with such tactics could the guerrillas be—as Frémont put it to a subordinate—exterminated.[3]

The relatively quick transition from McClellan's hope for an honorable conflict to Frémont's approval of a war of annihilation challenges a fundamental tenet of the traditional interpretation of the Civil War. Scholars in the past described an initially limited war fought by uniformed soldiers that over time metamorphosed into a "total war," in which armies used the harshest measures against civilians and soldiers alike in pursuit of victory. William Tecumseh Sherman's March to the Sea and Philip Sheridan's Shenandoah Valley Campaign often have been pointed to as the critical moments when the tactics of modern war seized the day. As writers such as James Reston, Jr., assure readers, it then was only a few steps from Sherman's Georgia to Hiroshima and My Lai.[4]

Recent works, however, call this interpretation into question. Mark E. Neely, Jr., for example, rejects the entire concept of total war as essentially presentist. Maintaining that "the distinction between soldiers and civilians, combatants and noncombatants" usually did not break down, Neely asserts that Civil War generals "waged war the same way most Victorian gentlemen did. . . . there was little new to report." Real total war is a twentieth-century phenomenon.[5] Mark Grimsley, meanwhile, suggests a three-stage model. Between "conciliation" and "hard war," Grimsley maintains, there existed an intermediate "pragmatic" stage, during which greater latitude was allowed soldiers in dealing with guerrillas or civilians possessing goods worth foraging. Otherwise, Federal commanders continued to believe that battle and not destruction would win the war.[6]

Other scholars have taken quite a different approach to the subject. Wayne K. Durrill, Michael Fellman, Reid Mitchell, and Charles Royster all depict a war not only much harsher than that described by Neely, but one routinely characterized from the first by chaos, destruction, and violence toward noncombatants. Civil War soldiers stole food and property, destroyed homes, terrorized civilians, and murdered prisoners almost from the beginning of the conflict. In this "destructive war," as Royster terms it, the only real change was in the escalation of hatred and violence towards noncombatants.[7]

"Destructive" or "hard" war, as defined by the latter scholars, often first grew out of confrontations with guerrillas. As the comments of both McClellan and Frémont suggest, guerrilla warfare was a mode of fighting familiar to Americans by 1861. It was hardly new or modern, and it required no great leap forward in military thinking. Indeed, conditioned by warfare in Europe, particularly the struggle in the Spanish Netherlands, the Thirty Years War, and the English conquests of Northern Ireland and the Scottish Highlands, European colonists in North America had practiced ambush,

destruction, surprise, and the rule of no quarter from the earliest settlement. The tactics of Native Americans themselves reinforced and made respectable what, by the eighteenth century, had come to be called "the
American way of war," especially when the opponent was an ostensibly
"inferior" Other and combatants could rationalize the cause as "just" or
"righteous." The American Revolution in the South, Florida's Seminole
Wars, the Mexican War, and conflicts growing out of the continuing westward movement had given the Civil War generation more familiar and
more recent examples of guerrilla war and counterinsurgency. Once the
war began, historical precedent helped condition secessionists in Union-
occupied areas to take to the bush. Moreover, the same precedent, coupled
with the anxiety, chaos, fear, frustration, and rage that grew out of personal
encounters with irregulars, almost immediately stimulated harsh retaliation on the part of Federals against their "savage" tormentors. Since guerrillas were hard to distinguish from the wider southern population, invariably a population considered inferior by northerners, counterinsurgency
quickly broadened into hatred and violent suppression of much of the citizenry, a localized total war. "Inside war" particularly was the dominant
mode of fighting in the southern mountain region, and West Virginia provided an early and especially graphic illustration of the transition from
noble hopes to violent reality.[8]

Western Virginia's corner of the mountain war began on May 26, 1861,
the day McClellan's Ohio regiments began to cross the Ohio River into
the northwestern section of the state. Augmented by Unionist Virginians
in blue, McClellan's troops quickly overcame their Confederate counterparts in the Battles of Phillipi, Rich Mountain, and Beverly. Within two
months, the northwestern quarter of the Old Dominion was firmly in
Union control; the region's Unionist leaders had set in motion the creation
of their new, loyal state; and McClellan had emerged as the North's first
hero. Occupation, however, did not mean an end to the fighting. Less than
forty-eight hours after the first Federal set foot on Virginia soil, secessionist guerrillas, universally called "bushwhackers," inaugurated a new dimension of the war when they burned two Baltimore and Ohio Railroad
bridges near Farmington.[9]

In the next weeks, Confederate bushwhackers remained active, and
McClellan lamented that they were "doing much damage in the region."
In response, he issued a warning. On June 23, only two days after he himself arrived in the region, he proclaimed that those engaged in guerrilla activities would be "dealt with in their persons and property according to
the severest rules of military law." Armed mountaineers, "unless of known

loyalty," and others caught assisting guerrillas would be arrested. "Houses, families, property, and rights," however, were to be "religiously respected" by his men, with violators promptly punished.[10]

Almost immediately, the military began to arrest suspected bushwhackers and their supporters, including men openly identified as "political prisoners." Most went to Camp Chase, four miles west of Columbus, Ohio, where they were held while higher authorities tried to decide what to do with them. Such arrests, however, did little to stop the bushwhacking. Indeed, in the month that followed, guerrilla activity increased in both tenor and ferocity.[11] Chilling stories of bushwhacker atrocities circulated widely among Union soldiers; one such story told of a murdered and mutilated Federal, "his abdomen . . . ripped open, his bowels extracted, his head severed from his body and placed all gashed and bleeding in the cavity."[12] Unwilling to admit the failure of his policies, McClellan continued to express confidence that the keys to taming the bushwhackers remained the same: appeals to the enemy's sense of decency and honor, military arrests of guerrillas, and especially the eventual defeat of regular Confederate units on the field of battle. Once the Rebel armies had been driven from the field, the guerrilla organizations must quickly disperse, and then his men would "have no great difficulty . . . securing the entire pacification of this region." Only if events proved him wrong would he then fall back on a secondary plan to "scour the country with small columns."[13]

McClellan never had the chance to follow through. Within days, he left for Washington and command of the Army of the Potomac. His replacement as commander of the Department of the Ohio was his able subordinate, William S. Rosecrans. Having spent the entire campaign in West Virginia—indeed, many now credit him and not McClellan with the army's successes—Rosecrans took over the Union's drive southward on the vital Virginia and Tennessee Railroad and, beyond that, East Tennessee. While occupied with tactical and strategic concerns, however, he also began to wrestle with the dilemma presented by the guerrillas.[14]

In general, Rosecrans's hopes and program were very similar to McClellan's. He continued to send prisoners to Camp Chase as well as to Wheeling, Virginia—although later he confessed that he thought many innocent of any crimes—and also began to dispatch companies from strongly fortified points to "scour" areas infested with bushwhackers and make arrests, as McClellan had suggested earlier.[15] As for the local population, Rosecrans promised to protect "unarmed and peaceful civilians" and to respect private property. In return, he called upon the region's population to turn against the bushwhackers, "raise the hue and cry, and pursue the offenders. . . . stand firm for law and order." Communities that sheltered guerrillas, in contrast, would be held responsible as "accessaries to the crime." Small committees of public safety, he suggested, not only would help preserve the peace, but also would bring a halt to what Rosecrans termed "needless arrests."[16]

Unhappy with reports of plundering, Rosecrans at the same time issued General Orders to set high standards of behavior for his troops, some of whom he asserted were "disgracing our arms." Soldiers were not to enter private homes unless invited. If the houses needed to be searched, a local commanding officer had to issue the order. Property could not be taken unless "in cases of absolute necessity," and then the owners had to be compensated in full. Stolen property must be returned. Officers who protected violators would themselves be charged with the same offenses.[17]

Many of Rosecrans's soldiers nonetheless ignored the wishes of their superiors and continued to steal. The theft of items such as food, fence rails for fires, and livestock was common, as was vandalism of businesses and homes. Poor provisions, including a lack of proper uniforms and shoes; unseasonably cold weather that included snow, sleet, and incessant rain; and ease of opportunity—large numbers of secessionist refugees had left homes and even towns vacant—all contributed to widespread pillaging and vandalism.[18] Rosecrans later would complain that "numerous claims for damages caused by the wanton destruction of private property . . . have been presented to me almost daily since I assumed the command of this Department."[19]

Rosecrans tended to blame his officers for the men's criminal behavior. He and other members of the high command must bear at least some of the responsibility, however. Certainly his own refusal to back up his orders with rigorous enforcement played a role in allowing disobedience to thrive. One case in point was the court martial of George Raines of the 12th Ohio Volunteer Infantry in November 1861. Finding Raines guilty of robbing a Roman Catholic church in Summersville, Virginia, of a host of items, the court punished him with only a reprimand and the loss of one month's pay. Rosecrans approved the light sentence, deeming the crime "pilfering, rather than robbery."[20]

While concerned with the behavior of his Ohio soldiers, Rosecrans and those around him particularly considered the Unionist Virginians within his ranks to be the major threats to order and good discipline. At the urging of Francis H. Pierpont, governor of the Unionist "restored" government of Virginia, the army had enlisted many local Unionists in Federal Virginia regiments and had provided still others with weapons for self-defense. Across occupied western Virginia, "Home Guard" units were the result of the latter policy. Like many of his subordinates, Rosecrans thought that the Virginians were unreliable, in that most wanted to remain in their neighborhoods and serve as guides or in Home Guard units, rather than join regular regiments. He also foresaw a greater potential for theft, violence, and revenge. Unless tightly controlled, Rosecrans feared, the Home Guards would become little more than Unionist bushwhackers,[21] "a mere armed mob coming & going where it pleased."[22]

Clearly, slipping the bonds of official control and countering the guerrillas with their own tactics was just what the Home Guards and their supporters wanted to do. William Keany, for example, wrote Rosecrans praising the Unionist Tug River Boys, "who can clean out the whole country and . . . are anxious to try the job on."[23] Another Home Guard supporter wrote the general suggesting that a force of one thousand Home Guard riflemen be raised to "meet [the bushwhackers] in their own mode of warfare. . . . give them a taste of the metal of our mountaineers, and give them a little bushwhacking."[24]

Local concerns, fear, and the desire for personal revenge, as well as a salary of one to two dollars per day for guides, motivated Unionist Virginians to champion guerrilla-style tactics. Home Guards fought to defend their families and neighborhoods and to avenge old wrongs. Capt. Thomas T. Taylor of the 47th Ohio confirmed Rosecrans's fears regarding the Home Guards in describing his guide, James R. Ramsey. Bushwhackers had murdered Ramsey's son near his home, stripped the body, and left it in the open for five days. They then had turned to the father, first robbing him and then hunting him "from place to place like a wild beast." Taylor concluded that "these men are bursting for vengence. . . . Oh, how strong is this passion, this desire for revenge."[25]

Nor was it a "passion" restricted to mountaineers. Increasingly, as the summer and autumn of 1861 passed, the desire to fight like bushwhackers rather than play by the rules gripped Rosecrans's northerners as well as his Virginians. Three factors combined to produce this new phase in the destructive war.

At its core was the very real fear and rage that grew out of fighting an invisible and dangerous foe. While probably emotionally prepared to face an enemy in line of battle across an open field, soldiers had a hard time adjusting to the guerrilla threat. Soldiers, baggage trains, and even boats were fired upon without warning; men were wounded and sometimes killed. Standing guard on cold nights without fires that could draw the attention of the guerrillas, pickets imagined a bushwhacker in every shadow. To the men in Rosecrans's army, this seemed less like war than cold-blooded murder.

Trapped in what increasingly seemed a backwater of the war, bored and bitter when they were not afraid, Federals grew to fiercely hate their tormentors.[26] As William H. Busby of the 23rd Ohio put it, "Men on pickets had been shot by rebels in the brush until our men became almost furious at this sneaking cowardly fighting. At last the tables turned."[27]

A second factor was the blurring of lines between combatants and noncombatants, as hatred of the bushwhackers degenerated into a general dislike of mountaineers, often including mountain Unionists. Seemingly, any civilian could be a bushwhacker. Northern soldiers almost always depicted western Virginians with a harshly negative "vocabulary of abuse" that implied cultural superiority, contempt, a developing callousness, and an ever present rage. Denigration made it easier for the soldiers to rationalize their treating mountaineers as inferior.[28] To be sure, they were not always consistent. Future President Rutherford B. Hayes, for example, once referred to mountaineers as "a helpless and harmless race," elsewhere described them as "timid but cunning," and then drew a distinction between the "kind-hearted, good-natured" upper class—"they have courage but no endurance, enterprise, or energy"—and the "cowardly, cunning, and lazy" lower class. Elsewhere, Hayes described lower class mountaineers as "unenterprising, lazy, narrow, listless, and ignorant . . . serfs." Hayes concluded, "The height of their ambition is to shoot a Yankee from some place of safety."[29]

Mountain women came in for particular censure from soldiers. Instead of remaining on their pedestal and acting appropriately, as northern middle-class values demanded, secessionist women were open in their hatred of Yankees. From Lewisburg, Virginia, Taylor reported that "the women say that they would like to cut our throats even said so in the presence of one of our officers."[30] Such behavior elicited both condescension and retaliation. One Federal wrote, "The women are worse than the men one old bitch said she wished all the union army were in hell. but she soon got over that. they took all her honey 11 scaps & hogs & chickens. She was union then thats the only way you can fix them."[31]

Mountaineers increasingly were seen not only as inferior, but as positively savage as well, as their appearance, behavior, and especially their bushwhacking atrocities seemed to prove. Mountaineers were "natives" living in "semi-barbarism."[32] Even other mountaineers agreed, when the enemy was concerned. Unionist S. C. McFadden of the 5th Virginia Infantry (U.S.A.) drew a particularly crucial analogy when he wrote that a secessionist "ran like an Indian when he saw us comeing."[33] The metamorphosis of mountaineers, in Federal eyes, from equals into savages, the white equivalent of Native Americans, was a rapid and major development. Once soldiers regarded all mountaineers as savages, it was possible to fight and punish all of them—men, women, and children—with tactics usually reserved for "inferior," nonwhite peoples: destruction, starvation, and killing.[34]

Finally, there was a third factor. Federals increasingly came to believe, literally, that the savage, terrifying mountaineers were getting away with murder. The disposition of prisoners became a raw point of contention. Time and again, Federals arrested suspected bushwhackers, only to see them later released by military or state authorities. Authorities in Washington, Wheeling, and at Camp Chase released selected prisoners to please prominent Unionists, to encourage the Confederates to release some of their prisoners, and for reasons of age, infirmity, or a professed change in allegiance. Federals in the field particularly suspected that those released for the last reason only feigned loyalty to avoid prison.[35] Thirty years after the war, this issue still rankled George Crook, who had molded the 36th Ohio into the counterinsurgent regiment *par excellence*. Noting the number of prisoners he had sent to Camp Chase, Crook remembered, "It was not long before they commenced coming back, fat, saucy, with good clothes, and returned to their old occupations with renewed vigor. . . . we were all disgusted at having our hard work set at naught, and have them come back in a defiant manner, as much to say, 'Well, what are you going to do about it?'"[36]

Even those kept in custody seemed to have an better life than Federal soldiers in the field. Early in 1862, news of a scandal involving Ohio Gov. David Tod's alleged coddling of Confederate prisoners at Camp Chase reached Washington. Captured officers were allowed to keep their black servants with them in the camp. Unsupervised, uniformed, and allegedly armed prisoners also received paroles to visit Columbus, reportedly with a disloyal woman on each arm. Some took rooms in the city's hotels. While some Central Ohioans paid to tour the camp as if it were a tourist attraction, many other citizens complained bitterly to Washington that the southerners constantly insulted them, not only with their mere presence but also by actively advocating secession and the Confederacy in their streets and bars.[37] "COLUMBUS TURNED OVER TO SECESH," a local newspaper proclaimed early in 1862, adding, "Our streets and hotels more resemble Richmond than a loyal city of the Northwest." While a War Department investigation found the charges exaggerated, the stigma remained. Certainly the Camp Chase scandal helped undermine Rosecrans's policy of arrests.[38]

These three factors—the fear and rage generated by the bushwhackers; the growing belief that all mountaineers were a savage, evil, un-American Other; and the conclusion that bushwhackers were avoiding punishment—

all combined to convince Federals that harsher measures were necessary if they were to survive and triumph. For most, the arena for the transformation to a more destructive war was the "scout."

Scouting involved small groups of Federals, usually one or more companies, although the participants could range from a single individual to groups numbering two or three regiments. Generally lasting between two days and a week, a scout had as its missions to engage in reconnaissance; to seize secessionist property, especially food and livestock; to capture or kill bushwhackers, especially ringleaders, often from ambush; and ultimately to eliminate the guerrilla menace. In practice, scouting involved arduous rides over mountains and through some of the roughest country imaginable, during an autumn and winter notable for torrential rains and early snow. Occasionally, scouts were punctuated by sharp and, to the Federals, often exhilarating action that provided a needed release from the usual tensions. Led by local Unionist guides such as James Ramsey, Federal scouts often rode from house to house in search of bushwhackers and their known supporters. Scouting, in short, approximated bushwhacking, except that the scouts belonged to organized, uniformed Federal regiments, and their superiors exerted theoretical control over scouting activities, through the chain of command and the keeping of mandatory journals.[39]

For some Federals, scouting became an intoxicating addiction. "I have had some royal times since I've been here, . . ." Thomas Taylor of the 47th Ohio wrote, "we had a real jolly time." To Taylor, scouting was an adventurous game of cat-and-mouse at which he excelled. "It is just the thing that suits me, . . ." he told his wife, "there is romance and adventure with it and you know I always used to be fond of reading adventure stories."[40]

Fueling Taylor's sense of adventure, however, was his deeper need for personal advancement. Deeply in debt back in Ohio, estranged from his wife, and convinced that he was friendless in his hometown, Taylor had entered the war more to improve his financial situation and regain his status than to save the Union. At first, he seemed destined to fail in realizing even these goals, as he barely recruited enough men to form his company. All this changed, however, one evening in early October. Dispatched on a scout to capture a bushwhacker, he learned that a more important prey, "the Chief of rebel bushwhackers," as Taylor referred to him, was at home with his family. On his way to the house, Taylor became separated from his men and arrived at the home alone. Undaunted, he knocked at the door, discovered the guerrilla, and pursued him from the house into the woods before killing him.[41]

Somewhat chagrined at first about shooting a man in front of his wife and children, Taylor discovered to his delight that killing the bushwhacker had made him a celebrity. "The Unionists and every man in the regiment wants to go under me," he exclaimed to his wife, adding that fellow officers such as George Crook suddenly were choosing him as a dinner companion. "I am anxious for the work," he continued. "I came out here to make a reputation some way and I am going to try for it." Before long, he was undertaking solo scouts into Confederate-held territory, ostensibly to steal horses but in reality to augment his reputation and for the sheer thrill of escaping pursuing Rebel cavalry.[42]

Taylor was an officer, but, importantly, it took the enlisted men of the 47th Ohio to certify and informally sanction his behavior. Taylor killed bushwhackers and bent the rules in doing it; thus, he was a desirable commander. Clearly, the transition from McClellan's textbook war to Frémont's war of extermination often rose from the bottom up, with ambitious or pliant officers like Taylor taking advantage of the desires of their enlisted men and fellow officers.

No better illustration of this process exists than the regiment destined to become most feared by the bushwhackers, the 36th Ohio. The regiment was organized and mustered in August 1861, at Camp Putnam, Marietta, Ohio, just along the state's southeastern border with Virginia. At the end of the month, the regiment crossed the Ohio into Virginia. While four companies temporarily remained in Parkersburg, the other six, under the unpopular command of Maj. A. J. Slemmer of Rosecrans's staff, marched into the interior with the clear purpose of fighting bushwhackers. They did not have to look far. During their first full day in Virginia, the regiment's cavalry escort was fired upon by guerrillas. One horse soldier was wounded. The next day was spent skirmishing with bushwhackers. Attacks continued until the companies arrived at their destination, Summersville, in Nicholas County, in the south-central part of West Virginia and near the front. On the march, men of the regiment went on their first scouts and also learned how to forage in the abundant peach orchards. They also suffered; as early as September 16, it snowed. By the time they reached Summersville, the men of the 36th were afraid, hungry, cold, and demoralized. They hated Slemmer, a martinet, as well. Many had turned to alcohol for relief.[43]

At about the same time, the regiment's new colonel arrived in Summersville. George Crook, West Point class of 1852, had spent his prewar career fighting Indians in the Rogue River and Yakima Wars in the Pacific Northwest. Anxious to get back east and into the war, Crook took a leave of absence from the 4th Infantry and, with the help of powerful friends, secured command of the 36th Ohio. He must have had second thoughts when he arrived in Summersville. "I found the regiment in rather a demoralized

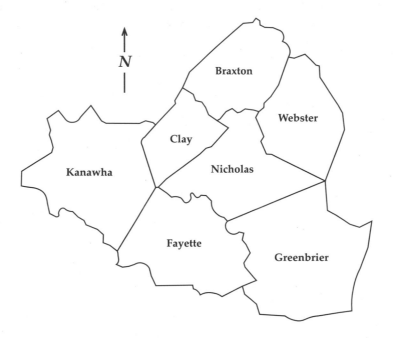

N

Braxton

Webster

Clay

Kanawha

Nicholas

Fayette

Greenbrier

Map 5.1. Central West Virginia, 1861. Map by The University of Tennessee Cartography Lab.

condition," he remembered. "They were mostly from the country, and had been taken from their plows with such clothing as they happened to have on. They were unused to discipline. . . . almost in a state of mutiny. . . . when I arrived and announced myself, I was regarded with much disfavor amongst them."[44]

Crook immediately went to work. He made repeated efforts to secure uniforms, shoes, and decent overcoats for his men, of whom fully one-third were sick at any given time with measles or typhoid fever. He introduced a strict schedule of drill and daily parades. Officers were required to meet regularly to learn about their craft. To keep his men busy, Crook also took over an abandoned sawmill and set them to work. Soon, they had constructed a 740-foot-long "drill house," where the men of the 36th drilled by day and attended recitations by night.[45]

Crook's efforts to rebuild his regiment's morale and win its favor worked. Capt. William H. Dunham praised him: "our Col. is a through military man, graduate of West Point . . . and unlike most West Pointers is not a swell head but a plain common sense man. . . . I think we are probably fortunate in our Col."[46]

What seemed to impress them most about Crook, however, was his background fighting Native Americans—experience that promised the stronger antiguerrilla methods most advocated. "Colonel Crook is a regular Old Indian fighter," John A. Palmer wrote; "I reckon he will 'Bushwhack' some of the Bushwhacking cusses in regular Bushwhacking stile if they venture across his war path."[47]

John Booth agreed: "I believe Colonel Crook could give cards and spades and then learn them something in the line of 'Surprising' in 'Bushwhacking,' he having been practising those warlike arts for over ten years among the Indians on our western frontiers."[48]

Indeed, Crook planned to do exactly what his soldiers expected. "The question was how to get rid of [the bushwhackers]," he wrote. "Being fresh from the Indian country, where I had more or less experience with that kind of warfare, I set to work organizing for the task. I selected some of the most apt officers, and scattered them through the country to learn it and all the people in it, and particularly the bushwhackers, their haunts, etc."[49]

In October, as Rosecrans's drive on Southwest Virginia literally became stuck in the mud, the 36th Ohio and other regiments embarked upon a rigorous schedule of scouting to counter a perceived upsurge in guerrilla activity. Jewett Palmer's Company G gained a particular reputation within the regiment for its prowess in seizing cattle, horses, and weapons. Once it brought in a reported $25,000 worth of property from a single scout.[50] Crook's Federals took several prisoners as well. At this juncture, however, some of his men began sporadically to shoot suspected bushwhackers in the field. "Our army still brings in prisoners," Dunham wrote, "and they are killing a good many. . . . Our fellows shoot them down wherever they find them with arms in their hands. . . . it is the most disgraceful outrageous mode of warfare imaginable."[51]

Crook, however, approved of his men's "no-prisoners" policy. "In a short time no more of these prisoners were brought in," he wrote. "When an officer returned from a scout he would report that they had caught so-and-so, but in bringing him in he slipped off a log while crossing a stream and broke his neck, or that he was killed by an accidental discharge of one of the men's guns, and many like reports. But they never brought back any more prisoners."[52]

As winter deepened, the cycle of violence escalated. After rescuing elements of the 30th Ohio from a bushwhacker ambush in mid-November, Company G burned barns and outbuildings and killed livestock "in reparation for encouraging rebel raids on Union people and otherwise aiding the enemy." A week later, Company G embarked upon a scout, during which they temporarily arrested every adult male they found and took away as many goods as they could carry. They also killed J. W. Beckley, a prominent local secessionist who in the darkness had tried to pass himself off as a slave. Confederate authorities branded it murder, a charge the Federals hotly denied. The following month, Crook sent out a force of 150 men from Companies B, E, and H, under the command of former college professor Ebenezer B. Andrews, to scout Confederate Gen. John B. Floyd's abandoned encampment at Meadow Bluff and also to secure horses and other livestock. Andrews burned the camp and returned home with livestock, captured weapons, two notorious bushwhackers, and other plunder.[53] "The people of Greenbrier County," Andrews reported, "seemed generally disposed to admit their helplessness as secessionists, and showed a disposition to make friends with Federal authorities as the stronger power."[54]

With the new year came even greater ferocity. On January 1, Crook personally led six companies out of Summersville and "into the very heart of Africa," as the *Marietta Home News* later tellingly put it. The column moved northward towards Sutton, Braxton County's seat, which reportedly had been occupied and burned by Confederates the previous day. The rumor proved false, and the next morning Crook returned to camp with two of the companies. After he left, a captain informed the remaining scouts that "Colonel Crook's orders were that every thing along the road was to be burned." Whether or not the orders actually were Crook's, the soldiers did their best to obey. John Booth of Company G wrote that "we simply burned every thing of worth, burnable. The destruction was complete."[55]

Now towns, as well as homes and barns, were put to the torch, as the men of the 36th moved toward Sutton. After heavy skirmishing with guerrillas, the Federals burned the small settlement of Chapman's Store, which was occupied, according to William H. Dunham, by no one but a small orphaned girl. They then moved on to another hamlet, Gardiner's Store. When Jewett Palmer ordered the residents there to vacate their homes, one woman took to her bed and refused to move. As John Booth reported it, a fellow soldier named Thornton "finally said, he'd throw hot coals on the bed. Calling him pretty stiff names, she defied him. Thornton took up a wooden shovel, that stood by the fire place, took upon it a lot of hot wood embers and tossed the hot coals upon the bed. The woman flew off and out, seemingly forgetting all she had threatened. The goods were set out and the house burned!"[56]

Indeed, the Federals burned the entire town, in retaliation for the bushwhacker attacks they had suffered. "The wounding of [Sergeant Thomas J.] Stanley was avenged," Booth continued, "and all the buildings here about burned, the women supplying a requiem . . . in loud, bitter and angry shouts and hurrahs for 'jeff davis' and the 'southern confederacy' [and] . . . calling us by the endearing name of 'BRUTE.'" The 36th then returned to Summersville, "burning everything that fire would destroy along line of march. Creating a broad path, marked with destruction and ruin, the earmarks of that . . . war they had . . . compelled the North to unwillingly engage in." It was the victims who were to blame.[57]

More than burning occurred during the scout just described. Booth reported that his fellow soldiers had killed up to twenty secessionists. While many were killed in skirmishes, at least one was an unarmed civilian prisoner whose links to the bushwhackers were circumstantial at best. Dunham, who had remained in camp during the scout but approved of burning the "miserable secesh hole," clearly was more uncomfortable with what followed. The Federals had captured a young man "running bullets, *evidence incontestable that he was a bushwhacker* (especially in this country of game where nearly all men are hunters)." When the companies had returned to within a few miles of Summersville, Dunham continued, "they . . . *in cold blood, barbariously shot him.* They put the dirty work on Co. D. as its commanding officer was not there. . . . the two Prices Andy and John were selected as executioners under the charge of a corporal of Co. G.—The corporal, executioners, with prisoner were instructed to fall back in the rear some distance. They did so, when the corporal told the fellow now was his time to escape and for him to run for his life . . . the Prices fired upon him and brought him to the ground. . . . they left him *unburied.* My God: has it come to this?"[58]

Letters such as Dunham's upset many of the home folks in and around Marietta. They wrote to their sons and husbands asking for the truth. In reply to one such letter, Jewett Palmer's brother John defended the activities of his sibling and his regiment. "Well mother," he wrote, "you wanted to know about a Bushwhacker that had been killed on a scout by some of Co. 'G'. . . . if we ant out here to kill Bushwhackers what are we for? . . . they may have shot a poor bushwhacking cuss, & I am one of the kind that believes in them doing so every chance they get,—If I did not, I would not have been here." Soldiers like Dunham who opposed killing bushwhackers, Palmer added, were either overly pious or cowards.[59] One soldier was even blunter. In his hometown newspaper, he wrote, "We never take any of their class prisoners. They have murdered our men and we have retaliated."[60]

In the 36th Ohio, in short, one sees in microcosm all the factors that contributed to the transformation to destructive war. The regiment had encountered bushwhackers and learned to fear and hate them. As time passed, that hatred broadened to include nearly all mountaineers, who were "bumpkins," "yokels," "natives," "savages," a distinct "race . . . dressed in the 'homespun' of our ancestors." Even avowed Unionists could not be trusted. Evidence to the contrary notwithstanding, all were guilty, all deserved punishment. With Crook offering both a symbolic justification of the soldiers' desired tactics—his experience in the Indian wars—and his willingness to participate in the vengeful release they craved, scouting quickly metamorphosed into an opportunity to enact justice and revenge. It was the secessionists' fault; after all, had they not first started the war and then unleashed the murderous bushwhackers? Only the faint-hearted and traitorous failed to comprehend that the harder the measures used to stop the guerrillas, the better. As far as the men of Crook's regiment were concerned, they were not "brutes" but rather patriots doing a dirty but important job that no-one else wanted.[61]

The 36th Ohio gained a reputation as the Federal regiment most feared by Virginia's secessionist mountaineers, but it hardly was alone in adopting the tactics of destructive war. Other regiments repeated the pattern, as the winter of 1862 passed into spring. While one admittedly is hard pressed to find an Ohio regiment that scouted with the zeal of Crook's men, both the official and the private correspondence are dotted with references to plundered goods, burned homes and towns, hostages, and captured or dead bushwhackers. Against the rising tide of destruction, Rosecrans vainly tried to hold the line. As late as March, he was still trying to punish thieves, retrieve stolen property, and free from jail avowed secessionists who nonetheless had committed no crimes.[62]

Rosecrans's tenure, however, had come to an end. On March 11, 1862, President Lincoln created the Mountain Department to supersede Rosecrans's Department of West Virginia, naming as its commander the celebrated explorer and former Republican presidential candidate, John C. Frémont. To many in Washington, it seemed a regrettable choice. As commander of the Department of the West from July to October 1861, Frémont had been a dismal failure. Weak, moody, isolated from reality by a large and incompetent staff, and, according to his most recent biographer, possibly under the influence of laudanum, the Pathfinder, after attempting on his own to emancipate Missouri's slaves, under pressure quickly had given way to Henry Halleck. Yet Frémont's political prestige and Radical Republican supporters had won him a second chance in the Appalachian Mountains.[63]

Frémont's record against Missouri Confederate guerrillas suggested that in West Virginia he would take a somewhat harder line than had McClellan or Rosecrans. While attempting to control the guerrilla war, in part through a gentlemanly arrangement with Confederate Gen. Sterling Price, Frémont also ordered harsher measures. Indeed, his celebrated emancipation proclamation of August 30 was aimed primarily at quelling guerrilla activities, with the forfeiture of slaves only one of the punishments threatened. In addition, he proclaimed martial law, ordered that captured bushwhackers be tried and shot if found guilty, and ordered southern sympathizers back to their homes, with absence to equal treason.[64]

Knowing all this, many of the soldiers in Frémont's new department anticipated that his command would mean that their unofficial war against the guerrillas finally would receive official sanction and support. Albert George of the 30th Ohio, for example, reacted with joy upon hearing the news, writing that "these cowardly devils will get what they deserve & that is instant *death*.... Hurrah for *Frémont* the man that ... shoots all bushwhackers."[65]

Frémont's "policy of annihilation," as Thomas Taylor called it, was not long in coming.[66] Bushwhacker activity once again was on the increase, spurred both by the resumption of the Union drive south and by the Confederacy's decision officially to recognize and recruit guerrillas as Partisan Rangers. Under increasing pressure from politicians such as Governor Pierpont to act decisively, Frémont on April 7 ordered that his men "use their utmost exertions to destroy the various bands of guerrillas.... to fight them in their own style."[67]

Immediately, just as Frémont turned to confront Stonewall Jackson and the main forces of the Federal Kanawha Division under Gen. Jacob Cox pressed towards Southwest Virginia and its important railroad, detachments of scouts moved out through southern West Virginia. Some dressed as Confederates. Their orders from Cox and Frémont's headquarters were clear: give no quarter, and eliminate the Rebel bushwhacker menace once and for all.[68]

Of particular importance was the attempt to drive the bushwhackers from one of their mightiest strongholds, Webster County. One of the most rugged places in all of western Virginia, Webster had been settled only recently, and it was sparsely populated. Secession had divided Webster irrevocably. Most of her citizens supported the Confederacy, but not all; several Webster Unionists found their way into the 10th Virginia Infantry (U.S.A.). As war approached in 1861, Webster County became base, headquarters, and refuge for many of the bushwhackers operating in southern West Virginia, particularly Duncan McLaughlin's notorious Webster Dare Devils. Violence and destruction were such that farmers were afraid to tend their fields.[69]

To eliminate the threat from Webster County, Frémont turned to none other than George Crook. On April 14, Frémont ordered Crook and Lt.

Col. Thomas Maley Harris—the latter a Unionist Northwest Virginian and commanding officer of the locally-based Federal 10th Virginia—to send a total of 375 bluecoats into the county, approaching the county seat of Addison from different directions. Elements of another Unionist regiment, the 1st Virginia Cavalry, later would join the expedition. Crook responded with some discomfiture and less hope. Not only would the bushwhackers disperse when they learned of his approach, Crook contended, but Webster was not the root of the problem anyway. A better approach, he suggested, would be to let him mount a traditional attack on the Confederate stronghold of Lewisburg, to the south in Greenbrier County. Crook's growing distaste for fighting guerrillas did not reflect second thoughts about his tactics, which he still advocated, but rather grew out of his ambition to lead his regiment into a real battle and his deepening disillusionment with mountain Unionists. By April 1862, the latter hardly seemed worth the effort of saving. Crook thus turned over his end of the onerous task to subordinate Ebenezer Andrews.[70]

On April 22, Andrews left Summersville with a little over two hundred men, drawn from Companies E, G, I, and K. Having stopped for the night near Gardiner's Store, the men of the 36th Ohio arrived in Addison the next afternoon. The others appeared the next day. What happened next remains open to debate, as reports conflict. Andrews officially reported to Crook that, after skirmishing with bushwhackers, the Federals loaded up goods previously stolen from Unionists and left town, leaving in ruins only a small saltworks owned by McLaughlin. William H. Dunham, who despised Andrews, nonetheless concurred in a letter written April 23, which adds strength to Andrew's report. In an April 26 communiqué to Secretary of War Edwin Stanton, however, Frémont indicated a higher tally of destruction, writing that seventeen houses were burned in Addison. In an 1865 report, Frémont went even further, claiming that his men had burned the entire town. Crook told yet another story. After the expedition, he played down the expedition's results, telling Jacob Cox that his men had returned from Addison without seeing any Rebels. A second foray in early May also proved disappointing, Crook maintained. However, years later, in his postwar memoirs, Crook boasted that his men "had to burn out the entire county."[71]

Whatever the scale of destruction in Webster County, Frémont's campaign against the guerrillas seemed at first to produce the results he and his men wanted, although Frémont himself resigned in a huff shortly afterward. By mid-May, many bands were dispersing; and at least one bushwhacker leader, George Downs of Calhoun and Roane counties, had proposed an eight-day truce, during which his men either would return home or cross the lines to join regular Confederate units. Col. J. C. Rathbone of the Federal 11th Virginia Infantry agreed to the armistice, but his superiors overruled him, in effect demanding unconditional surrender. New Home Guard units meanwhile were added to the antibushwhacker force, as many of Frémont's Federals took part in more traditional battles and marches. Cox's May dash for the upper Valley of Virginia also applied pressure on all Confederates, regulars or irregulars.[72]

Participation in battles such as Princeton and Lewisburg—the latter managed by the newly promoted brigade commander George Crook—produced among Federals both boredom and a craving to get out of western Virginia and into a more important theater of the war. The Federals' wish temporarily came true in August, when Cox's Kanawha Division raced eastward to support the Army of the Potomac at South Mountain and Antietam. In early 1863, after a brief return to West Virginia, many of those in the division were reassigned by the high command to Mississippi or Tennessee, with some rejoining Rosecrans. Most hoped that the mountain Unionists, together with a small contingent of unlucky northerners, could contain the bushwhackers and control the region's stalemated front.[73]

Their hopes proved illusory, however. The bushwhackers had not given up, nor would they until after Appomattox. As the autumn of 1862 approached, the bushwhackers regained their momentum and once again were terrorizing their Unionist neighbors and foes, just as before. As a result, many Union regiments had to remain in the region or return to it, and they continued to exact, with torch and rifle, an eye for an eye.

The final irony, perhaps, is that the tactics of destructive war failed. The Federal counterguerrilla campaign in West Virginia and elsewhere in Appalachia never succeeded in exterminating the bushwhackers, who remained active throughout the rest of the war. Indeed, it almost certainly was counterproductive, as it not only tied down regular troops needed elsewhere, but also fueled a vicious circle of violence and retribution. From a strictly military point of view, the Federals might well have been advised to ignore the region altogether.[74] More than military necessity shaped the Civil War, however. No politician north or south could afford to abandon a corner of his nation, and certainly Washington could not allow the Confederacy to control unmolested a region so close to the Ohio River, without damaging the Union's legitimacy. Once the struggle began, American military history from Roanoke Island on had pointed toward just such a war. Hardly inevitable, a destructive guerrilla war nonetheless was the surest bet in a civil conflict of such magnitude, as McClellan and Rosecrans initially realized.

It resulted in the kind of war perhaps summed up best by West Virginia Unionist Nancy Hunt, who, in September 1863, wrote, "Unless it is stopped I awfully fear another Lawrence massacre . . . I have not written of all the havoc that has been made here. It is awful to live the way we do."[75] Most Americans, however, had ignored that part of their past, at their peril; as recent events suggest, they continue to do so. Even most modern Civil War historians either downplay or romanticize the facet of the conflict that is examined here. In so doing, they distort the war as a whole. What George Crook did at Cedar Mountain or Chickamauga was important, but the war he fought in and around Summersville was no less significant.

Notes

This essay is a revised version of a paper presented at the Annual Meeting of the Southern Historical Association, Orlando, Fla., Nov. 11, 1993. I am grateful to Kenneth Bindas, Michael Fellman, John Ferling, Marion Smith, Altina Waller, and Shannon Wilson for their comments and suggestions.

1. U.S. Dept. of War, *The War of the Rebellion: A Compilation of the Official Records of the Union and Confederate Armies* (Washington, D.C.: U.S. Government Printing Office, 1880–1901; hereafter cited as *OR*), ser. 1, vol. 2, p. 251.

2. Mountain Dept., General Orders No. 11, Apr. 7, 1862, in Records of the U.S. Army Continental Commands, 1821–1920, Mountain Dept., 1861–62, RG 393, NA.

3. *OR*, ser. 1, vol. 12, pt. 1, pp. 5–7; *OR*, ser. 1, vol. 12, pt. 3, pp. 53, 55, 69, 75; *OR*, ser. 1, vol. 51, pp. 584–85.

4. James Reston, Jr., *Sherman's March and Vietnam* (New York: Macmillan, 1984). For a recent reiteration of the traditional model, see James M. McPherson, *Drawn with the Sword: Reflections on the American Civil War* (New York: Oxford Univ. Press, 1996), 66–86.

5. Mark E. Neely, Jr., "Was the Civil War a Total War?" *Civil War History* 37 (Mar. 1991): 5–28 (quotations from 27–28). While Neely admits that tactics resembling those of total war were used locally in suppressing guerrillas, he underrates that aspect of the war.

6. Mark Grimsley, "Conciliation and Its Failure, 1861–62," *Civil War History* 39 (Dec. 1993): 317–35. See also Grimsley's *The Hard Hand of War: Union Military Policy toward Southern Civilians, 1861–1865* (Cambridge: Cambridge Univ. Press, 1996).

7. Wayne K. Durrill, *War of Another Kind: A Southern Community in the Great Rebellion* (New York: Oxford Univ. Press, 1990); Michael Fellman, *Inside War: The Guerrilla Conflict in Missouri During the American Civil War* (New York: Oxford Univ. Press, 1988); Reid Mitchell, *Civil War Soldiers* (New York: Viking, 1988); Charles Royster, *The Destructive War: William Tecumseh Sherman,*

Stonewall Jackson, and the Americans (New York: Vintage, 1991). These works, and particularly Fellman's, inform this essay throughout. Note also Joseph T. Glatthaar's assertion, in *The March to the Sea and Beyond: Sherman's Troops in the Savannah and Carolina Campaigns* (New York: New York Univ. Press, 1985), xii, that Sherman's total war grew in part from his soldiers' "veteran character," an argument which Fellman, Mitchell, Royster, and this essay dispute.

8. For pre-1861 examples of guerrilla warfare and its consequences in America, see Robert F. Berkhofer, Jr., *Images of the American Indian from Columbus to the Present* (New York: Alfred A. Knopf, 1978), 28–29, 81, 119–25; John Ferling, *Struggle for a Continent: The Wars of Early America* (Arlington Heights, Ill.: Harlan Davidson, 1993), 1–60, 120, 163–65, 206; Gary B. Nash, "The Image of the Indian in the Southern Colonial Mind," *William and Mary Quarterly*, 3rd ser., 29 (Apr. 1972): 197–230; Robert M. Utley, *Frontiersmen in Blue: The United States Army and the Indian, 1848–1865* (New York: Macmillan, 1967), 7–11; Russell F. Weigley, *The American Way of War: A History of United States Military Strategy and Policy* (New York: Macmillan, 1973), 23–26; Russell F. Weigley, *The Partisan War: The South Carolina Campaign of 1780–1782* (Columbia: Univ. of South Carolina Press, 1970); and Robert Wooster, *The Military and United States Indian Policy, 1865–1903* (New Haven, Conn.: Yale Univ. Press, 1988), 141–43. On guerrilla war in the Civil War, in addition to the works cited above, see Stephen V. Ash, *Middle Tennessee Society Transformed, 1860–1870: War and Peace in the Upper South* (Baton Rouge: Louisiana State Univ. Press, 1988), 86–99, 143–66; Durwood Dunn, *Cades Cove: the Life and Death of a Southern Appalachian Community, 1818–1937* (Knoxville: Univ. of Tennessee Press, 1988), 127–41; Herman Hattaway and Archer Jones, *How the North Won: A Military History of the Civil War* (Urbana: Univ. of Illinois Press, 1983); Ralph Mann, "Family Group, Family Migration, and the Civil War in the Sandy Basin of Virginia," *Appalachian Journal* 19 (Summer 1992): 374–93; Ralph Mann, "Guerrilla Warfare and Gender Roles: Sandy Basin, Virginia, as a Test Case," *Journal of the Appalachian Studies Association* 5 (1993): 59–66; James B. Martin, "Black Flag Over the Bluegrass: Guerrilla Warfare in Kentucky, 1863–1865," *Register of the Kentucky Historical Society* 86 (Autumn 1988): 352–75; Kenneth W. Noe, *Southwest Virginia's Railroad: Modernization and the Sectional Crisis* (Urbana: Univ. of Illinois Press, 1994), 118–20, 128–30; Phillip Shaw Paludan, *Victims: A True Story of the Civil War* (Knoxville: Univ. of Tennessee Press, 1981), esp. 56–109; and Emory M. Thomas, *The Confederacy as a Revolutionary Experience* (Englewood Cliffs, N.J.: Prentice-Hall, 1971; reprinted Columbia: Univ. of South Carolina Press, 1992), xi, 53–56. Grimsley, "Conciliation," 335, notes that "hard war" appeared earliest in the Southern Mountains.

9. *OR*, ser. 1, vol. 2, pp. 2, 71, 195–96, 653. On the general war in western Virginia, see Hattaway and Jones, *How the North Won*, 36–39; James M. McPherson, *Battle Cry of Freedom: The Civil War Era* (New York: Oxford Univ. Press, 1988), 297–304; Noe, *Southwest Virginia's Railroad*, 109–38; and John Alexander Williams, *West Virginia: A History* (New York: Norton, 1984), 57–65.

10. *OR*, ser. 1, vol. 2, pp. 195–96.

11. Union Provost Marshall's File, Prison Records, 1862–65, Camp Chase, Ohio, Arrival Rolls 1–16, 18–20, 22–23, 25, 27, 29, 31–37, 39, 41, 44, 47, 56, 65, 68, 72, 78, War Dept. Collection of Confederate Records, RG 109, NA. *OR*, ser. 1, vol. 2, pp. 205, 211. *OR*, ser. 2, vol. 2, p. 39. W. S. Rosecrans, Clarksburg, Va., to Col. J. M. McConnell, June 27, 1861, Letters Sent, Mountain Dept., RG 393, NA. Edward McMobley, Harpers Ferry, Va., to Provost Marshall's Office, May 29, 1862[?], Letters Received, Mountain Dept., RG 393, NA. William K. Knauss, *The Story of Camp Chase: A History of the Prison and Its Cemetery, Together With Other Cemeteries Where Confederate Prisoners Are Buried, Etc.* (Nashville: Methodist Episcopal Church South, 1906), 111–25.

12. "Diary of Seargeant John Thomas Booth Company 'G' Thirty-Sixth Ohio Volunteer Infantry. In War of the Rebellion. Under the Name of 'Foot Prints of the Thirty-Sixth Ohio Volunteer Infantry in the War of the Rebellion,'" Dr. John Booth Papers, Folder 7, Box 1, Collection 180, Ohio Historical Society (hereafter, OHS), Columbus, Ohio.

13. *OR*, ser. 1, vol. 2, pp. 205, 211. McClellan hardly was alone; other Federal commanders pursued similar conciliatory policies. See Grimsley, "Conciliation," 317–23.

14. *OR*, ser. 1, vol. 2, pp. 762–63; William M. Lamers, *The Edge of Glory: A Biography of General William S. Rosecrans, U.S.A.* (New York: Harcourt, Brace and World, 1961), 20–39; Hattaway and Jones, *How the North Won*, 38–39; McPherson, *Battle Cry of Freedom*, 300–303.

15. W. S. Rosecrans, Wheeling, Va., to Lorenzo Thomas, Mar. 17, 1862, and A. H. Tomlinson, New Creek, Va., to Brig. Gen. Schenck, Mar. 17, 1862, both in Letters Sent, Mountain Dept., RG 393, NA. *OR*, ser. 1, vol. 5, p. 552. Lamers, *Edge of Glory*, 41–46.

16. *OR*, ser. 1, vol. 5, pp. 576–77.

17. General Orders No. 3, July 28, 1861, in *OR*, ser. 1, vol. 2, p. 766. General Orders No. 8, Aug. 5, 1861, and General Orders No. 21, Sept. 18, 1861, both in Mountain Dept., RG 393, NA. See also George S. Hartstuff, Wheeling, Va., to Lt. Col. J. C. Rathbone, Mar. 26, 1862, Letters Received, Mountain Dept., RG 393, NA.

18. "Diary of Booth," 84–89, in Booth Papers, OHS. George Crook, *General George Crook: His Autobiography*, ed. Martin F. Schmitt (Norman: Univ. of Oklahoma Press, 1946; reprinted 1986), 86. W. H. Dunham, Summersville, Va., to Henrietta, Oct. 28, Nov. 15, and Nov. 20, 1861, all in William H. Dunham Letters, U.S. Army Military History Institute (hereafter, USAMHI), Carlisle Barracks, Pa. Thomas T. Taylor, Camp Summerville, Va., to Wife, Sept. 25, 1861, Folder 2, Box 1, Thomas T. Taylor Papers, MSS 7, OHS. W. S. Rosecrans, Wheeling, Va., to Frank Blair, Mar. 4, 1862, Letters Sent, Mountain Dept., RG 393, NA. *OR*, ser. 1, vol. 5, pp. 669–70.

19. W. S. Rosecrans, Wheeling, Va., to Henry Wilson, Feb. 27, 1862, Letters Sent, Mountain Dept., RG 393, NA.

20. General Orders No. 13, Nov. 15, 1861; W. S. Rosecrans, Wheeling, Va., to M. C. Meigs, Feb. 28, 1862; and Rosecrans, Wheeling, Va., to Frank Blair, Mar. 4, 1862; all in Letters Sent, Mountain Dept., RG 393, NA.

21. *OR,* ser. 1, vol. 2, p. 767. George S. Hartstuff, Clarksburg, Va., to Col. Tyler, Aug. 12, 1861; and W. S. Rosecrans, Wheeling, Va., to M. C. Meigs, Feb. 28, 1862; both in Letters Sent, Mountain Dept., RG 393, NA. Jacob Dolson Cox, *Military Reminiscences of the Civil War,* vol. 1: Apr. 1861–Nov. 1863 (New York: Charles Scribner's Sons, 1900), 421–25.

22. W. S. Rosecrans, Clarksburg, Va., to Henry W. Westfall, Aug. 11, 1861, Letters Sent, Mountain Dept., RG 393, NA. Louis Reed, "Colonel Rathbone of Burning Springs," *West Virginia History* 23 (Apr. 1962): 208–11.

23. William Keany, Camp Pierpont, Va., to W. S. Rosecrans, Aug. 25, 1861, Letters Received, Mountain Dept., RG 393, NA.

24. L. Ruffner, Kanawha Salines, to Gen. Rosecrans, Oct. 26, 1861; and George Dennison, Columbus, Ohio, to W. S. Rosecrans, Aug. 9, 1861; both in Letters Received, Mountain Dept., RG 393, NA.

25. Thomas T. Taylor, Camp Scott, Va., to Wife, Oct. 16, 1861, Folder 2, Box 1, Taylor Papers, MSS 7, OHS. See also *OR,* ser. 1, vol. 12, pt. 3, p. 58; Mann, "Family Group," 374–75, 379–86; Paludan, *Victims,* 62–78; and Hila Appleton Richardson, "Raleigh County, West Virginia, in the Civil War," *West Virginia History* 10 (Apr. 1949): 227–29. William Griffee Brown, *History of Nicholas County, West Virginia* (Richmond, Va.: Dietz, 1954), 116–19, notes how Ramsey later became a celebrated Home Guard captain.

26. Jacob D. Cox, Marietta, Ohio, to Salmon P. Chase, Jan. 1, 1863, Jacob Dolson Cox Papers, Oberlin College Archives, Oberlin, Ohio (microfilm). Albert George, Camp Ewing, to Sister, Oct. 25, 1861, Albert George Letters, VFM 2040, OHS. John A. Palmer Diary, Sept. 1, 2, 5, 1861, in Lester L. Kempfer, *The Salem Light Guard: Company G, 36th Regiment, Ohio Volunteer Infantry, Marietta, Ohio, 1861–1865* (Chicago: Adams, 1973), 18–20. Wallace S. Stanley, diary, 100–107, in Dr. John Booth Papers, Box 2, Collection 180, OHS. Thomas T. Taylor, Camp at Sutton, Va., to Wife, Sept. 22, 1861; Taylor, Camp Summerville, to Wife, Sept. 25, 1861; Taylor, Camp Scott, Va., to Wife, Oct. 11, 1861; and Netta Taylor, Georgetown, Ohio, to Husband, Oct. 20, 1861; all in Folder 2, Box 1, Thomas T. Taylor Papers, MSS 7, OHS. *OR,* ser. 1, vol. 5, pp. 576, 615. Charles R. Woods, Camp Piatt, to Assistant Adjutant General, Headquarters, Dept. of West Virginia, Aug. 10 and 24, 1861, both in Letters Received, Mountain Dept., RG 393, NA. Henry Clay McDougal, *Recollections, 1844–1909* (Kansas City: Franklin Hudson, 1910), 220–21. Reid Mitchell, *Civil War Soldiers,* 132–34; John Alexander Williams, *West Virginia,* 65–67; T. Harry Williams, *Hayes of the Twenty-Third: The Civil War Volunteer Officer* (New York: Knopf, 1965), 62–63.

27. William H. Busby to Rice Lewis and Lewis Walker, Sept. 10, 1861, quoted in Theodore W. Blackburn, *Letters from the Front: A Union "Preacher" Regiment (74th Ohio) in the Civil War* (Dayton, Ohio: Morningside, 1981), 13–15.

28. Reid Mitchell, *Civil War Soldiers,* 133–39; T. Harry Williams, *Hayes,* 63. The term "vocabulary of abuse" is taken from Nash, "Image of the Indian," 220.

29. Rutherford B. Hayes, diary, Oct. 11, 1861 (first quotation); Aug. 13, 1861 (second quotation); and Jan. 15, 1862 (fourth quotation); and Rutherford B. Hayes, Birch River, to Uncle, Sept. 14, 1861 (third quotation), in *Diary and Letters of Rutherford Birchard Hayes, Nineteenth President of the United States,* ed. Charles Richard Williams (Columbus: Ohio State Archaeological and Historical Society, 1922; reprinted New York: Kraus, 1971), 114, 64, 92.

30. Thomas T. Taylor, Lewisburg, Va., to Margaret A. Taylor, May 15, 1861, Folder 6, Box 1, Taylor Papers, MSS 7, OHS. See also Fellman, *Inside War,* 193–201, 216–21.

31. Albert George, Camp Union, to Brother, Dec. 10, 1861, Albert George Letters, VFM 2040, OHS.

32. William H. Dunham, Summersville, W.Va., to H., Jan. 27 and Apr. 18, 1862, both in Dunham Letters, USAMHI.

33. S. C. McFadden, Head Quarters, Co. A, 5th Va. Regt., to John L. Ziegler, Apr. 27, 1862, Letters Received, Mountain Dept., RG 393, NA.

34. See Fellman, *Inside War,* 13–18, 148, 158–76; Reid Mitchell, *Civil War Soldiers,* 24–28, 133–39; Noe, *Southwest Virginia's Railroad,* 118–20; Sherry Lynn Smith, *The View from Officers' Row: Army Perceptions of Western Indians* (Tucson: Univ. of Arizona Press, 1990), 11–16, 40–41, 145–57. One question that emerges in any discussion of mountaineers as "savages" is how much wartime perceptions shaped the Appalachian stereotype that emerged later in the century. Was a persistent stereotype created in the war years? That is to say, were the celebrated feudists of popular lore only bushwhackers warmed over? Or was "savagery" a conceptual tool that disappeared after Appomattox, to be superseded years later by something similar but largely unrelated? I tentatively suspect the former, but clearly more research needs to be done in comparing wartime and postwar descriptions.

35. George S. Hartstuff, Wheeling, Va., to Theo Gaines, Mar. 1, 1862, and W. S. Rosecrans, Wheeling, Va., to E. M. Stanton, Mar. 17, 1862, Letters Sent, Mountain Dept., RG 393, NA. Joseph Darr, Jr., Wheeling, Va., to Albert Tracy, Letters of Apr. 1 and May 2, 1862; H. S. Samuels, Wheeling, Va., to W. S. Rosecrans, Dec. 4, 1861; and Edward McMobley, Harpers Ferry, to Provost Marshall's Office, May 29, 1862[?]; all in Letters Received, Mountain Dept., RG 393, NA. Albert George, M'Coys, to Sister, Mar. 13, 1862, in Albert George Letters, VFM 2040, OHS.

36. Crook, *General George Crook,* 87.

37. *OR,* ser. 2, vol. 3, pp. 219, 228, 258, 346, 410–11, 420, 427–29, 498–500. See also Knauss, *Camp Chase,* 125–39.

38. *OR,* ser. 2, vol. 3, p. 500.

39. *OR,* ser. 1, vol. 5, pp. 468–70, 501–3, 552. Maj. Hawkins, Camp Scott near Cross Lanes, Va., to Sir, Sept. 12, 1861, Letters Sent, Mountain Dept., RG 393, NA. Jewett Palmer, Jr., diary, Sept. 7–8 and Oct. 24–27, 1861; and John A. Palmer to Margaret Palmer, Oct. 27, 1891; all in Kempfer, *Salem Light Guard,* 20–21, 24–29, 32–35. Thomas T. Taylor, Camp Scott, Va., to Wife, Oct. 9, 1861, Folder 2, Box 1, Taylor Papers, MSS 7, OHS.

40. Thomas T. Taylor, Camp Scott, Va., to Son, Oct. 26, 1861 (first quotation); and Taylor, Head Quarters, 3 Brigade, Mountain Dept., to Margaret Taylor, May 17, 1862 (second quotation); both in Folder 2, Box 1, Taylor Papers, MSS 7, OHS.

41. Thomas T. Taylor, Camp Scott, Va., to Wife, Oct. 16, 1861, Folder 2, Box 1, Taylor Papers, MSS 7, OHS. Nearly all of Taylor's many letters touch on his financial difficulties, the growing estrangement in his marriage, his hatred for former friends and associates in Georgetown, Ohio, and his personal reasons for joining the army.

42. Ibid. See also Thomas T. Taylor, Camp Scott, Cross Lanes, Va., to Son, Oct. 26, 1861, Folder 2, Box 1, Taylor Papers, MSS 7, OHS.

43. "Diary of Booth," 22–42, in Booth Papers, OHS. Kempfer, *Salem Light Guard,* 7–10, 18–23. William H. Dunham, Parkersburg, Va., to Henrietta, Sept. 15, 1861, Dunham Letters, USAMHI. Whitelaw Reid, *Ohio in the War: Her Statesmen, Her Generals, and Soldiers* (Cincinnati: Moore, Wilstach and Baldwin, 1868), 2:233.

44. Crook, *General George Crook,* xix–xxiv, 3–85 (quotation, 85). There is no modern biography of Crook—one is sorely needed—but see two articles: James T. King, "George Crook: Indian Fighter and Humanitarian," *Arizona and the West* 9 (Winter 1967): 333–48; and James T. King, "Needed: A Re-Evaluation of General George Crook," *Nebraska History* 45 (Sept. 1964): 223–35. The Rogue River and Yakima wars are discussed in Utley, *Frontiersmen in Blue,* 93–111, 175–84, 187–200. Wooster, *Military and Indian Policy,* 50–51, 64, 127, notes that Crook's reputation as a humanitarian general developed only late in the general's career. Before the 1880s, he fought Native Americans as he fought West Virginia secessionists.

45. *Ohio Order Books, Cos. C, I, and K, 36th Infantry A.G.O.,* Orders No. 1, 2, 5, 8, 20, 27, RG 393, NA. Crook, *General George Crook,* 85–86. William H. Dunham, Summersville, Va., to Henrietta, Nov. 1, Nov. 24, and Dec. 4, 1861, all in Dunham Letters, USAMHI. Reid, *Ohio in the War,* 2:233.

46. William H. Dunham, Summersville, to William Odell, Nov. 15, 1861, Dunham Letters, USAMHI.

47. John A. Palmer, diary, Jan. 1, 1862, in Kempfer, *Salem Light Guard,* 38. Palmer earlier had compared mountaineers to Native Americans on Oct. 17, 1861; in ibid., 24.

48. "Diary of Booth," 50, in Booth Papers, OHS.

49. Crook, *General George Crook,* 87.

50. "Diary of Booth," 47–50, 80, in Booth Papers, OHS. John A. Palmer, diary, Oct. 17, 1861; and John A. Palmer to Margaret Palmer, Oct. 27–28, 1861; in Kempfer, *Salem Light Guard,* 24–27, 32–35. Thomas T. Taylor, Camp Scott, Va., to Wife, Oct. 11, 1861, Taylor Papers, Folder 2, Box 1, OHS; Cox, *Military Reminiscences,* 1:144–45.

51. William H. Dunham, Summersville, Va., to Henrietta, Oct. 28, 1861, Dunham Letters, USAMHI. *OR,* ser. 1, vol. 5, p. 995.

52. Crook, *General George Crook,* 87.

53. "Diary of Booth," 7, 52–70, 79–80, 84–89, 96–98, in Booth Papers, OHS. William H. Dunham, Summersville, Western Va., to H., Dec. 24, 1861, Dunham Letters, USAMHI. *OR,* ser. 1, vol. 5, p. 471. *OR,* ser. 1, vol. 51, pp. 54–56.

54. *OR,* ser. 1, vol. 51, p. 56.

55. "Diary of Booth," 100–104 (quotations from 102 and 104 respectively), in Booth Papers, OHS. William H. Dunham, Summersville, W.Va., to H., Jan. 1, 1862, Dunham Letters, USAMHI.

56. William H. Dunham, Letter Fragment, Jan. 1862, Dunham Letters, USAMHI. "Diary of Booth," 105, 122–25, in Booth Papers, OHS. The *Home News,* as transcribed in "Diary of Booth," 122–25, reported the skirmishing with guerrillas but not the destruction. Thornton's violation of a woman in her bed—what Stephen V. Ash refers to as "symbolic rape"—suggests the real possibility of rape or other violence aimed at the region's women. As of this writing, I have found no evidence of such crimes. For an assertion that "symbolic rapes" were common but actual rapes rare, see Ash, *When the Yankees Came: Conflict and Chaos in the Occupied South, 1861–1865* (Chapel Hill: Univ. of North Carolina Press, 1995), 197–203.

57. "Diary of Booth," 105–6, in Booth Papers, OHS.

58. William H. Dunham, Summersville, W.Va., to H., Jan. 14, 1862 (first quotation), and Dunham, Letter Fragment, Jan. 1862, Dunham Letters, USAMHI. See also "Diary of Booth," 106, in Booth Papers, OHS. Reid Mitchell, *Civil War Soldiers,* 134–35, depicts Dunham as a lone voice of decency amid the insanity of war. However, as Dunham's letters of Dec. 29, 1861, and Feb. 2, 1862, particularly demonstrate, much of his aversion to the advocates of destructive war was personal in nature. Many of the regiment's leading practitioners of scouting, notably Ebenezer Andrews, also were members of a group Dunham termed "the Marietta clique," a circle of officers whom Dunham ridiculed as incompetent and cowardly. Dunham, in turn, belonged to a rival faction of non-Mariettans, many of whom, like Dunham himself, soon would resign. Too, his aversion to scouting probably derived at least in part from practical concerns. As John Palmer put it, "Capt. Dunham being a very fat man is not adapted to climbing the mountains, & scaling rocks" (Kempfer, *Salem Light Guard,* 61). It also is important to note that the men of the 36th Ohio routinely did not kill all their prisoners, which suggests that, when prisoners were killed, it was a result of anger, frustration, and rage, rather than any coolly designed policy. See Oliver Parker, Camp Meadowbluff, to Father and Mother, July 25, 1862, Civil War Bound Notebook Series, vol. 1, Roy Bird Cook Collection, West Virginia and Regional History Archives (hereafter cited as WVU), Univ. Libraries, West Virginia Univ., Morgantown, W.Va.

59. J. A. Palmer, Summersville, W.Va., to Margaret, Feb. 12, 1862; and Palmer to Folks at Home, Mar. 31, 1862; both in Kempfer, *Salem Light Guard,* 39–41, 49–50.

60. "Diary of Booth," 135, in Booth Papers, OHS. While unidentified, the writer almost certainly was Wallace S. Stanley.

61. Ibid., 111–12, 134–35.

62. Albert George, M'Coys, to Sister, Mar. 13, 1862, Albert George Letters, VFM 2040, OHS. John Palmer Journal, May 14, 1862, in Kempfer, *Salem Light Guard,* 59. Oliver Parker, Meadow Bluff, to Father, July 29, 1862, Civil War Bound Notebook Series, vol. 1, Roy Bird Cook Collection, WVU. T. K. White, Camp Ruth Waddell, to Mother, Dec. 18, 186[1], Thomas K. White Letters, VFM 1298,

OHS. *OR*, ser. 1, vol. 5, pp. 468, 496, 501–3, 1052. *OR*, ser. 2, vol. 2, p. 1404. A. H. Tomlinson, New Creek, Va., to Brig. Gen. Schenck, Mar. 17, 1862; B. R. Duffee, Camp at Fork of Moorfield and Petersburg, to W. S. Rosecrans[?], Mar. 23, 1862; and E. B. Tyler, Charleston, Va., to W. S. Rosecrans, Oct. 31, 1861; all in Letters Received, Mountain Dept., RG 393, NA. W. S. Rosecrans, Wheeling, to Lorenzo Thomas, Mar. 17, 1862, and Rosecrans to Henry Wilson, Feb. 27, 1862, Letters Sent, Mountain Dept., RG 393, NA. General Orders No. 12, Feb. 17, 1862, and No. 14, Feb. 25, 1862, Dept. of West Virginia, RG 393, NA. G. Wayne Smith, "Nathan Goff, Jr., in the Civil War," *West Virginia History* 14 (Jan. 1953): 115.

63. Andrew Rolle, *John Charles Frémont: Character as Destiny* (Norman: Univ. of Oklahoma Press, 1991). See also Hattaway and Jones, *How the North Won*, 55, 97, 136–37; and McPherson, *Battle Cry of Freedom*, 150–51, 424–25.

64. *OR*, ser. 1, vol. 3, pp. 415–19, 466–67, 469–70, 492, 553. Rolle, *Frémont*, 191–210; McPherson, *Battle Cry of Freedom*, 352–53.

65. Albert George, M'Coys, to Mother, Mar. 16, 1862 (first quotation); and Albert George to Sam George, Jr., Mar. 22, 1862 (second quotation); both in Albert George Letters, VFM 2040, OHS.

66. Thomas T. Taylor, Camp Gauley Mountain, to Wife, Apr. 23, 1862, Box 1, Folder 6, Taylor Papers, OHS.

67. *OR*, ser. 1, vol. 12, pt. 1, p. 5. *OR*, ser. 1, vol. 12, pt. 3, pp. 41, 45, 53, 55, 62, 69. *OR*, ser. 2, pt. 3, p. 427. *OR*, ser. 4, vol. 1, pp. 1094–95, 1098. Cramer Trimble, Calhoun County, Va., to George L. Hartstuff, Apr. 7, 1862, Letters Received, Mountain Dept., RG 393, NA. The quotation is from General Order No. 11, Mountain Dept., 1862, RG 393, NA. See n. 2 above.

68. *OR*, ser. 1, vol. 12, pt. 1, pp. 6–7, 489–91, 496. *OR*, ser. 1, vol. 12, pt. 2, pp. 106–7, 114–18. *OR*, ser. 1, vol. 12, pt. 3, pp. 62, 69, 74–75, 84, 90, 165–67, 212, 369. *OR*, ser. 2, pt. 2, pp. 284, 286. Martin O. Holston, Spokane, Wash., to Dr. John Booth, Jan. 11, 1911, in Folder 3, Box 1; and "Diary of Booth," 169–76, in Folder 7, Box 1; both in Dr. John Booth Papers, Collection 180, OHS. "Transcriptions from James Ireland Diaries at Glendower," 14, 18, 20, 25, 29–36, VFM 2304, OHS. Elijah Warren, Camp Hayes, Va., to Col. H. Ewing, May 1, 1862, Letters Received, Mountain Dept., RG 393, NA.

69. U.S. Bureau of the Census, *Population of the United States in 1860* (Washington, D.C.: U.S. Government Printing Office, 1864), 518. U.S. Bureau of the Census, *Manufactures of the United States in 1860* (Washington, D.C.: U.S. Government Printing Office, 1865), 633. U.S. Bureau of the Census, *Statistics of the United States in 1860* (Washington, D.C.: U.S. Government Printing Office, 1866), 485–87. William Christian Dodrill, *Moccasin Tracks and Other Imprints* (Charleston, S.C.: Lowell, 1915), 17, 55, 90–91, 100–103, 144, 154). H. E. Matheny, *Major General Thomas Maley Harris* (Parsons, W.Va.: McClain, 1963), 25–26, 29, 33–40.

70. *OR*, ser. 1, vol. 12, pt. 1, pp. 4–5; and *OR*, ser. 1, vol. 12, pt. 3, pp. 78–79, 84–85, 439–40. Years later, however, Crook took complete responsibility for the expedition and its results; see Crook, *General George Crook*, 88.

71. *OR,* ser. 1, vol. 12, pt. 1, pp. 439–40. *OR,* ser. 1, vol. 12, pt. 3, pp. 108, 159–60. *OR,* ser. 1, vol. 51, pp. 584–85. William H. Dunham, Summersville, W.Va., to H., Apr. 23, 1862, Dunham Letters, USAMHI. Crook, *General George Crook,* 88. Matheny, *Harris,* 37–39. Commenting on an earlier version of this essay, Marion Smith suggested that Andrews actually may have burned a *saltpeter* works rather than a salt works.

72. *OR,* ser. 1, vol. 12, pt. 3, pp. 159–60, 212–13. S. W. Downey, Camp at Petersburg, Va., to Albert Tracy, May 16, 1862; Cramer Trimble, Calhoun Co., Va., to George L. Hartstuff, Apr. 7, 1862; and Elijah Warner, Camp Hayes, Va., to Col. H. Ewing, May 1, 1862; all in Letters Received, Mountain Dept., RG 393, NA.

73. *OR,* ser. 1, vol. 12, pt. 2, pp. 106, 114. *OR,* ser. 1, vol. 12, pt. 3, pp. 127–28, 337, 369, 435–37, 442–43, 445–46, 451, 457, 462–63, 471, 480, 508, 539, 545, 560–61, 570, 676–77. Jacob D. Cox, Charleston, W.Va., to George Thomas, Nov. 4, 1862, and Cox to Aaron F. Perry, Nov. 17, 1862, Jacob Dolson Cox Papers, Special Collections, Oberlin College Archives, Oberlin, Ohio. Reid, *Ohio in the War,* 2:88–90, 2:135, 2:195, 2:203–4, 2:223–24, 2:235, 2:241, 2:278.

74. James Ireland, diary, 29–36, VFM 2304, OHS. Nancy Hunt, Mountain Cove, W.Va., to ?, Sept. 28, 1863; Sarah Frances Young, diary, Sept. 8, 10, 12, 17, 22, and 29, and Oct. 6, 1862; and J. V. Young, Meadow Bluff, to Pauline Young, May 20, 1864; all in Young Civil War Papers, Civil War Bound Notebook Series, vol. 1, Roy Bird Cook Collection, WVU. William Davis Slease, *The 14th Pennsylvania Cavalry in the Civil War* (Pittsburgh: Art Engraving and Printing, 1915), 114. William E. Cox, "The Civil War Letters of Laban Gwinn: A Union Refugee," *West Virginia History* 43 (Spring 1982): 227–37.

75. Nancy Hunt, Mountain Cove, W.Va., to ?, Sept. 28, 1863, in Civil War Bound Notebook Series, vol. 1, Roy Bird Cook Collection, WVU.

6

An Execution in Lumpkin County: Localized Loyalties in North Georgia's Civil War

Jonathan D. Sarris

On the evening of October 22, 1864, a squad of Georgia militia led three prisoners out of their jail cell in the basement of the Lumpkin County courthouse and into the streets of the town of Dahlonega. The soldiers tied the captives and led them in a column through the small North Georgia community, heading eastward toward the Chestatee River. On a river bank outside of town limits, the prisoners were forced to kneel while a firing squad readied. If the executioners and the victims exchanged any words, history has not recorded them. In a moment, the soldiers unceremoniously finished their grim work. Solomon Stansbury, Iley Stuart, and William Witt were shot to death and their bodies hastily buried. Months, perhaps years, later, someone erected unadorned soapstone markers over the gravesite. They remain one of the few tangible records of the killings.[1]

Stansbury, Stuart, and Witt never were charged officially with any crime, but everyone in Dahlonega must have known why they were executed. Their deaths were the result of local militia leader James Jefferson Findley's desperate efforts to maintain order in a community rent by war. Findley, the citizens of Lumpkin County, and their neighbors largely were unscathed by the conventional armies and battles of the Civil War; yet, between 1861 and 1865, they knew no peace. They all were active combatants in a local civil conflict, mirroring to some extent the broader conflict and tied to its rhetoric, but fought on local terms. The soldiers in Lumpkin County's struggle included local pro-Confederate militia, state troops, loosely organized U.S. Army units, and rogue guerrilla bands from both sides. Each faction claimed to fight for certain causes, but all shared a common overriding concern for some particular concept of community. Most had fled the larger war and returned home, finding not peace but a different kind of warfare, one fought for local goals and local victories.

But this more accurately is a tale of two communities. As the war dragged on, Lumpkin's pro-Confederates increasingly identified "the enemy" with the more isolated frontier regions on Georgia's northern border, especially Fannin County. Lying deep in the Blue Ridge and at the time of the Civil War only recently settled, Fannin represented to many Georgians the epitome of the wild Appalachian frontier—uncivilized, backward, and full of pro-Union mountaineers. Lumpkin's secessionist citizens, afraid of being tainted by the dissent associated with mountain areas, acted to prove their loyalty in drastic and murderous ways. The execution of Stansbury, Stuart, and Witt, all Fannin County residents, was the ultimate expression of fealty to the Confederacy.

Several works have explored the dynamics of Civil War loyalties at the community level in recent years, including Wayne Durrill's study of Washington County, North Carolina; Robert McCaslin's analysis of the Great

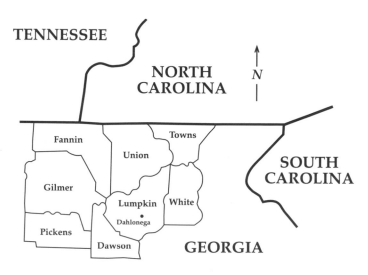

Map 6.1. Lumpkin and Fannin Counties, Georgia, 1864. Map by The University of Tennessee Cartography Lab.

Hanging in Cooke County, Texas; and Michael Fellman's book on the guerrilla war in Missouri. As for Appalachia, Martin Crawford, W. Todd Groce, Phillip Paludan, Ralph Mann, Kenneth Noe, and others have explored the effect of the war on communities from southwestern Virginia to western North Carolina and East Tennessee.[2] North Georgia, however, largely has been neglected. This article begins to redress that neglect. By examining the circumstances surrounding this 1864 execution in Lumpkin County, we can understand better the localism and violence of the civil wars that raged throughout the Southern Appalachian Mountains.

The town of Dahlonega derived its name from the Cherokee word for "yellow." It refers to the commodity which put the region on the map and which still draws tourists to this portion of the North Georgia mountains—gold. Settlers first discovered the ore there in 1828, and within months the region was booming in what was America's first genuine gold rush. Rude mining towns sprang up overnight, and one of them was Dahlonega, which in 1833 became the seat of newly created Lumpkin County. Like many settlements in the region, Dahlonega was in those early years a rough-and-tumble town where rival miners often shot it out in the streets and where "gambling houses, dancing houses, drinking saloons, houses of ill fame, billiard saloons, and tenpin alleys were open day and night."[3] But within a few years, a spirit of respectability replaced the controlled anarchy of the frontier. Flush with the temporary wealth of the gold mines, Dahlonegans built a courthouse, a jail, and, in 1837, an imposing granite edifice housing one of only three branch mints created by the federal government. Although the Mint never lived up to its proponents' economic expectations, it lent an aura of gilded sophistication to the North Georgia town.[4] It also represented the first of many efforts to dampen the crude, boom-town image which was Dahlonega's inheritance from the heady first days of the gold rush.

By 1860, the gold had run out, and Dahlonega had been transformed from a lawless mining camp into a peaceful frontier village of about a thousand people. Dahlonegans still were isolated—it could take days or weeks to get to Atlanta—but they craved development. In 1851, a committee of about sixty residents petitioned the Georgia Railroad Company to extend a line to the town, modestly asking for a once-daily route "running only during the day at from eight to ten miles per hour." Nothing came of the venture, however, and Dahlonega had to wait until 1879 for a railroad.[5] Nevertheless, as one of the last major towns on the southern slopes of the Blue Ridge mountains, Dahlonega was connected firmly to social and economic trends in the rest of Georgia. In surrounding Lumpkin County,

133

farming began to replace mining as the predominant occupation, and corn and potatoes supplanted gold and copper as the most abundant produce.[6] Compared to Georgia's Cotton Belt, slavery had a limited direct impact in Lumpkin—there were only 432 slaves, out of a population of 4,626, in 1860. However, compared to other mountain counties in the state, slavery played an important role there. In 1860, none of the six counties surrounding Lumpkin contained a slave population of more than 5 percent, and no individual in that region owned more than thirty slaves. By contrast, almost 10 percent of Lumpkin residents were slaves, and the county's largest slaveholder owned some eighty individuals.[7]

The secession crisis struck Lumpkin County hard, foreshadowing divisions which later would resurface in the Civil War. Residents voted solidly against leaving the Union by electing Cooperationist delegates to Georgia's secession convention of January 1861, by a margin of 538 to 137.[8] When Georgia did secede, fear spread among pro-Confederate Dahlonegans that dissenters would fight for the Union. That fear seemed to have been realized when one of the town's wealthiest and most influential residents, state senator Harrison Riley, threatened to seize the Mint building, with its fifty thousand dollars in gold, and hold it for the federal government. Georgia Gov. Joseph E. Brown, himself a North Georgian sensitive to the mountaineers' situation, was afraid to move forcefully against the popular Riley, for fear of losing local support.[9]

But Lumpkin County soon quieted. Despite the lingering stereotype of pervasive mountain Unionism, the facts indicate that most Dahlonegans soon fell into lockstep behind the Confederacy. As many students of secession elsewhere in the Southern Appalachians have shown, a vote cast against secession in early 1861 did not usually indicate pro-North sentiment.[10] Indeed, once the issue had been decided and Lincoln had called for troops, many who once had been conditional Unionists became fervent Confederates. Riley's attempt to take the Mint, if it ever had been a serious one, soon fizzled in the face of Governor Brown's quiet persuasion and the firm security measures taken by the pro-Confederate Mint assayer. All in all, any fear that Lumpkin County would be less than loyal to the Confederacy seemed muted by the summer of 1861. Recruiting for the Confederate army went smoothly in the region, and the first company of Lumpkin County men marched off to camp even before the first shot had sounded over Fort Sumter.[11]

The second Lumpkin company to form, proudly named "The Blue Ridge Rifles," marched through the streets of Dahlonega in July, in an emotional ceremony designed to draw the entire community into the war effort. "After the company assembled on the public square," the *Dahlonega Mountain Signal* reported, "Col. McMillan made the concluding speech . . . flash after flash of patriotic fire electrified the audience and held them spellbound." The paper went on to capitalize upon the image of the mountain man as a crack shot and a ruthless fighter, explicitly professing fealty to the Confederacy and countering the rumors of mountain disloyalty with images of mountain ferocity and devotion. "No company in the state is better qualified for destructiveness," the paper's editors commented; "every time they pull the trigger a man will fall." The day's activities culminated with the women of Dahlonega presenting a flag to the company. Ida Hamilton, daughter of the company commander, rose and spoke to the enlistees, urging them to "strike till the last armed foe expires" and to avenge with "burning zeal" the Yankee's "butchery of homeless ladies and smiling infants."[12]

In the war's early years, then, Lumpkin County hardly held itself aloof from the national trend toward militancy. Similar rhetoric was enunciated and similar rituals were enacted in hundreds of communities north and south. The commitment of family, and especially of women, formed a strong basis for enlistment and helped to establish popular concepts of courage and manhood.[13] The pro-Confederate women of Dahlonega preached hard war from the outset, and many of them continued to do so until Appomattox. Two weeks after the ceremony in Dahlonega, Fannie Boyd, daughter of a prominent local attorney, wrote her soldier brother a scalding letter in which she called Lincoln "his satanic majesty" and proclaimed that "the north means to crush us by superior numbers but they can't do it." She professed that even if the Yankees did "tryumph at times and there flag may wave for a while," a righteous God ultimately would save the South with "a voice louder than the thunder of their grand Niagra."[14]

One of the men who marched out of Dahlonega that first year of war to the cheers of women like Fannie Boyd was James Jefferson Findley, a lieutenant in Company D of the 52nd Regiment of Georgia Volunteer Infantry, which mustered into Confederate service in March 1862. Findley in 1860 was one of the most colorful and influential individuals in Dahlonega, a prominent member of the second generation of leaders who had arrived after the gold rush of the 1830s. He would become a dominant figure in Lumpkin County's civil war and would personify the localism and violence of that war for North Georgia as a whole.

James Jefferson Findley had migrated from South Carolina to North Georgia's Gilmer County as a teenager sometime during the 1840s. Eventually he abandoned the frontier and moved southeast to Dahlonega, where he read law and became an attorney.[15] In 1857, the ambitious young lawyer expanded into the gold business and led a small-scale rejuvenation of the region's declining mining industry. He discovered a rich vein of gold on some unclaimed land near the Yahoola River, an area which still is known as "The Findley Chute." Lawyer Findley did not let legal niceties prevent him from developing the site, even though its ownership was unknown. He formed a business partnership with the respectable Harrison Riley (the same man who would attempt to seize the Mint four years later), thus insulating himself from any potential legal disputes. Protected by this association, Findley's business flourished. The vein ultimately produced about $250,000 in gold, and by 1860, Findley was one of the richest men in town, worth almost $20,000. With some of his profits, he bought a twelve-year-old black slave girl to serve in his increasingly affluent household. Within ten years, James Findley had risen from being a small upcountry farmer to become an attorney, miner, slaveholder, and aspiring politician.[16]

In the tumultuous early months of 1861, the thirty-two-year-old Findley cast his lot with the Confederacy. He helped organize military recruitment in Lumpkin County and in October won a seat in the state House of Representatives, where he served as a vocal back-bencher and advocate of resistance to the U.S. government.[17] But Findley never divorced his concept of national service from his local concerns. He put off joining the military for as long as possible, preferring instead to organize Dahlonega's war effort and serve his community in the state legislature. Findley appreciated the comparatively cosmopolitan lifestyle of Milledgeville and wrote to a friend in Dahlonega that he greatly enjoyed the company of the capital's female inhabitants. "There are so many wants me and I cannot marry them all," he complained, "and they are all so pretty."[18] In March 1862, one month before the Confederate Congress passed the Conscription Act, Findley finally enlisted, gaining a commission in Company D of the 52nd Georgia Infantry, which was commanded by his friend and fellow Dahlonega attorney, Wier Boyd. Findley apparently was popular with his troops, who that summer elected him major. But he served for only eight months with the 52nd. He resigned his commission in November and returned home to Dahlonega with Boyd, who also had resigned. There Findley assumed command of the Lumpkin County militia, which he served when not representing his district in Milledgeville.[19]

Why would an ambitious politician resign from a prestigious position in the Confederacy's armed forces? That ambition itself was probably a large factor. The opportunity to command as a colonel must have beckoned impressively after months of serving at a lower grade. Also, as leader of the militia during wartime, Findley was perhaps the most powerful official in Lumpkin County and one of the most influential in north-central Georgia. Indeed, during the war years, Findley established a close political relationship with Governor Brown, who regarded the loyal Lumpkin County colonel as one of his confidantes on issues pertaining to the troublesome mountain regions. In short, the war made James J. Findley a success, capping a decade of ambition, profit, and hard work. For such an aspiring leader, local service probably seemed the most logical option.

But another factor, beyond personal ambition, drew men like Findley home in 1862. By the end of that year, Findley and many others were convinced that the real war was being fought in the mountains of North Georgia, and that they should be part of that effort rather than commit themselves to fight in Mississippi, Tennessee, or even other parts of Georgia. Although regular Union troops would not enter Dahlonega until after the war was over in 1865, the Confederate conscription act had instigated a crisis in the mountain counties which, by the beginning of 1863, would lead to internal warfare on a fairly wide scale.

The immediate problem was the veritable army of draft dodgers and deserters from all over the state who sought refuge from conscription in the mountains of Lumpkin, Fannin, Union, Gilmer, and neighboring counties. They subsisted off the countryside and fought a guerrilla war against militia, conscription agents, and pro-Confederate civilians.[20] This was the war that James J. Findley thought was important, and other Dahlonegans agreed with him. Wier Boyd, father of the strident Fannie Boyd, also resigned his commission in 1862 and ran for the state senate. Although he and Findley would come to oppose each other by war's end, in late 1862 both were concerned with maintaining stability and order in Lumpkin County, and toward that paramount goal they were united.

The potential for violent dissent always had existed in North Georgia. The large antisecession vote in 1861, although not necessarily expressive of outright Unionism, did indicate a core of dissent which continued to grow during the war's first year. In February 1861, a resident of Walker County in northwestern Georgia wrote to Governor Brown that he and his neighbors did not "intend to submit to . . . secession" and if necessary would oppose separation with "flint and steel."[21] That same month, a loyal Confederate from Fannin County, on Lumpkin's northwestern border, wrote Brown of "demagogues . . . telling [the people] that they are not interested in the nigger question, that this [secession] was all for the benefit of the wealthy."[22] Upon occasion, such sentiments incited violent response. In Dahlonega, Fanny Boyd heard from a friend in northeastern Georgia that a mob had "come within an ace of hanging a man" for speaking out against the Confederacy.[23]

However serious this early dissent may have been, the passage of the conscription act in 1862 incited truly widespread and violent disaffection in the mountains, and reports of violence and terrorism flooded Governor Brown's office. James Findley's brother Webster, who had stayed in Gilmer County, noted plaintively in the summer of 1862 that he and his neighbors had suffered greatly "on account of the tories and deserters who have taken up their abode in the mountains." These men had broken into homes, robbed the wives and families of loyal Confederate soldiers, senselessly killed large amounts of livestock, and "burnt up soldiers wives' houses and threatened their lives if molested." Findley blamed outsiders for the trouble, although he conceded that "some of our own citizens are with them." Like many others throughout the region, he begged the governor for arms and ammunition so that he and his neighbors could protect themselves.[24]

In Lumpkin County, Josiah Woody reported to the governor in late 1862 that "these blue mountains . . . are filled with tories and deserters and thieves and runaway Negroes, and they are robbing soldiers' families." As males of fighting age volunteered for military service and left the area defenseless, the "tories ran wild . . . shamefully abusing" women and "even ministers of the gospel." In response, the loyal Confederates of Lumpkin County "form[ed] mobs and taken up Union men and made them take the oath of allegiance." Whether or not these "mobs" engaged in more drastic measures at that point, Woody did not state.[25]

From the perspective of established citizens like the Findleys and Boyds, the dissenters were nothing but shirkers and criminals who had to be suppressed ruthlessly. But the mountaineers' dissent was based upon real issues of autonomy and security, and from the point of view of many "tories and deserters," it was the state and Confederate governments who threatened liberty and property. Early in the war, Confederate authorities had instituted an impressment system which empowered officials to seize needed supplies from citizens, with only minimal compensation. Later in the war, Richmond enacted a tax-in-kind program, under which farmers were obliged to give one-tenth of their produce and livestock to the government, in addition to other taxes.[26]

These measures were unpopular, of course, but what incited such violent opposition in North Georgia were the enforcement measures pursued locally by state authorities. Impressment officials, state militia, and regular troops often took these policies as licenses to plunder at will, especially if a families was rumored to be in some way "disloyal." Indeed, the depositions given by North Georgians to the Southern Claims Commission after the war abound with accounts of government depredations which are eerily similar to the charges pro-Confederates brought against the "tories and deserters." Civilians accused state troops of taking livestock and crops without any pretense of remuneration, breaking into homes, and stealing personal belongings. When challenged, troops often responded with violence. "They threatened to burn my house," one Fannin County claimant charged; when he protested, troops "knocked down and badly hurt" his daughters and "badly abused" his wife and other children. Here was a blatant example of the state's reaching into the homes of isolated, community-oriented mountain families. The state called it "impressment." Unionist mountaineers called it stealing. For them, the state was doing nothing less than making war on women and families. As with the charges brought against the tory raiders, the nature of the crime depended on the perspective of the victim.[27]

But the war measure that aroused the most strident opposition was conscription. Arguably the most revolutionary and far-reaching measure taken by the Confederate government, the draft symbolized in the most tangible manner possible the state's intrusion into the lives of citizens.[28] In the Appalachian Mountains, where central authority was minimal, community ties strong, and allegiance to national government limited, conscription was especially wrenching.[29] As with impressment, what incited the most violent reaction against the draft were increasingly harsh efforts at enforcement.

The hard hand of the state first rose against Lumpkin County and its environs in January 1863. There desertion and draft evasion had reached immense proportions. Reports reached Governor Brown that "a large force under the Union flag [was] laying waste to the country" in Lumpkin County and threatening Dahlonega itself. In response, the Confederate government in Richmond ordered Col. George W. Lee, commander of its Atlanta garrison, to round up deserters and draft evaders and to restore order in the region. Lee led a mixed column of regular troops and militia out of Atlanta and proceeded to Dahlonega, with orders to seek out and arrest those who were "committing acts of robbery and threatening to burn the dwellings of loyal citizens." Lee reached Dahlonega on January 26 and made the town a base of operations for further raids into Lumpkin and Fannin counties, quartering his troops in private homes and churches. Lee captured hundreds of deserters in and around Lumpkin County and dubbed his mission a success, but the intrusion of outsiders into the mountain communities left in its wake disrupted families, smoldering animosities, and mushrooming anti-Confederate sentiment.[30]

Not all North Georgians disapproved of harsh measures to suppress dissent. In Dahlonega, pro-Confederate citizens remained adamantly opposed to the Union and unrelenting in support of the war effort. Fannie Boyd spent the winter of 1862–63 knitting socks for Georgia's troops in the field and writing her brother earnest letters extolling the Confederate victory at Fredricksburg and the successes of Nathan Bedford Forrest.[31] Writing home in late 1862, A. J. Reece, a Dahlonegan fighting with the Army of Northern Virginia, expressed some war weariness but maintained diehard support for the Confederate cause. "The Yankees seem hard to convince that we intend to be free," Reece asserted, "but I guess they will find out in the end that the subjugation of the South is not as easy a thing as they suppose it is. It is costing us dearly but it only makes our men more determined to live free men or die fighting."[32] And in Dahlonega's churches, ministers continued to pray for the success of the Confederacy and to preach individual sacrifice for the good of the nation. One townsperson wrote of being especially moved by a patriotic sermon based upon Jonah 2:9: "But I with the voice of thanksgiving will sacrifice to thee; what I have vowed I will pay."[33] Clergymen thus enjoined their congregants to uphold their oath of loyalty, both to God and to the Confederacy.

Opinions also began to harden among Dahlonega's civilians regarding the proper treatment of enemies, including those "traitors" who roamed the North Georgia mountains. After two years of war and a year of enervating guerrilla conflict, Nancy Wimpy was in no mood for tolerance or compassion. When Robert E. Lee's army invaded Pennsylvania in the summer of 1863, Wimpy, the wife of Dahlonega's wealthiest attorney (he also was one of the town's largest slaveholders), expressed her fervent wish that "Gen'l Lee's mind may change in regard to destroying private property. I think everything ought to be left in ruins. Let them feel the war at home as our people have felt it."[34] And when state troops killed a deserter in the county in August, she stated matter-of-factly: "I think all deserters from state service ought to be shot, for they know nothing about suffering and hardship yet."[35]

The bitterness evident in these statements led to increased violence in the mountains. Indeed, 1863–64 was an unusually violent period in Lumpkin County, a time of shocks which paralyzed the community with fear and seemed to demand ever more drastic actions to insure law and order. George Lee's foray into the county in January 1863 restored order temporarily, but guerrilla activity soon resumed. Bands led by renegades Jeff Anderson and James Jackson terrorized the citizens of Lumpkin and White counties, often killing men without regard to their loyalty or affiliation. Colonel Lee returned with his troops to Dahlonega later that year and noticed that things had not improved since his last expedition. The region still was "overrun with Deserters, tories, and Rogues, who are stealing and running off horses[,] mules, and cattle."[36]

Nancy Wimpy, who was frightened by constant rumors of anti-Confederate irregulars operating in the area, welcomed Colonel Lee's soldiers. She told her nephew, with relief, that "there was four or five hundred soldiers sent up here a few weeks past to look up deserters and tories—they have plenty to do . . . I think we are safe now for a while at least."[37] But relief was short-lived. In August, word came that "the tories and deserters . . . are getting up a considerable force out about Murphy [North Carolina]. They are going around in squads and taking all the arms from the citizens."[38] After Colonel Lee's second expedition returned to Atlanta, disorder continued. Dahlonegans lived under continuous threat of real or imagined invasions by anti-Confederate bands. Wimpy wrote to her nephew again in March 1864, worrying that "every two or three weeks we hear they [the tories] are coming. The men that *are not for the Yanks* get their guns and make ready for them." She was prepared for the worst, but insisted, "I can't feel afraid of such cowardly rogues, though I don't expect any mercy from them if they come here." Wimpy viewed the approaching tories as savages who would war on women and children if left unchecked.[39]

For James Jefferson Findley, the increasing lawlessness of his county seemed overwhelming. Faced with the task of arresting deserters and fighting innumerable guerrillas, Findley found his efforts further handicapped by rebellious troops and inadequate supplies. In January 1864, he wrote Governor Brown that his militia were refusing to perform their duties because their terms of enlistment had expired. Meanwhile, disorder engulfed the defenseless county. "Our country is being overrun with deserters and tories, [who are] stealing horses and mules and cattle," Findley complained to Brown. Worrying about the economic future of the county he was pledged to defend, he estimated that, "if something is not done to relieve us[,] we will not be able to plant much less make a crop." Desperate to restore order, Findley considered other options, respectfully suggesting that "the home guards be compelled to perform active duty or at once be disbanded, [so] that other organizations may . . . relieve us of these troubles."[40] What "other organizations" Findley had in mind he did not say, but clearly he was unwilling to allow formal rules and regulations to hamstring efforts to keep the peace.

Lumpkin's crisis was exacerbated by the growing conviction among many citizens that some of their friends and neighbors were actively aiding and abetting the tories. The number of cases of treason brought in Lumpkin County courts grew dramatically in 1863, fanning the flames of fear and divisiveness. In January, four draft dodgers were arrested in Dahlonega for carrying weapons in the public streets and threatening treason; the following December, two more cases rocked the county. A grand jury first brought treason charges against John A. Wimpy, a member of the influential Wimpy clan. He was acquitted, but Dahlonegans must have been severely disturbed by the very thought of such a prominent name being associated with treachery. During that same session of court, James Findley headed a grand jury which indicted one John Woody for treason. The prosecution's case rested largely on the testimony of Josiah Woody, a relative of the defendant and the same pro-Confederate petitioner who had written Governor Brown so many worried letters about the situation in Lumpkin County. Josiah claimed that he had heard the defendant say "he wish[ed] the Confederacy to be subjugated and that we should be whipped." And although the accused admitted that he "would not fight if I could help it," the jury acquitted him. Dahlonegans' confidence in their community and their legal system was shaken.[41]

The specter of treason injected suspicion and distrust into daily life in Dahlonega, as citizens increasingly looked for the hidden enemy within. Nancy Wimpy thought she saw one in Amzi Rudolph, who planned to run for the state legislature in 1863. "I don't think any Yankee ought to hold office in the Confederacy," she proclaimed; "we have suffered enough by them already." Whether or not Rudolph was a northern sympathizer is unknown, but the fact that Wimpy thought to make such a serious charge against him suggests the atmosphere prevailing in and around Dahlonega in 1863. Combined with the rising tide of violent events in Lumpkin, charges of treason created a palpable fear that the county was disintegrating into disorder.[42]

Pro-Confederate Dahlonegans felt a measure of shame at this instability, as if all their work to transform the town from a lawless gold-rush hamlet into a respectable community had been in vain. At the opening of the February term of court in 1863, members of the Lumpkin County grand jury felt compelled to issue a lengthy explanation of the situation and to assure fellow Georgians of their loyalty. Referring to the troops of George W. Lee, who had come to Dahlonega to hunt deserters, the jury noted sadly that, "for the first time in the history of the county[,] its roads are patrolled by a military force . . . headquarter[ed] within sight of the courthouse." Ashamed that they required outside help to police themselves, the jurors lamented that "the good name of the county is hearby tarnished and its reputation lost" because of the action of a few "outlaws and traitors," but they stoutly professed the community's devotion to the Confederacy. "Against this stain on her name Lumpkin County protests. Her people are not traitors or disloyal." The statement concluded defensively that, although the town appreciated Colonel Lee's help, it should "be remembered that it was [Dahlonega's] hour of need and not of guilt and shame."[43]

Increasingly self-conscious about the disorder in their midst, Confederate Dahlonega craved stability and embraced any actions to achieve it. Although the treason cases of 1863 had taught them to look within for enemies, citizens of Lumpkin County continued to believe that the greatest danger came from outsiders. For many, the chief threat came from the counties which bordered Lumpkin on the north, a region underdeveloped in comparison to theirs and one in which anti-Confederate dissent had been vocal, violent, and widespread since the beginning of the war. Dahlonegans considered Fannin County particularly dangerous. Fannin served as a useful foil for Lumpkin County residents who wanted to prove their loyalty to the Confederacy and shift the label of treason from their backs onto those of other, less civilized Georgians. Thus, in late 1864, when Wier Boyd wanted to impress upon Governor Brown the seriousness of the situation in Lumpkin, he contrasted Lumpkin with the lost wilderness to the north. "Our county is approaching anarchy . . . and unless a favorable change occurs soon we will become *like Fannin . . .* on our northern and Western borders."[44] The example could not have been clearer. Fannin was synonymous with lawlessness, and without help Lumpkin would be contaminated by Fannin's contagious anarchy. Therefore, by 1864, Lumpkin County residents saw the source of their troubles in the wilds of the Blue Ridge. Soon their fears about that region would be realized.[45]

Fannin County, lying in the midst of what today is the Chattahoochee National Forest, seemed the definitive frontier region. Bordering portions of western North Carolina and Tennessee, the county was full of rugged peaks and deep gorges cut by the wild Toccoa River. Fannin had not been organized until 1854, when the state legislature carved it out of portions of Gilmer and Union counties and named it after a Georgian who had given his life in the War for Texas Independence.[46] Many early Fannin settlers emigrated from western North Carolina, and they named their new county seat Morganton, after a town in that region. A few copper and coal mines supplied raw materials to the Ducktown Copper Works just across the Tennessee line, but most Fannin residents made their living on small farms of less than fifty acres. By 1860, Fannin actually had a population larger than that of Lumpkin County and was approximately as wealthy. But there were important differences. Fannin had fewer slaves—less than 3 percent of the population, contrasted with Lumpkin's 10 percent—and no large slaveholders on the scale of some of Dahlonega's wealthiest citizens. Moreover, Fannin did not have a gold rush or any similar event to give it identity, history, and legitimacy. It was a new, unsettled county, with no towns of any size or status and no Federal Mint to establish a real or imagined significance outside the region or the state. Fannin County was even more isolated than Lumpkin, most of its area lying amid the sharp line of mountain ranges which rose just north of Dahlonega and continued on into Tennessee and North Carolina.[47] To some extent, Fannin truly was the wilderness Dahlonegans perceived it to be.

Like most of North Georgia, Fannin County split over the secession issue, and its vote in the 1861 state convention divided evenly between secession and antisecession candidates. But unlike Lumpkin County, where the citizenry seemed to close ranks after state seceded, Fannin County grew more and more divided after 1861. Fannin did send three infantry companies into the Confederate service, but they had dramatic desertion rates, especially after 1863. Lumpkin units had no such desertion rates.[48] By late 1862, Confederate loyalists considered Fannin county one of the most dangerous in the region, full of bushwhackers, deserters, and guerrillas. George W. Lee, in his 1863 forays into North Georgia, noted that Fannin was a source of "considerable trouble," a place where bands of deserters were "plundering and burning at will."[49] Some of its more respectable Confederate citizens concurred with this evaluation of their district, writing Governor Brown that tories were "at large in every part of the county, every night [stealing] every gun that can be found" and threatening to hang any that opposed them. "So soon as they get all our guns," one correspondent worried, "a regular system of robbery will be commenced by these scoundrels . . . Immediate action must be had or this county will be over soon!"[50] By the end of 1862, it was clear that even many of those who initially had supported the Confederacy in Fannin were becoming disillusioned with the cause.

One of those mountaineers who had turned from the Confederacy was Solomon Stansbury, a thirty-five-year-old Tennessee native who had migrated to Hot House Creek in northern Fannin County, where he made a lucrative living as a manufacturer and provider of charcoal to the Ducktown copper mines. His coal business had made him relatively wealthy (he was worth $4,500 in 1860) and enabled him to buy some farmland.[51] Neighbors recalled that Stansbury had been "before and at the commencement of the war a rebel sympathizer," but that his disaffection from the Confederacy grew after conscription was enacted in 1862. By that time, one neighbor remembered, Stansbury had become an open and vocal dissenter, attempting to disrupt the enlistment efforts of state officials and urging men not to submit to the draft but to "stay home and take care of their families."[52] Stansbury tried hard to avoid the draft, arguing to conscription agents that his value to the Ducktown mines should exempt him from military service. This worked initially, but in 1863 authorities arrested Stansbury for draft evasion and took him to Atlanta for trial. The head of the Ducktown mine personally intervened to get his employee released, but by that time Stansbury must have realized that his privileged days of exemption were numbered. He soon would find common cause with other dissenters who felt they had no choice but to leave North Georgia and seek protection behind the Union lines.[53]

Iley Stuart was another such fugitive. One of the many North Carolina migrants who entered what in the 1840s would become Fannin County, Stuart and his family settled in Morganton. There, by 1863, they had accumulated almost six hundred acres of farmland valued at over $1,300.[54] Unlike his future colleague Stansbury, however, Stuart consistently had opposed secession from the beginning. His wife and many neighbors remembered him as "a Union man from the first" who "cursed and abused the rebels for doing as they did." This "made him obnoxious" to pro-Confederate authorities in Fannin, who harassed the family constantly.[55] In September 1863, Stuart made a drastic and dangerous decision to leave North Georgia for the Union lines in Tennessee. Following the well-worn refugee trail along the Toccoa River and into East Tennessee, Stuart made his way to Athens, where he enlisted in the 11th Tennessee Cavalry (U.S.A.).[56]

Solomon Stansbury had made the same choice nine months earlier, leaving his family and fleeing to Cleveland, Tennessee, which had become a haven for anti-Confederate refugees. He worked as a railroad laborer for the U.S. Army, then joined the Union's 1st Tennessee Artillery Battalion.[57]

Stansbury and Stuart both deserted the Union Army within months of their enlistment. By the spring of 1864, they were back in Fannin, trying to organize local units to fight the Confederates in their home county. On their surface, their choice to desert seems puzzling. Both men had gone to great lengths to avoid joining or being drafted into the Confederate army, and both had made what seemed to be the most drastic and irrevocable choice a southerner could make in 1863: turning their backs on their state and joining the same army that was killing many of the their friends, neighbors, and relatives. But these two men simply were making the same choice that James Findley and Wier Boyd had made—leaving a conflict which did not involve their direct interests to fight for their community. Their decision to forsake the broader war for a local conflict thus mirrored a phenomenon occurring throughout North Georgia, and illustrates the power of localism in the mountain counties.[58]

Stuart and Stansbury had been rather ill-served by their ostensible Union allies. Stuart requested placement in a mounted regiment, but instead U.S. troops had confiscated his own horse and assigned him to an infantry unit.

More importantly, both these men soon realized that the war they were fighting in the Tennessee regiments only drew them farther away from their homes and from those they considered to be the real enemy: the pro-Confederate militia and guerrillas of North Georgia. While dissenting civilians were being victimized by conscription and impressment in Fannin County, Stuart and Stansbury suffered assignments to posts in Knoxville and Nashville, as far removed from their community as they had ever been and with no prospect of a quick return. This was not the war they had enlisted to fight.[59]

Both men claimed that they had not deserted their former units, but had been "reassigned" to recruit Union soldiers in North Georgia for service in a new regiment, the 5th Tennessee Mounted Infantry. Whether or not they had such an order, by the summer of 1864, both men had begun to recruit friends and neighbors into an indigenous home guard with which they hoped to wrest control of Fannin County from pro-Confederate forces.[60]

That autumn, they received help from an outside source. Capt. William A. Twiggs was a Fannin County native who at the war's beginning had enlisted in the Confederacy's 52nd Georgia Infantry (the same regiment to which James Findley, Wier Boyd, and most other Dahlonega soldiers belonged). But by 1863 Twiggs had become disenchanted, and soon after the Battle of Chickamauga, he defected to Union lines and enlisted in the 5th Tennessee Mounted Infantry. He soon convinced the 5th's commander that he could recruit a company of Union soldiers from among the disaffected population of his home county. Armed with authority to gather enlistees, he too returned to Fannin County in September 1864. Discovering that Stansbury and Stuart already were mobilizing the forces of dissent, Twiggs coordinated his efforts with theirs, lending them the stamp of authority that he carried from the U.S. Army, in return for their ability to identify and organize anti-Confederate sentiment in the county.[61]

At some point, the character of Twiggs's mission changed. Authorized only to recruit volunteers, the eager captain seized the opportunity to strike directly at pro-Confederate authority in Fannin county. Perhaps at the urging of Stansbury and Stuart, Twiggs decided to organize local citizens into a force which could "give protection to the Union people" and pursue retribution against pro-Confederates.[62] With that goal in mind, the three men rode into Morganton in late September to recruit manpower for their raid. Stuart and Stansbury were wearing parts of their old U.S. Army uniforms to lend authority to the mission. There they gave public speeches urging citizens to join them and "drive out rebels who were robbing the citizens." Playing on local resentment of impressment and conscription, the Twiggs party reminded Morganton residents of their duty "to protect their homes," and pledged to defend the county against further Confederate depredations.[63]

With a few dozen men, Twiggs rode out of Morganton and went into action in early October. The first priority was to gather horses, which the band enthusiastically liberated from "enemies of the government." Here the mission got out of hand, and the new recruits, "not being under the proper control, took the opportunity of repaying past injuries, if not on those who inflicted them, on their abettors."[64] What had begun as a recruitment drive degenerated into a destructive raid conducted by men who had lived with fear, humiliation, and disorder for three years.

Forty miles away in Dahlonega, word had reached authorities that Union raiders were "stealing horses and robbing houses." Once again, disorder threatened battered Lumpkin County. Once again, the source of the trouble was "uncivilized" Fannin County. Without hesitation, James Findley ordered his militia into Fannin to "capture the party or drive them out and take back the stock they had stolen." A squad of cavalry entered the mountains on October 20, 1864 to search for the raiders and headed for the Dial community on the Toccoa River at the county's southern end. There, the militia surprised and captured Stuart, Stansbury, and several others who had become separated from Twiggs's command and were having their horses shod at a local blacksmith's. The captives marched off under guard for Dahlonega that evening. When they reached the town the following afternoon, Findley imprisoned them in the basement of the courthouse.[65]

The Dahlonega colonel then faced the decision of what to do with the prisoners. Whether he agonized over the decision or not we do not know, but there must have seemed few options. The progress of the war and its psychological impact upon Lumpkin County residents dictated the response. By late 1864, Dahlonega was a town living in terror, cut off from the rest of the state by Sherman's forces, surrounded by actual or imaginary bands of tories, and victimized by a year-long series of disturbing, violent events in which some of their citizens had been implicated as traitors. Now, the "savages" of the Blue Ridge threatened to spread disorder into their homes and return Dahlonega to the unruliness of its frontier days. No measures seemed too extreme to prevent this disintegration.[66]

Pro-Confederate Dahlonega also had something to prove. As its grand jury had noted in 1863, the region had suffered "a stain upon her name" due to the actions of the tories. In the past, Lumpkin had been forced to accept help from outside the community to establish order, and they were determined not to suffer that dishonor again. They would prove that they could keep order in their own house, and that Lumpkin's sons were as brave and devoted as any in the Confederacy.[67]

On a personal level, Findley felt a paternalistic responsibility for the people of Lumpkin County and took his pledge to protect them seriously.

As a legislator, he had learned to take care of his constituents, and he often had intervened on their behalf with the state government. He sought draft exemptions for iron workers in his district, constantly petitioned Governor Brown for more supplies, and worried over the problems faced by Lumpkin's farmers.[68] A day before the Stansbury-Stuart party was captured, Findley took the time to write the governor and request rations for his soldiers, who were denied food by the regional commander because they were "not mustered into the Confederate service."[69] Findley took great pride in his ability to care for his people and his troops, and bragged to Brown that "no one can controll them but me . . . I have got them out of the woods and have more men than any boddy. The men will follow me any where." Part of that authority rested on the fact that he protected the community from men like Twiggs, Stansbury, and Stuart, and it was an obligation he was bound by honor to fulfill.[70]

All these factors seem to leave Findley little choice. The prisoners were criminals who had threatened the order of the region and were residents of a county known to be "treasonous." If attorney Findley saw fit to offer the prisoners the semblance of a trial, there is no record of it. On October 22, the colonel ordered William R. Crisson of his command to "take the following named of those prisoners—Solomon Stansbury, Iley Stuart, and William Witt—and have them shot for being bushwhackers."[71] Crisson was a former mining partner of Findley's and a justice of the peace who had presided over the treason trials of the previous year. He had ample motivation to follow the order. But why these three were picked for death is unclear. Stuart and Stansbury obviously were leaders of the raid, but William Witt was simply a volunteer they had picked up during the recruitment drive. There was at least one other raider in the cell with these men who was not executed. For whatever reason, these three were chosen as examples to the tory element.

On the evening of the 22nd, Crisson and a seven-man firing squad took the prisoners out to a small knob called Bearden's Bridge Hill, overlooking the Chestatee. There, in compliance with Findley's orders, Crisson's soldiers shot the three to death. Soon afterward, the widows of Stuart and Stansbury traveled to Dahlonega to inquire about their husbands. Crisson told them matter-of-factly of the men's fate and allowed them to visit the site and view the bodies. It may have been they who erected the soapstone markers, although Stuart family tradition claims that the widows simply covered the men with rocks and returned home.[72]

Findley did not rest there. In early November, he mobilized his militia for action against the anti-Confederate guerrilla band of J. H. Ashworth, "whose thieving, burning, and other depredations had been so extensive in the upper counties." Findley invaded yet another county, Dawson, to the southeast, and captured a dozen guerrillas, as well as five local citizens who the aggressive militia colonel accused of being "engaged in secret negotiations with the enemy." On November 7, Findley summarily hanged twelve of these prisoners.[73] For the time being, Lumpkin County was secure.

Not everyone in Dahlonega supported Findley's actions. Wier Boyd, a fellow attorney who had served with Findley in both the Confederate Army and the state legislature, complained to Governor Brown in December 1864 that his comrade's zeal oppressed the citizens and exacerbated the very disorder it was intended to quell. "Some of the officers of the regiment organized under your authority, as I understand commanded by Col. Findley, have arrogated to themselves the power of forcible impressment of the property of our citizens," Boyd complained. Findley was "compelling citizens who are not subject to [his] orders to do military service and attempting to arrest others who have the courage to assert their rights." Boyd suggested that Findley's force be disbanded and replaced with one more observant of the law and less inclined toward "military despotism."[74] Boyd's concept of law and order apparently did not include the summary execution of citizens, and he blamed these actions on the void left by Lumpkin County Judge Stephen Rice. The judge apparently had abdicated his authority and refused to hold court regularly, due to the "unsettled conditions in this peculiar crisis."[75] Perhaps in response to this angry letter, the relationship between Boyd and Findley chilled and, after the war, remained icily formal.

The people of Lumpkin and Fannin counties had taken actions which made sense in the context of their local conflict, actions which were dictated by the changing dynamics of a community at war with itself. That they professed larger, national goals is indisputable. Fannie Boyd and Nancy Wimpy never wavered in their support for the secessionist cause and eagerly followed the fortunes of the Confederate armies from Virginia to Mississippi. To the end of the war, James Findley professed loyalty to the Confederacy, as late as January 1865 urging Governor Brown to take any measures necessary to "sustain our independence."[76] Iley Stuart had been a vocal "Union man" from the beginning, couching his dissent in terms of the national conflict and national loyalties. But although these individuals echoed the rhetoric of the broader conflict, they saw national events refracted through the prism of their local perspective. They may not have recognized a contradiction between their professed loyalties and their determination to focus on local issues. But when the two ends did conflict, they had no difficulty choosing between them. All were refugees from the Civil War, the war which is spelled in capital letters and read about in textbooks highlighted by names like "Gettysburg" and "Chancellorsville" and "Shiloh." For the people of mountain Georgia, the war was not on these fields, but in their towns and on their farms and homesteads. Their battlegrounds were their communities. Their enemies were those who threatened the latter—or, more accurately, those who offered a conflicting definition of what those communities should be.

The first postwar session of the Lumpkin County Superior Court was called to order in February 1866. Among the first cases on the docket was *The State v. William Crisson, Macy Crisson, Benjamin Van Dyke, Hardy Forrester, J. A. Hollifield, Ferdinand McDonald, J. R. Pruitt and W. H. Worley.* The charge was murder. Over a year after the incident, the Reconstruction government of Georgia had decided to try the men who had carried out the wartime execution of Stansbury, Stuart, and Witt.

For some reason, James Findley was not among the accused. Perhaps his still-formidable influence served to insulate from prosecution the man locals still called "the Colonel." Or perhaps the lack of a written execution order explicitly linking Findley with the killing allowed him plausibly to deny guilt in the case. At any rate, he did not join his erstwhile colleagues at the bar of justice and spent the next several years trying to maintain the wealth and power he had accumulated before and during the war. He was not always successful, and creditors sued the former soldier several times for nonpayment of debt. His old nemesis Wier Boyd often represented the plaintiffs. With his financial situation insecure and some future prosecution for his wartime actions still a possibility, Findley in 1868 fled south to Gainesville. There he set up a successful law practice with his son William and by 1870 had managed to regain his prewar wealth and status. Not all the Findleys were so fortunate or so successful at putting the war's legacy behind them, however. In the 1880s, Findley's father and brother both were arrested and tried for assaulting former North Georgia Unionists.[77]

William Crisson and his fellow executioners were brought to trial in August 1866, but the grand jury refused to indict the group. Although no record of the jury's deliberations exists, its rationale for the acquittal can be found in another war-crimes decision it issued that summer: "We the jury chosen and selected for the August 1866 term of the County of Lumpkin recommend the solicitor general to enter a 'not pros.' on all old war prosecutions."[78] The message was clear. The people of Dahlonega wanted to forget about the recent events which so brutally had torn their community apart.

In 1871, Dahlonegans founded North Georgia Agricultural College, a school where military discipline prevailed and whose leaders consciously fostered the myth of the Confederacy and Lost Cause in Lumpkin County.

In doing so, they rewrote history to obscure the fact that so many local citizens had opposed that cause during the war.[79] The community's crisis of memory revealed itself most tellingly in an 1894 series of articles about the history of the region, written by William Crisson for the *Dahlonega Signal*. Then one of the oldest living citizens of Dahlonega, Crisson had commanded the firing squad that day on Bearden's Bridge Hill. But he hardly mentioned the war years in his memoir. Indeed, the only reference to the period between 1861 and 1865 was his praise for "the noble, untiring efforts of our patriotic southern ladies . . . to vindicate our just cause."[80] For Crisson and the rest of Dahlonega, what the war had done to them was best forgotten.

Notes

1. Depositions of S. B. Boyd, William R. Crisson, Mary Stansbury, Margaret Stuart, William A. Twiggs, Francis Williams, and Thomas N. Wilson, located in U.S. Pension Bureau files of Solomon Stansbury and Iley Stuart, NA. Robert S. Davis, Jr., "Forgotten Union Guerrilla Fighters from the North Georgia Mountains," *North Georgia Journal* 5 (Summer 1988): 30; William S. Kinsland, "Murder or Execution? A Tale of Two Counties," *North Georgia Journal* 1 (Fall 1984): 13–30; Ethelene Dyer Jones, *Facets of Fannin: A History of Fannin County, Georgia* (Dallas, Ga.: Curtis Media, 1989), 533.

2. Wayne K. Durrill, *War of Another Kind: A Southern Community in the Great Rebellion* (New York: Oxford Univ. Press, 1990); Michael Fellman, *Inside War: The Guerrilla Conflict in Missouri During the American Civil War* (New York: Oxford Univ. Press, 1989); Richard B. McCaslin, *Tainted Breeze: The Great Hanging at Gainesville, Texas, 1862* (Baton Rouge: Louisiana State Univ. Press, 1994); Martin Crawford, "Confederate Volunteering and Enlistment in Ashe County, North Carolina, 1861–1862," *Civil War History* 37 (Mar. 1991): 22–29; Martin Crawford, "Ashe County, North Carolina's Union Volunteers: A Study in Mountain Unionism" (paper presented at the 59th Annual Meeting of the Southern Historical Association, Orlando, Fla., Nov. 11, 1993); W. Todd Groce, "Mountain Rebels: East Tennessee Confederates and the Civil War, 1860–1870" (Ph.D. diss., Univ. of Tennessee, 1992); Ralph Mann, "Family Group, Family Migration, and the Civil War in the Sandy Basin of Virginia," *Appalachian Journal* 19 (Summer 1992): 374–93; Kenneth W. Noe, "Red String Scare: Civil War Southwest Virginia and the Heroes of America," *North Carolina Historical Review* 69 (July 1992): 301–22; Kenneth W. Noe, "Exterminating Savages: The Union Army and Mountain Guerrillas in Southern West Virginia, 1861–62" (paper presented at the 59th Annual Meeting of the Southern Historical Association, Orlando, Fla., Nov. 11, 1993); Kenneth W. Noe, *Southwest Virginia's Railroad: Modernization and the Sectional Crisis* (Urbana: Univ. of Illinois Press, 1994); and Phillip Shaw Paludan, *Victims: A True Story of the Civil War* (Knoxville: Univ. of Tennessee Press, 1981).

3. David Williams, *The Georgia Gold Rush: Twenty-Niners, Cherokees, and Gold Fever* (Columbia: Univ. of South Carolina Press, 1993), 97; Andrew Cain, *History of Lumpkin County for the First Hundred Years: 1832–1932* (Atlanta, Ga.: Stein, 1932), 57–78.

4. Sylvia Head and Elizabeth Etheridge, *The Neighborhood Mint: Dahlonega in the Age of Jackson* (Macon, Ga.: Mercer Univ. Press, 1986), 1–46; John C. Inscoe, "Northeast Georgia: Appalachian 'Otherness,' Real and Perceived," in Editorial Board of Georgia Humanities Council, *The New Georgia Guide*, (Athens: Univ. of Georgia Press, 1996), 181–210; David Williams, *Georgia Gold Rush*, 105–9, 118.

5. *Dahlonega Mountain Signal*, Nov. 1, 1851, quoted in Cain, *History of Lumpkin County*, 135.

6. U.S. Bureau of the Census, *Agriculture of the United States in 1860: Compiled from the Original Returns of the Eighth Census* (Washington, D.C.: U.S. Government Printing Office, 1864), 26–28.

7. Ibid., 227. Counties averaged are Dawson (8 percent), Fannin (3 percent), Gilmer (2 percent), Towns (4 percent), Union (3 percent), and White (8 percent). John Inscoe has shown how slavery, although less prevalent in western North Carolina than in the rest of the state, did have a disproportionate influence and linked that area closely to the state and to the South as a whole. See Inscoe, *Mountain Masters: Slavery and the Sectional Crisis in Western North Carolina* (Knoxville: Univ. of Tennessee Press, 1989), 9.

8. Michael P. Johnson, "A New Look at the Popular Vote for Delegates to the Georgia Secession Convention," *Georgia Historical Quarterly* 56 (Summer 1972): 259–76. See also Michael P. Johnson, *Toward a Patriarchal Republic: The Secession of Georgia* (Baton Rouge: Louisiana State Univ. Press, 1977); and Roy R. Doyton and Thomas W. Hodler, "Secessionist Sentiment and Slavery: A Geographic Analysis," *Georgia Historical Quarterly* 73 (Summer 1989): 323–48.

9. Head and Etheridge, *Neighborhood Mint*, 182. Riley, one of the founders of Dahlonega, actually was a bluff opportunist who probably wanted to take advantage of the confusion to seize the gold for himself.

10. Daniel W. Crofts, *Reluctant Confederates: Upper South Unionists in the Secession Crisis* (Chapel Hill: Univ. of North Carolina Press, 1989), 104–29; Crawford, "Ashe County's Federal Volunteers," 3; Groce, "Mountain Rebels," 53–89; Inscoe, *Mountain Masters*, 231–57; Noe, *Southwest Virginia's Railroad*, 98–108.

11. Muster Roll of Company H, 1st Regiment Georgia Volunteer Infantry, in *Roster of the Confederate Soldiers of Georgia, 1861–1865*, ed. Lillian Henderson (Hopeville, Ga.: Logino and Porter, 1964), 1:283–90. Martin Crawford, "Ashe County's Union Volunteers," 4, records similar enthusiasm in western North Carolina.

12. The entire ceremony is described in the *Dahlonega (Ga.) Mountain Signal*, July 6, 1861.

13. Reid Mitchell, *The Vacant Chair: The Northern Soldier Leaves Home* (New York: Oxford Univ. Press, 1993), xi–39; Bell I. Wiley, *The Life of Johnny Reb: The*

Common Soldier of the Confederacy (New York: Charter, 1943), 15–27. For an analysis of how a lack of family and specifically female support eroded military morale in the Civil War, see Drew Gilpin Faust, "Altars of Sacrifice: Confederate Women and the Narratives of the War," in *Divided Houses: Gender and the Civil War*, ed. Catherine Clinton and Nina Silber, 171–99 (New York: Oxford Univ. Press, 1992).

14. Fannie Boyd to Augustus Boyd, July 21, 1861, Madeleine Anthony Collection, Lumpkin County Public Library (hereafter, MAC-LCPL), Dahlonega, Ga. For other evidence of women's sometimes fanatical support of the war, see George Rable, "Missing in Action: Women of the Confederacy," in Clinton and Silber, *Divided Houses*, 134–44.

15. U.S. Bureau of the Census, *7th Census of the Population of the United States, 1850: Gilmer County, Georgia*; Cain, *History of Lumpkin County*, 136; *Dahlonega (Ga.) Mountain Signal*, July 6, 1861.

16. Cain, *History of Lumpkin County*, 112–13; Head and Etheridge, *Neighborhood Mint*, 175–76; U.S. Bureau of the Census, *8th Census of the Population of the United States: 1860*, Free and Slave Population Schedules, Lumpkin County, Ga., 1860; William R. Crisson, *Report of W. R. Crisson on the Mineral Resources Around Dahlonega: A Few Practical Thoughts and Figures* (Dahlonega, Ga.: Mountain Signal, 1875).

17. *Milledgeville (Ga.) Southern Recorder*, Nov. 4, 1861.

18. James J. Findley to J. H. Worley, Apr. 14, 1863, MAC-LCPL.

19. Muster Roll of Company D, 52nd Regiment Georgia Volunteer Infantry, in Henderson, *Roster of Confederate Soldiers*, 5:474–84.

20. T. Conn Bryan, *Confederate Georgia* (Athens: Univ. of Georgia Press, 1953), 137–55.

21. Ibid., 139.

22. W. A. Campbell to Joseph E. Brown, Feb. 23, 1861, quoted in Ethelene Dyer Jones, *Facets of Fannin*, 32.

23. Emily Hughes to Fanny Boyd, May 15, 1861, MAC-LCPL. Similar examples of community-based sanctions against anti-Confederate dissent are cited in both Mann, "Family Group," 380–81; and Lee Kennett, *Marching Through Georgia: The Story of Soldiers and Civilians During Sherman's Campaign* (New York: Harper Collins, 1995), 34.

24. Webster Findley to Joseph E. Brown, July 26, 1862, Executive Correspondence, Georgia Dept. of Archives and History (hereafter, EC-GDAH).

25. Josiah Woody to Joseph E. Brown, Sept. 6, 1862, quoted in Mills Lane, ed., *Times that Prove Men's Principles: Civil War in Georgia, a Documentary History* (Savannah, Ga.: Beehive Press, 1993), 125.

26. Bryan, *Confederate Georgia*, 90–93; Peter Wallenstein, *From Slave South to New South: Public Policy in Nineteenth-Century Georgia* (Chapel Hill: Univ. of North Carolina Press, 1987), 118–20.

27. U.S. Commissioner of Claims, Case File of Rickles Stanley, Fannin County, Georgia, Southern Claims Commission Approved Claims, National Archives Microfilm, M1658, NA; Jonathan D. Sarris, "Anatomy of an Atrocity: The Madden Branch Massacre and Guerrilla Warfare in North Georgia, 1861–1865," *Georgia Historical Quarterly* 78 (Winter 1993): 694–95. For similar instances of Appalachian women being drawn into mountain warfare, see Ralph Mann, "Guerrilla Warfare and Gender Roles: Sandy Basin, Virginia, as a Test Case," *Journal of the Appalachian Studies Association* 5 (1993): 59–66.

28. Emory M. Thomas, *The Confederacy as a Revolutionary Experience* (Englewood Cliffs, N.J.: Prentice-Hall, 1970), 61. For an exploration of how the draft affected Appalachia specifically, see Paludan, *Victims,* 69.

29. For a look at how community ties influenced conscription and desertion in Civil War armies, see Peter S. Bearman, "Desertion as Localism: Army Unit Solidarity and Group Norms in the U.S. Civil War," *Social Forces* 70 (Dec. 1991): 321–42.

30. William Harris Bragg, *Joe Brown's Army: The Georgia State Line, 1862–1865* (Macon, Ga.: Mercer Univ. Press, 1987), 18–21. Reports reached North Carolina Gov. Zebulon Vance in 1863 that conscription officers from Georgia had even crossed into North Carolina in search of conscripts. See Joe A. Mobley, ed., *The Papers of Zebulon Baird Vance* (Raleigh, N.C.: Division of Archives and History, 1995), 2:93–97.

31. Fannie Boyd to Augustus Boyd, May 10, 1863, MAC-LCPL.

32. Andrew Reece to Nancy Wimpy, Oct. 9, 1862, MAC-LCPL.

33. Nancy Wimpy to Andrew Reece, Aug. 27, 1863, MAC-LCPL.

34. Nancy Wimpy to Andrew Reece, July 6, 1863, MAC-LCPL. Some Confederates with the Army of Northern Virginia felt the same way as Mrs. Wimpy, and would express those feelings a year later in the burning of Chambersburg, Pa. See Everard H. Smith, "Chambersburg: Anatomy of a Confederate Reprisal," *American Historical Review* 96 (Apr. 1991): 432.

35. Nancy Wimpy to Andrew Reece, Aug. 27, 1863, MAC-LCPL. For a further exploration of civilian commitment to harsh war measures, see Charles Royster, *The Destructive War: William Tecumseh Sherman, Stonewall Jackson, and the Americans* (New York: Knopf, 1991), 232–95.

36. Henry Wayne to George Lee, Sept. 1863, quoted in Bryan, *Confederate Georgia,* 146; William S. Kinsland, "The Civil War Comes to Lumpkin County," *A North Georgia Journal of History* (Woodstock, Ga.: Legacy Communications, 1989), 180–81.

37. Nancy Wimpy to Andrew Reece, Oct. 5, 1863, MAC-LCPL.

38. Nancy Wimpy to Andrew Reece, Aug. 27, 1863, MAC-LCPL.

39. Nancy Wimpy to Andrew Reece, Mar. 12, 1864, MAC-LCPL.

40. James J. Findley to Joseph E. Brown, Jan. 18, 1864, EC-GDAH.

41. Grand Jury Presentments for Lumpkin County, Ga., Dec. 1863, Lumpkin County Courthouse, Dahlonega, Ga.; Kinsland, "Civil War Comes to Lumpkin County," 181–82.

42. Nancy Wimpy to Andrew Reece, Aug. 2, 1863, MAC-LCPL. Richard McCaslin has documented a similar case of mass hysteria inspired by charges of pro-Union "treason" in Civil War–era Cooke County, Texas. See McCaslin, *Tainted Breeze.*

43. Grand Jury Presentments for Lumpkin County, Ga., Feb. 1863, Lumpkin County Courthouse, Dahlonega, Ga.

44. Wier Boyd to Joseph E. Brown, Dec. 19, 1864, EC-GDAH.

45. Kenneth Noe has documented a similar dehumanizing ethic prevalent among Union Army troops fighting guerrillas in Southwest Virginia. See Noe, "'Exterminating Savages,'" 8–9.

46. Ethelene Dyer Jones, *Facets of Fannin*, 11–19.

47. Ibid., 12; R. E. Barclay, *Ducktown Back in Raht's Time* (Chapel Hill: Univ. of North Carolina Press, 1946); U.S. Bureau of the Census, *Agriculture of the U.S. in 1860*; Sarris, "Anatomy of an Atrocity," 687–91. Slaveholding was not necessarily an indicator of pro-Confederate sentiment. Indeed, in Fannin County, some of the most prominent slaveholders were Unionists.

48. Michael P. Johnson, "New Look at the Popular Vote," 268. Henderson, *Roster of Confederate Soldiers*, 1:283–90; 2:105–13; 5:462–513; 6:585–97; 6:628–37.

49. George W. Lee to Joseph E. Brown, June 12, 1863, quoted in Bryan, *Confederate Georgia*, 146.

50. Elijah Chastain to Joseph E. Brown, Aug. 5, 1863, EC-GDAH.

51. U.S. Bureau of the Census, *8th Census of the Population of the United States, 1860: Fannin County, Ga.*

52. Dept. of Interior, U.S. Pension Bureau, Deposition of Thomas Anderson, Feb. 8, 1877, and Report of Special Agent John G. Wager, Mar. 8, 1877, Pension Case File of Solomon Stansbury, RG 15, NA. For a discussion of the importance of familial concerns in effecting loyalty, see Mann, "Family Group."

53. Some of Stansbury's associates claimed that he had run for the state legislature in 1862 but had been defeated by a pro-Confederate candidate. This is unsubstantiated by any other source. U.S. Pension Bureau, Deposition of Levi Wilson, Feb. 13, 1877, and Report of Special Agent John G. Wager, Mar. 8, 1877, Pension File of Solomon Stansbury, NA.

54. Ethelene Dyer Jones, *Facets of Fannin*, 533; U.S. Bureau of the Census, *Census of the Population of the United States, 1860: Fannin County, Ga.*

55. U.S. Pension Bureau, Deposition of Margaret Stuart, Feb. 9, 1877, Pension File of Iley Stuart, RG 15, NA.

56. Report of Commissioner of Pensions, Sept. 11, 1891, Pension File of Margaret Stuart, RG 15, NA; Sarris, "Anatomy of an Atrocity," 681–83.

57. U.S. Pension Bureau, Deposition of Mary Stansbury, Feb. 13, 1877, Pension File of Solomon Stansbury, RG 15, NA. The most thorough treatment of southerners who joined the Union Army is Richard Nelson Current, *Lincoln's Loyalists: Union Soldiers From the Confederacy* (Boston: Northeastern Univ. Press, 1992).

58. Mann, "Family Group," 385–89; Paludan, *Victims*, 62–63.

59. U.S. Pension Bureau, Deposition of John Wilson, Feb. 10, 1877, Pension File of Iley Stuart, RG 15, NA. For similar views of how localism affected loyalty, see Paludan, *Victims*, 56–71; Mann, "Family Group"; Bearman, "Desertion as Localism," 336–41; Crawford, "Ashe County's Federal Volunteers."

60. Kinsland, "Murder or Execution," 13–30.

61. U.S. Pension Bureau, Deposition of William A. Twiggs, Nov. 17, 1886, Pension File of William A. Twiggs, RG 15, NA; Kinsland, "Murder or Execution," 13–30.

62. U.S. Pension Bureau, Deposition of Thomas Wilson, Feb. 12, 1877, Pension File of Solomon Stansbury, RG 15, NA.

63. At the same time they denounced Confederate oppression, the Twiggs raiders threatened to conscript Union men in Fannin County if none volunteered. U.S. Pension Bureau, Deposition of John Merrel, Feb. 10, 1877, and Deposition of Margaret Stuart, Feb. 9, 1877, Pension File of Iley Stuart, RG 15, NA.

64. U.S. Pension Bureau, Report of Special Agent John G. Wager, Mar. 9, 1877, Pension File of Solomon Stansbury, RG 15, NA.

65. U.S. Pension Bureau, Deposition of Francis Marion Williams, Feb. 28, 1877, Pension File of Solomon Stansbury, RG 15, NA.

66. Richard B. McCaslin notes a similar confluence of events leading to a hanging in Cooke County, Texas, two years before Findley's executions. See McCaslin, *Tainted Breeze*, 35–60.

67. W. Todd Groce documents a similar inferiority complex among pro-Confederate mountaineers in East Tennessee. See Groce, "Mountain Rebels," 105–7.

68. James J. Findley to Governor Brown, Jan. 24, 1864, EC-GDAH.

69. Findley to Brown, Oct. 19, 1864, EC-GDAH.

70. Findley to Brown, Jan. 11, 1865, EC-GDAH.

71. U.S. Pension Bureau, Deposition of William R. Crisson, Feb. 28, 1877, Pension File of Solomon Stansbury, RG 15, NA. Findley was hardly unique in his treatment of "bushwhackers." By 1864, Union and Confederate troops throughout Appalachia and the South were taking similarly brutal measures against guerrillas. See Kennett, *Marching Through Georgia*, 99; Paludan, *Victims*; Noe, "Exterminating Savages."

72. U.S. Pension Bureau, Deposition of Thomas N. Wilson, Feb. 9, 1877, and Deposition of William and Macy Crissom, June 8, 1869, Pension File of Iley Stuart, RG 15, NA; Ethelene Dyer Jones, *Facets of Fannin*, 533.

73. *Athens (Ga.) Southern Watchman*, Nov. 30, 1864; Robert Davis, "Forgotten Union Guerrilla Fighters," 32.

74. Wier Boyd to Joseph E. Brown, Dec. 19, 1864, EC-GDAH.

75. Lumpkin County Grand Jury Presentments, May 1864, Lumpkin County Courthouse, Dahlonega, Ga.

76. James J. Findley to Joseph E. Brown, Jan. 26, 1865, EC-GDAH. In the same letter, he professed his loyalty to the Confederacy. Findley also urged the governor to suspend Confederate Army conscription in the mountains, arguing that the region's fighting men could be employed best in local defense.

77. James Findley to Wier Boyd, Dec. 25, 1868, MAC-LCPL; U.S. Census Bureau, *9th Census of the Population of the United States, Hall County, Georgia, 1870*; Robert Davis, "Gunfight at Doublehead Gap," *North Georgia Journal* 8 (Autumn 1991): 62–64.

78. Lumpkin County Grand Jury Presentments, Feb. and Aug. 1866, Lumpkin County Courthouse, Dahlonega, Ga.

79. Cain, *History of Lumpkin County,* 263–322; Rod Andrew, "Citizen Soldiers: Military Training at North Georgia Agricultural College, 1871–1915" (unpublished paper, Univ. of Georgia, 1994).

80. William R. Crisson, "Memories of Dahlonega in Early Days and Surroundings," *Dahlonega (Ga.) Signal,* May 4, 1894.

7

"Moving Through Deserter Country": Fugitive Accounts of the Inner Civil War in Southern Appalachia

John C. Inscoe

Outside observers have been vital to both our understanding and our misunderstanding of Appalachian society. Particularly valuable as source material on the Southern Highlands in the nineteenth century, their works range from the amply descriptive antebellum travel accounts of Caroline Gilman, James Buckingham, and Frederick Law Olmsted, through the local-color fiction and nonfiction of the post–Civil War popular press, to the more socially conscious tracts of missionaries, social workers, and journalists in the latter part of the century. While all these works have been and remain essential to scholars seeking to understand preindustrial highland life, all too often they have been sources of the many stereotypes, misconceptions, and distortions to which this region, more than almost any other in the country, has been subjected.

Among the most overlooked of regional commentaries by outside observers are those documenting one of the chapters most crucial in the Southern Appalachian experience (as of course it was for the South and the nation as a whole), the Civil War.[1] No other epoch in our history has elicited written records from so vast a number of participants. Edmund Wilson, in the introduction to his *Patriotic Gore,* asked, "Has there ever been another historical crisis of the magnitude of 1861–1865 in which so many people were so articulate?" Or, as Louis Masur more recently stated, "The Civil War was a written war," one in which hundreds of participants and observers "struggled to capture the texture of the extraordinary and the everyday."[2]

Among the vast literature that indeed did capture the texture of the extraordinary and the everyday is a considerable body of prison narratives. The most scholarly authority on the subject, William Hesseltine, noted in 1935 that the Library of Congress catalog listed almost three hundred titles of published reminiscences or personal narratives by former prisoners, most of them Union soldiers in Confederate prisons.[3] Remarkably, almost a fourth of those works were by men who escaped from such prisons and whose narratives cover their post-prison experiences as fugitives. Among these, I have located twenty-five accounts by Union soldiers (for a listing, see the "Prison Escape Accounts" at the end of this chapter) whose escape routes led them through the Southern Appalachian Mountains.

Published as early as 1863 and as late as 1915, these books and articles often are sensationalistic in nature and melodramatic in tone. Their titles reflect their various approaches, which range from the stark minimalism of W. H. Parkins's *How I Escaped*, Alonzo Cooper's *In and Out of Rebel Prisons*, and John Ennis's *Adventures in Rebeldom* to J. Madison Drake's *Fast and Loose in Dixie*, which bears a typical mid-nineteenth-century subtitle that doubles as a synopsis: *An Unprejudiced Narrative of Personal Experience as a Prisoner of War . . . With An Account of a Desperate Leap from a Moving Train of Cars. A Weary Tramp of Forty-five Days Through Swamps and Mountains. Places and People Visited. Etc.. Etc.,* and Junius Browne's *Four Years in Secessia: Adventures Within and Beyond the Union Lines: Embracing a Great Variety of Facts. Incidents. and Romance of the War. Including . . .* six more lines of subtitle. The literary merit of these works, like their scope and format, varies considerably, reflecting in part the very different types of experiences their authors had as soldiers, as prisoners, and as fugitives.

Yet the narratives of those whose escape routes took them through Southern Appalachia share a great deal. In crossing what was for most unknown and perilous territory, these fugitive-authors observed and experienced the region in ways quite different from those of the more casual antebellum travelers or the late-nineteenth-century mission workers and journalists. Union escapees found themselves in the highlands not by choice but by necessity. For many, the risk of capture or death was all too immediate, and their treks through this treacherous terrain were as surreptitious as they could make them. Their judgments of the people and situations they encountered often were matters of life and death. Miscalculating the lay of the land or the loyalties of those upon it could—and on occasion did—

prove fatal for these men, whose survival depended on knowing which residents they could trust and which they should avoid. As literature, their writings often are seriously flawed and amateurish; yet, because these men proved so astute in their perceptions of the country through which they traveled, their accounts, taken together, provide an unusually detailed and full-bodied portrait of a section of the Confederacy that suffered as much turmoil, devastation, and deprivation as any area of the South not overrun by Union armies.

Of the twenty-five fugitives whose narratives are considered here, just over half escaped from Camp Sorghum, a Confederate prison for Union officers in Columbia, South Carolina; most of the rest broke out of a similar facility in Salisbury, North Carolina. Two narratives involve groups of Federal soldiers who fled from a tobacco warehouse-turned-prison in Danville, Virginia. By 1864, all three of these makeshift prisons were vastly overcrowded; in both structure and manpower, security was grossly inadequate, and escapes were commonplace. The Columbia site was so poorly guarded that 373 of the 1,200 officers incarcerated there escaped before the prison was abandoned for more secure quarters.[4]

For escapees from these three prisons, the mountains of North Carolina, Virginia, and Georgia offered the most obvious escape routes, if only because they had to be crossed in order to reach East Tennessee and eastern Kentucky beyond, the most accessible areas with predominantly Unionist populations. By the latter half of the war, the Tennessee highlands were occupied by Union forces and thus offered even more reliable sanctuary. In addition, the rugged, sparsely settled terrain en route to those Unionist strongholds offered good hiding places, remote roads, and a populace sufficiently sympathetic to lend support and assistance along the way. In North Carolina's highlands, there developed a network among the pro-Union minority that one "passenger," a New York cavalry captain, described as "an underground railway, as systematic and as well arranged as that which existed in Ohio before the war." It served two purposes, he wrote: "first to protect or secrete loyal North Carolinians who wished to avoid the rigid conscription of the south; and second, to aid in the escape of such Yankee prisoners as might choose that precarious route to freedom."[5]

Thus, a variety of circumstances made the Southern Appalachians havens for refugees of all sorts—those Ella Lonn once (oddly ignoring the escaped prisoner faction) described as "marauders, bummers, strolling vagabonds, negroes, rebel deserters, Union deserters, all bent on committing outrages."[6] These elements, combined with the divisive character of local sentiment, created an unusually volatile environment that turned the war into an intensely localized guerrilla campaign fueled by personal animosities, vandalism, and other atrocities that had little bearing on military strategy or even ideological commitment beyond regional or even community concerns.

The prison escape narratives provide an abundance of detail and insight into the dynamics of this inner war. This essay focuses specifically on how their authors treated the three groups of mountain residents with whom they had the most direct contact, and who thus emerge as the dominant and most sharply etched characters: Unionists, women, and blacks. Because it was those segments of the mountain populace upon whom the success of their escapes and their chances of survival hinged, the fugitive writers, not surprisingly, portrayed all three in the most sympathetic, admiring, and often idealized terms. Despite the obvious bias apparent in these accounts, however, the graphic detail, expansive coverage, and relative consistency of the portrayals of southern highlanders in these twenty-five works make them valuable and generally credible source materials. No other contemporary coverage of the Civil War in Southern Appalachia portrays as vast a spectrum of the population as vividly or with as much complexity and nuance as do these works.

Among the more elusive aspects of the war in the highland South are the extent and nature of Unionist sentiment in the region. These aspects, too, have been among those most subjected to myth and distortion since the conflict ended. While the fugitive narratives are no more helpful than those of later scholars in explaining why certain highlanders pledged allegiance to either the Union or the Confederacy, they do provide a great deal of descriptive detail and generous commentary on the many individuals and groups encountered by the fugitives. Like so many other treatments of the subject, their narratives often exaggerated the extent of Unionist sentiment in the region or tended to see the populaces of all highland locales as committed to the Union.

A New York officer, moving westward after escaping from Salisbury, stated that western North Carolina "was to the full as loyal as West Virginia."[7] Such an assessment is a distortion and, in part, may typify attempts made by many of these authors, particularly those publishing their work during or just after the war, to stress to northern readers the diversity of southern views, the strength of pro-Union loyalties in some parts of the South, and the deteriorating support for the Confederate government among southern civilians.

Such distorted assumptions were sufficiently widespread that some escapees actually entered highland areas with a false—and dangerous—sense of security about the prevalence of Unionist sentiment, only to have this complacency shaken once they encountered a very different reality. During his 1864 escape from Columbia en route to Knoxville, Maj. Charles Mattocks of Maine stated in his journal that, in crossing into North Carolina, "our Rubicon is passed. . . . We now feel highly encouraged and think we have accomplished the most dangerous portion of our journey. Visions optimistic begin to loom up." His optimism proved premature, though; he and several companions were captured ten days later by Rebel scouts deep in the Smoky Mountains, just a mile and a half from the Tennessee state line.[8]

A Salisbury escapee noted that, as he and his fellow fugitives entered western North Carolina, "we experienced little trouble in finding 'friends,' for they were everywhere." Soon thereafter, they were startled to find themselves face to face with a with a local Confederate officer, who charged them with being "d——n Yankees." The prisoners panicked, but the officer quickly alleviated their fear by informing them that, as the father of three sons killed in battle and another dying of fever in a Delaware prison, he had lost all interest in the war. He allowed the Union men to proceed unharmed, but, once out of his sight, they raced away, still unsure of his intentions or truthfulness. They agreed that "hereafter we must be more careful, and not act on the hypothesis that every person we meet is devoted to the Union, even though he is a *North* Carolinian."[9]

It is hardly surprising that these authors so often romanticized the heroism and self-sacrifice of the resident Unionists they encountered. J. Madison Drake met "hundreds of this class" in Caldwell County, North Carolina, along with many of their "boon companions, the lyers-out." "In all my wanderings," Drake wrote, "I had never seen a more intelligent or determined people. Mingling with them, as I did for weeks, I thought of the brave defenders of the Tyrol, of the hardy Waldenses, fighting and dying among the hills for dear Liberty's sake." Although many had been comfortable farmers before the war, during the conflict their loyalties had reduced them to poverty and ruin, he claimed, and forced them to abandon everything—their homes and their families—to go into hiding, all "because of their devotion to the Government."[10]

A Wisconsin colonel, fleeing through the mountains of North Georgia in hopes of reaching Sherman's army, confirmed this description, noting that "with few exceptions, these were rough, unlettered men . . . but generous, hospitable, brave, and Union men to the core; men who would suffer privations, and death itself, rather than array themselves in strife against the Stars and Stripes, the emblem of the country they loved. . . . Uneducated though they were, under their homespun jackets beat hearts pure as gold, and stout as oaks."[11]

For some, such praise was a bit more forced and required some rationalization. In a chapter on "Union Bushwhackers," Junius Browne acknowledged that these southern allies were hardly passive victims of Confederate harassment. He admitted that they often took the offensive and that their aggression, like that of their Confederate oppressors, "was treacherous, coldly calculating, brutal." Yet, he wrote, "I cannot find it in my heart to blame many of the men who resort to it in the mountainous regions of North Carolina and Tennessee." He explained their transformation: "They were quiet, peaceable, industrious, loyal; opposed to the doctrine of Secession, and all its attendant heresies; the natural antagonists of the Slaveholders; lovers of the Union for the Union's sake, and regarded as an enemy whoever would seek its destruction. . . . Domestic by nature and habits, they were unwilling to quit their firesides and the few acres that had been their World. They would rather die than surrender all they valued in life. Yet they could not stay at home." After describing the harassment to which they had been subjected by their neighbors and by Home Guard troops, Browne concluded, "It is not difficult to conceive how a few months of such experience would transform a man from an enduring saint to an aggressive demon."[12]

Albert Richardson, a *New York Tribune* correspondent (and Browne's companion in many of their southern exploits), was perhaps the worst offender in patronizing the "Union mountaineers" he met. "Theirs was a very blind and unreasoning loyalty, much like the disloyalty of some enthusiastic Rebels . . . They had little education; but when they began to talk about the Union their eyes lighted wonderfully, and sometimes they grew really eloquent. . . . They regarded every Rebel as necessarily an unmitigated scoundrel, and every Loyalist, particularly every native-born Yankee, almost as an angel from heaven." Richardson perhaps strains readers' credibility most in asserting the mountaineers' great affection for the North. "How earnestly they questioned us about the North!" he wrote. "How they longed to escape thither! To them, indeed, it was the Promised Land."[13]

The more Unionists Richardson encountered in moving westward toward Tennessee, the more noble they became. He much belabored the extent of their suffering: "Almost every loyal family had given to the Cause some of its nearest and dearest. We were told so frequently—'My father was killed in those woods;' or 'The guerrillas shot my brother in that ravine,' that, finally, these tragedies made little impression upon us." Later on, after listening to a woman along the Blue Ridge relate stories of her family's trials and tribulations, Richardson waxed poetic: "The history of almost every Union family was full of romance. Each unstoried mountain stream had its incidents of daring, of sagacity, and of faithfulness; and almost every green hill had been bathed in that scarlet dew from which ever springs the richest and ripest fruit."[14]

Despite the exaggeration and sentimentality that infects much of this work, the fugitive accounts offer some of the most thorough assessments we have of both the extent of Unionist sentiment in the mountains and the varying degrees of commitment associated with it. Despite the fact that Unionists are the central and most vividly portrayed figures in these narratives, their authors make it quite clear that they were very much a minority in most parts of the Southern Highlands. Although some areas of North Georgia and western Carolina were known as strongholds of Unionist sentiment (one fugitive, for instance, noted that Wilkes County, North Carolina, had acquired a reputation among the rebels as "the old United States"[15]), there never was a highland area where local Unionists felt safe or comfortable among their neighbors, or where the fugitives themselves felt that they were not in enemy territory until they crossed the state line into Tennessee.

In traveling through the Georgia mountains, John Azor Kellogg of Wisconsin was surprised to see "three or four men at work digging sweet potatoes—*each man with a musket strapped to his back*" [Kellogg's emphasis]. He went on to compare the situation with that of the early pioneers, who "were compelled to defend themselves against the North American savages in a war prosecuted without regard to the laws governing civilized nations." "But this," he continued, "was in the interior of Georgia, one of the older States, in the noon-tide of the nineteenth century. These men were not warring with savages, but with their fellow men of the same race, with their neighbors, their former friends and acquaintances."[16]

Most fugitives quickly recognized and acknowledged the distinctions between the truer Unionists and the disaffected "out-liers" who had deserted from the Confederate army or were hiding in the hills to elude conscription officers. Although usually sympathetic to the position forced by Confederate authorities upon these more localized refugees, they demonstrated less compassion for them than for the more "noble" and consistent Unionist stalwarts. Some softened their judgments of individual deserters and other out-liers by stressing instead what wavering loyalties or even cowardice indicated about the Confederate cause and its power to sustain the type of devotion the Union inspired.

After encountering a group of young men "lying out" along the North Carolina–Virginia border, Richardson noted that they included both deserters from the Army of Northern Virginia and individuals evading conscription. At least one of their number admitted to having "foolishly acquiesced in the Revolution because at first it seemed certain to succeed, and he wished to save his property . . . now he heartily repented." Such men, Richardson concluded, were an index of the change that recently (as of December 1863) had come over Confederate sympathizers in that area, and suggested only a superficial commitment to either cause.[17]

On a number of occasions, the Union escapees found themselves dependent upon these deserters, sharing their mountain hideouts and their limited resources, benefiting from their wilderness survival skills and their guidance through the troublesome terrain. In such cases, their gratitude overshadowed any contempt the authors might have felt for the less than ideologically pure motives that brought them together. Madison Drake noted the irony in such circumstances: "Here we were, four Yankee officers, in the heart of the enemy's country, in a mountain fastness, surrounded by some of the men whom we had encountered in battle's stern array at Bull Run, Roanoke, Newbern, Fredericksburg, and on other ensanguined fields, who now were keeping watch and ward over our lives, which they regarded as precious in their sight—willing to shed their blood in our defense."[18]

Among the more striking aspects of these mountain-based narratives is the extent to which fugitives encountered slaves throughout the region. While such contacts with blacks were frequent and to be expected among escaped prisoners moving through other parts of the South, the fact that such contacts were equally prevalent in highland areas seems unusual, given the much smaller slave population in the highland South. Yet blacks seemed to be everywhere. Only one of these twenty-five descriptions of Appalachian escape routes notes a scarcity of slaves. In moving into the mountains of northeastern Georgia, a New York lieutenant bemoaned the fact that "the people in that section were generally very poor, and owned no negroes. We missed the assistance of the slaves very much."[19] Almost all other narratives relate incidents in which black residents aided their efforts in the mountains.

There are a number of explanations for what at least was perceived as little difference in racial demographics between lowland and highland escape routes. One is simply that these fugitives were intent on finding slaves and sought them out wherever possible. Another is that the black populace of Confederate Appalachia swelled greatly as lowland slaveholders in areas vulnerable to Union interference sent their human property—under various arrangements of hire, sale, or temporary guardianship—to the seemingly safer environment of the remote highlands.[20]

Slaves often guided fugitives through the rugged and treacherous mountains as they moved through the Carolinas or North Georgia toward

Knoxville. Many opened their homes to these men, sometimes hiding them for days at a time and feeding them generously. Others provided passersby with clothing, foodstuffs, or other supplies (more often than not, their masters' property) or offered medical care if needed. To a number of fugitives, slaves' information on the political persuasions of residents of their area was the most valuable service they offered. Slaves usually were well aware of which white residents of their areas were Unionists and therefore useful to those making inquiries, and which were not. Upon encountering a lone white Unionist, to whose mountain cabin he had been directed by helpful slaves west of Greenville, South Carolina, a Rhode Island fugitive was exasperated with "this most ignorant man I had ever met, black or white." While the hermit expressed his willingness to help, the soldier wrote that he was too ignorant to do so and that "we could do better with the negroes" in terms of information and advice.[21]

John Kellogg found that what he called the slave "telegraph line" in Georgia's northeastern highlands was equally useful in reporting on military activity within the region. From slaves near Carnesville, his party learned at what points Sherman's occupation forces still held strong between Atlanta and Chattanooga, and used that information to plan the route to take in maneuvering through the northern part of the state. "We also obtained from them accurate knowledge of Sherman's troops only five days previous; and this, too, a hundred and fifty miles from the scene of action." So impressed was Kellogg with the informational services they provided that he wrote that, in his opinion, "they were, as a class, better informed of passing events and had a better idea of questions involved in the struggle between North and South, than the majority of that class known as the 'poor white' of the South."[22]

Of course it was not only in the highland South that slaves proved to be such valuable collaborators. They engaged in such subversive activity wherever opportunity arose throughout the Confederate South. Most escaped prisoners already had benefited from collusion with friendly blacks long before they moved into mountain regions, and those experiences had taught them to seek out black allies once there. A group of six escaped prisoners, in flight to West Virginia from a Danville, Virginia, prison, were forced to abandon one of their number in a "crippled and almost helpless condition" during the harsh winter of 1864, leaving him alone "in a bleak mountain country" of the Virginia Blue Ridge. In speculating upon his chances for successful escape, one of his former companions remarked that his only "difficulty . . . will be in avoiding Rebel citizens and finding a true Union friend to care for him for a few days." To this another in the company replied, "He must have nothing to do with any body but a negro, or he's a goner."[23]

Albert Richardson practically gushed over the African Americans he encountered in western North Carolina. "By this time," he wrote, "we had learned that every black face was a friendly face. So far as fidelity was concerned, we felt just as safe among the negroes as if in our Northern homes. Male or female, old or young, intelligent or simple, we were fully assured they would never betray us."[24]

It was not simply kindness toward strangers that motivated the hospitality and aid bestowed by highland blacks, slave or free. Recipients of those kindnesses were convinced that it was the cause for which they had fought that determined the extent of black assistance. As Richardson saw it, "they were always ready to help anybody opposed to the Rebels. Union refugees, Confederate deserters, escaped prisoners—all received from them the same prompt and invariable kindness. But let a Rebel soldier . . . apply to them, and he would find but cold kindness."[25] Junius Browne was more eloquent in describing black partisanship as he witnessed it: "The magic word 'Yankee' opened all our hearts, and elicited the loftiest virtues. They were ignorant, oppressed, enslaved; but they always cherished a simple and beautiful faith in the cause of the Union and its ultimate triumph."[26]

In some cases, the slaves encountered by escaped prisoners were on the run themselves, a factor that made not only for sympathy but also for empathy on the part of some fugitive-authors. On more than one occasion, soldiers who had found shelter in slave cabins shared those tight quarters with escaped slaves, or "travelers," as blacks called runaways.[27] In some cases, slaves begged to accompany the fugitives as they moved toward Union

Fig. 7.1. "Escaping Prisoners Fed by Negroes in Their Master's Barn." From Albert D. Richardson, *The Secret Service, the Field, the Dungeon, and the Escape* (1865).

lines and freedom. Such requests elicited mixed reactions from those whites who suddenly found themselves asked to help those from whom they had received such vital assistance.

William Burson met five slave men in Wilkes County, North Carolina, who asked if they could accompany him to East Tennessee. After having hidden out for several days under the care and protection of these slaves, Burson and his party were joined by local Confederate deserters. He asked their advice about taking the black men with him. One assured him that "they were all good fellows and belonged to rebel masters whom they would be glad to see robbed of their slaves" but went on to warn him about the added risks in his own escape if he were accompanied by runaway slaves. Their presence probably would assure that all would be hanged if captured. This frightened Burson's companions, who urged him to abandon the idea, but Burson reiterated his own resolve to contribute in this small way to the emancipation process, maintaining that "to anybody who had treated me as well as the negroes had, I would do all in my power to assist them out of bondage." His commitment remained firm, but upon receiving a warning of impending arrest by the Home Guards and hence needing to make a quicker retreat from the area than he had anticipated, Burson "informed the darkies of our danger. 'Well, well,' they said, 'nebber mind us, massa, we'll come arter awhile.'" They never appear again in Burson's aptly titled narrative, *A Race for Liberty*.[28]

Michael Egan found it more difficult to shake off unwanted black company. In moving into the Carolina highlands, Egan, a Union captain from West Virginia, met two young slave men who had decided to make a "joint effort to escape into the Union lines" and asked Egan if they could join him. Egan resisted their pleadings, stating that, even though he "fully appreciate[d] the sad predicament of the unfortunate negros . . . I could not allow my sympathies to jeopardize my own safety." "Whatever chance of life they might have owing to their commercial value," he reasoned, "I could expect none" as a presumed smuggler of slave property, "an unpardonable offense in the South." Egan bid the two black youths good-bye and "spurted ahead," only to find "to my surprise and annoyance they still follow close on my heels, making prodigious efforts to keep me in sight." He finally resigned himself to accepting the company of these "persistent darkies" but stuck with them only until they heard "the sickening sounds of the barbarous Siberian hounds" of their master, at which point he abandoned them to their fates.[29]

The courage and generosity exhibited by some slaves led their white beneficiaries to reassess their own racist assumptions. Alonzo Cooper, a

New York cavalryman captured in 1864 by local Home Guards and imprisoned in Asheville's flimsy jail, was ashamed of the way his companions treated a fellow black prisoner. A local slave who shared a cell with several Union captives paid a heavy price for his attempt to aid them. In accord with a preconceived plan of escape, this "large, powerful negro" seized the guard and held him, while his white cellmates took his keys and made their exit. Intimidated by the threats of another guard, the "cowards" retreated back to their cell. Assuming that the slave alone had instigated the attack that allowed the white prisoners to escape, the guard ordered that he be given a hundred lashes.[30]

In his postbellum account of the incident, Cooper expressed genuine revulsion at the slave's punishment. He claimed to be "astonished to find such brutality among those who professed civilization," calling it "the most sickening transaction I ever witnessed." He was particularly offended by the complacency with which the southern jailers carried out this "exhibition of fiendish cruelty." Only after witnessing it, Cooper claimed, was he "ready to believe that the system of human slavery was capable of developing total depravity into the hearts of slave holders." He was almost as harsh in passing judgment on his own companions' role in the incident. "The poor ignorant black man's only fault," he wrote, "had been his confidence in the courage of his white associates. . . . if any one should be punished it should be those whose lack of *sand* had got this poor fellow into a scrape and then like cowards basely deserted him."[31]

Fig. 7.2. "The Escaped Correspondents Enjoying the Negro's Hospitality." From Junius H. Browne, *Four Years in Secessia: Within and Beyond Union Lines* (1865).

More positive encounters with African Americans inspired similar abolitionist sentiments. Richardson was taken in by "a peculiarly intelligent mulatto woman" he encountered near Wilkesboro, North Carolina. After an hour's conversation with this slave wife (who he noted also was forced to be the mistress of her master), he concluded: "Using language with rare propriety, she impressed me as one who would willingly give up life for her unfortunate race. With culture and opportunity, she would have been an intellectual and social power in any circle." Inspired by this and other contacts with highland blacks, Richardson extolled the race as a whole and expressed his optimism for their prospects, once emancipated:

> Some one has said that it needs three generations to make a gentleman. Heaven only knows how many generations are required to make a freeman! But we have been accustomed to consider this perfect trustworthiness, this complete loyalty of friends, a distinctively Saxon trait. The very rare degree to which the negroes have manifested it, is an augury of brightest hope and promise for their future. It is a faint indication of what they may one day become, with Justice, Time, and Opportunity.[32]

John Kellogg prided himself on the liberalization of his attitude toward blacks, declaring of those who had aided his escape efforts: "Those men and women who succored us in our great peril are my friends, and will be met and treated as such, wherever found, though their skins be darker, and their hair curl tighter than my own." After extolling their generosity toward him, he avowed, "May my right hand wither and my tongue cleave to the roof of my mouth, when I forget to be grateful to that people, or fail to advocate their cause, when their cause is just!"[33]

Massachusetts Lt. James Gilmore's manuscript account of his escape from Richmond's Libby Prison and his subsequent flight through the mountains of Virginia was so filled with stories extolling the character and courage of the blacks who aided him that abolitionist Edmund Kirke acquired it and published it in 1866. "It gave me," Kirke proclaimed in an introduction to the volume, "my first vivid idea of the present disposition and feelings of the Southern negroes." He informed Gilmore's brother, who had delivered the manuscript to him, that it should be published, "for it tells what the North does not as yet fully realize—the fact that in the very heart of the South are four millions of people—of strong, able-bodied, true-hearted people,—whose loyalty led them, while the heel of the 'chivalry' was on their necks, and a halter dangling before their eyes, to give their last crust, and their only suit of Sunday homespun, to the fleeing fugitive, simply because he wore the livery and fought the battles of the Union."[34]

In her recent study of the impact of the Civil War on Victorian Americans, Anne Rose notes that few of those who wrote of their wartime experiences mentioned blacks, free or slave. Even those who became involved in legislative or social efforts to aid freedmen after the war had little to say about their own encounters with them during the war.[35] If that was indeed the case, the fugitive narratives are even more distinctive in their forthright and detailed descriptions of their interactions with highland slaves. In aiding, guiding, and confiding in the Union refugees who moved into their midst, these mountain blacks contributed more to their own cause and ultimately were more indebted to the fugitives they helped than they ever could have suspected at the time. They had no way of knowing that their good deeds would be commemorated in print, or that such testimony on their behalf might serve to win northern sympathies and respect, as the nation wrestled with the issue of black status and benefits after the war.[36]

Of all of the mountain residents observed by these fugitives, however, their most profuse adulation was reserved for the white women they encountered. Wives and mothers were often left at home alone, as the men of their households were engaged in military service, had become casualties of such service, or were avoiding it, often by hiding in caves and forests near their homes. Fugitives seem to have approached women with less trepidation than they did men, especially when the loyalties of those with whom they were forced into contact were in doubt. Michael Fellman has written of women caught up in the guerrilla warfare that characterized the Civil War in Missouri: "Disintegration, demoralization, and perverse adaptation engulfed women's behavior and self-conceptions as it assaulted the family and undermined male-female and female-female . . . relationships." Women, as both victims and actors, "were compelled to participate, which they did with varying degrees of enthusiasm, fear, and rage."[37]

Such an assessment is equally applicable to the women of Appalachia, and the escaped prisoner narrators depicted that full range of responses among the women they encountered. While most accounts of the plight of Appalachian women during the war have stressed their victimization, these fugitive narratives suggest that just as often they, like Fellman's Missouri women, were assertive and effective participants in local conflicts. Although they never neglected, and often movingly conveyed, the sacrifices and hardships endured by highland women during the war, the fugitive-narrators were even more impressed with the strength, resourcefulness, and courage of the women—both Unionist and Confederate—they encountered. No doubt because the Federal fugitives so were often the recipients of their aid, Unionist women were among the figures most celebrated in these narratives. More significantly, perhaps, these works demonstrate the extent to which such women played key roles in the subversive activity that undermined Confederate strength in the region, often in surprisingly militant and physically aggressive ways.

Women were among the most outspoken partisans in the region, and the fugitives never resisted the temptation to quote their tough talk expressing devotion to the cause. A "voluble, hatchet-faced, tireless woman" in Cashiers, North Carolina, hosted a group of refugees who "listened in amused wonder to the tongue of this seemingly untamed virago, who . . . cursed, in her high-pitched tones, for a pack of fools the men who had brought on the war."[38] Aunt Becky, an elderly woman in Henderson County, North Carolina, was quoted by another fugitive as having said: "I ain't afraid of those rebels. I tell them, 'you may hang old Aunt Becky if you want to, but with the last breath I draw I will shout, Hurrah for the Union!'"[39]

A young girl who guarded the entrance to beleaguered Cades Cove in Tennessee's Smoky Mountains, using a horn to warn her community of approaching danger, told a Massachusetts fugitive that she would tell anyone attempting to take her horn to go to hell. The reply of this young "sentinel," he claimed, "was rather a surprise to me as I had always had a great respect for women, but had met only the kind that used soft words." Yet he obviously admired her and understood the situation which induced such manly language, noting that the soft-spoken women he had known up to that point "had not been on the 'battle line,' so to speak," and lived in pleasant homes and surroundings.[40]

In some instances, such defiance conveyed vindictive intent. In an 1887 memoir, Frank Wilkeson, a Union private who had served at an Alabama refugee camp for southern Unionist civilians, wrote of the Appalachian women who had sought safe haven there. They were determined that the Confederate neighbors from whom they had fled should pay for their actions. "I heard them repeat over and over to their children the names of men which they were never to forget, and whom they were to kill when they had sufficient strength to hold a rifle," he recalled. "These women, who have been driven from their homes by the most savage warfare our country had been cursed with . . . impressed me as living wholly to revenge their wrongs."[41]

An intriguing dimension of many of these descriptions of highland women lies in two features that, in terms of Victorian values, seem contradictory. While fully documenting the ways in which these women assumed the roles of protector, provider, and guardian of their homes, their families, and often their husbands, the fugitives spared no romantic cliché or florid Victorian flight of prose in describing the femininity and sexual allure of these hearty belligerents in skirts.

Under the chapter heading "A Noble Woman," for example, J. Madison Drake recounted an incident in which a woman discovered him and his companions as they hid in a ravine near her remote cabin. "She was a typical woman of the North Carolina mountains," Drake wrote. "No shadow of fear manifested itself in her somewhat masculine features, as she boldly advanced toward us." Mrs. Estes, as he later learned to call her, demanded that the Union prowlers identify themselves and offered them food if they could assure her that they were not in the area to round up deserters. "You must not use any deceit [or] you will be shot down where you stand. A dozen true rifles are now levelled on you, and if I raise my hand you will fall dead at my feet . . . if you turn out to be spies, seeking the life of my husband and his friends, you will rue the day you ventured into this wild." Drake concluded, "We had never met before such a woman . . . certainly the bravest of her sex."[42]

Once Drake and his companions had affirmed their northern identities and assured Mrs. Estes that they posed no danger to her deserter husband, she became a kind and generous ally. Her hospitality proved boundless; once ensconced as a comfortable, well-fed guest in her cabin, Drake focused less on her masculine features and fearless demeanor, remarking instead that "she looked quite handsome now, having combed her hair smoothly down her ruddy cheeks, and with her comely form robed in a green dress . . . and a gracious smile, worthy of a queen."[43]

Other physically enticing women proved equally hardened to the realities of the conflict encroaching upon their remote highland homes. Along the Nolichucky River in western North Carolina, William Parkins, a fugitive from South Carolina, was taken in by a Unionist sympathizer known as "Old Yank" and his daughters, described by Parkins as "three comely, bright-eyed, lithe but buxom mountain maidens." In relating the harassment he had endured at the hands of Confederates as a result of his nickname and well-known sympathies, Old Yank told Parkins that, in response to one attempt to force him into service, "I just reached 'round the door and pulled out my Henry rifle, an' my gals understood it an' got their double-barreled shotguns, an' I just told them boys I had lived too long in the mountains to be scared that way, an' if they . . . laid hands on an ole man like me they'd never do it agin, fur my gals had the bead on 'em."[44]

Junius Browne wrote of "A Nameless Heroine" in East Tennessee, who, though only sixteen or seventeen years old, "had assisted many true men out of awkward predicaments and dangerous situations, and had shown herself willing at all times to aid them." Working closely with that most notorious of mountain Unionist guides, Daniel Ellis, "she had often arisen at night when she obtained intelligence of importance, and communicated it

173

to loyalists some miles distant, preventing their capture or murder by the enemy." Browne, obviously quite taken with this teenager's courage and capabilities, devoted several pages of his book to recounting her exploits in much detail. Clearly, he was much taken with her demeanor, noting that she was "decidedly fair, intelligent, of graceful figure, and possessed of that indispensable requisite to an agreeable woman—a sweet voice." He confessed to gazing at her "as she sat there, calm, smiling, comely, with the warm blood of youth flushing in her cheek, under the flood of mellow moonlight that bathed all the landscape in poetic softness and picturesque beauty."[45] While such descriptions likely reflect the natural proclivities of military males too long denied female companionship, it is obvious that much of the attraction had to do with more substantive and less sexual qualities.

Soon after moving into North Carolina after an escape from Columbia's Camp Sorghum, Capt. J. V. Hadley and a group of fellow fugitives approached three young women in Flat Rock, in Henderson County, taking the opportunity "to investigate the Union sentiment in the mountains." The men identified themselves as Confederate soldiers and were surprised to receive a stern lecture from one of the girls, who blamed the men for bringing on the war. Her tirade serves as one of the few explicit declarations of mountain Unionists' opposition to the Confederate cause. "For a few niggers," she charged the soldiers, "you've driven this country to war, and force men into the army to fight for you who don't want to go, and you've got the whole country in such a plight that there's nothing going on but huntin' and killin' . . . all the time."[46]

Pleased with the girl's response and impressed with her courage in confronting what she thought were enemy soldiers, Hadley and his companions revealed their true allegiances to her and her sisters. The young women, two of whom were married to Confederate soldiers, quickly agreed to provide the fugitives with a guide across the mountains to Knoxville, and fed and sheltered them for the three days until the guide was available to make the journey. Despite the fact that the girls' parents were tenants on the palatial estate of Christopher G. Memminger, the Confederacy's treasury secretary, they were committed to the Union, according to their daughters. Their father, in fact, had been arrested on several occasions for sheltering deserters and other fugitives; because of that, they refused to inform him of their present charges or allow Hadley and his companions to approach their home. Instead, they undertook on their own all care of the men and arrangements for their continued escape.[47]

In this and other cases, the fugitives' interest in the women they encountered lay in their independent and often outspoken views regarding the war and their equally independent actions. Several such instances confirm the prevalence of divided loyalties, not only within mountain neighborhoods but also within households, with those splits often falling along gender lines. Jennette Mabry of Knox County, Tennessee, was among the more notable examples. Although her husband was a Confederate colonel and most of her family pro-southern in sentiment, she was an invaluable resource for Union guides. No guide, it was said, considered his mission complete unless he stopped to trade intelligence with Mrs. Mabry. "She always had the latest news from the front," and many a Federal fugitive was surprised at how much information she gave him to relay to those beyond, as he moved ever closer to Union territory.[48]

Madison Drake wrote of a pro-Confederate "vixen" who gave him and his party a vehement tongue-lashing once she learned their identities. She took special pleasure, he said, in telling them of a Yankee who had escaped from Salisbury, only to be captured and hanged near Lenoir. Once she confirmed "that we were Yankees, she would gladly assist in hanging us on the same tree." But all hope of aid from this particular household was not lost, for this defiant Rebel's husband, a cripple, witnessed this scene. "While his spouse was declaiming against us so virulently," Drake wrote, "he remained a passive listener; and when she concluded her tirade, he winked at us significantly, and hobbling off the stoop, bade us follow him." Once safely out of earshot of the cabin, this "happy or unhappy husband," as Drake labeled him, informed his visitors that he had served in the Confederate army until he was wounded and discharged. Two of his brothers had been captured in battle, had "taken the oath," and now were doing good business in the North, and he was determined to do likewise. With the threat of conscription looming, this Confederate veteran "resolved to befriend us." He proposed helping them get through to Union lines and asked that they then return with other forces and take him prisoner, so that he, like his brothers, could move North and escape not only the Confederacy but also his shrewish bride, whom he had married only six weeks before.[49]

Michael Egan told of a somewhat different division—one between a Confederate son and his Unionist mother. Egan and his companions encountered Henry Grant, a "fire-tried Unionist, brave, prudent, determined, and inflexible," in Macon County, North Carolina, who wanted to "relieve our distress and give us the shelter of his hospitable roof at once, but there is a slight obstacle in the way—there is an armed rebel soldier in the house." This young Confederate was a neighbor, home on leave, and the dilemma was resolved only when the Grants confided in his widowed mother, who lived in an adjoining house. To their surprise, they found that

Fig. 7.3. "Meeting with Deserters." From J. Madison Drake, *Fast and Loose in Dixie* (1880).

she "had no real sympathy with the Southern cause," despite the fact that her only child was fighting for that cause, and she agreed to help conceal the identities of the fugitives as long as he remained at home.[50]

Drew Gilpin Faust has noted the number of southern women who expressed a yearning to be men during the course of the Civil War. While none of the women encountered and quoted here ever articulated a wish for what Faust calls "a magical personal deliverance from gender restraints," many demonstrated to the Union fugitives whom they aided just how capable they were of crossing the lines of traditional gender roles to meet the new demands imposed on them by the war.[51] Of equal significance, though, is the degree to which the fugitives admired and celebrated the manly virtues and masculine role-playing—the practical and ideological independence, the assertiveness, and even the militancy—of the Union women whom they encountered, particularly when these women were serving the fugitives' interests and needs so well.

How, then, are we to assess the value of this "subgenre" of Civil War literature as a commentary on Southern Appalachian society? In contrast to most depictions of mountaineers during the nineteenth century, these accounts present appraisals of their subjects that are far more positive than most. Northern fugitive soldiers brought fewer preconceptions and prejudices concerning southern mountain life into the region. Their intent at the time was neither to observe, comment upon, nor improve what they found. In the midst of a war in which their lives were very much at stake, the escaped prisoners characterized mountaineers in terms of their behaviors and

attitudes, noting the extent to which both served to alleviate their own predicaments. Their status as hunted men was crucial to their powers of observation and criteria for assessment.

Other Union soldiers who moved through Appalachia had far different
reactions to the highlanders with whom they had to interact. Southwestern Virginia was inundated with Federal troops intermittently throughout
the war, with major incursions into the region in late 1861 and early 1864.
Kenneth Noe has analyzed the letters, diaries, and regimental histories produced by those soldiers and finds their characterizations of the highland
populace they observed "by far some of most degrading depictions of
mountain people ever penned." They dismissed their subjects in much
harsher terms than did those who moved through the same area before the
war. Typical of the former commentaries is that of Rutherford B. Hayes,
who served in the area with the 23rd Ohio Volunteer Infantry in 1861 and
1862. "What a good-for-nothing people the mass of these western Virginians are!" he wrote, going on to refer to them as "unenterprising, lazy, narrow, listless and ignorant, members of a helpless and harmless race."[52]

Nor were Union troops as tolerant or as generous as the fugitives toward the blacks or white women with whom they came in contact in moving through the Confederacy. In his study of the behavior and attitudes of
Sherman's troops, Joseph Glatthaar found that, while attitudes toward the
many slaves and former slaves with whom the troops came in contact varied
greatly, they harbored a great deal of resentment toward blacks and often mis-
treated them. An Ohio captain confirmed that "the silly prejudice of color is
as deeply rooted among northern as among southern men. Very many of our
soldiers have as yet no idea of treating this oppressed race with justice."[53]

In his recent book on Federal soldiers' experiences and perceptions of
the war, Reid Mitchell, in a chapter entitled "She-Devils," notes the extent
to which northern troops condemned southern women for their savagery,
their treachery, and the "irrational zeal" with which they supported the
rebellion and drove their men to do likewise. Such contempt for these
women, whom many Federals saw as the most determined and even dangerous of Rebels, cast them as little more than prostitutes or "loose
women" devoid of the virtues characteristic of northern womanhood.[54]

In all such cases, both in and outside Appalachia, invading or occupying forces were fully secure and in control of their situations. No doubt,
they rarely were intimate with, or particularly dependent upon, those into
whose communities they had intruded. One wonders whether Hayes and
his comrades would have been so contemptuous of those remote Virginia
highlanders had they been forced to move through the same territory as

escaped prisoners. By the same token, one wonders how differently the men of Sherman's army of liberation would have reacted toward slaves and slavery, had they, as prisoners on the run in enemy territory, found the aid of those slaves vital to their survival. Ironically, too, the qualities that Union troops found so contemptible in Confederate "she-devils"—their toughness and stubborn resolve—were the very ones that the fugitives, grateful to their female allies, celebrated in their descriptions of those women. The physical allure of these highland heroines seems to have been directly correlated with their ideological correctness. An Illinois private's observation from East Tennessee—"There is some good looking girls down heare, union girls that is"—is a blatant example of the interplay of sexual and political biases conveyed with only slightly more subtlety in many of the fugitive narratives.[55]

Dependency and gratitude tend to breed tolerance and open-mindedness. No other travelers through Southern Appalachia ever were so dependent upon the highlanders they met or had as much reason for gratitude toward them as did these escaped prisoners of war. The aid they received, the kindnesses bestowed upon them, and the collusion with those of like loyalties assured the safe passage, and even saved the lives, of many Union fugitives; hence they were predisposed to portray those responsible in a generous light. As a result, mountain Unionists appear as men of intelligence, courage, and steady resolve; their wives as both "angels of mercy" and strong, determined, and capable fighters; and mountain slaves as intelligent, cunning, defiant, and patriotic allies.

But such impressions, if they registered at all, proved fleeting in the national mindset. William Hesseltine, in assessing the propagandistic purposes of the prison narratives, maintains that their authors wrote of the atrocities they endured in southern prisons in order to assure the South's punishment during Reconstruction, and to keep alive public resentment of Rebel cruelties. "No group in America furnished more gore for the bloody shirt," Hesseltine claimed, "than ex–prisoners of war."[56] Such motives may also have inspired the neo-abolitionist tone of several of the narratives.

The prison passages of these works, along with others, served as effective antisouthern propaganda; curiously, though, the post-prison sections dealt with here had little or no influence in shaping more positive perceptions of the one group of southerners they consistently portrayed in a favorable light—those in Appalachia during this very period in which a national consciousness of the region was emerging, but in very different terms. The literary and socially conscious "discovery"—or, as Allen Batteau terms it, the "invention"—of Appalachia by northerners in the late nineteenth century served "to provide American society with colorful characters for its fiction, perfect innocents for its philanthropy, and an undeveloped wilderness in which to prove its pioneering blood."[57] It took demeaning and distorted imagery to do so. By the 1870s and 1880s, just as many of the fugitive narratives were being published, other accounts were printed, portraying Appalachia as "a strange land and peculiar people."[58] In such accounts, southern mountaineers emerged as depraved and semibarbaric people, notable for their moonshining, feuding, and inbreeding, as well as for their poverty and ignorance.

At the same time, a more uplifting aspect of Appalachian myth making also was underway: the creation of "Holy Appalachia."[59] Much of the appeal to those discovering the region in the latter half of the nineteenth century was its apparent ethnic purity, its whiteness. Historian James Klotter has reasoned that rampant racism and other barriers thwarted philanthropic impulses toward southern freedmen during Reconstruction. Those impulses then were transferred to another group of southerners perceived as equally needy and perhaps more deserving—the mountaineers who were, in the words of a turn-of-the-century ethnographer, the "purest Anglo-Saxon stock in all the United States."[60]

Other northerners, intent upon sectional reconciliation with the South, found its highlanders' wartime loyalty, that "union column thrust deep into the heart of the Confederacy," vital to its mission of bringing the country together. They were quick to exploit a corollary of Appalachia's image as a solid bastion of Unionism by suggesting that this lack of support for the Confederacy was due to highlanders' opposition to slavery. According to one lofty assertion, Appalachians "cherish liberty as a priceless heritage. They would never hold slaves and we may almost say they will never be enslaved."[61]

The fugitive prison narratives could not be used to buttress such views of the highland South. Their depiction of regular and constant contact between slaves and free blacks throughout the mountains clashed with the image of Appalachia as both a slaveless region and a racially pure populace. By the same token, those who championed Appalachians' unwavering commitment to the Union would have found these narratives questionable sources of validation. While mountain Unionists emerge as the heroes and heroines of the fugitive accounts, those works make all too apparent their minority status within their region; their heroism stems from the fact that they were forced to cope within an ideologically hostile environment.

In short, there seems to have been little place in the rapidly evolving imagery of postbellum Appalachia for the more complex and nuanced narratives of the Civil War fugitives. Not only did these accounts undermine the stereotypes of a primitive, violent, and depraved people; they also showed a populace more diverse in terms of race, political ideology, and socioeconomic circumstances than the dictates of regional stereotyping and image making could bear. While these narratives contradict—and might have provided useful correctives for—much of the simplistic condescension with which the region was being perceived during the postbellum decades, there is no evidence that they were ever put to such use.[62] One can speculate that, upon close scrutiny, such sources proved less useful because their complexities, contradictions, and variables would have diluted the simplicity of the myth that, when the war came, "Appalachian America clave to the old flag."[63]

The very depth and credibility of those narratives, in effect, diminished their polemical value during an era in which less ambivalent and multilayered messages were in vogue. Yet their very rich and often powerful portraits of Appalachians—along with the sheer volume of material they contain—have encouraged recent historians of the war and of the region to utilize the narratives in challenging the very mythology that was created at the same time when they, too, were being produced and read.

Notes

1. Three of the most comprehensive treatments of the 19th-century literature on Appalachia make no mention of the Civil War fugitive narratives. They are Cratis D. Williams, "The Southern Mountaineer in Fact and Fiction" (Ph.D. diss., New York Univ., 1961); Henry D. Shapiro, *Appalachia on Our Minds: The Southern Mountains and Mountaineers in the American Consciousness, 1870–1920* (Chapel Hill: Univ. of North Carolina Press, 1978); and Allen W. Batteau, *The Invention of Appalachia* (Tucson: Univ. of Arizona Press, 1990).

2. Edmund Wilson, *Patriotic Gore: Studies in the Literature of the American Civil War* (New York: Farrar, Straus, and Giroux, 1962), ix; Louis P. Masur, *"The Real War Will Never Get in the Books": Selections from Writers During the Civil War* (New York: Oxford Univ. Press, 1993), iv. For other treatments of the Civil War as conveyed in memoir and autobiography, see Daniel Aaron, *The Unwritten War: American Writers and the Civil War* (New York: Knopf, 1973); and Anne C. Rose, *Victorian America and the Civil War* (Cambridge, England: Cambridge Univ. Press, 1992), ch. 6. On the high literacy rate of Civil War soldiers, see James M. McPherson, *What They Fought For, 1861–1865* (Baton Rouge: Louisiana State Univ. Press, 1994), 1, 4–6.

3. William B. Hesseltine, "The Propaganda Literature of Confederate Prisons," *Journal of Southern History* 1 (Feb. 1935): 56. In the bibliography of Hesseltine's earlier *Civil War Prisons: A Study in War Psychology* (Columbus: Ohio State Univ. Press, 1930), 261–80, he lists 212 such works—148 books, 55 articles, and 9 nineteenth-century accounts of others' experiences.

4. Hesseltine, *Civil War Prisons*, 165–67; W. B. Hesseltine, "The Underground Railroad from Confederate Prisons to East Tennessee," *East Tennessee Historical Society's Publications* 2 (1930): 55–69.

5. James W. Savage, *The Loyal Element of North Carolina During the War*, a pamphlet (Omaha, Neb.: Privately published, 1886), 4. For other accounts of this network, see William Burson, *A Race for Liberty; or, My Capture, My Imprisonment, and My Escape* (Wellsville, Ohio: W. G. Foster, 1867), 80; Hesseltine, "Underground Railroad"; Paul A. Whelan, "Unconventional Warfare in East Tennessee, 1861–1865" (Master's thesis, Univ. of Tennessee, 1963), ch. 5; and Arnold Ritt, "The Escape of Federal Prisoners Through East Tennessee, 1861–1865" (Master's thesis, Univ. of Tennessee, 1965).

6. Ella Lonn, *Desertion During the Civil War* (New York: Century, 1928), 200–201.

7. Savage, *Loyal Element of North Carolina*, 4. Savage cites a Captain Hock of the 12th New York Cavalry as the source of this information.

8. Philip N. Racine, ed., *"Unspoiled Heart": The Journal of Charles Mattocks of the 17th Maine* (Knoxville: Univ. of Tennessee Press, 1994), 236–37, 246–47.

9. J. Madison Drake, *Fast and Loose in Dixie* (New York: Published by the author, 1880), 177, 117–18.

10. Ibid., 178.

11. John Azor Kellogg, *Capture and Escape: A Narrative of Army and Prison Life*, Original Papers, no. 2 (Madison: Wisconsin Historical Commission, 1908), 165.

12. Junius Henri Browne, *Four Years in Secessia: Adventures Within and Beyond the Union Lines* (Hartford, Conn.: O. D. Case, 1865), 351–52.

13. Albert D. Richardson, *The Secret Service, the Field, the Dungeon, and the Escape* (Hartford, Conn.: American, 1865), 458.

14. Ibid., 470, 473.

15. Ibid., 451.

16. Kellogg, *Capture and Escape*, 165–66.

17. Ibid., 459.

18. J. Madison Drake, *Fast and Loose in Dixie*, 160.

19. A. O. Abbott, *Prison Life in the South: At Richmond, Macon, Savannah, Charleston, Columbia, Charlotte, Raleigh, Goldsborough, and Andersonville During the Years 1864 and 1865* (New York: Harper and Bros., 1865), 236.

20. For a fuller account of such transactions, see John C. Inscoe, "Mountain Masters as Confederate Opportunists: The Profitability of Slavery in Western North Carolina, 1861–1865," *Slavery and Abolition* 16 (Apr. 1995): 85–110.

21. James M. Fales, *The Prison Life of James M. Fales*, ed. George N. Bliss (Providence, R.I.: N. Bangs, Williams, and Co., 1882), 55–56.

22. Kellogg, *Capture and Escape*, 147, 149.

23. William H. Newlin, *An Account of the Escape of Six Federal Soldiers from Prison at Danville, Va.: Their Travels by Night through the Enemy's Country to the Union Pickets at Gauley Bridge, West Virginia, in the Winter of 1863–64*, rev. ed. (Cincinnati, Ohio: Western Methodist Book Concern, 1886), 54, 56.

24. Albert D. Richardson, *Secret Service*, 444.

25. Ibid., 445. See also Racine, *Unspoiled Heart*, 237–39, for Charles Mattocks's account of similar instances of slave aid in western North Carolina.

26. Browne, *Four Years in Secessia*, 368.

27. See Charles O. Hunt, "Our Escape from Camp Sorghum," in *War Papers Read Before the Commandery of the State of Maine, Military Order of the Loyal Legion of the United States* (Portland, Me.: Thurston Press, 1898), 1:96.

28. Burson, *Race for Liberty*, 79–82.

29. Michael Egan, *The Flying Gray-Haired Yank; or, The Adventures of a Volunteer* (Marietta, Ohio: Edgewood, 1888), 279–82. See also W. H. Parkins, *How I Escaped*, ed. Archibald C. Gunter (New York: Home, 1889), 118, for an account of a similar incident.

30. Alonzo Cooper, *In and Out of Rebel Prisons* (Oswego, N.Y.: R. J. Oliphant, 1889), 188–97.

31. Ibid., 197–98.

32. Albert D. Richardson, *Secret Service*, 444–45.

33. Kellogg, *Capture and Escape*, 148.

34. James R. Gilmore, *Adrift in Dixie; or, A Yankee Officer among the Rebels* (New York: Carleton, 1866), 11–12. (Edmund Kirke's name appears on the title page of the book and the author's name does not. The author is identified by two different names elsewhere—as Gilmore in the copyright citation, and as Henry L. Estabrooks in Kirke's introduction.)

35. Rose, *Victorian America*, 242–44.

36. Nina Silber, *The Romance of Reunion: Northerners and the South, 1865–1900* (Chapel Hill: Univ. of North Carolina Press, 1993), discusses factors contributing to beneficent impulses of northern whites toward southern blacks after the war. Interestingly, Silber includes analyses of northern attitudes toward both blacks and mountaineers in a single chapter (ch. 5, "Of Minstrels and Mountaineers: The Whitewashed Road to Reunion," 124–58), but within the chapter makes no attempt at linking the two.

37. Michael Fellman, *Inside War: The Guerrilla Conflict in Missouri During the American Civil War* (New York: Oxford Univ. Press, 1989), 193.

38. W. H. Shelton, "A Hard Road to Travel Out of Dixie," *Century Magazine* 40 (Oct. 1890): 937.

39. Hunt, "Our Escape from Camp Sorghum," 113.

40. Charles G. Davis, "Army Life and Prison Experiences of Major Charles G. Davis," typescript, n.d., in Special Collections, Univ. of Tennessee Library, Knoxville; quoted in Durwood Dunn, *Cades Cove: The Life and Death of a Southern Mountain Community* (Knoxville: Univ. of Tennessee Press, 1988), 137–38.

41. Frank Wilkeson, *Recollections of a Private Soldier* (New York: Putnam, 1889), 232–33, quoted in Phillip Shaw Paludan, *Victims: A True Story of the Civil War* (Knoxville: Univ. of Tennessee Press, 1981), 23.

42. J. Madison Drake, *Fast and Loose in Dixie,* 148–50.

43. Ibid., 152.

44. Parkins, *How I Escaped,* 116–17. Parkins calls this book a novel, but it varies only slightly from his autobiographical narrative, "Between Two Flags; or, The Story of the War by a Refugee," and his 1885 typescript in the William H. Parkins Papers, Atlanta History Center, Atlanta, Ga.

45. Browne, *Four Years in Secessia,* 421–23. Daniel Ellis identifies this "nameless heroine" as Melvina Stephens, the daughter of a "good Union man" at Kelly's Gap, Tenn. See Daniel Ellis, *Thrilling Adventures of Daniel Ellis, The Great Union Guide of East Tennessee For a Period of Nearly Four Years During the Great Southern Rebellion* (New York: Harper and Brothers, 1867), 357–58.

46. J. V. Hadley, *Seven Months a Prisoner* (New York: Charles Scribners' Sons, 1898), 180–81.

47. Ibid., 182–86.

48. Georgia Lee Tatum, *Disloyalty in the Confederacy* (Chapel Hill: Univ. of North Carolina Press, 1934), 151; Whelan, "Unconventional Warfare in East Tennessee," 139.

49. J. Madison Drake, *Fast and Loose in Dixie,* 140–41.

50. Egan, *Flying Gray-Haired Yank,* 325–28. For other wives whose loyalties differed from those of their husbands, see Gordon B. McKinney, "Women's Role in Civil War Western North Carolina," *North Carolina Historical Review* 69 (Jan. 1992): 52–53.

51. Drew Gilpin Faust, "On the Altars of Sacrifice: Confederate Women and the Narratives of War," *Journal of American History* 76 (Mar. 1990): 1200–1228, quotation 1206–7. For treatments of similar demands and the responses to them by Confederate women in Appalachia, see McKinney, "Women's Role"; Ralph Mann, "Guerrilla Warfare and Gender Roles: Sandy Basin, Virginia, as a Test Case," *Journal of the Appalachian Studies Association* 5 (1993): 59–68; and John C. Inscoe, "Coping in Confederate Appalachia: Portrait of a Mountain Woman and Her Community at War," *North Carolina Historical Review* 59 (Oct. 1992): 388–413.

52. Kenneth W. Noe, "'Appalachia's' Civil War Genesis: Southwest Virginia as Depicted by Northern and European Writers, 1825–1865," *West Virginia History* 50 (1991): 102. See Noe's essay in this volume for other equally explicit examples of Union soldiers' contempt for Appalachian residents.

53. Quoted in Joseph T. Glatthaar, *The March to the Sea and Beyond: Sherman's Troops in the Savannah and Carolina Campaigns* (New York: New York Univ. Press, 1985), 55–56. James McPherson, *What They Fought For,* 58–67, documents considerably more variety in Union soldiers' attitudes toward southern blacks, noting that sentiment opposing emancipation was based on "a mixture of racism, conservatism and partisan politics," while support for emancipation among northern troops was the result more of pragmatic than of altruistic motives.

54. Reid Mitchell, *The Vacant Chair: The Northern Soldier Leaves Home* (New York: Oxford Univ. Press, 1993), ch. 6. For other treatments of Union soldiers' interactions with southern women, see George C. Rable, *Civil Wars: Women and the Crisis of Southern Nationalism* (Urbana: Univ. of Illinois Press, 1989), ch. 8; Nina Silber, "Intemperate Men, Spiteful Women, and Jefferson Davis," in *Divided Houses: Gender and the Civil War,* ed. Catherine Clinton and Nina Silber, 283–305 (New York: Oxford Univ. Press, 1992); Charles Royster, *The Destructive War: William Tecumseh Sherman, Stonewall Jackson, and the Americans* (New York: Knopf, 1991), 86–87; and Glatthaar, *March to the Sea,* 71–76.

55. Reid Mitchell, *Vacant Chair,* 98, using this quotation, notes a correlation among virtue, prettiness, and a pro-Union stance in Federal perceptions of southern women. Quotation from Albertus A. Dunham and Charles LaForrest Dunah, *Through the South with a Union Soldier,* ed. Arthur H. DeRosier, Jr. (Johnson City, Tenn.: East Tennessee State Univ. Research Council, 1969), 48.

56. Hesseltine, "Propaganda Literature of Confederate Prisons," 64–65.

57. Batteau, *Invention of Appalachia,* 1.

58. This term was coined by Will Wallace Harvey in his "A Strange Land and a Peculiar People," *Lippincott's Magazine* 12 (Oct. 1873): 429–38.

59. Batteau applies this term to Berea College President William G. Frost, a "latter-day abolitionist" whose turn-of-the-century chronicles of mountain life made him one of the era's most influential image-makers. Batteau, *Invention of Appalachia,* 74–78.

60. James C. Klotter, "The Black South and White Appalachia," *Journal of American History* 66 (Mar. 1980): 832–49; Ellen Churchill Semple, "The Anglo-Saxons of the Kentucky Mountains: A Study in Anthropogeography," *Bulletin of the American Geographical Society* 42 (Aug. 1910): 566. See also Silber, *Romance of Reunion,* 143–52.

61. William G. Frost, "Our Contemporary Ancestors in the Southern Mountains," *Atlantic Monthly* 83 (Mar. 1899): 314.

62. Among the proponents of the myth of Unionist Appalachia were Frost, "Our Contemporary Ancestors," 311–19; Julian Ralph, *Dixie; or, Southern Scenes and Sketches* (New York: Harper and Brothers, 1896); and Samuel T. Wilson, *The Southern Mountaineers* (New York: J. J. Little and Ives, 1914). Scholarly analyses of these and other works include Shapiro, *Appalachia on Our Mind,* 87–90; Batteau, *Invention of Appalachia,* 77–79; Klotter, "Black South and White Appalachia"; Silber, *Romance of Reunion,* 143–52; and Kenneth W. Noe, "Toward the Myth of Unionist Appalachia, 1865–1883" *Journal of the Appalachian Studies Association* 6 (1994): 73–80.

63. Quotation from Frost, "Our Contemporary Ancestors," 314.

Prison Escape Accounts

Abbott, A. O. *Prison Life in the South: At Richmond, Macon, Savannah, Charleston, Columbia, Charlotte, Raleigh, Goldsborough, and Andersonville During the Years 1864 and 1865.* New York: Harper and Brothers, 1865.

Burson, William. *A Race for Liberty; or, My Capture, My Imprisonment, and My Escape.* Wellsville, Ohio: W. G. Foster, 1867.

Browne, Junius Henry. *Four Years in Secessia: Within and Beyond the Union Lines: Embracing a Great Variety of Facts, Incidents, and Romance of the War.* Hartford, Conn.: O. D. Case and Co., 1865.

Conley, Isaiah. "Captain Isaiah Conley's Escape from a Southern Prison, 1864." Part 2. Edited by George D. Harmon and Edith Blackburn Hazlehurst. *Western Pennsylvania Historical Magazine* 47 (July 1964): 225–47.

Cooper, Alonzo. *In and Out of Rebel Prisons.* Oswego, N.Y.: R. J. Oliphant, 1888.

Davis, Charles G. "Army Life and Prison Experiences of Major Charles G. Davis." N.d. Typescript of journal. Special Collections, Univ. of Tennessee Library, Knoxville, Tenn.

Drake, J. Madison. *Fast and Loose in Dixie.* New York: Authors' Publishing Co., 1880.

Egan, Michael. *The Flying. Gray-Haired Yank; or, The Adventures of a Volunteer.* Marietta, Ohio: Edgewood Publishing Co., 1888.

Ellis, Daniel. *The Thrilling Adventures of Daniel Ellis: The Great Union Guide of East Tennessee . . .* New York: Harper and Brothers, 1867.

Ennis, John W. *Adventures in Rebeldom; or, Ten Months Experience of Prison Life . . .* New York: "Business Mirror" print, 1863.

Fales, James M. *The Prison Life of Lieut. James M. Fales.* Edited by George N. Bliss. Personal Narratives of Events in the War of the Rebellion, no. 15. Providence, R.I.: N. Bangs, Williams, and Co., 1882.

Gilmore, James R. *Adrift in Dixie; or, A Yankee Officer among the Rebels.* Edited by Edmund Kirke. New York: Carleton, 1866.

Hadley, J. V. *Seven Months a Prisoner.* New York: Charles Scribner's Sons, 1898.

Hunt, Charles O. "Our Escape from Camp Sorghum." In *War Papers Read Before the Commandery of the State of Maine, Military Order of the Loyal Legion of the United States.* Portland, Me.: Thurston Press, 1898.

Johnson, Hannibal A. *The Sword of Honor: A Story of the Civil War.* Worcester, Mass.: Blanchard Press, 1906.

Kellogg, John Azor. *Capture and Escape: A Narrative of Army and Prison Life.* Original Papers, no. 2. Madison: Wisconsin Historical Commission, 1908.

Langworthy, Daniel Avery. *Reminiscences of a Prisoner of War and His Escape.* Minneapolis, Minn.: Byron Printing Co., 1915.

McTeer, Will A. "Among Loyal Mountaineers." Undated pamphlet. Civil War Collection, Special Collections, Univ. of Tennessee Library, Knoxville.

Newlin, William H. *An Account of the Escape of Six Federal Soldiers from Prison at Danville, Va.: Their Travels by Night through the Enemy's Country to the Union Pickets at Gauley Bridge, West Virginia, in the Winter of 1863–64.* Rev. ed. Cincinnati, Ohio: Western Methodist Book Concern, 1886.

Parkins, W. H. *How I Escaped.* Edited by Archibald C. Gunter. New York: Home Publishing Co., 1889.

Racine, Philip N., ed. *"Unspoiled Heart": The Journal of Charles Mattocks of the 17th Maine.* Knoxville: Univ. of Tennessee Press, 1994.

Richardson, Albert D. *The Secret Service, the Field, the Dungeon, and the Escape.* Hartford, Conn.: American Publishing Co., 1865.

Shelton, W. H. "A Hard Road to Travel Out of Dixie." *Century Magazine* 40 (Oct. 1890): 931–49.

Stafford, David W. *The Defense of the Flag: A True War Story [of] Thrilling Experiences During Escape from Southern Prisons.* Kalamazoo, Mich.: Wellington Bros., 1904.

Younce, W. H. *The Adventures of a Conscript.* Cincinnati, Ohio: Editor Publishing Co., 1901.

8

A Former Slave in Federal Service: John McCline's Experience in Appalachia

Jan Furman

In late December 1862, John McCline, ten years old and a slave at Clover Bottom Plantation not far from Nashville, Tennessee, walked out of slavery and into the Union army.[1] For McCline, running away was the culmination of months of war talk and frantic activity around the plantation. Lincoln's election in 1861, the appearance of a comet (which the slaves interpreted as a sure sign of war) in 1860, and John Brown's raid the year before increasingly, over three years, had raised hopes of either a full-scale war on slavery, a slave insurrection, or, at the very least, conditions favorable for escape.

Despite (or perhaps because of) the real and long-anticipated drama of war which finally came, McCline's escape was largely unpremeditated. During a routine errand to one of the outlying grazing pastures to round up a herd of cattle and bring it back to the barn, McCline noticed a regiment of Union soldiers passing along the Lebanon Pike, which ran adjacent to the plantation. These were not the first soldiers he had seen; in a year and a half of fighting, armies from both sides in that part of Tennessee often had stopped at Clover Bottom to forage for food and supplies. Whenever troops appeared, McCline always was impressed by the aura of authority created by so many men in uniform. They never failed to excite his boyish instinct for adventure.

On that day in 1862, trying to get as close as possible, McCline positioned the mule he was riding next to a fence and watched the regiment pass. After several minutes, one of the soldiers, seeing McCline, called out, "Come on Johnny and go with us up North, and we will set you free" (55).[2] Taking the invitation literally, McCline climbed down from Nell and joined the march. In later years, McCline remembered with humor and disbelief that he had mistaken the Confederate appellation, Johnny, for his own name.

McCline looked back once to see his owner, James Hoggatt; Hoggatt's wife; her two nieces; and the house servants standing on the lawn—unconsciously caught, as it seems now, in the final days of a familiar but fleeting way of life. With the white plantation house looming large in the background and columns of Federal soldiers passing at the gate, Hoggatt's position in the middle suggests his inevitable destruction by the clash of slavery and freedom.[3] Noting some of the symbolism of that moment, McCline, concealed from view, observed his master "looking at us Union soldiers pass, for I was one of them, in deed, and in action" (55–56).

Only one time during the fifteen-mile walk to camp did McCline fear detection; at the toll station near Clover Bottom, two white boys recognized him and threatened to tell Hoggatt. Perhaps they did, but by then McCline had gotten away. In a single act, to which he had given little if any forethought, McCline had been transformed, at least in his own imagination, from slave into Yankee soldier.

The regiment which took McCline in was the 13th Michigan Volunteers, part of the Army of the Cumberland under Gen. William S. Rosecrans. The 13th Michigan, organized in January 1862, since that time had been deployed primarily in Alabama, Kentucky, and Tennessee, serving in Charles G. Harker's brigade of Thomas J. Wood's division. McCline encountered it en route to Nashville. A week later he would be with the regiment at the Battle of Stones River, where, between December 29, 1862, and January 2, 1863, it would fight one of its two most devastating encounters (the other was Chickamauga) and be cited for gallantry. In four days, eighty-nine men, a third of the regiment, would be wounded or killed.[4]

Of course, McCline was too inexperienced and, more to the point, too young actually to enlist and fight, even if he had not been a "contraband." He was issued a uniform, however, and put to work almost immediately in Company C as a teamster on the six-mule supply wagon. Always eager to learn, McCline found the work of a teamster difficult but exciting. What he did not know about mules, he learned; within a few weeks, he could more than carry his share of responsibility on a two-man wagon team. He and a veteran teamster named Dick drove one of ten regimental supply wagons, with McCline usually mounted on one of the large brown mules closest to the wagon, called the near-wheeler, and Dick walking beside the team, coaxing its leaders along, especially over mountainous or rough terrain.

For nearly two years, McCline was Dick's assistant, except on one remarkable occasion when the child took on the awesome burden of handling the team alone. Late on the night of September 16, 1863, Dick was absent from camp and no other teamster was available. With a battle brewing, the quartermaster ordered McCline to deliver bacon, coffee, and hardtack loaded on his wagon to troops positioned somewhere in the vicinity of Chickamauga Creek, near Lee and Gordon's Mills. (McCline does not give the exact location, and the *Official Records* make no mention of the 13th Michigan's activities on that date).[5] Without questioning the order, McCline in the dark hitched the team to the wagon and was on his way. The effort of driving alone at night was intensified by the sound of gunfire, which made the mules nervous. "My team wanted to run," McCline remembers, "but I managed with some difficulty to keep it down to a slow trot" (88). McCline delivered the supplies without mishap and returned to camp. Years later, in chronicling that evening, he captured the compelling incongruity of a man's work being done by a boy his age:

> Reaching the camp in safety, I unhitched, watered and fed my team and
> went to bed. I looked around, and called, but none of the teamsters had put
> in an appearance. I didn't go to sleep for a long time; and, for the first time
> since I left Murfreesboro, I had a bad spell of the blues. First, the regiment
> was out there on the battle field and, perhaps was being cut to pieces by the
> enemy, and I wanted to be with it. All were so kind to me. Many of them I
> knew by name. I think I cried myself to sleep. (88)

When it counted, McCline had acted with a man's courage. Afterward, however, he had longed for the comforting reassurance of some adult. A few days later, on September 19 and 20, McCline's regiment, "the last in the field, suffered heavily, losing a hundred and seven men, killed, wounded, and missing" (89). According to McCline, the regiment took its greatest losses at Lee and Gordon's Mills. Many of the dead and wounded later were found there.[6]

As a noncombatant, distant from the battlefield, McCline was an observer, reporting the aftermath of fighting—winners, losers, casualties—as well as an occasional shelling which sometimes reached his position behind the lines. But what his depiction lacks in immediacy, it gains in emotional depth. He despairs over the loss at Chickamauga of the young soldier who first called him Johnny at Clover Bottom. In losing him, McCline loses a significant link to his new life. He writes movingly of the dead lying on the field at Murfreesboro and of the thousands of wounded, "heads bandaged, arms in slings, and many on crutches . . . stirring about in the warm sunshine" (69) outside the hospital where the "more desperately wounded" lay dying. He is equally affected by the sight, late on a snowy afternoon, of "two thousand Rebels" being marched into Chattanooga. These were the first prisoners McCline had seen, and he observed them closely. "It was a pathetic sight," he writes, with only a hint of condescension, "and in my heart I pitied them. Poor and thin, many without coats, hats, or shoes, plodding dejectedly along the rough, winding mountain road" (90). In the intervals between fighting, he describes in vivid detail the people he encounters, the countryside, and the routine of life in camp—all of which leave a stronger impression on the reader than the battles.

The camp rendered in most detail (probably because he stayed there longest) is Appalachian Chattanooga, where McCline spent the final months of 1863 and most of 1864. Since he had joined the 13th Michigan, that unit, as part of Rosecrans's army, had been on the offensive against Gen. Braxton Bragg's Confederate Army of Tennessee, attempting to push it out of Middle Tennessee. Moving to Alabama from Murfreesboro, the army then had headed east across the Cumberland Mountains toward Chattanooga. McCline's approach through Dayton to the mountains of East Tennessee, the first mountains he had seen, was stunning. He characterizes the view as amazing, and an adjacent valley where he camped for a night is "a most beautiful bit of country, with low, flat meadows, extending from north to south along the base of the mountains" (80). The area is made more pleasant by "a stream of cool, clear water" which "flowed directly from under the mountains" (80). McCline declares it "the most delicious drinking water" he has ever tasted.

A full day of slow progress on a steep, dangerously narrow, deeply rutted path the next day brought McCline and the other supply wagons to the regiment's temporary camp on a mountain plateau, from which Dayton could be seen "slumbering in the valley below" (81). There McCline's sense of the war was shaped by his sense of the place. The familiar, elaborately appointed plantation houses and fields of Middle Tennessee, where slaves always were in evidence, had been replaced by cabins and winding paths leading to springs "with wooden troughs arranged so that the water could be carried a good ways down the mountain side" (81). Amid huge expanses of smooth mountain rock, heavy timber, and the largest chestnut trees he had ever seen, war seemed remote. Myriad campfires illuminating the countryside created a picturesque scene and imparted a feeling of security, despite Confederate activity throughout the mountains. Even when McCline's wagon lost a wheel during its descent down the opposite side of the mountain and he and Dick had to spend the night on a steep path until a new wheel could be brought the next day, McCline felt protected as much by the mountain elevation as by the presence of troops. That night, after a refreshing swim in the warm waters of the Tennessee River, he slept without concern.

On the following morning, the regiment's final destination appeared in the distant valley below. Chattanooga's "long straight macadamized streets . . . and the occasional church spires" were interspersed incongruously with "long rows of tents and many soldiers" moving about (86). McCline recalls that, as the soldiers entered the occupied city later in the day, "the large population of women, children, and old men, seeing the 'Yankees' for the first time, so crowded the streets that the cavalry had to gallop along with swords drawn and force them back so that the troops and [wagon] train could pass" (86). As soon as he was settled in the regimental camp, an open field protected by a stand of woods near the battlefield, McCline explored the city. He was thrilled to see steamboats for the first time. Several, anchored on the Tennessee River, were loaded with cotton and other freight. Peddlers on the bank sold fruits and vegetables, giving life in the city a deceptive air of normalcy.

McCline remained in Chattanooga and its vicinity for nearly a year, and his narrative account of his military residence in the southern mountains is expansive. Following the battles of Chickamauga and Chattanooga, Union soldiers turned from war to building. The men of the 13th Michigan were redeployed as engineers. Organized squads with axes and saws cut logs for a large chapel. They fortified the city and built comfortable sleeping quarters. Artisans in the Michigan regiment were detailed to construct several hospitals on Lookout Mountain. New recruits came, and veterans went home on furlough. For McCline, the camp was at once a whir of exciting activity and simultaneously an idyllic respite. "In no camp," McCline writes, "during my time in the service, were there so many pleasant and varied attractions. One could go about wherever he liked with such perfect freedom, and without the least danger or fear of being captured or fired upon by sharpshooters" (95). He foraged for huckleberries which "grew everywhere in abundance." He found an ice-cold mountain stream "bubbling up beneath the great mass of a rock covering it" (96). One day he chased a long blue racer snake into a hole in the mountainside. As the snake ran, to McCline's amazement, it seemed to stand, and was as tall as the boy. During that same afternoon, upon his return to camp, McCline "found most of the regiment engaged in the exciting game of baseball" (96). Unlike previous camps in Middle Tennessee and Alabama, and those to come in Georgia and the Carolinas, Chattanooga and its mountain wonders measured up to the dream of adventurous freedom McCline must have entertained long before he left the plantation.

In subtle ways, McCline was transformed further during this period. For one thing, he learned to read. Roaming the countryside one day in August 1863, in the vicinity of a temporary camp in the woods where the men could have target practice, McCline came upon a cabin that previously had been occupied by Confederates. Searching around inside, he found a blueback speller and a letter, neither of which he could read. Back at camp, McCline learned from Larkin, the cook, that the missive, a love letter, had been written to a Tim Allen by his sweetheart in Bridgeport, Alabama. Larkin kept the letter and passed it around the company, apparently to everyone's amusement, but McCline kept the speller, and with Larkin's help, he began rudimentary reading. "During our two week stay [in the temporary camp]," McCline writes, "Larkin taught me the alphabet so that I could say it by heart, forward and backward. . . . We returned to our original camp and for ten days I was making splendid progress with my spelling book—got so far advanced I could spell words of one syllable" (100). The reading lessons then were interrupted by orders to move, and later McCline lost the speller when it fell from the train during an overnight transfer from Franklin, Tennessee, to Dalton, Georgia. In his disappointment, McCline the next day retraced the train route for a mile or so, but he never recovered the knapsack containing the book. It would be nearly fifteen years before he could study again, but, once literate, McCline read avidly—newspapers and all the popular fiction he could obtain.

During this Chattanooga period, McCline also saw black soldiers for the first time. He reports that he came upon them, three regiments of infantry, quite unexpectedly, camped in open country several miles away from McCline's own regiment's elevated location. McCline walked into one of many large tents and, in effect, into a world very different from any he had known. He recalls that "there were four or five [men] in the great tent, and to my great surprise, some were reading, and others writing. All were neatly dressed and looked so nice in their uniforms—their shoes were even polished. This was a custom that did not prevail in my regiment—none seemed to take pride in polishing their shoes. They were very kind and asked me many questions about myself. . . . I told them of my regiment, of its many engagements, before and since I joined. They asked if I would not like to be with them—enlist and be a real soldier. Yes, I told them, but I didn't think I was quite old enough; also, having been with the 13th a year and a half, I hated to leave it" (97). Outside the tent, McCline observed drill and saw the chapel tent, which doubled as a schoolroom "where they were taught by the Chaplain to read and write" (97). Unfortunately, by the time he writes this account in the 1920s, McCline does not remember the identities of the regiments. Only the images and impressions of the afternoon remain strong, perhaps even romanticized. Obviously, proud black men in uniform carried their own force of authority for McCline, quite apart from their real association with any army.

Around this same time, McCline was reunited briefly with his older brother Jeff, who also had run away from Clover Bottom Plantation and for six months had been nearby "with the Sixth Ohio Battery." It seemed incredible to McCline that the two brothers should meet, quite by accident, on top of an East Tennessee mountain during a civil war. From Jeff, McCline learned that James Hoggatt had died and that his wife and nieces had moved to Mississippi. The plantation house, in Jeff's words, had "become a rat hole." Promising to meet again when John McCline returned from a foraging expedition, the brothers parted; later, back in camp, McCline unsuccessfully looked for Jeff. They did not see each other again until many years after the war. At the time, McCline felt utterly dejected, but perhaps he also felt relieved. Jeff's report of Clover Bottom in a sense had brought closure to an unpleasant part of the past.[7]

When orders eventually came to move in October 1864, everyone in the 13th Michigan felt disillusioned, irrational though it might have been to expect such a hiatus to continue in the middle of a war. Breaking camp was especially poignant for McCline, because the wagon train, all but two teams, had been disbanded, and the horses that he loved so well were to be left behind in a corral. "Our leaving one of the most delightful of camps," McCline recalls, "was sad in the extreme" (100). Officers' wives who had been visiting for more than a month were left behind in tears. One of McCline's last memories was the "sad forlorn" women, standing "on the edge of the mountain" weeping "as the regiment moved down the winding road" (100).

After a year serving as engineers and as an occupying force at Chattanooga and atop Lookout Mountain, McCline's regiment briefly returned to Middle Tennessee before heading to Georgia to join William Tecumseh Sherman's Savannah campaign. The first stop in North Georgia was Dalton, which the 13th reached by train. McCline was there on November 8, 1864, for the presidential election, which he recalls as "spirited and lively," with the "majority of the regiment" (like the majority of the army) voting for Lincoln. A week later, the 13th Michigan, now attached to the XIV Army Corps, was moving again, heading south toward Atlanta, destroying bridges and railroad tracks as they went. McCline recounts every detail:

On leaving camp, we marched to the railway track, a little to the north, and when the regiment reached it, it was halted and stacked arms. Then orders were given to tear up the tracks. Picks, hammers, and crowbars were brought up by four mule teams, and when the spikes had been loosened, every man taking hold, it was raised [and] tipped over. The ties were then torn up and placed around a tree and the long iron rails placed on top of them, and a big fire built under them. When the rails were red hot in the middle, one end of them would be chained to a tree and the mule team hitched to the other, and they would be bent around it, thus making them entirely useless. (111)

For three days and over twelve miles, McCline's regiment tore up track by day and used the ties for fuel at night. On the fourth day, having reached the Chattahoochee River, they left the railroad and took a dirt road "across the river into Atlanta, some ten miles to the South" (111).

McCline depicts the destruction in North Georgia even as he observes the region's beauty. As a "Yankee soldier," destruction of the Confederate South was logical. But as an impressionable boy, he was compelled to acknowledge the beauty of the landscapes that he was seeing for the first time. At the top of a hill overlooking the Chattahoochee, for example, McCline surveys the aesthetically pleasing scene below. "The view from the hill overlooking the river below, winding its way carefully to the southwest, through a fine strip of level farming country, was beautiful in the extreme," he writes. "It was Saturday," he continues, "and the sun was setting, throwing its golden rays over miles of the fine valley as far as the eye could trace" (111–12). By midnight, when all the troops had descended the hill and crossed the "little stream" below, the bridge, an integral part of the pastoral scene which had enchanted McCline a few hours earlier, "was blown up and the great mass of heavy beams rose and fell into the stream" (112).

In other descriptions of Atlanta, too, this context of extremes predominates. McCline saw the city for the first time and declared it "a great city in complete ruins" (112). In one notation, he remarks upon the splendor and the decimation. All the structures which had lent Atlanta an aura of grandeur "were burned to the ground—not a single building was standing" (112). The noteworthy exception was a storehouse of provisions, a long, low shed filled to capacity with "barrels of flour, hogsheads of brown sugar, sacks of coffee, and . . . great heavy cords of bacon" (113). This bounty supplied each soldier with as much as he could carry on the march south. After that, McCline declares, "its valuable contents [enough to ration a large army for months] was set on fire and burned to the ground" (113), offering another drama in the tragic inevitability of things.

Curiously, McCline appreciated the charm and grace of southern life even as he unselfconsciously recalled participating in its destruction. Perhaps this kind of uncomplicated delineation of paradoxical experience is the province of childhood, or perhaps it reflects a mature acceptance of competing realities. Whatever its source and meaning, the strength of McCline's narrative and of his personality is this willingness to treat successive, contradictory episodes of his life honestly and completely and, while the reader is still absorbed in one episode, move on to the next— without regret. He always is prepared to go forward.

From Atlanta to Savannah, McCline was part of a mammoth army whose epic and destructive force lay in its numbers as much as in any actual display of power. The several corps under Sherman stretched along miles of road, covering an average distance sometimes of no more than five miles a day, according to McCline. Along the way, everything in the army's path, from livestock to Confederate dollars, was swept away. Milledgeville, Saundersville, Savannah, the Carolinas—all in turn are rendered by McCline, who often remembers each time and place in remarkable detail.

One event, however, was especially memorable. Ten days out of Atlanta on the March to the Sea, he spoke with General Sherman himself, whom McCline describes as "magnificent in appearance on horseback." Seeing him for the first time was "a real sensation" for many of the men in McCline's regiment, who had not participated in the Atlanta campaign. "His attitude on horseback," McCline recollects, "was striking. He seemed to be a very tall man, when seen mounted on his big bay horse with one white hind leg. He rode perfectly erect in the saddle and seemed to be looking directly ahead of him" (115–16).

During a short rest, the general and his staff took refuge under a large oak; as McCline passed on his return from a nearby creek, the general called to him. Here is McCline's account:

> "Here boy. I have seen you a good many times. What regiment do you belong to?"
> I was taken completely by surprise, but stepped up, came to attention, took off my cap and said "I belong to the fighting Thirteenth."
> "Oh you do, do you? How old are you?"
> "I don't know, sir."
> "Well, you are nearly big enough to carry a gun."
> "Yes sir. I do carry one once in a while, when a tired soldier drops behind."
> "That's right," he said, "help all you can."
> I then saluted and passed on. (115)

Here and nearly throughout the memoir, McCline strongly embraces patriotism, military duty, and the idealized Union soldier. Sherman, who in reality was not a friend to blacks and who rejected the notion of black men in uniform, is "the grand old man."[8] Rosecrans, whom McCline had seen at Chattanooga before the general was cashiered for Chickamauga, is "the great little man." The "fighting Thirteenth" is his regiment, and the men of Company C his comrades and "dear friends." Incredibly for some readers, perhaps, nowhere is there the minority perspective, the black soldier's point of view. Freedmen and freemen alike, serving as soldiers in segregated regiments and as servants in white regiments, routinely struggled against injustices: brutal impressment, humiliation, inferior pay, forced labor, Confederate slaughter.[9] Yet, if McCline experienced any of these problems, he does not say so. Either he was consistently treated well, or he was willing years later to overlook the exceptions. He willingly worked the first fifteen months with the 13th Michigan without wages, and the eight dollars per month he received during the second and third years were an unexpected windfall for an eleven-year-old boy who considered freedom compensation enough. McCline thus perceived military life from the confined perspective of his tender years and his own experience. It stood in stark contrast to slavery: one made him fearful and dependent; the other instilled initiative and daring.

The 13th Michigan, and McCline, remained with Sherman through the end of the war. The unit was camped in North Carolina when Joseph E. Johnston surrendered to Sherman. McCline was thirteen or fourteen then, and, instead of returning to Tennessee to look for his family, he remained with the 13th through the grand review in Washington and until it was mustered out of service at Louisville, Kentucky, in July 1865. McCline and Bart, another black teenager, even went "home" to Michigan with a colonel and found employment in a small-town hotel. Nine years later, McCline moved to Chicago, where, four years after the fire of 1871, workers still were needed to help rebuild the city. McCline went to work immediately as a waiter at the Madison Hotel, which later became the Palmer House. After two years in Chicago, he learned that his brother Jeff was alive but ill and living in St. Louis. McCline went to him, and the two of them returned to Tennessee to find their family members and to attend school. Two years of instruction qualified McCline to teach, but, with no teaching jobs available, he returned to St. Louis and certainly would have remained there if a persistent cough and malaria had not forced him west to Colorado Springs in 1890. His last move, in 1906, was to Santa Fe, New Mexico, to manage the territorial governor's residence for Herbert Hagerman, whose family had employed him in Colorado. McCline lived in New Mexico until his death in 1948.

At some time during the 1920s, in surveying the seventy or more years of his life, McCline settled upon slavery and the Civil War as subjects of his memoir. As an ex-slave, he knew intuitively what the Lincoln government had discovered only reluctantly—that slavery and the Civil War were inextricably intertwined. The fate of one had determined the outcome of the other, and both had influenced the course of McCline's life. Slavery had taught him to expect very few rewards, but army life, in contrast, had brought freedom, wages, and education, among other things. In 1862, during his escape, McCline had allowed himself only a furtive glance back at slavery, preferring instead to look forward toward his future. During the 1920s, living in a future that McCline could not have imagined sixty years earlier, he looked back once more, this time from the broad perspective of old age to realize that the entire episode of war, and notably his service in the Southern Mountains, had been an apprenticeship for the rest of his life.

Notes

1. Clover Bottom, a 1,500-acre farm owned by James Hoggatt, was one of the largest plantations in Davidson County, Tenn. With about 60 slaves, Hoggatt bred mules, raised large herds of cattle and pigs for market, and produced thousands of bushels of vegetables and grain annually. The State of Tennessee, which now owns Clover Bottom, recently restored Hoggatt's Greek Revival plantation house, and several offices of the Tennessee Historical Commission are located there.

2. All quotations are from John McCline's unpublished memoir, "Slavery in the Clover Bottoms," presently being editing for publication by the Univ. of Tennessee Press. The original has disappeared, but a typescript is held by the Kit Carson Museum, Taos, N.M. Parenthetical citations are page numbers of the unedited typescript.

3. Hoggatt died at Clover Bottom early in 1863, about a month after McCline's escape.

4. U.S. Dept. of War, *The War of the Rebellion: A Compilation of the Official Records of the Union and Confederate Armies* (Washington, D.C.: U.S. Government Printing Office, 1880–1901; hereafter cited as *OR*), ser. 1, vol. 20, pt. 1, pp. 180, 205, 212, 462, 511–12. See also Michigan Adjutant-General's Dept., *Michigan in the War*, rev. ed. (Lansing: W. S. George, 1882), 331–41.

5. Although McCline is clear, in broad terms, about the role his regiment played at Chickamauga, he is less clear about the chronology of events. In his account, the evening during which the quartermaster orders him to supply the troops and the battle occur on successive days. In fact, the first event most likely happened as he remembers on Sept. 16, while the battle began on the Sept. 19. This is one of several instances in which he condenses time. Peter Cozzens notes that on the evening of Sept. 16, in anticipation of an attack, all corps commanders were ordered to give each soldier three days' rations and 20 rounds, plus a cartridge box full of ammunition. See Peter Cozzens, *This Terrible Sound: The Battle of Chickamauga* (Urbana: Univ. of Illinois Press, 1992), 94; and *OR*, ser. 1, vol. 30, pt. 1, pp. 653–54.

6. McCline—whose estimate of casualties was off by only one—was not wrong to worry about the fate of his regiment in what has been described as the bloodiest battle in the Western Theater. See *OR,* ser. 1, vol. 30, pt. 1, pp. 44, 175, 652–58, 66–67.

7. After the war, Mrs. Hoggatt and many former slaves (including McCline's grandmother and uncles) returned to Clover Bottom plantation.

8. For Sherman's views of African Americans in uniform, see Michael Fellman, *Citizen Sherman: A Life of William Tecumseh Sherman* (New York: Random House, 1995), 149–70.

9. For detailed treatments of the black soldier's experience, see Ira Berlin, Joseph P. Reidy, and Leslie S. Roland, eds., *Freedom: A Documentary History of Emancipation, 1861–1867,* ser. 2: *The Black Military Experience* (New York: Cambridge Univ. Press, 1982); Dudley Taylor Cornish, *The Sable Arm: Negro Troops in the Union Army, 1861–1865* (New York: Norton, 1966); James M. McPherson, *The Negro's Civil War: How American Blacks Felt and Acted During the War for the Union* (New York: Ballantine, 1991). Edwin S. Redkey, *"A Grand Army of Black Men": Letters from African-American Soldiers in the Union Army, 1861–1865* (New York: Cambridge Univ. Press, 1992). Howard C. Westwood, *Black Troops, White Commanders, and Freedmen During the Civil War* (Carbondale: Southern Illinois Univ. Press, 1992).

9

"Oh! Ours Is a Deplorable Condition": The Economic Impact of the Civil War in Upper East Tennessee

Robert Tracy McKenzie

Few problems troubled white southerners more than the pervasive, suffocating poverty that settled upon their region after the end of the Civil War. Levels of income there were scarcely half the national average for the next three-quarters of a century.[1] Similarly, few issues have generated greater interest among twentieth-century historians of the South than the disputed causes of its sustained economic backwardness.[2] Until quite recently, however, in investigating this question, historians focused almost exclusively on the large plantation sections of the Deep South. They were interested primarily in the war's effect on two population groups—white planters and black slaves—and paid little attention to areas of the South in which neither group was numerous.

Happily, during the last decade or so, due primarily to a rejuvenation of interest in the southern white "yeomanry," scholars have exhibited a heightened appreciation for the South apart from the Black Belt and have produced a number of important studies of nonplantation regions, most notably the "upcountry" (Piedmont) portions of Georgia and South Carolina. Although interest in the Appalachian South also has been stimulated as part of this trend, most scholarly investigation of this neglected area continues to concentrate on the period of capitalist transformation at the very close of the nineteenth century. It is but a slight exaggeration to say that the history of the region's preindustrial period has yet to be written.[3]

To address this deficiency, this essay explores the economic impact of the Civil War on the white farm population of upper East Tennessee, a portion of the South that was far removed—figuratively as well as literally—from the world of cotton fields and plantations that traditionally has captivated modern scholars. In striking contrast to so much of the future Confederacy, the area's white population was predominantly Unionist (more than two-thirds of voters opposed secession), overwhelmingly nonslaveholding (less than one-tenth of households owned slaves), and almost universally uninvolved in the cotton economy. Fiercely proud of their homeland's uniqueness, East Tennesseans labeled the region—with a forgivable measure of exaggeration—the "Switzerland of America."[4]

Geologically and agriculturally, the region actually encompasses not one but two distinct sections. The eastern one consists of the Unaka (or Smoky) Mountains, which rise to a height of several thousand feet along the border with North Carolina. On the eve of the Civil War, Smoky Mountain farmers generally had access to few passable roads and no railroads. Largely, if not perfectly, isolated from external markets, they concentrated on grazing livestock, while growing modest quantities of food crops for local consumption. Farther west lay the far less sequestered and far more prosperous Valley of East Tennessee, a fluted region of alternating wooded ridges and narrow, fertile valleys. Characterized by census officials as the "poor man's rich land," this section of the state not only was well suited to the production of corn, wheat, and hogs, but also was well connected by both water and rail to major regional markets. As a consequence, for much of the antebellum era, it rivaled the Shenandoah Valley of Virginia as one of the leading food-producing areas in the entire South. In sum, despite a significant measure of geographic and economic diversity within the region, on the eve of the Civil War, upper East Tennessee as a whole constituted the very antithesis of the Cotton South. Yet, when war came, the region was every bit as profoundly affected by the chain reaction of events inexorably set in motion.[5]

Into the Vortex of Civil War

As white East Tennesseans reflected upon their Civil War experience, they undoubtedly found the cruelest irony in the knowledge that they had suffered economic ruin while fighting on the winning side.[6] In no other area of the Confederacy was Unionism consistently stronger than along the wooded ridges and mountain valleys of upper East Tennessee. Only slightly dependent upon slavery and resentful of the disproportionate political power wielded by the wealthier central and western sections of the state, East Tennesseans from the start overwhelmingly opposed the movement toward secession gaining momentum farther west. Even after the fall of Fort Sumter and President Lincoln's call for volunteers to suppress the rebellion, a large majority of East Tennesseans still denied that there were sufficient grounds for disunion. They would have agreed with the resolution of a Johnson County convention that their "rights and liberties [could] be better maintained in the Union and under the Constitution, than by any revolution or separate organization." When voters in Middle and West Tennessee strongly endorsed secession in the state referendum of June 8, 1861, East Tennesseans opposed separation from the union by more than two to one.[7]

Nine days after the secession referendum, a convention of Unionists from throughout the region gathered at Greeneville, issued a "Declaration of Grievances," and forwarded to the state legislature a petition requesting that the counties of East Tennessee be allowed to form a separate state. When the petition predictably was ignored, the majority of Unionists in the region—critical of "ultra men" on both sides, sobered by thoughts of the repercussions certain to follow overt resistance to Confederate rule, and conscious of the obstacles to joining the Union Army in Kentucky—initially sought to avoid involvement of any kind.[8] Even the vituperatively combative "Parson" William Brownlow moderated (relatively) the tone of his Unionist newspaper and spoke both of "yield[ing] to the necessity upon us" and of "retiring to a position of neutrality."[9]

A position of neutrality is notoriously difficult to maintain in the midst of civil war, however, and ultimately it proved an impossible one for the Unionists of East Tennessee. In particular, the crucial strategic importance of the East Tennessee Valley—both as a center of food production and as a railroad and communications corridor connecting Virginia with the trans-Appalachian Confederacy—insured that both Union and Confederate armies would vie for control of the region. Indeed, the first Confederate "army of occupation" entered the area within a month after the state's secession, thus setting off the first major movement of Unionists through mountain passes to Kentucky and the Union Army. Although the Confederate military commander in East Tennessee, Gen. Felix K. Zollicoffer, consciously pursued a policy of conciliation toward the local population, two particularly polarizing events, in November 1861 and April 1862, dashed any remaining hope of meaningful neutrality and forced East Tennesseans into the vortex of civil war.

201

First, on the night of November 8, small bands of Unionists, anticipating an aborted Union invasion from Kentucky, burned five strategic railroad bridges between Bristol and Chattanooga, including one spanning Lick Creek in Greene County.[10] This premeditated campaign of resistance "startled the whole Confederacy" and resulted, not surprisingly, in an escalation of political repression by Confederate authorities. Determined that "this rebellion must be crushed out instantly," Governor Isham Harris promised to send ten thousand troops to the region to insure that its leaders were arrested and "summarily punished." General Zollicoffer immediately declared martial law throughout the district, and over the next several weeks, hundreds of prominent East Tennesseans were arrested and sent to prison in Tuscaloosa, Alabama, for conspiracy against the Confederacy. Gen. Edmund Kirby Smith, who succeeded Zollicoffer as Confederate commander of the region in early 1862, actually stepped up the pace of arrests and threatened to send all disloyal males into the Deep South. Although not without provocation, the Confederate crackdown understandably deepened the latent resentment of area Unionists.[11]

Five months after the bridge burnings, the Confederate Congress in Richmond further alienated mountain Unionists with the passage, on April 16, 1862, of the first Conscription Act, a measure which made every white male in the Confederacy between the ages of eighteen and thirty-five subject to military service. Anticipating the furor that the legislation would evoke, on April 8 Jefferson Davis had designated East Tennessee as enemy territory and had authorized the temporary suspension of habeas corpus throughout the region. When Congress followed the Conscription Act with legislation authorizing exemptions from the draft for all who could hire substitutes or who owned twenty or more slaves, East Tennesseans understandably concluded that the Richmond government had determined to force poor mountaineers to finish a war that wealthy slaveholders had begun.[12] Ultimately, no other single factor was as important as this widespread perception in pushing East Tennesseans toward a position of overt resistance to the Confederacy. By convincing them that neutrality no longer was an option, the Conscription Act set off a second and far larger wave of emigration into Kentucky by mountaineers who now literally believed that they had no acceptable choice but to join the Union Army. Even Kirby Smith quickly recognized the act's disastrous consequences for the Confederacy, estimating that, within ten days of its passage, more than seven thousand East Tennesseans fled the region to volunteer for the Union. By war's end, this number would exceed thirty thousand, a figure higher than those of such officially loyal states as Delaware, Minnesota, or Rhode Island.[13]

The Economic Imprint of War

"No Section of our Country has Suffered more," a Blount County minister wrote to Andrew Johnson in the fall of 1864, "no people hated more [by the Rebels,] and no country more exposed to their ravages and plundering than all E[ast] Tennessee."[14] Despite their fervent hopes of being left alone, by the spring of 1862, white East Tennesseans found themselves inextricably entangled in the coils of civil war. Before peace could be restored to the land some three years later, war would exact its customary price, as measured in waste, destruction, and human suffering. For those who endured it, the economic shock that the war inflicted on the region seemed a costly price indeed.

Broadly speaking, the Civil War affected the wealth and income of white East Tennesseans in one of two primary ways: through the emancipation of area slaves and through the destruction or confiscation of nonslave property by Union and Confederate armies or paramilitary guerrilla forces. Of the two, the first clearly was of less importance to the region. Emancipation adversely affected the southern economy both by reducing the individual wealth of former masters and by profoundly disturbing traditional labor patterns; yet in neither respect was its impact unduly severe in East Tennessee. A Congressional investigating committee after the war estimated that, for the state as whole, the value of emancipated slaves exceeded the value of nonslave property losses by a ratio of approximately three to two. In East Tennessee, however, the reverse ratio still would have exaggerated greatly the relative economic impact of emancipation.[15] When the war began, less than 10 percent of white households in the section owned slaves, and those that did typically owned four or fewer; throughout the region, only one out of every five hundred household heads met the standard definition of a "planter" by owning twenty slaves or more. Thus, in contrast to the former plantation areas of the Deep South, emancipation's direct effect on the wealth of white East Tennesseans was limited to a tiny proportion of the free population. Nor was its disruptive effect on the labor system appreciably greater. Unlike areas in which slavery had been more prevalent, in upper East Tennessee landless white labor had been superabundant before the Civil War, making most rural employers independent of black workers.[16]

If East Tennessee suffered less from emancipation than most southern areas, it definitely experienced more than its share of material devastation. For much of the war, Confederate and Union armies struggled for control of the Valley of East Tennessee, marching almost the whole length of the region on four separate occasions and waging major campaigns in both

1863 and 1864. The valley was not permanently under Federal control until late 1864, and it was March or April 1865 before Union forces "liberated" the remote mountain counties along the state's northeastern border.[17]

Confederate control of the region largely went unchallenged during the first two years of the war, allowing Confederate forces basically unrestricted access to the first fruits of the land. Foraging details roamed the countryside, "impressing" livestock, food crops, fodder, and firewood for use by the army. In return for their "contribution" to the cause, mountain Unionists received either curses for their "tory" sympathies or rapidly depreciating Confederate currency, the latter worth but slightly more than the former and hardly less insulting. Confederate troops took four horses and seven cattle from Greene County widow Margaret Ripley, for example, and robbed her house on five separate occasions. Unionist Enos Rambo was treated but little better. In 1863, Rebel soldiers took corn, wheat, oats, rye, fodder, bacon, tobacco, hay forks, and horses from his farm southeast of Greeneville, compensating him with fifty-five dollars in worthless Confederate notes. As Rambo related to federal claims agents after the war, it was "hard to call that pay."[18]

Unchallenged Confederate domination of the region finally ended in late summer, 1863, when Gen. Ambrose Burnside led fifteen thousand Federal soldiers of the Army of the Ohio from southeastern Kentucky into the East Tennessee Valley, occupying Knoxville on September 3. In terms of their material welfare, however, East Tennesseans found Union occupation no more desirable than Confederate. Although Unionists thronged along the course of march to cheer the Yankees' arrival, they rapidly became disillusioned by the ill treatment they received at the hands of their deliverers. A young officer in Burnside's army glowingly wrote to his father of how "some of the people would scarcely ask for pay for the forage which we had seized to feed our animals, although the corn we had taken was all they had to look to for their winter's food." Perhaps "some of the people" exhibited such patriotic generosity for a season, but as the burden of Union occupation grew more cumbersome, a larger number grew resentful at the idea that starvation apparently was to be the price of their liberation. Prominent East Tennessee Unionist T. A. R. Nelson complained to a Union general:

> The Union Army is more destructive to Union men than the rebel army ever was. Our fences are burned, our horses are taken, our people are stripped in many instances of the last vestige of subsistence, our means to make a crop next year are being rapidly destroyed, and when the best Union men in the country make appeals to the soldiers they are heartlessly cursed as rebels. . . . If nothing is done & promptly done, starvation and ruin are before us, and there will be nothing here to support the army next summer.[19]

Profoundly disappointed by the behavior of Burnside's army, loyal East Tennesseans were inclined to attribute such behavior to a callous indifference to civilian suffering. According to Nelson, area Unionists were beginning to believe that the government they had "loved and trusted . . . had at last become cruel and unjust, and cares nothing for [their] sorrows and sufferings." Although this was an understandable conclusion, and one at least partially justified, much of the damage inflicted by Burnside's men reflected the exigencies of war more than personal insensitivity. As Union Gen. Gordon Granger observed, although nothing had troubled him "so much as being compelled to strip the country[,] friend and foe must fare alike, or the army must starve."[20]

What East Tennesseans learned by experience was that it mattered little whether the color of the uniforms was blue or gray; the proximity of soldiers invariably resulted in the extensive confiscation of livestock and crops. Consequently, the only fate worse than occupation by either army was occupation by both, which was precisely what lay in store for the region during the winter of 1863–64. In an attempt to reclaim upper East Tennessee, Confederate Gen. James Longstreet in early November led nearly twenty thousand soldiers up the East Tennessee Valley from North Georgia, eventually laying siege to Burnside's army at Knoxville around the middle of the month. Longstreet was forced to break off the siege in early December, however, when Ulysses Grant dispatched reinforcements to Knoxville in the form of two Union army corps under the command of William T. Sherman. With Sherman's two corps astride the return route to Georgia, Longstreet retreated toward the Virginia line, spending the winter between Russellville and Greeneville, some seventy-five miles north of the Union Army's winter headquarters in Knoxville.[21]

Forced to feed not one but two armies, during the winter of 1863–64 the civilians of East Tennessee were introduced to a new level of privation and suffering. Assuming that they were leaving the region for good after the failed siege of Knoxville, Longstreet's forces took everything they could with them from the region to the north and east of the city. As Longstreet recalled in his memoirs, "Wheat and oats had been hidden away by our Union friends, but the fields were full of maize, still standing. . . . Our wagons immediately on entering the fields were loaded to overflowing." A Union officer stationed in the region at the time reported of "the ravages of both Union and rebel armies and the extreme destitution produced by them among the people." A Confederate officer concurred, observing that "East Tennessee is bleeding at every pore" and "is literally eaten up."[22]

In many respects, the situation worsened rather than improved as winter gave way to spring. In April 1864, Longstreet's army was ordered to the Virginia theater to assist Robert E. Lee in the defense of Richmond, while Union troop strength around Knoxville also was gradually reduced to support Sherman's invasion of Georgia. Although small units of both armies continued to vie with desperate intensity for control of the region, the absence of a major military presence in the region encouraged an escalation of both guerrilla warfare and outright banditry. Both Unionist and Confederate civilians believed that they were suffering the greater amount of depredations, and both sides characteristically attributed to the enemy the thievery and destruction that plagued the region. Greene County Unionist Samuel Milligan, for example, recalled that the evacuation of Longstreet's army "left the country open to a set of marauders" that made life more difficult for loyal mountaineers than it had been when the regular Confederate Army had occupied the region. Parson Brownlow agreed that a "spirit of demons seems to possess the rebel guerrillas in upper East Tennessee. . . . Property they can't carry off they destroy." In contrast, a southern sympathizer complained that, ever since the area had been "abandoned" by Confederate troops, it had been "infested by lawless gangs who call themselves home-guards" and who "plunder and terrorize our southern people."[23]

By the time that the Union Army reclaimed control of most of the region in December 1864, upper East Tennessee was almost entirely destitute. Although the East Tennessee Relief Association had been created in February 1864 to funnel northern charitable contributions into the region, a poorly developed transportation network combined with a continuing Confederate military presence to prevent most relief supplies from going any farther north than Knoxville.[24] Consequently, Union and Confederate veterans returned from the war in the spring of 1865 to find dilapidated buildings, deteriorated soil, broken-down work stock, and seriously depleted food supplies. When veteran Joel Henry arrived at his home, for instance, he found that "conditions were awful—fences burned, provisions about all taken—stock driven off, houses burned—nothing to make a crop on." Similarly, after getting back home to Bulls Gap, Lewis Gulley discovered that the "Federals had stold every thing most my father had."[25]

The suffering of the civilian population did not end with the return of husbands, sons, and fathers from the war. Because most veterans did not reach their homes until after the spring planting, the 1865 crop was planted primarily by women and children. It was restricted in size not only by the shortage of male labor, but also by the severe deficiency of work stock caused by the depredations of both armies. Nor was plenty restored in

1866. As a Federal officer stationed in the area reported, the discharged soldiers typically "absorbed the little money paid them at their muster out in repairing their fences and buildings, as well as eking out the scanty stores for winter consumption, so that the Spring [of 1866] dawned upon them with barely sufficient means to procure the requisite seeds for planting." Indicative of the persistence of food shortages in the area, the Freedmen's Bureau still was distributing foodstuffs among East Tennessee whites as late as the summer of 1866. For example, in the month of June alone, agents dispensed eighteen thousand rations in Greene County and eleven thousand in Johnson. The bureau estimated that the number of destitute families in the latter county approached 150, roughly one-fifth of its entire population. Even as late as the following spring—i.e., fully two years after the war's conclusion—a Freedmen's Bureau official who visited Greeneville was forcibly struck by the extent of destitution in the town. The abandoned (windowless) buildings of old Greeneville College had become the home of more than fifty vagrants, who now subsisted entirely by "begging and digging roots for 'greens.'" As northern journalist John Trowbridge described it, the poverty-stricken town, replete with its "old, dilapidated, unpainted houses," appeared "eminently disagreeable."[26]

Keeping in mind the age-old adage that "to the victor belongs the spoils," many ex-Confederates probably expected such prolonged hardship and resigned themselves to a predictable fate.[27] But for those who had remained loyal to the Union throughout four years of civil war, such extended privation was a bitter pill to swallow. Having seen their homeland decimated while the economy of the officially loyal states flourished, East Tennessee Unionists looked to the federal government not for a demeaning handout, but for their rightful due. At a minimum, they believed that they should be reimbursed for the extensive foodstuffs and forage they had provided the Union Army between the time of Burnside's 1863 invasion and the end of the war.

In the end, such hopes were largely disappointed. Although Congress finally, in 1871, did establish a commission to consider the claims of southern Unionists, the more than four thousand Tennesseans who applied for compensation before the Southern Claims Commission discovered that it defined Unionism so strictly, and determined the boundaries of acceptable claims so narrowly, that all but the most persistent and best-documented appeals ultimately were frustrated. As citizens of a state that had been part of the insurrection, all East Tennesseans were assumed to have been disloyal and required to pass a loyalty test, which, according to the most thorough assessment of the commission, literally "demanded a life of treason to the Confederacy."[28] In a ruling that was particularly galling, the commission determined to exclude all claims for damage that resulted from the "unauthorized or unnecessary depredations" of the federal troops. So, for example, when Unionist James Park requested compensation for seventeen hogs taken by soldiers in Burnside's Army of the Ohio in October 1863, the commissioners rejected the claim on the grounds that the soldiers probably had shot the hogs "for their personal satisfaction." In like manner, the commission disallowed payment for hogs confiscated from Reuben Rader, ruling that they had been "killed in a promiscuous way by the soldiers" rather than "regularly taken as supplies." In other words, if Union soldiers officially had impressed foodstuffs or other supplies, then payment might be justified; if they had simply stolen such goods without authorization, then their victims were out of luck. After more than six years of deliberations, the commission ultimately awarded approximately $4.6 million to southern Unionists—roughly 8 percent of the total amount requested.[29]

Assessing War's Impact

"Our once beautiful and happy country is so defaced that you would scarcely recognize it," a Greene County farmer wrote to Andrew Johnson in late 1864. "Oh! ours is a deplorable condition—the people mourning in sackcloth and ashes—destitute of the comforts of life."[30] If Americans living in other times and places frequently have been able to regard history as "something unpleasant that happens to other people," white East Tennesseans who survived the Civil War did not hold this view, as even the most superficial survey of contemporary perceptions makes evident. Like white southerners generally, they knew unquestionably that "history had happened" to them and that it had been painful.[31] Although the recognition and appreciation of East Tennesseans' perceptions is critical to understanding the war's economic impact, the historian's task does not end there. Rather, it is imperative not only to make use of the perspective afforded by hindsight but also to take into consideration forms of evidence not widely available to contemporaries in order to craft an analysis of the past that transcends, whenever possible, the understanding of the historical actors themselves.

Toward that end, the remainder of this essay employs statistical information from the manuscript schedules of the United States Census to assess the Civil War's long-term economic impact on the white farm population of upper East Tennessee. To reduce the task to manageable proportions, the assessment is limited to three sample counties: Johnson, which lies wholly within the Unaka Mountain chain; Greene, which is situated partially within the Unakas but predominantly in the Valley of East Tennessee; and Grainger, which is entirely a valley county. Although the counties are not representative of the region in a statistically verifiable sense, they do reflect many of the political and economic characteristics that contributed to the area's uniqueness on the eve of the war. (See map 9.1 and table 9.1.) An analysis of census data from these counties—one that concentrates on changes in the level and distribution of wealth and in the incidence of household self-sufficiency—should allow not only more precise estimates of the war's economic impact but also greater insight into the Civil War's social meaning for the region's inhabitants.

Table 9.1
Profile of Sample East Tennessee Counties, 1860

	Grainger	Greene	Johnson
Median Farm Size in Improved Acres	81.0	75.0	50.0
Farm Households Owning Slaves* (%)	13.3	8.7	7.5
Farm Operators Planting Cotton (%)	2.1	0.0	0.0
Voters Opposing Secession, June 1861 (%)	71.8	78.3	87.6

NOTE: *Figures apply to slaves owned or rented within the county of enumeration only.
SOURCES: Owsley Charts, Frank L. Owsley Papers, Special Collections, Jean and Alexander Heard Library, Vanderbilt University, Nashville, Tenn.; Mary E. R. Campbell, *The Attitude of Tennesseans Toward the Union, 1847–1861* (New York: Vantage Press, 1961), 291.

Map 9.1. Upper East Tennessee, 1860. Map by The University of Tennessee Cartography Lab.

Predictably, census data indicate that the overall level of wealth among white farm households in the sample counties fell dramatically during the 1860s. Mean total wealth per household (including the value of both real and personal property) fell from $2,907 to $1,772, a decline of approximately 39 percent (see table 9.2).[32] Because undoubtedly there was a measure of recovery during the latter half of the decade, the decrease during the war years alone was assuredly even greater. All forms of wealth were not affected equally, of course. Personal (movable) property per household fell by half, a decline caused primarily by the loss of slaves and the decimation of livestock, more than two-fifths of which was destroyed during the war. By comparison, the average value of real property—land and buildings—dropped "only" by about one-third. Less straightforward than the changes in personal wealth, the reduction in real wealth reflected a variety of factors, including increasing landlessness among the farm population, shrinking farm size, soil deterioration, damage to buildings and fences, and falling market values caused by diminished expectations of future profitability.[33]

A decline of nearly two-fifths in the overall level of wealth during the 1860s is certainly suggestive, yet, of various indicators of the war's economic impact, this statistic probably is the least helpful. To begin with, it tells us very little about the war's effect on *individual* white farmers. The figures in the top half of table 9.2 summarize cross-sectional data, i.e., "snapshots" taken at two discrete points in time. They convey accurate information concerning the overall level of wealth in 1860 and 1870, yet it would be dangerous to infer from them the changing wealth position of individual farmers during the intervening ten years. The population that they describe was demographically dynamic, not static; its composition was perpetually being altered due to inmigration, outmigration, natural increase, mortality, and the aging process inherent in the life cycle. Of the household heads

Table 9.2
Mean Value of Wealth among White Farm Households, Sample East Tennessee Counties, 1860 and 1870

	Real Estate	Personal Estate	Total Estate
All Farm Households			
1860	$1,716	$1,191	$2,907
1870	$1,182	$591	$1,772
Geographically Stable Farm Households*			
1860	$2,300	$1,634	$3,934
1870	$2,601	$962	$3,563

NOTE: *Household in same county in both 1860 and 1870.
SOURCE: Three-county sample of Grainger, Greene, and Johnson counties; see nn. 32 and 34, this essay.

present in the sample counties in 1860, just under one-half had died or moved away by 1870.[34] Of those present in 1870, more than one-half had not been among local household heads a decade before.[35] As a result, trustworthy insight into individual experiences can be ascertained only by longitudinal analysis, i.e., by tracing individual farmers across time.

Longitudinal analysis shows that the cross-sectional figures in table 9.2 substantially exaggerate the losses typically experienced by individuals during the war decade. Mean total wealth among household heads who were present in the sample counties in both 1860 and 1870 decreased by only 9 percent (from $3,934 to $3,566), as opposed to the 39 percent decline for the counties as a whole. (Indeed, among the 53 percent of white farm household heads who remained in the same county throughout the decade, more than one-half—54 percent, to be precise—actually experienced an *increase* in total wealth.) Because those who suffered large economic losses were less likely to stay put geographically than those who prospered, the longitudinal figures given in the lower half of table 9.2 almost certainly understate the average magnitude of individual loss. Even so, the estimates indirectly yield important insight into the overall decline in wealth among white farmers in the sample counties: the falling level of wealth during the 1860s was due at least as much to diminished opportunities for wealth accumulation among new or transient households as to devastating losses by established wealthholders. Among geographically persistent heads of farm households, the probability that a landless farmer would acquire land fell from 44.4 percent during the 1850s to 35.7 percent during the 1860s. The decline in the incidence of land acquisition was probably even greater among individuals who recently had moved to the community or who had just left the households of their parents.

Although it contributed to drastically reduced overall levels of wealth among the white farm populations of upper East Tennessee, the cataclysm of civil war had surprisingly minimal effect on patterns of wealth distribution. Although modern historians frequently have described Southern Appalachia prior to the late nineteenth century as akin to a Jeffersonian utopia, the distribution of wealth in antebellum upper East Tennessee was literally indistinguishable from that which characterized the plantation belt of the Deep South (see table 9.3).[36] Contemporary boosters were correct to point out that the minimal importance of slavery to the region precluded the growth of a class of "great lordly proprietors."[37] They conveniently failed to note, however, that landlessness was more pronounced in East Tennessee than almost anywhere else in the antebellum South. In 1860, the landless constituted 43 percent of all free farm households in the sample East Tennessee counties, compared with an estimated 37 percent in the Georgia Piedmont, 33 percent in Mississippi's northeastern hill country, 26 percent in eastern Texas, 25 percent in the Mississippi Delta, 24 percent in the Alabama Uplands, 24 percent in the Georgia Black Belt, and 19 percent in the Alabama Black Belt.[38]

Statistically speaking, then, East Tennesseans' frequent claims that "all were equals" before the Civil War were preposterous and should not be taken seriously as indicators of wealthholding structure.[39] They appear most frequently in appeals to immigrants or in political commentaries that reflect a marked resentment of the disproportionate influence of plantation districts in the state's politics. With regard to the latter, East Tennesseans' assertions of local egalitarianism were analogous to Republicans' glorification of the antebellum North. Both were intended to underscore slaveholders' social and economic domination of plantation regions; neither were particularly accurate representations of their own society. Parson Brownlow, for example, altered his characterization of the socioeconomic structure of East Tennessee according to his immediate object. In February 1864, for instance, Brownlow blasted local secessionists by denouncing the "aristocracy founded alone upon the nigger" that had "cursed" eastern Tennessee "for the last forty years." In an appeal to immigrants in the *very next issue* of his newspaper, Brownlow lauded the advantages of the region over the rest of the South, noting that, "as a general thing, before the introduction of this rebellion, the people were very nearly upon an equality as to their possessions."[40]

As table 9.3 shows, the patterns of economic inequality that obtained in 1860 stubbornly persisted throughout the war decade. Because such a tiny proportion of the region's households had owned slaves prior to the war, emancipation did cause a noticeable diminution in the concentration of

Table 9.3
Distribution of Wealth among White Farm Households, Sample East Tennessee Counties, 1860 and 1870

	Real Estate	Personal Estate	Total Estate
% Share of Richest 5%			
1860	39.1	48.7	40.7
1870	41.1	32.6	36.3
% Share of Poorest 50%			
1860	1.7	6.7	4.9
1870	0.6	12.3	6.0
Gini Coefficient			
1860	0.71	0.70	0.69
1870	0.74	0.57	0.67

SOURCE: Three-county sample of Grainger, Greene, and Johnson counties; see n. 32, this essay.

personal wealth between 1860 and 1870, as the Gini coefficients in the table reveal. (The Gini coefficient is a standardized measurement of wealth concentration that ranges from 0.0, when each household owns an equivalent share of locally owned wealth, to 1.0 when one household owns 100 percent and all others are propertyless.[41]) The proportion of personal property owned by the wealthiest 5 percent of households—who had owned more than nine-tenths of all slaves in the sample counties in 1860—fell sharply, whereas the proportion controlled by the bottom half of households very nearly doubled. This trend toward a less concentrated distribution of wealth was partially mitigated, however, by a minor increase in the concentration of real wealth during the war decade, due largely to a slight increase in the proportion of landless households, which increased in the sample counties from 43 to 47 percent. The combined result of these offsetting trends was an imperceptible, almost inconsequential decline in the overall concentration of wealth. At the close of the Civil War, as at its beginning, the white farm population of East Tennessee was characterized by a highly concentrated distribution of economic resources.

Before the Civil War, however, this highly uneven distribution of wealth had coexisted with a social order sufficiently fluid to sustain the democratic ideal that hard work should bear fruit in economic independence. If upper East Tennessee ever truly was home to a spirit of egalitarianism, it was not an egalitarianism rooted in an equality of wealth and material circumstances, despite the frequent claims of contemporary boosters (and some modern-day historians). Rather, it was an egalitarianism grounded in the perception that the local economy afforded industrious producers the realistic prospect of economic independence, both for themselves and for their descendants. Ideally, hardworking farmers could expect to accumulate over time the amount of worldly goods necessary to feed and clothe their families, support themselves in their old age, and provide a proper inheritance for their children.[42]

As late as 1860, the economy of upper East Tennessee still afforded enough economic opportunity to sustain at least the perception that the ideal remained viable. The region was not a utopia—more than two-fifths of free farm households were landless, after all. Yet, for those with the necessary diligence and patience, the chances of eventual landownership were good. The proportion of farm household heads who owned land rose steadily by age cohort and reached extremely high proportions toward the end of the life cycle; although less than one-third of household heads under thirty years of age owned their own farms, more than three-quarters of household heads over sixty were independent proprietors. Furthermore, those who successfully acquired land typically owned plots at least large enough to sustain a bare subsistence for their families. The median size of owner-operated farms in the sample counties was seventy improved acres, and about four-fifths of these (81 percent) had generated sufficient quantities of foodstuffs during the preceding year to satisfy minimum household requirements.[43]

The material underpinnings of this ideal were tenuous at best, however, and they crumbled rapidly within a generation after 1860. This was not so much because landownership per se became substantially less common. Indeed, after falling during the 1860s, the frequency of land acquisition among persisting farmers increased during the 1870s to approximate the pattern of the 1850s; among geographically persistent heads of farm households who were landless in 1870, 43.6 percent had acquired farms of their own by 1880, a rate of success less than one percentage point below that of the final antebellum decade. Similarly, the overall proportion of white farm households without land, which had risen from 43 to 47 percent during the 1860s, actually dropped below prewar levels during the next ten years, so that only 39 percent were landless by 1880.

If the dream of farm ownership still was realized widely as late as 1880, the related ideal of economic independence had become increasingly unattainable, however. Although East Tennessee as a whole remained self-sufficient in foodstuffs immediately after the war, the individual incidence of self-sufficiency among white farmers plunged dramatically.[44] By 1879, the first postbellum year for which reliable agricultural data are available, the proportion of farm operators (including tenants) who were self-sufficient in the production of foodstuffs had dropped by more than one-third, from 77 to 49 percent. No longer a pervasive characteristic, self-sufficiency by 1880 characterized scarcely half of farm operators in the "Switzerland of America."[45]

Although a dramatic reduction in food production characterized the entire South after the Civil War, the decline in upper East Tennessee is particularly intriguing because it could not possibly have been caused by the factor most frequently cited to explain plummeting food production elsewhere in the former Confederacy. As with so many other issues of importance in southern history, the most prominent investigations of declining postbellum food production have concentrated on the major cotton-producing regions of the Deep South. In attempting to explain the decreasing output of foodstuffs, scholars have posited a fundamental tension between production for household subsistence (concentration on grain and livestock) and production for market exchange (concentration primarily upon cotton). Although there is little agreement concerning either the causes or the economic rationality of the change, historians do widely agree that a pronounced shift in emphasis among southern farmers from food crops to inedible cash crops largely explains the postbellum deterioration of self-sufficiency.[46]

In upper East Tennessee—an area where the production of both cotton and tobacco was almost nonexistent—the answer certainly lies elsewhere. A careful statistical investigation suggests that the decline in self-sufficiency stemmed less from the production decisions of individual farmers than from two impersonal trends: dwindling supplies of livestock and land, relative to the farm-operating population. This conclusion is suggested indirectly by regression analysis of production patterns in 1859 and 1879, which indicates that, in both years, the value of livestock per capita and the number of improved acres per capita were the two most crucial determinants of food production on white-operated farms.[47]

With regard to both variables, the position of farm operators in upper East Tennessee deteriorated badly after 1860. As already noted, the depredations of both Union and Confederate armies, as well as of guerrillas on both sides, literally decimated livestock holdings. As late as 1880, on sample county farms the median per-capita number of swine (the most important source of meat) still was 42 percent below 1860 levels, having fallen from 2.4 to 1.4 per household member. Total per-capita meat production (including pork, beef, and mutton) had dropped by fully 50 percent, from 393 to 196 pounds. Similarly, farm size also plunged dramatically during the same two decades. The median size of white-operated farms decreased by nearly half, from seventy to thirty-eight improved acres, whereas median per-capita improved acreage fell by one-third, from ten acres to less than seven. The proportion of farms with fewer than fifty improved acres approximately had doubled, so that, by 1880, nearly three-fifths of white farmers in the sample counties operated such small plots (see figure 9.1).

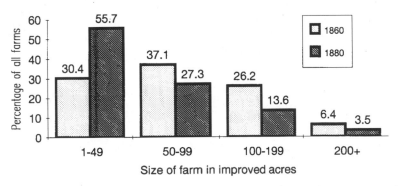

Fig. 9.1. Size Distribution of White-Operated Farms, Sample East Tennessee Counties, 1860 and 1880.

Significantly, whereas the severe decrease in livestock holdings can be attributed directly to the Civil War, the decline in farm size cannot. Average farm size falls whenever the number of farm units in a given area grows proportionally more rapidly than the supply of cultivable land. In the sample East Tennessee counties, for example, farm size plunged between 1860 and 1880, because the number of farm operators increased by 72 percent, while the amount of improved acreage grew by only 20 percent. Although something similar happened all across the former Confederacy during these years, in most other areas of the South, the breakup of the plantation system after emancipation was an essential catalyst, as former masters subdivided their holdings into small plots and rented them to the freedmen. In such areas it is appropriate to think of the Civil War as causing—or at least contributing significantly to—the dramatic decline in farm size.[48] The decline in upper East Tennessee, on the other hand, resulted primarily from two trends—one structural and one demographic—that were largely, if not entirely, independent of the war *per se.*

To begin with, between 1860 and 1880, there was a noticeable relative shift among landless whites from wage labor to tenancy. Although historians generally have assumed that white farm labor was inconsequential in the antebellum South, in 1860 nearly three-quarters (72 percent) of all landless white farm households in the sample counties were headed by farm laborers who hired out by the day, month, or year. For reasons not immediately apparent, that proportion fell over the next twenty years to 54 percent, as farm tenants increased in importance relative to wage laborers. Put another way, landowners in need of labor became relatively more likely to rent portions of their land than previously, contributing both to the increase in farm operators and the resulting decline in farm scale. The importance of this shift should not be exaggerated—wage labor still was more common than tenancy as late as 1880—but it does explain as much as one-fifth of the large increase in farm units.[49] The remainder can be explained almost entirely by an increase of more than 46 percent in the overall size of the white farm population (including both farm operators and farm laborers).[50] Although landownership continued to be widespread (as already noted, the rate of ownership actually rose between 1860 and 1880), this was made possible less by the new cultivation of virgin lands than by the extensive subdivision of existing farms.

Despite the extensive military destruction visited upon the region during the Civil War, in the long run no factor did more to undermine household subsistence in upper East Tennessee than the inexorable pressure of population growth against the region's increasingly rigid land constraint.[51]

Table 9.4 presents rates of self-sufficiency and median per-capita income (in constant 1860 dollars) for various farm size categories in 1860 and 1880. To provide a comparative context for the income figures, it is telling to note that in 1860 the typical Tennessee slave consumed thirty-one to thirty-three dollars' worth of food and nonfood items annually (exclusive of the value of housing). With this benchmark in mind, it becomes painfully clear that the economy of upper East Tennessee was undergoing a serious agricultural crisis by 1880 (well before the substantial penetration of extractive industry, incidentally). The crisis was especially severe on farms with fewer than fifty improved acres, which, by 1880, included nearly 60 percent of the total. Whereas on larger farms (units of fifty or more improved acres) self-sufficiency remained the rule and per-capita levels of income remained respectable, on farms of fewer than fifty improved acres, the rate of self-sufficiency was less than 25 percent, and the average per-capita income generated from on-farm production stood at approximately one-half the value of consumption among antebellum slaves.[52]

Even before the Civil War, however, self-sufficiency on such small farms had been precarious, to say the least; a bare majority of operators had produced enough foodstuffs to fulfill household needs, and the per-capita income from on-farm production already had fallen slightly below that of typical plantation slaves. The point is not that small farmers were, materially speaking, worse off than slaves (either before or after the war), but rather that, as early as 1860, most small farmers already must have been dependent on off-farm sources of income (hiring out, for example); on plots of less than fifty improved acres, farm operations alone simply could not provide adequately

Table 9.4

Rate of Self-Sufficiency and Median Per-Capita Income (in Constant Dollars) among White Farm Operators in Sample East Tennessee Counties, by Size of Farm, 1860 and 1880

	Proportion Self-Sufficient (%)		Median Income per Capita ($)	
	1860	1880	1860	1880
All farms	76.6	48.5	43.6	26.8
1–49 improved acres	55.7	28.1	24.7	16.6
50–99 improved acres	79.9	64.0	39.1	37.8
100–199 improved acres	91.5	86.8	60.1	70.7
200+ improved acres	97.2	99.2	107.7	120.0

SOURCE: Three-county sample of Grainger, Greene, and Johnson counties; see nn. 43, 45, and 52, this essay.

the necessities of life. Although the extensive loss of livestock incurred during the war certainly exacerbated the hardships of individual small farmers, in the long run the most salient economic development after 1860 for the region as a whole was the dramatic proportional increase in farmers relegated to such small plots. In addition to the looming specter of sectional conflict, East Tennesseans in 1860 faced another "impending crisis," one spawned not by political controversy but by population growth; its inevitable outcome would be poverty and economic dependency.

Conclusion

Our knowledge of the past, the distinguished historian Bernard Bailyn has observed, subdivides naturally into two basic categories. On the one hand, much of what we claim to know about the past might be labeled *manifest* history, a form of historical insight that relates exclusively to events in the past, of which contemporaries undoubtedly were aware and to which they consciously responded—congressional elections, military campaigns, or reform crusades, for example. On the other hand, unlike contemporary participants, modern historians also often are able to assess the impact of *latent* events, occurrences "that contemporaries were not fully or clearly aware of . . . and did not consciously struggle over, however much they might have been forced to grapple with their consequences." Examples of latent events would include subtle alterations in birth rates, sex ratios, labor markets, patterns of wealth distribution, or global terms of trade—developments profound in their impact and yet typically recognized imperfectly, if at all, at the time of their occurrence, even by those most directly affected. Although conceptually distinct elements of the past, the spheres of manifest history and latent events are complementary and overlapping, rather than mutually exclusive, and an effort to integrate the two offers the promise of a richer, fuller understanding of the complexities of the past.[53]

If the history of East Tennessee during the Civil War is at all indicative, such an approach may lead to a deeper appreciation of the tragic irony that frequently marks the human past. Undoubtedly, the American Civil War dominated the collective memory of those white East Tennesseans who endured the hardships and suffering of the years 1861–65. Their lives had been changed—intensely, rapidly, profoundly. They had been invaded by both Union and Confederate armies, victimized by prolonged guerrilla warfare, and subjected to pervasive military destruction and widespread destitution. In the space of four short years, in other words, they had witnessed a whole series of vividly manifest occurrences that had violently disturbed their world and shattered their prosperity. In 1861, the foreknowledge that they would survive the cataclysm of civil war was a source of encouragement unfortunately denied them. The additional recognition that imperceptible demographic forces unrelated to the war would silently—and permanently—undermine the very foundations of their existence was a cruel truth of which they were equally, but in this case mercifully, unaware.

Notes

1. Richard Easterlin, "Interregional Differences in Per-Capita Income, Population, and Total Income, 1840–1950," in Conference on Research in Income and Wealth *Trends in the American Economy in the Nineteenth Century* (Princeton, N.J.: Princeton Univ. Press, 1960), 74.

2. Recent surveys of the literature include Harold D. Woodman, "Economic Reconstruction and the Rise of the New South, 1865–1900," in *Interpreting Southern History: Historiographical Essays in Honor of Sanford W. Higginbotham*, ed. John B. Boles and Evelyn Thomas Nolen, 254–307 (Baton Rouge: Louisiana State Univ. Press, 1987); and Lee J. Alston, "Issues in Postbellum Southern Agriculture," in *Agriculture and National Development: Views on the Nineteenth Century*, ed. Lou Ferleger, 207–28 (Ames: Iowa State Univ. Press, 1990).

3. The number of works that deal seriously with southern Appalachia prior to 1880 is small but growing. See Margaret Ripley Wolfe, "The Appalachian Reality: Ethnic and Class Diversity," *East Tennessee Historical Society's Publications* 52–53 (1980–81): 40–60; Dwight Billings, Kathleen Blee, and Louis Swanson, "Culture, Family, and Community in Preindustrial Appalachia," *Appalachian Journal* 13 (1986): 154–70; Durwood Dunn, *Cades Cove: The Life and Death of a Southern Appalachian Community, 1818–1937* (Knoxville: Univ. of Tennessee Press, 1988); Altina L. Waller, *Feud: Hatfields, McCoys, and Social Change in Appalachia, 1860–1900* (Chapel Hill: Univ. of North Carolina Press, 1988); John C. Inscoe, *Mountain Masters: Slavery and the Sectional Crisis in Western North Carolina* (Knoxville: Univ. of Tennessee Press, 1989); Mary Beth Pudup, "The Boundaries of Class in Preindustrial Appalachia," *Journal of Historical Geography* 15 (1989): 139–62; Mary Beth Pudup, "The Limits of Subsistence: Agriculture and Industry in Central Appalachia," *Agricultural History* 64 (1990): 61–89; Paul Salstrom, "The Agricultural Origins of Economic Dependency, 1840–1880," in *Appalachian Frontiers: Settlement, Society, and Development in the Preindustrial Era*, ed. Robert D. Mitchell, 261–83 (Lexington: Univ. Press of Kentucky, 1991); Ralph Mann, "Mountains, Land, and Kin Networks: Burkes Garden, Virginia, in the 1840s and 1850s," *Journal of Southern History* 58 (1992): 411–34; and Robert Tracy McKenzie, "Wealth and Income: The Preindustrial Structure of East Tennessee in 1860," *Appalachian Journal* 21 (1994): 260–79.

4. See, e.g., *New York Times,* Jan. 28, 1866; Hermann Bokum, *The Tennessee Handbook and Immigrants' Guide* (Philadelphia: J. B. Lippincott, 1868), 8; John Trowbridge, *The Desolate South* (Hartford, Conn.: L. Stebbins, 1866), 124; and William G. Brownlow, *Sketches of the Rise, Progress, and Decline of Secession, with a Narrative of Personal Adventures among the Rebels* (Philadelphia: George W. Childs, 1862), 213.

5. For agricultural and geological characteristics of the area, see J. B. Killebrew, *Introduction to the Resources of Tennessee* (Nashville: Tavel, Eastman, and Howell, 1874; reprinted Spartanburg, S.C.: Reprint Company, 1974), 1–6, 423–47; Eugene W. Hilgard [Special Agent], *Report on Cotton Production in the United States* (Washington, D.C.: U.S. Government Printing Office, 1884), 409–11.

6. A point deftly made by William C. Harris in "The East Tennessee Relief Movement of 1864–1865," *Tennessee Historical Quarterly* 48 (1989): 86–96.

7. *Brownlow's Knoxville Whig,* May 11, 1861; Mary Emily Roberston Campbell, *The Attitude of Tennesseans Toward the Union, 1847–1861* (New York: Vantage, 1961), 291–94. The proportion of voters supporting secession was 88 percent in Middle Tennessee and 83 percent in West Tennessee; in East Tennessee, 69 percent of voters cast ballots opposing secession.

8. On the Greeneville Convention, see James W. Patton, *Unionism and Reconstruction in Tennessee, 1860–1869* (Chapel Hill: Univ. of North Carolina Press, 1934), 24–25; Charles Faulkner Bryan, Jr., "The Civil War in East Tennessee: A Social, Political, and Economic Study" (Ph.D. diss., Univ. of Tennessee, Knoxville, 1978), 60–63; Wilma Dykeman, *The French Broad* (New York: Rinehart and Co., 1955), 85–86. The Convention's "Declaration of Grievances" is reproduced in Oliver P. Temple, *East Tennessee and the Civil War* (Cincinnati, Ohio: Robert Clarke Co., 1899), 565–71.

9. *Brownlow's Weekly Whig,* Sept. 7, 1861.

10. Jesse Burt, "East Tennessee, Lincoln, and Sherman," pt. 1, *East Tennessee Historical Society's Publications* 34 (1962): 3–25; Temple, *East Tennessee and the Civil War,* 375–85; Bryan, "Civil War in East Tennessee," 74–91; Charles Faulkner Bryan, Jr., "'Tories' Amidst Rebels: Confederate Occupation of East Tennessee, 1861–1863," *East Tennessee Historical Society's Publications* 60 (1988): 3–22; David Madden, "Unionist Resistance to Confederate Occupation: The Bridge Burners of East Tennessee," *East Tennessee Historical Society's Publications* 52–53 (1980–81): 22–39.

11. Temple, *East Tennessee and the Civil War,* 386; Burt, "East Tennessee, Lincoln, and Sherman," 18; Bryan, "'Tories' Amidst Rebels," 8–11. Zollicoffer, an East Tennessean himself and a popular prewar Whig politician, was killed at the Battle of Mill Springs, Ky., in Jan. 1862.

12. Bryan, "'Tories' Amidst Rebels," 12–13; Dykeman, *French Broad,* 90–91.

13. U.S. Dept. of War, *The War of the Rebellion: A Compilation of the Official Records of the Union and Confederate Armies* (Washington, D.C.: U.S. Government Printing Office, 1880–1901; hereafter cited as *OR*), ser. 1, vol. 10, pt. 2, pp.

453–54, 521; Dykeman, *French Broad,* 79. Although there are no precise figures relating to Federal enlistments by East Tennessee Unionists, Richard Current conservatively estimates the number of white Union volunteers from the entire state at about 42,000. Because nearly three-quarters of the ballots against secession in the state referendum were cast in East Tennessee, it seems reasonable to suppose that at least three-quarters of Union enlistments originated from there as well. See Richard N. Current, *Lincoln's Loyalists: Union Soldiers from the Confederacy* (Boston: Northeastern Univ. Press, 1992), 215.

14. Spencer Henry to Andrew Johnson, Sept. 20, 1864, in *Papers of Andrew Johnson,* ed. LeRoy P. Graf and Ralph W. Haskins (Knoxville: Univ. of Tennessee Press, 1976), 4:176.

15. U.S. Congress, Joint Select Committee on the Condition of Affairs in the Late Insurrectionary States, "Affairs in the Late Insurrectionary States," H.R. 22, 42d Cong., 2d sess., 1872, pt. 1, pp. 110–11.

16. On the surplus of white farm labor in upper East Tennessee before the Civil War, see McKenzie, "Wealth and Income."

17. For example, Union troops first entered Taylorsville, the county seat of Johnson County, on Apr. 4, 1865, only five days before Lee's surrender to Grant at Appomattox, Va. See Thomas Smith Hutton Diary, Tennessee State Library and Archives, Nashville; and Samuel W. Scott and Samuel P. Angel, *History of the 13th Regiment, Tennessee Volunteer Cavalry* (Philadelphia: P. W. Ziegler, 1903).

18. See claims no. 13,864 and no. 14,119, Records of the General Accounting Office, RG 217, NA. Although filed in hope of receiving compensation for items taken by Union forces, affidavits of East Tennessee Unionists filed with the Southern Claims Commission invariably mention the depredations of Confederate troops.

19. *Harper's Weekly,* Oct. 24, 1863; Thomas A. R. Nelson to Brig. Gen. S. P. Carter, Dec. 26, 1863, in *OR,* ser. 1, vol. 31, pt. 3, p. 508. On Burnside's invasion generally, see Harold S. Fink, "The East Tennessee Campaign and the Battle of Knoxville in 1863," *East Tennessee Historical Society's Publications* 29 (1957): 79–117; Jesse Burt, "East Tennessee, Lincoln, and Sherman," pt. 2, *East Tennessee Historical Society's Publications* 35 (1963): 54–75; and Digby Gordon Seymour, *Divided Loyalties: Fort Sanders and the Civil War in East Tennessee* (Knoxville: Univ. of Tennessee Press, 1963).

20. *OR,* ser. 1, vol. 31, pt. 3, p. 508; Dykeman, *French Broad,* 112. See also Gen. W. T. Sherman to Gen. U. S. Grant, Dec. 1, 1863, and Dec. 11, 1863, *OR,* ser. 1, vol. 31, pt. 3, pp. 297, 382.

21. Seymour, *Divided Loyalties,* 191–221; Bryan, "Civil War in East Tennessee," 124–31.

22. James Longstreet, *From Manassas to Appomattox: Memoirs of the Civil War in America* (Bloomington: Indiana Univ. Press, 1960), 520; J. E. Jacobs to Clinton B. Fisk, May 28, 1866, microfilm roll 38, microcopy T142, Records of the Assistant Commissioner for the State of Tennessee, Bureau of Refugees, Freedmen, and Abandoned Lands, RG 105, NA; Bryan, "Civil War in East Tennessee," 133.

23. Dykeman, *French Broad,* 119; Samuel Milligan Memoirs, 103–5, Tennessee State Library and Archives, Nashville; *Brownlow's Knoxville Whig and Rebel Ventilator,* July 23, 1864; William E. Sloan Diary, May 18, 1865, Tennessee State Library and Archives, Nashville. See also M. S. Temple to Dear Sir [O. P. Temple], Aug. 31, 1864, O. P. Temple Papers, Special Collections, Univ. of Tennessee Library, Knoxville; "Officers of 2nd TN Cav" to Andrew Johnson, Aug. 1, 1864, and William G. Brownlow to Andrew Johnson, Nov. 21, 1864, both in *Papers of Andrew Johnson,* ed. LeRoy P. Graf (Knoxville: Univ. of Tennessee Press, 1986), 7:65–66.

24. Bryan, "Civil War in East Tennessee," 142–47; Thomas W. Humes, *Report to the East Tennessee Relief Association at Knoxville* (Knoxville: N.p., 1865), 8.

25. Colleen Morse Elliot and Louis Armstrong Moxley, eds., *Tennessee Veterans Questionnaires* (Easley, S.C.: Southern Historical Press, 1985), 3:1081, 3:974.

26. J. E. Jacobs to Clinton B. Fisk, May 28, 1866, microfilm roll 38; Wm. A. Maloney to J. E. Jacobs, May 20, 1866, microfilm roll 40; D. Burt to William P. Carlin, Apr. 30, 1867, microfilm roll 38, microcopy T142, Records of the Assistant Commissioner, Bureau of Refugees, Freedmen, and Abandoned Lands, RG 105, NA; Trowbridge, *Desolate South,* 124.

27. See, e.g., the remarks of Confederate sympathizer O. R. Broyles, in Broyles to T. A. R. Nelson, July 24, 1865, in T. A. R. Nelson Papers, East Tennessee Historical Society, Knoxville.

28. Frank W. Klingberg, *The Southern Claims Commission* (Berkeley: Univ. of California Press, 1959), 17.

29. Claims no. 14,115 and no. 13,549, Records of the General Accounting Office, RG 217, NA; Klingberg, *Southern Claims Commission,* 19, 192. Klingberg concludes that there were so many restrictions and limitations on filing that "it is probable that for every man or woman who filed an honest claim, there were at least four who, with equal qualifications of Unionism and property, failed to do so" (164).

30. Jacob M. Bowley to Andrew Johnson, Dec. 2, 1864, in Graf, ed., *Papers of Andrew Johnson,* 7:325–26.

31. The quotations are from Arnold J. Toynbee, quoted in C. Vann Woodward, *Origins of the New South, 1877–1913* (Baton Rouge: Louisiana State Univ. Press, 1951), viii.

32. The overall wealth figures are based upon estimates made by heads of farm households and given to the census enumerator; the estimates are supposed to represent the "full market value" of property owned by that household, regardless of "any lien or encumbrance," and regardless of whether the property actually was situated within that enumeration district or county. I define the "farm population" to include all households in which one or more members reported an agricultural occupation—whether "farmer," "tenant," "farm laborer," or "farm hand"—to the census enumerator. The ratio of farm households to total households in 1860 was .77 in Grainger County, .76 in Greene, and .83 in Johnson. The total number of households studied was 4,216 in 1860 and 5,099 in 1870. For instructions to census enumerators, see Carroll D. Wright and William C. Hunt, *The History and Growth of the United States Census,* S. Doc. 194, 56th Cong., 1st sess., 1900.

33. Serious defects in the 1870 agricultural census prevent an accurate comparison of 1860 and 1870 farm values or farm sizes. Tax assessments on real estate constitute a potential alternative but appear highly unreliable. Between 1859 and 1867 (the date of the first complete postwar assessment), the assessed value per acre of land fell approximately 21% in the three sample counties. The accuracy of these figures, it must be stressed, is highly suspect. See *Appendix to Senate and House Journals, Tennessee, 1859–1860* (Nashville: E. G. Eastman and Co., 1860), 26–27; *Appendix to Senate Journal, Tennessee, 1867–1868* (Nashville: N.p., 1868), 55.

34. The precise proportion present in both census years was 53%. This conclusion, as well as the subsequent discussion of economic mobility among geographically persistent households, is based on an analysis of a random sample of 1,487 heads of farm households drawn from the three sample counties. The total sample represents a weighted composite of separate random samples for each of the counties. Each county sample is stratified by tenure category: *farm owners* (those who appeared in the agricultural census and reported ownership of real estate on the population census), *tenants* (those who appeared on the agricultural schedule but reported no real estate), and *farmers or farm laborers without farms* (household heads who reported agricultural occupations on the population schedule, but who were absent from the agricultural schedule). In searching for sample household heads in 1870, I confined my examination to the county of origin and made no further attempt to locate farmers who emigrated. To verify instances of persistence, I checked not only the name and age of the household head but also the names and ages of spouses and dependent children.

35. This estimate is based on a backwards-linkage analysis of sampled 1870 households in Greene and Johnson counties. See Robert Tracy McKenzie, "From Old South to New South in the Volunteer State: The Economy and Society of Rural Tennessee, 1850–1880" (Ph.D. diss., Vanderbilt Univ., 1988), 225.

36. The Gini coefficients given in table 9.3 compare closely with those for other rural areas in 1860. Randolph B. Campbell and Richard G. Lowe, e.g., compute a Gini coefficient of total wealth concentration of 0.74 for East Texas in 1860. Jonathan Wiener does not include Gini coefficients in his study of landholding in the Alabama Black Belt, but one can calculate from his published decile table a coefficient of 0.68. See Randolph B. Campbell and Richard G. Lowe, *Wealth and Power in Antebellum Texas* (College Station: Texas A&M Univ. Press, 1977), 46; and Jonathan Wiener, *Social Origins of the New South: Alabama, 1860–1885* (Baton Rouge: Louisiana State Univ. Press, 1978), 15. Works emphasizing the egalitarian structure of preindustrial Appalachian society include Harry M. Caudill, *Night Comes to the Cumberlands: A Biography of a Depressed Area* (Boston: Atlantic Monthly, 1963); Jack E. Weller, *Yesterday's People: Life in Contemporary Appalachia* (Lexington: Univ. Press of Kentucky, 1965); John Gaventa, *Power and Powerlessness: Quiescence and Rebellion in an Appalachian Valley* (Urbana: Univ. of Illinois Press, 1980); Ronald D Eller, *Miners, Millhands, and Mountaineers: Industrialization of the Appalachian South, 1880–1930* (Knoxville: Univ. of Tennessee Press, 1982); and Waller, *Feud.*

37. Temple, *East Tennessee and the Civil War,* 80–81.

38. Frederick A. Bode and Donald L. Ginter, *Farm Tenancy and the Census in Antebellum Georgia* (Athens: Univ. of Georgia Press, 1986), app. D; Randolph B. Campbell and Lowe, *Wealth and Power in Antebellum Texas,* 108–11.

39. See, e.g., Temple, *East Tennessee and the Civil War,* 80–81; Brownlow, *Sketches of the Rise, Progress, and Decline of Secession,* 211.

40. *Brownlow's Knoxville Whig and Rebel Ventilator,* Feb. 20 and 27, 1864. On the Republican critique of northern free-labor society, see Eric Foner, *Free Soil, Free Labor, Free Men: The Ideology of the Republican Party before the Civil War* (New York: Oxford Univ. Press, 1970), ch. 1.

41. For a brief explanation of the Gini coefficient, see Charles M. Dollar and Richard J. Jensen, *Historian's Guide to Statistics: Quantitative Analysis and His-torical Research* (New York: Holt, Rinehart, and Winston, 1971), 122–26.

42. On the pervasiveness of such values, esp. outside the Black Belt, see Barbara Jeanne Fields, "The Nineteenth-Century American South: History and Theory," *Plantation Society* 2 (1983): 7–27; Forrest McDonald and Grady McWhiney, "The South from Self-Sufficiency to Peonage: An Interpretation," *American Historical Review* 85 (1980): 1095–1118; Steven Hahn, *The Roots of Southern Populism* (New York: Oxford Univ. Press, 1983), 29–39; Harry L. Watson, "Conflict and Collabo-ration: Yeomen, Slaveholders, and Politics in the Antebellum South," *Social His-tory* 10 (1985): 273–98; Lacy K. Ford, Jr., *Origins of Southern Radicalism: The South Carolina Upcountry, 1800–1860* (New York: Oxford Univ. Press, 1988), 49–51.

43. Estimates of food self-sufficiency in 1860 (crop year 1859) are based on a ran-dom, stratified sample of 1,041 farm operators drawn from the agricultural and popu-lation censuses for the three sample East Tennessee counties. Employing census data for livestock inventories and crop outputs, and relying on contemporary esti-mates concerning the consumption requirements of animals and humans, I have esti-mated the frequency with which individual farm operators produced adequate quan-tities of grain and meat to sustain their families without reliance on off-farm sources. I estimate total food production by summing the yield of grains, peas and beans, and potatoes (reduced to reflect seed allowances for the following year and converted to corn-equivalent units for comparability) and adding to that total the estimated out-put of beef, mutton, and pork (inferred from livestock inventories and grain sur-pluses and also converted to corn-equivalent units, at the ratio of 7.6 net pounds of meat per bushel of corn.) I also assume that, on average, tenants paid one-third of all major grains to their landlords as rent. For a full discussion of the methodology, see Robert Tracy McKenzie, *One South or Many? Plantation Belt and Upcountry in Civil War–Era Tennessee* (New York: Cambridge Univ. Press, 1994), app. B.

44. Using aggregate, county-level census data on crop and livestock produc-tion, I calculate an "index of self-sufficiency" in total foodstuffs (the index is a ra-tio of total food production to the estimated quantity of food necessary for the subsistence of both humans and livestock). For all of East Tennessee in 1879, the

index is 1.15. Although substantially lower than that for 1859 (1.39), the index clearly suggests that the region as a whole remained self-sufficient in basic food-stuffs. For a discussion of the self-sufficiency index, see Sam Bowers Hilliard, *Hog Meat and Hoecake: Food Supply in the Old South, 1840–1860* (Carbondale: Southern Illinois Univ. Press, 1972), 158

45. Estimates of food self-sufficiency in 1880 (crop year 1879) are based on a random, stratified sample of 1,211 white farm operators, drawn from the agricultural and population censuses for the three sample East Tennessee counties. The method of computing self-sufficiency is identical to that outlined in n. 43 above, except that the grain output of all share tenants is reduced by one-half, rather than by one-third, to reflect rent.

46. See, e.g., Robert Higgs, "Race, Tenure, and Resource Allocation in Southern Agriculture, 1910," *Journal of Economic History* 33 (1973): 149–69; Roger Ransom and Richard Sutch, "The 'Lock-in' Mechanism and Overproduction of Cotton in the Postbellum South," *Agricultural History* 49 (1975): 405–25; Gavin Wright and Howard Kunreuther, "Cotton, Corn, and Risk in the Nineteenth Century," *Journal of Economic History* 35 (1975): 526–51; and Robert McGuire and Robert Higgs, "Cotton, Corn, and Risk in the Nineteenth Century: Another View," *Explorations in Economic History* 14 (1977): 167–82.

47. The equations below show the crucial influence of livestock holdings and farm size on food output, after controlling for variations in crop mix and form of tenure.

$$1860: \quad F = 11.3 + 3.5A + 0.3L + 0.1C - 1.8T, \qquad R^2 = 0.59$$
$$(3.4) \quad (19.0) \quad (12.3) \quad (0.03) \quad (-0.2)$$

$$1880: \quad F = -13.9 + 2.9A + 0.8L + 0.1C + 8.6F + 13.9S, \qquad R^2 = 0.62$$
$$(-4.6) \quad (13.7) \quad (16.2) \quad (0.2) \quad (0.6) \quad (2.8)$$

where F equals net per-capita food production (the total amount of grain and meat produced, reduced to reflect livestock feed and seed requirements and converted to corn-equivalent bushels); A represents improved acreage per capita; C is the number of pounds of cotton grown per bushel of corn; L equals value of livestock per capita; T is a dummy variable distinguishing tenants from owner-operators (used only for 1860); F and S are dummy variables distinguishing fixed-rent tenants and share tenants or sharecroppers, respectively (used only for 1880).

T-statistics are in parentheses. The standardized beta coefficients in the 1880 equation for L and A are 0.46 and 0.40, respectively, indicating that per-capita livestock holdings and improved acreage exercised a roughly comparable influence upon food production in that year.

48. Figures on farm size may be derived from U.S. Bureau of the Census, *Report on the Production of Agriculture in the United States at the Tenth Census [1880]* (Washington, D.C.: U.S. Government Printing Office, 1883), 25.

49. That is, the increase in farm operators between 1860 and 1880 would have been approximately one-fifth smaller had the ratio between tenants and farm laborers remained constant.

50. Undoubtedly, this vigorous growth rate was primarily the result of natural increase. For evidence of dynamic population growth in southern Appalachia during the late 19th century, see Paul Salstrom, *Appalachia's Path to Dependency: Rethinking a Region's Economic History, 1730–1940* (Lexington: Univ. Press of Kentucky, 1994), esp. xv–xvii.

51. The best brief explication of this point is in Salstrom, "Agricultural Origins of Economic Dependency."

52. The census does not provide enough information to construct an exact evaluation of farm income. By applying regional wholesale price data (published in Knoxville newspapers), however, it is possible to produce a rough estimate equal to the total value of grain production, meat production, and household manufactures per farm. To derive a crude approximation of net farm income, the value of total production has been reduced to account for crops fed to livestock or retained for seed. The production of tenants has been modified further to reflect rent payments, whereas that of slaveowning operators (for 1860) also has been adjusted to account for the costs of slave maintenance, including not only the value of food that the slaves consumed but also estimated costs of clothing and medical supplies. For a more extended explanation of the method of computation, see McKenzie, *One South or Many?*, app. C.

53. Bernard Bailyn, "The Challenge of Modern Historiography," *American Historical Review* 87 (1982): 1–24, quotation from 10.

10

Premature Industrialization in Appalachia: The Asheville Armory, 1862–1863

Gordon B. McKinney

When Robert E. Lee's army retreated toward its surrender at Appomattox, it had no food but plenty of weapons and ammunition.[1] This seeming paradox—that an agricultural nation could not feed its armies but was capable of supplying its armaments—has been noted by many observers. There is general agreement that this surprising result is due in large part to the personnel overseeing Confederate government departments in these areas. Many historians credit Josiah Gorgas, chief of ordnance of the Confederate army, with the imaginative policies that provided the military supplies for the soldiers in gray.[2] While most of the rifles used by Confederate soldiers were brought through the blockade from Europe or "liberated" from captured or fallen Union soldiers, approximately seventy-five thousand pieces of ordnance were produced at small factories scattered throughout the southern states.[3] Gorgas took great pride in establishing an arms industry where none had existed before. In a self-congratulatory note in his diary entry for April 8, 1864, Gorgas listed all the manufacturing concerns that he had started. These included "a rifle factory at Ash[e]ville."[4] The Asheville Armory, then, was a significant part of the Confederate war effort.

At the same time, the development of an armory in western North Carolina was one of the first attempts to establish a modern integrated manufacturing concern in the Southern Mountains. The ultimate failure of this experiment tells us a great deal about the limited options available to the Confederacy, and about the obstacles in the way of anyone who sought to bring industry to the mountain South. Mary A. DeCredico, in her study of Confederate Georgia, asserts that one of the most important preconditions for the success of Confederate armories in Georgia was the existence of a diversified urban business community capable of providing the managerial skills needed to run a large business.[5] While some mountain men had developed successful trading networks, virtually no one had organized and run a factory. This was especially true in western North Carolina, including Asheville.[6] Equally important, mountain men and women had not developed the skills, attitudes, or discipline necessary for them to work successfully in a factory setting. In addition, modern transportation in the form of railroads had just reached the edge of the mountains in the late 1850s, and no tracks had crossed the Blue Ridge to Asheville.

Despite similar obstacles in other sections of the Southern Mountains, recent studies of antebellum Appalachia have concluded that industrial activity was much more widespread than previously had been thought. More than a dozen iron-making bloomery forges were located in the western North Carolina counties of Ashe, Cherokee, and Watauga in the 1850s. These small concerns produced iron used by blacksmiths and other craftspersons for local and regional markets.[7] A study of a large iron forge in southwestern Virginia provides details concerning the production methods used by these businesses.[8] Another scholarly investigation of that same region documents the existence of firms sending lead, iron, copper, salt, and coal to market over the recently completed Virginia and Tennessee Railroad.[9] In northwestern Virginia, the salt workers of the Kanawha Valley produced a large volume of their commodity for a national market.[10] It is important to point out that most of these establishments were involved in extracting raw materials, with relatively few workers being engaged in the production of finished items.[11]

A small number of factories did produce for sale directly to the consumer, but they did not require highly skilled labor. In western North Carolina, for example, three textile mills were in operation before 1860 in Wilkes and Caldwell counties.[12] Most of the workers in these factories were unskilled, younger members of neighboring farm families. Not unexpectedly, they did not develop into a reliable and productive labor force during this period. It is also important to note that these factories were located east of the Blue Ridge escarpment, and they had relatively greater access to railroads than did businesses west of the mountain chain.

Ironically, Asheville's location west of the Blue Ridge was one of the reasons why the Confederacy established an armory in the North Carolina highlands. By the fall of 1862, military pressure by the Union armies left large segments of Tennessee, Virginia, and Louisiana unavailable for Confederate use. In addition, raids by Union cavalry units threatened many other areas. The result was that the Confederacy was forced to locate its most of its major factories in the relatively safe states of Georgia, Alabama, South Carolina, and North Carolina. Asheville appeared an unlikely destination for a Federal army and from that perspective was an attractive site. But the primary impetus came from local businessmen, who, without any direct government assistance, created their own arms-making concern. As early as July 1861, William L. Henry of Asheville was corresponding with Gov. Henry T. Clark of North Carolina about a proposal to manufacture "Rifle guns" for the Confederacy.[13] Nothing came of this particular venture, but the idea of constructing an arms factory was not forgotten. It was resuscitated when, on August 5, 1861, Col. Robert W. Pulliam became the agent for the Confederate Ordnance Bureau in his home region of western North Carolina. To assist with his task of obtaining and repairing small arms, he contracted with a company in which he had a financial interest. His fellow entrepreneurs were Col. Ephraim Clayton and Dr. George Whitson of Asheville. Clayton, who specialized in producing finished timber and directing small construction projects, was put in charge of adapting his large wood-planing building to house workers involved in the project.[14]

Like most businessmen in the mountains of this time, Pulliam, Clayton, and Whitson ran their organization with a minimum of structure. Pulliam, for example, did not submit his contract to Richmond for approval and purchased all of his supplies locally and without authorization. In addition, he ran the fiscal side of the business out of his store and often issued the workers store script instead of currency for wages.[15] According to a list submitted by Pulliam in November 1862, 107 workers were employed at the factory. Not surprisingly, 87 of the workers were eligible for the Confederate draft and 8 others subject to service in the state militia.[16] While these figures do not prove that one of the motivations behind the initiation of the business was to avoid military service, undoubtedly some, if not many, of the laborers welcomed their exempt status. By January 1862, this concern was functioning well enough to start producing rifles.[17]

All of this was revealed to an astonished Gorgas in November 1862, when A. W. King, the master armorer of the Asheville factory, wrote to Gorgas to ask him where he should ship the two hundred rifles recently completed at the works. The meticulous Gorgas was stunned to discover the existence of an arms-producing factory in the Confederacy that previously had been unknown to him.[18]

He immediately dispatched W. S. Downer, superintendent of armories, to inspect the plant and to report back to him. Downer's report was devastating. Downer stated that "Mr. Pulliam has a great deal of private business to attend to, which from what I can learn, keeps him absent from the Armory the greater portion of the time." Downer's assessment of Whitson was equally unnerving: "[He] is a gentlemen of general genius but no practical knowledge of mechanics." Despite this latter disability, Downer discovered that Whitson had directed part of the operations of the gun making until recently. Nor were the workers any better at their work. The obviously dismayed Downer relayed to Gorgas that "the tools and machines . . . were mere makeshifts and the work carried on almost at the discretion of the men employed." The result was that "the guns were made worthless and the labor performed . . . worse than thrown away."[19] It is probable that Pulliam and his associates were not deliberately defrauding the government of the Confederacy. They were simply doing business in the pattern normal for western North Carolina. It was most unusual for managers and workers in highland commercial establishments to be highly skilled specialists. Instead, they and the farming population they served found that talented generalists—jacks-of-all-trades—were more useful in the local economy than highly skilled workers in a single trade.

Clearly, the Confederacy could not afford to allow resources to be used in this manner. Within a month, Capt. Benjamin Sloan was appointed to assume command of the newly discovered works. Sloan, a former Confederate ordnance inspector at the large Tredegar Works outside Richmond, understood how a modern factory should be organized.[20] Unlike the other small businesses located in western North Carolina before the war, which were characterized as "small, poorly capitalized, [and] short-lived," the armory now would be well capitalized and would maintain a large labor force.[21] Sloan estimated that, in the first three months of operation, he would require $32,000 to run the armory. Among the larger items in the budget were: $18,000 for "Labor & Stock fabricating new rifles," $6,500 for "Pur. & fabrication of new machy. & Tools," and $1,000 for "Completing New Smithery."[22] Nor was this request simply inflated by unusual startup costs. Sloan's request for funds for April through June 1863 rose to nearly $46,000.[23] The first task of the commander was to complete building the two brick structures to house the parts of the manufacturing process and to secure the machine tools necessary to fabricate the weapons.

Sloan reported to Gorgas on April 15, 1863, that all the tools and machines needed to begin production had been purchased or had been made at the armory.[24] Now all that was needed was an adequate work force and the materials necessary to produce the rifles.

A skilled work force was essential for the manufacture of rifles in the Confederacy. Because each factory had its own set of specially created tools—obviously the case at Asheville—"Confederate guns were all practically hand-made, with very little interchangeability of parts."[25] To help secure an adequate work force, Sloan reappointed Clayton to a key managerial position, overseeing "all Carpenters work and control of teams and teamsters, wood choppers, Coal Burners and saw mill hands."[26] Sloan defended his choice of Clayton to Gorgas by noting his "knowledge of the people and his influence with them."[27] Further considerations were that the main building of the armory was Clayton's reconditioned planing factory and that the armory was located on his land.[28]

Clayton's role was absolutely crucial, because many of the local men never had worked in a carefully structured environment like that governing many of the work practices. For example, Sloan found it necessary to decree that workmen no longer would receive their pay at Pulliam's store.[29] A couple of months later, an obviously irritated Sloan announced that workers who left their work area without the permission of their foreman and the master armorer were to forfeit double their pay for the time missed.[30] Despite Clayton's knowledge of the local people, many workers proved unable to accept the demands imposed upon them by the new workplace. Of the approximately 123 workers employed by the armory in January 1863, Sloan fired 20.[31] This 16-percent turnover in one month is a clear indication that many local men resisted the new discipline required by factory work.

Since most of the workers at the armory were subject to conscription and would be liable for military duty if they lost their positions, a semblance of discipline was maintained among the remaining workers. The men worked a ten-hour day during the winter and eleven hours during the summer when daylight hours were longer.[32] Apparently they were expected to work on Saturday but were granted time-and-a-half pay when they worked longer hours and double pay for any Sunday work. They were paid on a sliding scale from $5.15 a day for a foreman to as little as $1.00 a day for an unskilled laborer. A teamster with his own wagon and four horses could earn as much as $8.00 a day.[33] Even considering the high rate of inflation that plagued the Confederacy during this period, these wages were very substantial. This seems especially true when one realizes that a private in the Confederate army was paid $11.00 a month.

Despite the ample wages and the threat of conscription, Sloan found it difficult to retain an adequate work force. Part of the reason for this was that he did not prove to be efficient in sending those who lost their jobs into the army.[34] To secure a more compliant work force, Sloan, like many upper-class southerners for more than two centuries before him, turned to hiring African Americans.[35] In March 1863, he placed an advertisement in the *Asheville News* for "Ten negro men."[36] Black workers were resented, however, by a local community that suddenly found itself overwhelmed by slaves whose masters had removed them from eastern and central North Carolina and from lowland South Carolina to the relative safety of the mountains.[37] Allen, a worker at the armory and an enslaved person owned by W. F. M. Galbraith of Yorkville, South Carolina, was severely whipped by a mob during the evening of January 13, 1863. He was caught by some local roughs without a "pass" from the armory. He ran away from the factory for one day, but he soon returned and proved to be a reliable worker.[38]

Even when a more reliable work force had been secured, Sloan's problems did not abate. Many of the mountain workers at the factory now were expected to master a specialty. The workers were divided into four departments—Locks, Stocks and Machine, Smith Shop, and Barrel.[39] Each of these specializations was directly related to the production of rifles, the chief product of the armory. In addition, the armory required substantial numbers of people to purchase supplies, cut wood, haul materials, and perform other nonmanufacturing tasks that allowed the factory to function. These jobs included constructing the buildings and tools needed to run the business. Correspondence found in the armory's letterbook indicates that skilled personnel were scarce and difficult to retain.

Even when all of the proper personnel were in place, Colonel Sloan could not guarantee that they would be able to work. Just a few weeks after he took over, Sloan requested weapons for his workers from the government in Richmond. In early January, Unionists had raided the nearby community of Marshall to secure salt and other supplies denied them by their Confederate neighbors.[40] In the tense atmosphere of the wartime South, inhabitants of Asheville assumed that further raids would be directed at them.[41] In response, Sloan reported, "The operatives have been organized into a company to resist any attempt to destroy Government Property at this place, by disloyal persons."[42] Five months later, Sloan was appealing to Richmond for some artillery which he felt would be most useful to "intimidate the disloyal."[43] Thus, Sloan and his workers were forced to take time out of their demanding schedule to insure that their facility was safe from hostile raiders.

While the loss of production was a major concern for the worried commander, it was not the only one. He reported to his superiors that "many of these men indeed will embrace the first opportunity of joining the enemy[.]"[44] That Sloan's assessment of the Unionist sympathies of some of his workers and part of the general population was accurate was clearly demonstrated when three peace meetings were held in the Asheville area in July and August 1863.[45] While technically protests against Confederate policies, these gatherings generally were viewed as welcoming the end of the war, even if it meant the loss of southern independence. An election campaign for Confederate Congress was going on at the same time that the protest meetings were being held. One of the candidates, George W. Logan, was widely perceived as the candidate of those opposed to the Confederate government. His supporters called for a peace negotiated through a peace convention outside the regular political institutions.[46] While the political leanings of the individual workers at the armory are unknown, it is safe to conclude, with Sloan, that they were not enthusiastic supporters of the Confederacy. Thus, even under the best of circumstances, the work force at the Asheville Armory must be viewed as poorly prepared, in terms of both skills and motivation, to perform its tasks efficiently.

Even if the dubious loyalty and lack of industrial discipline of the workers could have been overcome, that would not have guaranteed that the products would be produced efficiently. Sloan's successor, Capt. C. C. McPhail, was asked to evaluate the mountain laborers in December 1863 and concluded: "There are, I find, very few first class workmen among the employees here, they are mostly novices & learning the various branches of the profession."[47] Sloan himself fired one engineer at the plant for "repeated and dangerous neglect of duty."[48] There is no reason to doubt the validity of these assessments that the general absence of industrial skills among mountain workers was a formidable barrier to the success of manufacturing entities requiring skilled workers.

Nor was this incompetence limited to workers at the immediate site. The most glaring example of this problem was the poor performance of a local company that produced pig iron, a crucial material used at the armory. McKinna and Orr—soon to become McKinna and Patton—operated a small mill owned by Leonard Cagle in the Davidson's River community of Henderson County. Sloan was so displeased with their performance at one point that he fired everyone in the business and ordered them into the army.[49] Apparently he did not follow through on this threat, because they were still contractors when McPhail took control. In his usual frank manner, McPhail evaluated their performance as follows: "The quality of your iron is, I must say, miserable, arising from palpable neglect & want of exercise of proper attention & skill in forging it. The quantity also falls below what might be reasonably expected."[50]

Although the problems posed by the employees were substantial, they were not the only ones faced by the embattled commanders of the Asheville Armory. A second and equally vexing conundrum was the transportation system that served the arms factory. Since the Asheville area of western North Carolina did not provide many of the raw materials and finished products needed to produce rifles, these supplies had to be brought in from outside. The most efficient way to do this was to ship the goods to the edge of the mountains in East Tennessee, upper South Carolina, or Burke or Rutherford County in North Carolina. From there the goods would have to travel "by stage line" to Asheville.[51] At best, this was a cumbersome system, and, under the pressures of the war, transportation in the mountains proved problematical. One correspondent reported in the spring of 1863 that many of the bridges on the turnpike leading to Asheville were "entirely gone" and that travel was quite hazardous.[52] Even government officials were forced to admit that the normal pattern of travel to western North Carolina had been thoroughly disrupted. Nicholas W. Woodfin, North Carolina salt commissioner at Saltville, Virginia, conceded that he could not ship his precious cargo to many highland counties.[53]

Such difficulties forced Sloan and his successor to rely upon local producers as much as possible, and these often proved to be unreliable and recalcitrant. One glaring example of this phenomenon was the behavior of Pulliam's tanning company, Gains and Deaver. This concern refused to do business with the armory at all after its owner was replaced as the director of the armory; as a result, most of the factory's employees were forced to go without shoes during the harsh mountain winter.[54] Even when local suppliers did agree to furnish needed items, Sloan and McPhail learned that the articles would not necessarily be produced. This was particularly true in regard to foodstuffs. Volunteering and conscription removed many farm owners and agricultural laborers from the population, and food supplies began to decline rapidly. By 1863, the threat of starvation was quite real in many sections of western North Carolina. The situation became so serious that the state government of North Carolina provided money, food, and other necessities to county committees to distribute to the needy.[55] Under these circumstances, it is not surprising that both Sloan and McPhail resorted to threats to obtain food for which they previously had contracted.[56] Sloan even resorted to the strategy of prepaying for part of a farmer's crop as an inducement for the agriculturalist to sign a contract with the armory.[57]

Even this expedient was not sufficient to insure a steady supply of food and fodder for the armory, however. Sloan was forced to contract with out-of-state farmers to supply the goods he was unable to obtain in western North Carolina. When this policy was pursued, the inadequacy of the transportation system once again intervened. While the factory was able to purchase corn from a South Carolina farmer, the commandant was forced to pay the farmer to store the grain until Sloan could secure a sufficient number of wagons to transport the foodstuffs.[58]

Equally vital to the functioning of the armory was securing local supplies of the materials needs to construct the rifles. Three primary ingredients were needed by the armory: iron for the barrels, copper for the mountings, and hard wood for the stocks. Sloan scoured the mountains looking for every scrap of iron that could be found. Seeking a constant flow of the precious material, he was in contact with at least seven different suppliers. Finally, he was able to secure a contract with the Cranberry Iron Work in eastern Tennessee to supply three thousand pounds of iron a month.[59] Even this solution proved to be temporary, since his successor was forced to report six months later that no iron could be obtained from that source.[60] Copper was even more difficult to obtain, and the two commanders of the factory were driven to confiscating small supplies held in private hands.[61] Ironically, some delays in production even occurred when Sloan had difficulty obtaining supplies of walnut wood for stocks in the midst of one of the great hardwood forests in the world.[62] One is forced to conclude, therefore, that the Asheville Armory probably would have faced substantial difficulties even if it had had a highly skilled and highly motivated work force. The difficulties of obtaining and transporting supplies were quite significant and would have limited the production capabilities of the best craftsmen.

No sooner had the armory reached a relatively acceptable rate of production in the summer of 1863 than the exigencies of war intervened and halted production at the Asheville site. In early September, a small Union army under the command of Ambrose Burnside entered and occupied Knoxville, Tennessee.[63] The civilian population of Asheville panicked. Assuming that Burnside's next objective would be the factory complex in Asheville, they deluged North Carolina Gov. Zebulon Vance with demands that the armory be better defended or closed.[64] Sloan apparently was caught up in the same anxiety and wrote to Gorgas suggesting "the propriety of removing the Government Machinery from Asheville to some safer place."[65] Sloan followed up that letter with one to the director of Confederate conscription in North Carolina, releasing nearly the entire work force to the army.[66] Subsequent events would demonstrate that Burnside was in no position to send raiders toward Asheville immediately. However, Unionists living near Asheville did obtain weapons from Tennessee and posed a potential threat to the armory.[67] As several weeks passed, Sloan attempted to resume a lower level of production, while being prepared to leave at a moment's notice.

Removing the armory from Asheville once again demonstrated the difficulties surrounding the entire enterprise. Apparently this development was the final straw for Gorgas, who was becoming increasingly dissatisfied with Sloan's management of the facility. Sloan's successor, McPhail, generously absolved Sloan of any failure in administration and concluded that his predecessor had done as well as he could under the circumstances.[68] McPhail was given no time to try to improve the performance of the factory. In late October, a Union army force was discovered near Warm Springs in nearby Madison County. While the Federal unit was driven out of the area with relative ease, McPhail recognized that the armory was a magnet that drew the enemy toward Asheville.[69] On October 24, he ordered Master Armorer A. W. King to make the machinery ready to be transported to another location.[70] McPhail's determination to relocate is apparent, since the anticipated orders from Gorgas authorizing the move did not arrive until early November.[71] McPhail, with evident satisfaction, then released all of the workers remaining at McKinna and Patton.[72]

The armory was now closed, but it would be more than a month before any machinery would leave western North Carolina. McPhail found it impossible to secure transportation to carry the heavy cargo to South Carolina. In late November, he appealed to Confederate Gen. James Martin to provide him with the authority to impress teams and wagons. Martin apparently refused to do so, but Gen. Robert B. Vance, an Asheville resident and brother of the North Carolina governor, gave McPhail the necessary orders.[73] On November 26, McPhail reported to Gorgas that the first wagons had started on their way to Columbia, South Carolina.[74] Not until five months later, however, were the most important pieces of machinery—the boiler and the engine—transferred.[75] Thus the inefficiencies and the transportation problems that had plagued the Asheville Armory from the beginning remained a problem to the very end. The armory buildings later were used to house Union prisoners, and they finally were destroyed by a Federal cavalry unit nearly three weeks after Lee's surrender.[76]

An assessment of the role played by the Asheville Armory would appear to be a very straightforward task. The armory was a failure in every conceivable way. It used precious resources at a time of crisis and failed to

236

produce the needed product in a timely manner. These failures were not the result of human cupidity or venality. Instead, the culprits appear to have been the absence of adequate material and human infrastructure to support an integrated industrial enterprise. There is little dispute about any of this. Why this virtually impossible task was attempted is also easy enough to explain. Pulliam and his associates started their business without any idea of the proper way to conduct it. They adapted traditional mountain skills and work habits to this new challenge. The result was inadequate workmanship and scale of production.

Although the armory did not prove to be a viable business, mountain businessmen sought to take advantage of its existence. The owners of a defunct and deeply indebted newspaper eagerly sold their offices to Sloan when the new commander was looking for temporary office space.[77] Other enterprising souls were willing to attempt to build a powder mill in Asheville to complement the armory.[78] Despite these small indications of collateral development, the Confederate Ordnance Bureau adopted the Asheville Armory only as a temporary expedient and as a possible partial solution to a desperate problem.

Although the results and the motivations of the participants are clear, the insights offered into Confederate policies and the requirements for successful industrialization beyond the extraction of natural resources in the mountains need further explication. One of the first points to be noted about this unsuccessful venture is how well it was capitalized. Counting both money granted to the armory and overruns that had to be covered, the Confederacy poured more than $375,000 into the arms factory.[79] This was a very large sum of money for the time and was a much larger amount than was invested in any other western North Carolina enterprise until well after the war. Nearly two hundred men were employed in an enterprise that lasted approximately twenty-six months and produced only nine hundred rifles.[80] One is forced to conclude that, in this instance, the Confederacy, to secure its independence, was willing to resort to revolutionary changes in southern business practices.

For western North Carolina in particular and Appalachia in general, the insights to be gleaned from this episode are particularly important. Clearly, manufacturing and many other types of industrialization could come to the mountains only with a tremendous commitment of capital and outside expertise. The failure of the Asheville Armory demonstrates without question that no local elite could command the resources and work skills and instill the habits necessary for launching widespread industrialization. The first prerequisite for industrial expansion in the Southern Mountains would have to be a greatly improved transportation system. In western North Carolina and most of the remainder of the mountain South, the railroad would be the ingredient crucial for improved travel and for commercial and industrial expansion. In most of the region, large outside corporations would be the active agents of this change. In western North Carolina, however, it would be the state government, under the active leadership of Gov. Zebulon Vance, that breached the Blue Ridge. The railroads would not reach Asheville until 1880, and the economic expansion that followed was startling. The small mountain village became a bustling small city of nearly ten thousand people in less than a decade.[81] Cotton mills and other industrial enterprises appeared almost as if by magic. This same transportation system also greatly expanded the tourism business that provided alternative employment opportunities to the region's increasingly hard-pressed farming population. The most successful of the new businesses were large timber companies, often from outside Appalachia, which purchased large holdings of land and offered wage-paying jobs to the highland people. As far as can be ascertained, none of the individuals who started the armory was involved in the new enterprises. These momentous developments came at huge cost to the mountain people who were caught in the pressures of unplanned change. These pressures were due in part to the fact that control of the resources of the region had passed to outsiders. The events surrounding the creation and troubled life of the Asheville Armory were a warning that industrialization was unlikely to come to the mountain South in any other way.

Notes

1. Emory M. Thomas, *The Confederate Nation: 1861–1865* (New York: Harper and Row, 1979), 212.

2. The most complete biography of Gorgas is Frank E. Vandiver, *Ploughshares into Swords: Josiah Gorgas and Confederate Ordnance* (Austin: Univ. of Texas Press, 1952).

3. Russ A. Pritchard, "Small Arms: Confederate Long Arms," in *Encyclopedia of the Confederacy,* ed. Richard N. Current (New York: Simon and Schuster, 1993), 4:1455.

4. Frank E. Vandiver, ed., *The Civil War Diary of General Josiah Gorgas* (University, Ala.: Univ. of Alabama Press, 1947), 91.

5. Mary A. DeCredico, *Patriotism for Profit: Georgia's Urban Entrepreneurs and the Confederate War Effort* (Chapel Hill: Univ. of North Carolina Press, 1990), 21–46.

6. See David L. Carlton, "The Revolution from Above: The National Market and the Beginnings of Industrialization in North Carolina," *Journal of American History* 87 (Sept. 1990): 450–54.

7. H. Tyler Blethen and Curtis W. Wood, "The Antebellum Iron Industry in Western North Carolina," *Journal of the Appalachian Studies Association* 4 (1992): 79–87.

8. Charles B. Dew, *Bond of Iron: Master and Slave at Buffalo Forge* (New York: Norton, 1994).

9. Kenneth W. Noe, *Southwest Virginia's Railroad: Modernization and the Sectional Crisis* (Urbana: Univ. of Illinois Press, 1994), 60–64.

10. John E. Stealey, III, *The Antebellum Kanawha Salt Business and Western Markets* (Lexington: Univ. Press of Kentucky, 1993).

11. The exception was at Buffalo Forge, where approximately half the workers produced finished iron and related products. Dew, *Bond of Iron*, 63–82.

12. Richard W. Griffin and Diffee W. Standard, "The Cotton Textile Industry in Ante-Bellum North Carolina: Part II, An Era of Boom and Consolidation, 1830–1860," *North Carolina Historical Review* 34 (Apr. 1957): 161–63.

13. Wm. L. Henry to H. T. Clark, July 22, [18]61, Governor's Papers (Clark), North Carolina Division of Archives and History, Raleigh.

14. William B. Floyd, "The Asheville Armory and Rifle," *Bulletin of the American Society of Arms Collectors* 44 (1981): 21.

15. Floyd, "Asheville Armory," 22.

16. William R. Young to Zebulon B. Vance, Nov. 13, 1862, in *The Papers of Zebulon Baird Vance*, ed. Frontis W. Johnston (Raleigh: North Carolina Department of Archives and History, 1963), 1:341–44.

17. [Raleigh] *North Carolina Standard*, Jan. 29, 1862.

18. Floyd, "Asheville Armory," 22.

19. Downer's entire report is reproduced in Floyd, "Asheville Armory," 22–23.

20. Floyd, "Asheville Armory," 23.

21. H. Tyler Blethen and Curtis Wood, "The Antebellum Economy of Southwestern North Carolina" (paper delivered at meeting of Society for the History of the Early American Republic, Gettysburg College, Gettysburg, Pa., June 1992), 6.

22. "Estimate of Funds for the Asheville Armory for the First Quarter 1863," Letterbook, Confederate States of America Armory, Asheville, N.C., Accession no. 20091, Military Records, in Archives and Records Division, Library of Virginia, Richmond.

23. "Estimate of Funds for the Asheville Armory for the Second Quarter 1863," Armory Letterbook, 80.

24. B. Sloan to J. Gorgas, Apr. 15, 1863, Armory Letterbook, 82.

25. Pritchard, "Confederate Long Arms," 1455.

26. B. Sloan to E. Clayton, Dec. 31, 1862, Armory Letterbook, 9.

27. B. Sloan to J. Gorgas, Jan. 13, 1863, Armory Letterbook, 18.

28. Floyd, "Asheville Armory," 21–23.

29. B. Sloan to R. W. Pulliam, Dec. 29, 1862, Armory Letterbook, 7.

30. B. Sloan, Order No. 15, Feb. 16, 1863, Armory Letterbook, 46.

31. B. Sloan to Peter Mallett, Jan. 2, 4, and 8, 1863; Sloan, Order No. 11, Jan. 15, 1863; Sloan, Order, Jan. 22, 1863; all in Armory Letterbook, 10–11, 13–15, 23, 27–28.

32. B. Sloan to J. Gorgas, May 25, 1863, Armory Letterbook, 96.

33. "Rates of Wages, June 1863," Armory Letterbook, 126.

34. B. Sloan to Peter Mallett, Apr. 27, 1863, Armory Letterbook, 87.

35. Both the managers at the Kanawha salt works and Buffalo Forge preferred slave workers to native white mountaineers. See Stealey, *Kanawha Salt Business,* 133–57; Dew, *Bond of Iron,* 67.

36. B. Sloan to Editor of *Asheville (N.C.) News,* Mar. 21, 1863, Armory Letterbook, 70.

37. A runaway slave advertisement in the *Asheville (N.C.) News,* July 17, 1862, indicated that the escaped slaves were from the eastern North Carolina city of New Bern—just one reminder of this demographic change.

38. B. Sloan to W. F. M. Galbraith, Jan. 14 and 19, 1863, Armory Letterbook, 19, 25.

39. B. Sloan, Order, Feb. 21, 1863, Armory Letterbook, 51.

40. The most complete account of the Unionist raid on Marshall is Phillip Shaw Paludan, *Victims: A True Story of the Civil War* (Knoxville: Univ. of Tennessee Press, 1981), 84–85.

41. *Asheville (N.C.) News* reported that the Unionists "are threatening to pay Asheville a visit, and have been expected for several days." Quoted in (Raleigh) *Daily Progress,* Jan. 19, 1863.

42. B. Sloan to J. Gorgas, Jan. 10, 1863, Armory Letterbook, 17.

43. B. Sloan to J. Gorgas, June 24, 1863, Armory Letterbook, 110.

44. B. Sloan to J. Gorgas, Sept. 14, 1863, Armory Letterbook, 147–48.

45. [Raleigh] *North Carolina Standard,* August 4, 21, and 28, 1863.

46. One spokesman for the Logan campaign phrased his position as follows: "As for myself, I am in favor of peace on the best terms that can be had and at the earliest day we can get it." L. S. Gash to Zebulon B. Vance, Sept. 7, 1863, Reel no. 19, *The Papers of Zebulon Baird Vance,* ed. Gordon B. McKinney and Richard M. McMurry (Frederick, Md.: Univ. Publications of America, 1987).

47. C. C. McPhail to W. S. Downer, Dec. 2, 1863, Armory Letterbook, 220.

48. B. Sloan, Order 11, Jan. 15, 1863, Armory Letterbook, 23.

49. B. Sloan to Peter Mallett, Sept. 10, 1863, Armory Letterbook, 145–47.

50. C. C. McPhail to McKinna and Patton, Oct. 17, 1863, Armory Letterbook, 176.

51. B. Sloan, Memorandum, Feb. 11, [18]63, Armory Letterbook, 41.

52. S. H. Miller to Zebulon B. Vance, Mar. 23, 1863, Reel no. 16, McKinney and McMurry, *Papers of Zebulon Baird Vance.*

53. Nicholas W. Woodfin to Zebulon B. Vance, Oct. 1, 1863, Reel no. 20, McKinney and McMurry, *Papers of Zebulon Baird Vance.*

54. B. Sloan to J. Gorgas, Feb. 7, [18]63, Armory Letterbook, 38.

55. Paul Escott, "Poverty and Government Aid for the Poor in Confederate North Carolina," *North Carolina Historical Review* 61 (Oct. 1984): 462–80. For a contemporary comment on the legislation, see [Salem, N.C.] *People's Press,* Mar. 13, 1863.

56. B. Sloan to McKean Johnson, Jan. 29, 1863, and C. C. McPhail to C. B. Brank, Oct. 15, 1863, both in Armory Letterbook, 30, 173.

57. B. Sloan to W. Hughes, Feb. 18, 1863, Armory Letterbook, 48.

58. B. Sloan to S. S. McClanahan, Apr. 29, 1863, Armory Letterbook, 88–89.

59. B. Sloan to J. Gorgas, May 20, 1863, Armory Letterbook, 94.

60. C. C. McPhail to J. Gorgas, Oct. 21, 1863, Armory Letterbook, 180.

61. B. Sloan to G. H. A. Adams, Oct. 3, 1863, Armory Letterbook, 158.

62. B. Sloan to J. Gorgas, Feb. 2, 1863, Armory Letterbook, 33.

63. The best account of Burnside's occupation of Knoxville is William Marvel, *Burnside* (Chapel Hill: Univ. of North Carolina Press, 1991), 267–80.

64. A. S. Merrimon to Zebulon B. Vance, Sept. 7, 16, and 18, 1863; J. W. McElroy to Vance, Sept. 10, 1863; R. W. Pulliam, et al., to Vance, Sept. 16, 1863; W. Murdock to [Vance], Sept. 18 and 20, [18]63; all in Reel no. 19, McKinney and McMurry, *Papers of Zebulon Baird Vance.*

65. B. Sloan to J. Gorgas, Sept. 5, 1863, Armory Letterbook, 143.

66. B. Sloan to Peter Mallet, Sept. 10, 1863, Armory Letterbook, 145–47.

67. W. Murdock to [Zebulon B. Vance], Sept. 21, 1863, Reel no. 19, McKinney and McMurry, *Papers of Zebulon Baird Vance.*

68. C. C. McPhail to J. Gorgas, Oct. 15, 1863, Armory Letterbook, 172–73.

69. [Raleigh] *Daily Progress,* Oct. 28, 1863; [Raleigh] *North Carolina Standard,* Oct. 30 and Nov. 3, 1863.

70. C. C. McPhail to A. W. King, Oct. 24, 1863, Armory Letterbook, 187.

71. J. Gorgas to C. C. McPhail, Nov. 4, 1863, Armory Letterbook, 192.

72. C. C. McPhail to McKinna and Patton, Nov. 24, 1863, Armory Letterbook, 202.

73. C. C. McPhail to R. B. Vance, Nov. 24, 1863, and [Robert B.] Vance, Special Order, Nov. 24, 1863, both in Armory Letterbook, 201, 203.

74. C. C. McPhail to J. Gorgas, Nov. 26, 1863, Armory Letterbook, 208.

75. Floyd, "Asheville Armory," 25.

76. Ibid.

77. Jo[h]n D. Hyman to Zebulon B. Vance, Apr. 20, 1863, Reel no. 3, in McKinney and McMurry, *Papers of Zebulon Baird Vance.*

78. A. J. and W. Greenwood to Zebulon B. Vance, May 8, 1863, Reel no. 17, in McKinney and McMurry, *Papers of Zebulon Baird Vance.*

79. See a variety of reports, Armory Letterbook, 16, 29, 37, 65, 80, 91, 100, 123, 125, 139, 185, 212.

80. Floyd, "Asheville Armory," 25.

81. Ina W. Van Noppen and John J. Van Noppen, *Western North Carolina Since the Civil War* (Boone, N.C.: Appalachian Consortium Press, 1973), 257–59.

11

Lincoln's Sons and Daughters: Berea College, Lincoln Memorial University, and the Myth of Unionist Appalachia, 1866–1910

Shannon H. Wilson

My friend is asking you to send me to school and to show your love for Mr. Lincoln.
> —Fundraising postcard, Lincoln Memorial University, 1909

And no less is it consistent for us to turn . . . to devising ways and means for benefiting the unknown Lincolns, lesser but significant, who are living in our mountains.
> —"Lincoln a 'Mountain White,'" *Berea Quarterly,* 1909

For the generation who fought the Civil War and the generations who followed, there remained a problem of coming to terms not only with what happened, but with what the war meant. This task was one of memory, both individual and collective, and we may view what was forgotten as being equal in importance with what was remembered.

After Reconstruction, a tension remained between sectional and national appeals—or, put another way, between regional loyalties and national reunion. The sectional appeal, on a national level, revolved around, on the one hand, the Union's reverence for the "bloody shirt," the sacrifice of noble patriots in preserving the Union; and, on the other hand, the tragic romance of the Confederate "Lost Cause." In counterpoint to these preoccupations was the sentiment of reunion, reflected in changing attitudes and emerging social contacts between North and South, particularly in educational reform and economic development. Berea College and Lincoln Memorial University (LMU) symbolized these appeals to section and nation.

Founded by southern abolitionists, Berea College projected a vision of a New South that was to be built upon the educational and moral uplifting of blacks and mountaineers who embraced "loyal" views of northern sentiments and institutions. Lincoln Memorial University, founded by former Union Gen. O. O. Howard and Rev. A. A. Myers, an Ohio-born missionary sponsored by the American Missionary Association, sought to serve the "loyal" mountaineers of East Tennessee, western Virginia, and eastern Kentucky. Inspired by Lincoln's wartime concern for Unionist East Tennessee, LMU's founders believed their school to be symbolic of a reunited North and South. In their publicity and fundraising efforts, Berea College and Lincoln Memorial University interpreted Appalachia in ways that reflected both national "progress" and regional loyalty, ultimately defining, for many, why and by whom the Civil War was fought.

For the Union soldiers who had tramped and fought through the South, the landscape had seemed a peculiar place. Northern soldiers regarded the environment as hostile, "queer," and "foreign."[1] Within the larger confines of this "foreign" place existed an even "stranger" landscape—the "Southern Mountains." At the same time the nation began to wrestle with the experience of the Civil War and its meaning, local colorists and missionaries brought Appalachia and its people before the reading and donating public. Southern mountaineers were "peculiar," inhabiting a "strange" land. The life of the hills was an echo of frontier settlement "surviving" in the midst of national change and "progress." Romantic images of Appalachia produced in the 1870s and 1880s gave way to tales of savagery and viciousness in the 1890s, giving rise to numerous "studies" —sociological and historical— which, along with novels and short stories, portrayed the region as "different" from mainstream American middle-class society.[2] An additional "southern problem" now emerged: the white people of the mountain South. Although busy establishing schools, churches, and other useful institutions for the freedmen, northern philanthropy was called upon to restore or "uplift" the fortunes of the "hardy and loyal" mountaineers, people who "had fought for the Union though their homes were in the heart of slave territory" and "who owned the land but did not own slaves." Mountaineers finally would be ennobled as "the people that Lincoln loved" and who inhabited what Allen Batteau has termed a "Holy Appalachia."[3]

People in the mountains remembered the Civil War differently from people in other areas of the South. Rather than the national Armageddon at Gettysburg, guerrilla raids and skirmishes with partisan rangers were the archetypal highland battles, prefiguring for some early observers the feuds, which were regarded as representative of the region's "Saxon" or "Elizabethan" heritage. Further, the war had widened the horizons of those mountaineers who had "penetrated the barrier" and followed Sherman's March to the Sea. Yet the remembrance of all these events, by and large, was articulated to the larger world not by those who had participated in them, but by philanthropists who regarded Appalachia as an exotic region apart from the wider South.

The memory of the war experience was manipulated artfully to project a way of seeing and perhaps a means of thinking about Appalachia in a defined and particular manner. For northern philanthropists, the image of the "loyal South" was particularly attractive in view of renewed social and economic ties with the South, the sentiment for reunion, and the growing discomfort with "foreign" immigration. As Henry Shapiro suggests, this view also denied the realities of sectionalism "and the relevance of the Confederate past to the southern present."[4]

The image of the "loyal South" was portrayed by numerous individual writers, educators, and missionaries but perhaps most notably by Berea College in Kentucky and Lincoln Memorial University in Tennessee. Both Berea and LMU were established among southerners who were perceived as having been loyal to the Union. The location of the schools characterized their founders' efforts to "efface sectional lines" by bringing together students from North and South for the greater good of the nation. Both institutions wrapped themselves in the symbolic mantle of Abraham Lincoln, who, at least according to the publicity literature, had roots deep in the culture and traditions of the mountain people. In their location, publicity, and student recruitment, both institutions brought Appalachia and the Civil War together to form a compelling image for the generations who struggled to understand the war and its results.

Berea's appeal was founded upon the bloody sacrifice of mountain Unionists, dramatically portrayed as the heroes of Lookout Mountain and Sherman's March to the Sea. LMU, on the other hand, lauded the nobility of character of both Unionists and Confederates, shaping a message of national reunion and reconciliation.

Founded by John G. Fee, J. A. R. Rogers, and others in 1855, Berea College from the beginning was dedicated to abolitionist principles, so much so that, in December 1859, local proslavery sympathizers, fearing another John Brown–style uprising, forced the Bereans to leave their homes. Returning in 1866, Fee and his companions reopened the institution, admitting both black and white students on an equal basis. Berea's efforts were supported heavily by the American Missionary Association (AMA), the Freedmen's Bureau, and individual northern philanthropists. Further, the school found itself endorsed not only by Union Gen. O. O. Howard, but also by such luminaries as Horace Bushnell, Henry Ward Beecher, and Frederick Douglass. The college's biracial mission ended only in 1904, with the Kentucky legislature's passage of the Day Law. This law forced Berea to make an agonizing choice—to close, to change location, or to become "merely" a white school or a black school. Under the leadership of President William Goodell Frost, the son of abolitionists and grandson of abolitionist William Goodell, the trustees voted to maintain the college's efforts among mountain students, and to found Lincoln Institute in Simpsonville, Kentucky, for the displaced black students. In fact, the college's interest in biracial education had begun to wane even before passage of the Day Law. The publicity literature of Berea clearly emphasizes the college's interracial mission and philosophy from 1866 to 1892, but thereafter these publications speak only of Berea's work among the mountaineers.[5]

In 1897, the Cumberland Gap witnessed the beginning of a new school. Established on the grounds of a defunct resort, Lincoln Memorial University grew out of the expansive dreams of A. A. Myers, another AMA missionary and principal of the Harrow School at Cumberland Gap, and O. O. Howard, who traced his interest in the project back to Abraham Lincoln's concern for the people of East Tennessee. As Howard recalled in his *Autobiography,* upon his transfer from the Army of the Potomac to the Union armies near Chattanooga, Lincoln had expressed a notable compassion for the mountaineers of East Tennessee. Howard remembered the president's exclaiming, "They are loyal, there, General, they are loyal!"[6] Assisting Myers in the acquisition of the property, Howard, Darwin James, and Frederick Avery laid the foundations for a school that would serve primarily the mountain people of western Virginia, eastern Kentucky, and East Tennessee. According to its charter, drafted in 1897, LMU was to exist as "a memorial to Abraham Lincoln, . . . as an expression of renewed good will and fraternal feeling between the people of sections of this country once opposed to each other in civil war."[7]

Hardy and Loyal Men

Both Berea and LMU defined Appalachian people as "loyal." The fact that many mountaineers had not been devoted to the Union cause either was treated as largely irrelevant or merely set the stage for touching stories of reconstructed Confederates who assisted the institutions' efforts on behalf of the Unionist mountaineers. This "historical" interpretation of mountain life was cast in sharp contrast to the presumed depravity of southern culture in general. Instead of being lazy, slaveholding aristocrats and bold, impetuous cavaliers, mountaineers were depicted as industrious though poor yeoman farmers and sturdy, constant patriots. For Berea and LMU, these images of Appalachia provided an entree into the circles of support and sympathy that would sustain their prospects for mountain education.

Berea's connections to Appalachian Unionism were basic to its founding. The land given to John G. Fee by Cassius Clay, a prominent politician and emancipationist, was located near persons agreeable to Fee's abolitionist cause: the mountain people of Jackson, Owsley, and Rockcastle counties. Thus it was no accident that the first Berea "Literary Institute" catalog, published in 1867, described the area and its people in a manner that would be echoed for over thirty years:

> It [Berea] is needed scarcely less for the loyal white people of the mountainous portion of Eastern Kentucky and the similar regions in the other states adjoining, not a few of whom are eager to secure its advantages. The "hill country" of Eastern Kentucky alone, . . . has an area equal to that of Massachusetts and Connecticut combined, and though occupied by hardy and loyal men, is singularly destitute of educational advantages, which hitherto in the South have been monopolized by the wealthy class of planters. Several of these counties, not far from Berea, sent more men to the Union army, than were subject to military service. Can any part of the North show so good a record? Now that these men, their ideas enlarged and energies developed by the War, are asking for the key of knowledge, their wants must be met. Having periled their lives for the Union, the least their grateful countrymen can do, is to give them those Christian Seminaries necessary to the full development of their manhood.[8]

For Berea, several themes were introduced. First, nearly all mountaineers were "loyal" southerners, persons neglected by "the wealthy class of planters." Second, they were volunteers rather than draftees, presumably spurred by patriotic devotion in their desire to defend the Union. Moreover, mountain loyalists were numerous, adding weight to the Union cause. Fourth, the newly reunited nation was indebted to these "men of the mountains" for the price paid in blood for their patriotism. Finally, mountain people hitherto had been undeveloped, and education was the key to helping them realize their "manhood." Before the Spanish-American War and to a lesser extent before World War I, these themes formed an essential part of Berea's portrayal of mountain people to the donating public.

Lincoln Memorial University, in contrast, had no heroic past to draw upon; before Gen. O. O. Howard's visit during a speaking tour of Kentucky and Tennessee in 1896, it had been only a dream. The dreamer was A. A. Myers, who, along with his wife Ellen, had been toiling obscurely in the Harrow School at Cumberland Gap, Tennessee. The school's financial prospects were particularly bleak in the wake of the collapse of a British syndicate that had speculated in mining and timber interests in nearby Middlesboro, Kentucky. The Four Seasons Hotel property, a relic of a resort for the Middlesboro entrepreneurs and their European visitors, appeared to Myers a perfect site for a college for mountain students. Howard, impressed with Myers's fervor and apparently recalling Lincoln's interest in East Tennessee, said, "Friends, if you will make this school a larger enterprise I will take hold and do what I can."[9] Myers and Cyrus Kehr, Howard's speaking agent, secured the six hundred acres of the Four Seasons property, which included a sanitorium suitable for a classroom and residence hall. In 1898, the fledgling LMU promoted its work as an "expression of renewed good will and fraternal feeling between the North and the South." The school described mountain people in this manner:

> During the Civil War they showed great bravery and their country was desolated by the contending armies. They are a warm-hearted loyal race . . .
> On the ground of fraternity and patriotism the Highlanders must receive the co-operation of their fellow Americans. The fact is recognized that our own country draws recuperative power from the rural districts and from the "strength of the hills;" that the mountains beget a spirit of liberty and morality . . . Here are a numerous people with a good heredity and a sympathy with our traditions and institutions. Among their youth must be more Lincolns, more great minds for crises, more great hearts for humanity.[10]

Southern mountain people, as seen from LMU's perspective, then, were "brave," "warm-hearted," and "loyal," although overt Unionism was not emphasized. The heroism of these people, moreover, seems almost genetic. As in Berea's view, mountaineers were owed the debt of a grateful nation on the grounds of "fraternity" and patriotism. Among them might be "more Lincolns" to resolve the new crises facing the country as a whole. Furthermore, LMU asserted that liberty and morality were basic to mountain life and so created a foundation that would make mountaineers sympathetic to northern traditions and institutions. Finally, mountaineers were a distinguished "race" with a "good heredity." These views were fundamental to LMU's promotional efforts. Eventually, they set Berea College and Lincoln

Memorial on a collision course with regard to donors and the authority to interpret Appalachia within the parameters of the Civil War experience.

Berea's vision of hardy Unionist mountaineers, firmly established from the reopening of the college in 1866, pervaded its literature until World War I, being emphasized particularly in the 1890s. Circulars, handbills, and catalogs told the story of Berea's heroic commitment to interracial education in a slave state and of the special bond between Appalachians and African Americans:

> Located where it can to the best advantage invite the colored man from the "Blue-grass" region and the loyal whites from the mountains, the number of students has always been greater than its limited facilities could well accommodate . . .
>
> This experiment of co-education in the South is regarded by the management as the most important educational problem of the present, and toward its complete solution they ask the aid of all Christian men, and lovers of true national prosperity.[11]

Before 1895, as noted above, Berea's work was fundamentally interracial. The role of the mountain people thus was defined in terms of a love of the Union and its causes, and a respect—if not support—for the college. Berea claimed the credit for galvanizing loyalist sentiment among the mountain people during the immediate crisis of the war's outbreak: "It is not too much to say that under God, as a result in great part, of the heroic work, and patient and self-sacrificing spirit of these missionaries, a large majority of the men in Madison, and four or five adjoining hilly counties were found to be unconditional Union men when the war commenced. . . . More men went from some of the Mountain Counties into the Union Army than were subject to military service."[12]

It is clear that, some twenty years before William G. Frost's "discovery" of Appalachia, Berea College was creating an image of southern mountain people. Perhaps inspired by the writings of Rebecca Harding Davis, Edward King, and Will Wallace Harney, as well as by the experiences of his father, Edward H. Fairchild, who had been president of Berea College, Charles G. Fairchild in 1883 addressed his colleagues at the American Missionary Association: "You should remember, too, that the men who made an antislavery church and school in a slavery state years before the war were these mountain whites. The Association nursed its firstborn on these mountain slopes. As patriots, some of whose sons sleep on that southern soil, you should remember that this whole section was loyal in the battle for a united country unstained by slavery."[13]

Fairchild's speech summarized this first phase of Berea's interpretation of southern mountaineers. They had been loyal to the Union and they would be amenable to northern ideals. Mountain people had resisted slavery while not becoming abolitionists and were participating freely in the coeducation of the races, recognizing a mutual bond of suffering inflicted upon themselves and their black associates by the "wealthy class of planters."[14] Even more hopeful for northern donors was the fact that mountaineers were both numerous and Republican. A. D. Mayo, a prominent Unitarian educator and reformer, observed that "some of the [mountain] counties [were] turning out more soldiers than the entire number of voters; and today they are almost as decided in their adhesion to Republican politics."[15]

Berea's depiction of Unionist Appalachia was in keeping with sectional northern attitudes toward institutions supporting the freedmen and financed by northern philanthropy. As Nina Silber and others have shown, an inclusive type of Americanism was at work during the Reconstruction era and into the 1890s. Blacks, like mountaineers, initially were seen as loyal, hardworking Americans and were welcomed in the new reunited nation.[16] Berea was careful to be even-handed in depicting the college's work, asserting itself as:

> The OLDEST INSTITUTION in the South open to the colored race.
> The ONLY INSTITUTION in the South having equal numbers of White and Colored.
> The ONLY INSTITUTION in Kentucky reaching the White people of the Mountain districts who were loyal to the Union, but very destitute of educational advantages.[17]

The Unionist mountaineer also formed an integral part of LMU's imagery. Indeed, LMU, unlike Berea College with its interracial mission, from the first devoted itself exclusively to mountain whites. From its beginnings in 1891 as the Harrow School, LMU described mountaineers as "much retarded and crippled" by the contending armies that had pushed through the Cumberland Gap, and further isolated by the lack of railroads and markets. It was the purpose of Myers and his colleagues to furnish a school "at a price low enough to be within reach of all, and in part to pay our country's debt to these Highlanders of America by educating the children of the G.A.R. [Grand Army of the Republic] on slave soil."[18]

O. O. Howard's initial fundraising efforts on behalf of LMU were even more eloquent. Relying upon his own wartime experiences, Howard took great pains to describe the sacrifices of mountain families in their support of the Union cause. Particular qualities of the mountaineers that northern donors would find of interest were patriotism, isolation, and the need for educational opportunity. Howard wrote, for example, of his journey with the XI Corps to join the Union forces at Chattanooga: "All throughout that mountain country, . . . the people met us with extraordinary manifestation of kindness and favor. They brought out hidden Stars and Stripes; they placed tubs and pails filled with water for us by the roadside; they gathered provisions and freely offered them to the soldiers, and many sat down upon the ground and pulled off their shoes to give them to some of the men who had none. I had nowhere else met with such enthusiasm for our cause."[19]

Within this same account, Howard designated the educational work at Cumberland Gap as a "Gettysburg, a strategic point" upon which to place "monuments" of "education and all its accompaniments."[20] These basic sentiments were echoed in the university's own literature, which proclaimed that "there is no place in the land where schools will be more appreciated" and cast LMU as a school of "educational and moral influence" equipping young men and women of the mountains to "keep their beautiful section abreast with the progress of our land."[21] For Myers, Howard, and their colleagues—like the early workers at Berea College—Appalachia's people were the key to a New South and a new nation.

Effacing Sectional Lines

Reunion, the integration of northern and southern interests to form a sense of American nationalism, dominated the generation following the Civil War.[22] William Goodell Frost, O. O. Howard, and the other leaders of Berea College and LMU were workers in this task of reuniting the nation. These two men and the institutions they represented expressed particular views of mountaineers and a particular idea of what the new nation would be. The views of Frost and Howard also formed part of a struggle for memory—a contest to determine how the war would be remembered or forgotten. This process of memory was significant not only to reunion, but also in how Appalachia was presented to the public consciousness.[23]

The arrival of William G. Frost at Berea usually is associated with the nation's "discovery" of Appalachian America and with his labeling the inhabitants "our contemporary ancestors," a term Frost used in the *Berea Quarterly* in 1895.[24] The appearance of his article, "Our Contemporary Ancestors in the Southern Mountains," in the *Atlantic Monthly* in 1899 not only popularized the Appalachian discussion, but also established Frost in some circles as the major authority on the region of the Southern

Fig. 11.1. "Mountain Types. Union Veterans of the 8th K.V.I." Photograph taken at Berea Decoration Day, 1895, reproduced in *The Berea Quarterly* 1 (May 1896): 11. Reprinted here courtesy of Berea College Archives, RG 11, Berea, Ky.

Mountains. While the impact of this image has been explored elsewhere, less often noted is Frost's assertion that mountain whites were a key to the "effacing of sectional lines." The phrase was intended to persuade northern philanthropists to support southern education, in a cooperation emblematic of reunion.[25]

Berea College was not a prosperous enterprise when Frost took the reins in 1892. Nevertheless when he became president, he expressed commitment to Berea's interracial purposes. Writing to the college's trustees, Frost noted that "the peculiar work of Berea for years to come, . . . is for the colored race." He further emphasized Berea's efforts in "teaching the races to live and work together, and to afford an object lesson to the whole country."[26] In asserting Berea's work in interracial education, this perspective was consistent with the college's earlier publicity.

Frost suggested a third constituency for Berea, too—northern students who would "give a good tone to the school." As their numbers increased, their presence might help bring more southern whites to Berea as well.[27] Frost's suggestion regarding northern students, no doubt a reflection of his own northern abolitionist background, was not unlike the views of other northerners who believed that immigration of northerners into the South would "civilize" the region, insuring its loyalty and patriotism within the Union.[28] For himself, Frost clearly became convinced shortly thereafter that the mountaineer would be decisive in the effort to build a "New England" in the South.

Frost regarded the education of mountaineers as the answer to the "Southern Problem," which he defined as "the divergence and estrangement of the two halves of our country—it is the impact of the two sets of dominant ideas."[29] The South, in Frost's view, could not be "intellectually subjugated," but its problems could be resolved by a liberal southern leadership educated at Berea College.[30] Publicity literature labeled Berea College as a "Work That Wins," an institution escaping the "opprobrium of a 'carpet-bag' institution" because it was founded by antislavery southerners "before the war" and because it was located "in the edge of that inland mountain realm which did so much to save the Union, and which is to affect the South and the whole country so deeply in coming years."[31]

The coming years, into the first decade of the twentieth century, saw this same message consistently repeated. The *Berea Quarterly*, established in 1895 as an "organ" for Berea's fundraising efforts and sent to the college's friends and supporters, quickly became a pioneer journal of Appalachian life and culture. Before it ceased publication in 1916, the quarterly printed no less than twenty articles discussing, or at least substantially mentioning, the Civil War, including several works celebrating Abraham Lincoln's alleged connections to Appalachia. Notable among these pieces were Gen. Jacob D. Cox's 1895 essay, "The Mountain People in the Struggle for the Union," and William E. Barton's 1897 article, "The Cumberland Mountains in the Struggle for Freedom." Cox, a member of Union Gen. Ambrose E. Burnside's staff during the Knoxville campaign of 1863, lauded the devotion of mountain people, asking, "What better security for a great future can there be than devoted and self-sacrificing patriotism, constancy in suffering, patience under tribulation, courage in honest strife, modest simplicity when the victory is won?"[32] Meanwhile, Barton, a Berea trustee and ultimately a noted Lincoln scholar, placed Berea and its founders among the largely unknown or unrecognized abolitionist elements of the South, while citing statistics concerning loyal troops from various states in the Confederacy. Subsequent issues featured Barton's novel, *A Hero in Homespun,* an "authentic" story of a loyal mountaineer soldier, and articles by Barton on "Old Plantation Hymns" and "Hymns of the Slave and the Freedman," as well as Thomas Higginson's "John G. Fee: A Southern Abolitionist."[33] These articles by Cox and Barton, among others, reflected a serious effort by Berea to present documentary evidence of the worthiness of Appalachian southerners and of their need for educational support, based primarily upon their contributions during the Civil War. The views reiterated in the college's publicity literature possibly were best summarized by Henry Brock, who was described as "A Mountaineer of the New Type" when he wrote in the *Berea Quarterly:*

Kentucky is not a region of desperate deeds; it is not to be despaired of . . . It was this same region that gave birth to Abraham Lincoln. Better times will come again to Kentucky; do not let us drift in ignorance. We have boys and girls who could be Abraham Lincolns, and who are as brave as any in America. All they need is the training which your boys and girls have. The North will not forget us. The mountaineers stood by the Union in '61. We may be ignorant, but we are patriotic and love the flag.[34]

Fig. 11.2. Oliver O. Howard and William Goodell Frost at Berea College, Memorial Day, 1898. Photograph in Berea College Archives, RG 11, Berea, Ky. Reproduced courtesy of Berea College.

If "effacing sectional lines" was a goal touted prominently in Berea's publications, "fraternal feeling" was LMU's catch phrase. From the composition of the charter to the choosing of blue and gray as school colors, LMU was to be a monument to reunion and the sentiments associated with it. These ideas were prefigured in a *Harrow School Catalog for 1894–1895*. In providing an educational opportunity for the district, the school's founders promised, in language reminiscent of the Berea publications, that the school would act "in part to pay our country's debt to these Highlanders of the G.A.R. on slave soil."[35] Yet, for the founders of LMU, southerners and northerners were praised and honored equally. This evenhandedness contrasted with the Berea viewpoint, which emphasized that those "who once favored the Confederacy now feel glad that the Union was saved."[36] At LMU, the sanitorium building was converted to a residence hall and dubbed Grant-Lee Hall because, as Howard claimed, "We want them joining hands. The Confederate and Union men are in the same board, working actively and harmoniously together to build up the institution."[37] The LMU charter points out the intention of the institution "to promote good society and good citizenship and the ability to develop the abundant natural resources of the Southern States."[38] Catalogs called upon donors to "aid the worthy sons and daughters of those noble heroes who wore the blue and gray."[39] As late as 1915, LMU was holding exercises in celebration of Robert E. Lee's birthday, the speeches emphasizing Lee's character as an "American rather than as a soldier" and asserting that "growing esteem" for Lee in the North was similar to the "great love and esteem" for Lee in the South. The ceremonies fittingly ended with the singing of "Dixie."[40]

Fig. 11.3. Grant-Lee Hall, Lincoln Memorial University. Photograph in Southern Appalachians Photo Archives, Accession 70, Berea College, Berea, Ky. Reproduced courtesy of Berea College.

Also indicative of LMU's interest in "fraternal feeling" was the composition of LMU's board of directors. Of the seventeen members in 1897–98, six lived within easy reach of the university, while the others resided throughout the Northeast and Midwest. Notable among the locals was Capt. Robert F. Patterson, C.S.A., a native of Claiborne County, Tennessee. Cited twice during the war for "meritorious conduct" and "marked and distinguished gallantry," Patterson had been present at the surrender of Lee's Army of Northern Virginia at Appomattox. He then followed Lee to Washington College, studied law, and returned to his extensive landholdings near Cumberland Gap. Patterson was an early supporter of Myers's efforts at the Harrow School and was named a charter member of LMU's board in 1897. O. O. Howard's relationship with Patterson was cordial, and the two soldiers had a keen shared interest in reunion.[41] Dedicating a bust of Lincoln donated to LMU in 1908, Patterson accepted the Confederacy's defeat as part of "God's foreordained purposes" and extolled the virtues of Lincoln and Jefferson Davis, Lee and Ulysses Grant, Stonewall Jackson and O. O. Howard alike, consigning "their faults and mistakes to the deep grave of oblivion." Patterson concluded his remarks by observing, "I hope, my young friends, that you may see the glorious day, if I do not, when the last vestige of sectional strife and war prejudice will be swept from the hearts of the people, and that the statues of all our great men, both North and South, may be placed in every capital of every state in the Union."[42]

Patterson's remarks were by no means idiosyncratic. Frederick Avery, an Ohio-born Episcopal priest and former trustee of Berea College, who in 1935 was the last surviving member of the original LMU board, recalled a visit by Confederate Gen. John B. Gordon. Gordon was on his way to Knoxville to give a speech on "Pickett's Charge," and his train stopped en route at Cumberland Gap. Avery, Howard, and others from LMU met Gordon to exchange pleasantries. Avery described the scene for the *Middlesboro Daily News:* "Howard said, 'Gordon, we tried to whip you once,' and Gordon replied, 'Well, you succeeded mighty well, but we are now all under one flag, "Old Glory,"' and we all cheered as the General's train pulled out. I have often thought that this would make a fine epic picture of the North and South. He 'sailed into the fiery sunset, into the purple vapors, into the dusk of evening.' God be with you till we meet again."[43]

It would be unwise to regard the observations of Patterson and Avery as mere sentimentality. Indeed, both were representative of incidents or beliefs consistent with "forgetfulness," the phenomenon Nina Silber attributes to northern progressive attitudes that regarded the immediate needs of the southern people while overlooking past faults and mistakes.[44] The comments of Avery and Patterson, as well as LMU publicity literature, reveal the rhetoric of reunion, with its idea that education somehow would repay the debt owed by the nation to "loyal southerners" and erase the sectional feeling that had brought about the war in the first place. Patterson observed to O. O. Howard that Lincoln himself no doubt would approve of Howard's efforts to "educate the descendants of the old mountain soldiers who left their own state and stood by him [Lincoln] for the Union."[45] In the end, it was the linkage of mountain heroism with Abraham Lincoln that would remain the enduring image of Appalachia's Civil War.

Mountaineer Emancipator

In their efforts to educate mountain youth, both Berea College and LMU came to claim Abraham Lincoln as a central figure. For Berea, the Lincoln connections were based upon his Kentucky birth and his emancipation of the slaves, the freedmen, and their descendants, whom Berea educated until 1904. LMU's use of the Lincoln image was more direct; Lincoln's interest in East Tennessee and his "commissioning" of O. O. Howard to provide for these loyal people had led to the creation of LMU, which Howard and others regarded as a "living memorial" to Lincoln among "the people of his birth." At both schools, Abraham Lincoln symbolized the promise of the mountaineer, who, like Lincoln, "thirsted for education." The education of the Appalachian people would develop "real" Americans and perhaps new Lincolns in a period when uneasiness over immigration was growing and blacks were being displaced as "foreign" or, as historian Reid Mitchell has observed, "as, at best, only distant kin."[46]

Berea College had not been slow to connect Abraham Lincoln with the worthiness of southern mountaineers. As early as 1888, publicity literature noted that "no truer type of manhood can be found than is found in the mountains of Kentucky—the same region that gave birth to Abraham Lincoln."[47] William Goodell Frost trumpeted the Lincoln image in the *Berea Quarterly* and in speeches on behalf of the college. Mountaineers were "Abe Lincoln's kindred," having the "native capacity" of English and Scotch-Irish ancestry to make "their way to greater opportunities, as Lincoln and Stonewall Jackson."[48] By 1901, Frost and Berea College were articulating the institutional mission on the college's letterhead stationery: "In Lincoln's State for Lincoln's People," illustrated with Eastman Johnson's portrait of "The Boy Lincoln." In 1908 and 1909, a spate of articles appeared in the *Berea Quarterly* asserting that Lincoln was "sociologically, if not geographically, a mountain man."

The college, moreover, suggested that Lincoln would have been familiar with the pioneer conditions still extant in Appalachia, and connected the mountain people with Lincoln as those who "owned land but did not own slaves."[49] In Lincoln, and in southern mountaineers, Frost found "the purest Americans,"[50] a people who would change the South: "And has not Lincoln hallowed the log cabin? I can never pass one of those humble cabins in the mountains without thinking of the possible Lincoln that it holds, and renewing my resolution . . . to shed the light of education into every mountain home."[51]

Meanwhile, LMU was intent on being a "living" memorial and not a mere stone monument. Howard recalled the intensity of Lincoln's identification with the mountain people: "General, if you come out of this horror and misery alive, . . . I want you to do something for these mountain people who have been shut out of the world all these years. I know them. If I live I will do all I can to aid, and between us perhaps we can do the justice they deserve."[52]

Before justice could be done, however, money was needed. Howard plunged into the work of raising an endowment, using his old connections from the army and from his Freedmen's Bureau days. University publicity characterized the educational experience at LMU: "Just as Lincoln studied: so these boys in the mountain district are seeking the light and paying part of their tuition at LMU in farm products."[53] The mountaineers who were being assisted by LMU were labeled "real" Americans; donors could "show [their] love for Mr. Lincoln" by sending "a DOLLAR or more."[54] Lincoln himself was "the highest and truest" of the mountaineer "type," and supporters were asked, "How can his memory be more splendidly and fittingly perpetuated and honored than in providing for the uplift of the people in whose loins resides the purest germ of unadulterated Americanism?"[55]

The connections between Lincoln and the "pure American" mountaineer

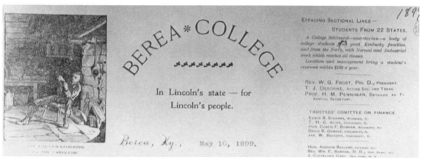

Fig. 11.4. Berea College Letterhead Stationery, 1899. Reproduced courtesy of Berea College Archives, RG 13, Berea, Ky.

reflected an emerging "Anglo-Saxonism" at the turn of the century. Northern observers, impressed with the patriotism, loyalty, and Scotch-Irish heritage of mountain "folk," donated heavily to both Berea and LMU. Administrators were not hesitant to use this racial appeal. Frost extolled mountaineers as "familiar"—like the great-grandfather who had fought in the Revolution. "Uncontaminated with slavery, they are not Catholics, nor aliens, nor infidels. They come of vigorous English and Scotch-Irish stock, and only need the touch of education to make them what the Scotch are to England."[56] Likewise, LMU, besides praising the "purest germ of unadulterated Americanism," found among the mountaineers "the truest, purest, unpolluted, type of pioneer American citizenship"[57] and proclaimed the inhabitants of Cumberland Gap as the "descendents of the Revolutionary fathers."[58]

The two schools jostled for funds in New York, Boston, and Philadelphia, applying to the same donors for support and warily eyeing each others' progress. William Frost saw LMU as a considerable threat to the progress of Berea. Writing to an associate in 1898, Frost said that he believed LMU would draw money away from both Berea and the American Missionary Association, ending "in a way that will bring discredit upon all benevolent educational work in the South."[59] Both Frost and William Barton wrote to O. O. Howard in an effort to weaken his support of LMU. Barton saw the issue as a division of educational efforts in a "sparsely settled region"; if LMU were a success, "it must be at the exclusion of colored students."[60] Frost regarded LMU as potentially "fatal," not because LMU would draw away funds but because "it would *rob us of our white students,* and leave Berea no longer a southern school practically illustrating the possibility of overthrowing caste."[61] Frost further bemoaned the prospect that "we [Berea] cannot compete with a school of northern methods and support which practically excludes the Negro."[62] Competition for the same donors reached such intensity that Howard attacked Frost's "ardent desire to raise his endowment and to have it thoroughly understood that all the wants of the mountain boys and girls can be attended to at Berea." The former general also scoffed at Frost's impression that LMU would "injure" Berea by drawing away mountain students. Concluding that "there is more than room enough for all," Howard regarded Frost as "utterly mistaken" in his concerns.[63]

Frost persisted, however, dashing off a general letter to the LMU trustees in 1900 airing his concern that LMU was so close to Berea that an "unseemly rivalry" might result and expressing the hope that LMU would operate only "South of the Cumberland Gap." He went on to declare that the former Berea College treasurer, Eugene P. Fairchild, at the time employed by LMU, was diverting funds and alienating donors from Berea, "causing more harm to us than good to you." Finally, Frost lectured LMU on its failure to recruit black students, asserting, "It is an essential part of the education of every white boy in the South that he should see colored people treated like men and women."[64] This last point is particularly ironic since, under Frost, Berea publicity literature had shifted away from discussing the college's interracial mission, and its black enrollment was declining.[65]

The matter ended, officially at least, with a signed communication from the LMU trustees, remonstrating that Frost's letter "has both surprised and grieved us." Flatly denying Fairchild's complicity in diverting funds from Berea, LMU noted him as "devoted, earnest and faithful." The trustees then avoided being drawn into any further controversy by declaring, "Shaping the policy and dictating the management of our institution are our responsibilities and we feel that they must remain with us."[66] The fundraising rivalry continued, however, and Frost remained convinced that LMU was nothing more than "a money making scheme of real estate men in [Cumberland Gap]" and "spite work" on the part of the turncoat E. P. Fairchild.[67] That both schools eventually were successful in reaching their financial goals seems to confirm Howard's observation that there was room enough for both.

For all the dispute over recruiting white mountaineers, Frost's observation concerning African-American students is significant. The appeals to the mountaineers' heritage and "pedigree" also reflected the declining status of support for African-American educational projects and the distancing of the Bereans and some white northerners from blacks in general. Even stout-hearted northern educational advocates such as A. D. Mayo lamented that "the 'Industrial Education of the Negro' is now about the only Educational spectacle the Boston mind recognizes looking southward."[68] Booker T. Washington criticized Frost for Berea's emphasis on mountaineer education at the expense of interracial education, while Mayo later despaired of the success of black education until "the white 'third estate' that now is in complete control can be educated into American christian [sic] ideas of their obligation and opportunity with respect thereto."[69] LMU did not recruit African-American students at all in its early years, instead focusing entirely on its mountain constituency.

Both institutions, then, to a certain extent reflected the retreat of northern leadership from racial concerns. They could benefit from northern philanthropy by shifting their emphases to respond to a redefined "southern problem"—the education of economically disadvantaged and isolated rural whites.[70] Ironically, the Lincoln legacy of emancipation became a metaphor for freedom from ignorance, rather than a tangible witness to a "new birth of freedom."

Stumbling in These Dark Hills

For Berea College and LMU, the "myth of Unionist Appalachia" was central to their depiction of southern mountaineers. Abraham Lincoln provided a personal embodiment of the qualities attributed to mountain people—loyalty, patriotism, bravery, plainness, and lack of opportunity. Mountaineers, moreover, represented the key to reuniting the sections of the nation divided by the Civil War. They embraced beliefs compatible with northern principles and institutions, while usefully offsetting the "foreignness" of blacks and immigrants. The way in which the Civil War was remembered through the heroic deeds of southern mountaineer loyalists created a monolithic interpretation of the region's experience of the war which only now is being scrutinized.

The Civil War was fought in dozens of coves and hillsides, the names have long since been forgotten. Berea College and LMU, however, at least reminded the generation after the Civil War that something important *had* happened in the mountains of Kentucky, Tennessee, North Carolina, the Virginias, and Georgia. The educational efforts of both schools represented both the victories and losses of educational reform in the South. The experiences of these institutions further represented the "road to reunion," by drawing northern money and leadership to southern schools and students. In the end, both Berea and LMU not only reflected the myths and realities of the Civil War, but also shaped the idea of the mountain war for generations to come.

Notes

The author wishes to thank Stephen Hague, formerly of the Abraham Lincoln Museum, and Wilma Patton of the University Library, Lincoln Memorial University, Harrogate, Tenn. (hereafter, LMU); and Susan Ravdin of the Bowdoin College Archives, Bowdoin College, Brunswick, Maine.

1. For further discussion of this topic, see Reid Mitchell, *Civil War Soldiers: Their Expectations and Their Experiences* (New York: Simon and Schuster, 1988) esp. 107ff. See also Reid Mitchell, *The Vacant Chair: The Northern Soldier Leaves Home* (New York: Oxford Univ. Press, 1993).

2. Henry Shapiro, *Appalachia on Our Mind: The Southern Mountains and Mountaineers in the American Consciousness, 1870–1920* (Chapel Hill: Univ. of North Carolina Press, 1978), 18; and Allen Batteau, *The Invention of Appalachia* (Tucson: Univ. of Arizona Press, 1990), 57–58.

3. Batteau, *Invention of Appalachia*, 77–78.

4. Shapiro, *Appalachia on Our Mind*, 16.

5. Berea's founding and early years are discussed in Elisabeth Peck and Emily

Ann Smith, *Berea's First 125 Years* (Lexington: Univ. Press of Kentucky, 1980); Richard Sears, *The Day of Small Things: Abolitionism in the Midst of Slavery, Berea, Kentucky, 1854–1864* (Lanham, Md.: Univ. Press of America, 1986); and James M. McPherson, *The Abolitionist Legacy* (Princeton, N.J.: Princeton Univ. Press, 1975). The shifting of the college's focus and the Day Law crisis are discussed in detail in Jacqueline G. Burnside, "Philanthropists and Politicians: A Sociological Profile of Berea College, 1855–1905" (Ph.D. diss., Yale Univ., 1988); and Paul David Nelson, "Experiment in Interracial Education at Berea College," *Journal of Negro History* 59 (1974): 13–27. Images of blacks and mountaineers at Berea also are traced in James C. Klotter, "The Black South and White Appalachia," *Journal of American History* 66 (1980): 832–49; and Shannon H. Wilson, "Window on the Mountains: Berea's Appalachia, 1870–1930," *Filson Club History Quarterly* 64 (July 1990): 384–400.

6. O. O. Howard, *Autobiography of Oliver Otis Howard, Major-General, United States Army* (New York: Baker and Taylor, 1907), 1:452–53.

7. "Charter of Incorporation, LMU," *Mountain Herald* 4 (May 1903): 17. Narratives of the founding of LMU can be found in Howard, *Autobiography*, 2:568–69; Robert L. Kincaid, *The Wilderness Road* (Indianapolis: Bobbs-Merrill, 1947), 339–46 ; John A. Carpenter, *Sword and Olive Branch: Oliver Otis Howard* (Pittsburgh: Univ. of Pittsburgh Press, 1964), 293–98.

8. *First Catalog of Officers and Students of Berea College for 1866–1867* (Cincinnati, Ohio: Gazette Steam Printing, 1867), 21.

9. Howard, *Autobiography*, 568. While it is unclear why Howard ended his connection with Berea, his role at the college may have ended with the closing of the Freedmen's Bureau. William G. Frost describes Howard as having "ceased to feel a personal responsibility or practical interest in the school." Frost to O. O. Howard, Dec. 29, 1896. O. O. Howard Papers, Bowdoin College Library, Bowdoin College, Brunswick, Maine.

10. "Lincoln Memorial University: Cumberland Gap, Tenn.," Appalachian Vertical Files, in Southern Appalachian Archives (hereafter, SAA), Berea College, Berea, Ky.

11. "Berea College" (ca. 1869), Office of Information Records, Berea College Archives, Berea, Ky. (hereafter, OIR-BCA).

12. "Berea College, Kentucky" (ca. 1870), OIR-BCA.

13. Charles Fairchild, "Address of C. G. Fairchild," *American Missionary* 36 (1883): 393. See Kenneth W. Noe, "Toward a Myth of Unionist Appalachia, 1865–1883," *Journal of the Appalachian Studies Association* 6 (1994): 73–80.

14. "Berea College, Kentucky, 1858–1861; 1865–1888," OIR-BCA.

15. A. D. Mayo, "The Other Folk of Kentucky," in "Berea College: A Brief History of Its Origin and Progress" (1882), OIR-BCA.

16. Nina Silber, *The Romance of Reunion: Northerners and the South, 1865–1900* (Chapel Hill: Univ. of North Carolina Press, 1993), 124–58. See John Higham, *Strangers in the Land: Patterns of American Nativism, 1860–1925* (New York: Atheneum, 1969), 19–23.

17. "Berea College: A Brief History of Its Origin and Progress," OIR-BCA.

18. *Harrow School Catalogue, 1893–94* (Middlesboro, Tenn.: News Printing Company, 1893), n.d.; and *Harrow School Catalogue, 1894–95* (Leominster, Mass.: Enterprise Print, 1894), in Univ. Archives, Lincoln Memorial Univ., Harrogate, Tenn. (hereafter, UA-LMU).

19. "Lincoln University," *New York Tribune,* Dec. 1, 1899. Clipping in Appalachian Vertical File, LMU, in SAA.

20. Ibid.

21. *LMU Catalogue, 1898–99* (N.p.: Faith and Works Print, n.d.), 5, in UA-LMU.

22. Paul H. Buck, *The Road to Reunion, 1865–1900* (New York: Vintage, 1959), vii–viii.

23. The relationship between historical memory and the Civil War is discussed in Silber, *Romance of Reunion,* 3–4, 61–63, 96, 99, 156–58; 163–66. See also Thomas Connelly and Barbara L. Bellows, *God and General Longstreet : The Lost Cause and the Southern Mind* (Baton Rouge: Louisiana State Univ. Press, 1982).

24. William G. Frost, "Berea College," *Berea Quarterly* 1 (May 1895): 24.

25. Shapiro, *Appalachia on Our Minds,* 124–25; Buck, *Road to Reunion,* 166–75.

26. William G. Frost to "Dear Brethren," July 16, 1892. William Goodell Frost Papers, Berea College Archives (hereafter, BCA), Berea College, Berea, Ky.

27. Ibid.

28. Reid Mitchell, *Civil War Soldiers,* 107.

29. Frost, "Berea College," 72.

30. Ibid.

31. "Work that Wins" (1896), OIR-BCA.

32. J. D. Cox, "The Mountain People in the Struggle of the Union," *Berea Quarterly* 1 (Nov. 1895): 7–8. Cox wrote in a letter of reference for Frost, "They (the people of Appalachia) are poor, shut out from ordinary means of liberal education, they are an important element in the southern population, their improvement is necessary to make the country in that region what it ought to be." J. D. Cox, Dec. 3, 1898, in Frost Papers, BCA.

33. William E. Barton, *A Hero in Homespun,* was reviewed in *Berea Quarterly* 2 (Nov. 1897): 22–26. The Nov. 1897 issue was devoted to "Southern Life in Fiction." See William E. Barton, "Old Plantation Hymns," *Berea Quarterly* 4 (Feb. 1899): 3–16; William E. Barton, "Hymns of the Slave and the Freedman," *Berea Quarterly* 4 (May 1899): 17–32; Thomas Wentworth Higginson, "John G. Fee: A Southern Abolitionist," *Berea Quarterly* 4 (Feb. 1900): 18–21. Barton's career as a Lincoln scholar is traced in Merrill Peterson, *Lincoln in American Memory* (New York: Oxford Univ. Press, 1994).

34. Henry Brock, "A Mountaineer of the New Type," *Berea Quarterly* 8 (Nov. 1903): 25.

35. *Harrow School Catalogue, 1894–95* (n.p.), UA-LMU.

36. "People's Institutes, Extension Department of Berea College," in *Bulletin of Berea College,* Aug. 1908, 13; in BCA.

37. O. O. Howard, "The Folk of the Cumberland Gap," *Munsey's Magazine* 27 (July 1902): 508.

38. "Charter of Incorporation," *Mountain Herald* 4 (May 1903): 17.

39. *Catalogue of LMU, 1905–1906*, 35, in UA-LMU.

40. "Robert E. Lee's Birthday," *Mountain Herald* 18 (Jan. 1915): 12.

41. U.S. Dept. of War, *The War of the Rebellion: A Compilation of the Official Records of the Union and Confederate Armies* (Washington, D.C.: U.S. Government Printing Office, 1880–1901; hereafter cited as *OR*), ser. 1, vol. 17, pt. 1, p. 678; and ser. 1, vol. 24, pt. 2, p. 100. "A Tribute to Colonel Robert F. Patterson," *Mountain Herald* 18 (May 1915): 7–10.

42. "Capt. Patterson's Address, Feb. 12, 1908," *Lincoln Herald* 57 (Fall 1955): 24.

43. F. B. Avery, "Concerning Mr. Fairchild and LMU," *Middlesboro (Ky.) Daily News*, July 30, 1935. Clipping in Appalachian Vertical Files in SAA.

44. Silber, *Romance of Reunion*, 62–63.

45. Quoted in Robert L. Kincaid, *The Lincoln Heritage in the Cumberlands* (Los Angeles: Lincoln Fellowship of Southern California, 1951), 15.

46. Reid Mitchell, *Vacant Chair*, 133.

47. "Berea College, Kentucky, 1858–1861, 1865–1888," OIR-BCA.

48. "Abe Lincoln's Kindred" (1896), OIR-BCA. This item contains a quotation from George Washington Cable: "In many ways, Berea is doing the most important work in the South." Also see "A Discovery" (1903), OIR-BCA.

49. "The Boy Lincoln," *Berea Quarterly* 12 (Apr. 1908): 1. See also "Lincoln a 'Mountain White,'" *Berea Quarterly* 12 (Jan. 1909): 5–8. Klotter, "Black South," 845–46.

50. "Lincoln's Kin, and Ours," *Berea Quarterly* 19 (Apr. 1916): back cover.

51. "Address of President Frost," *Berea Quarterly* 15 (Apr. 1911): 20.

52. Quoted in Kincaid, *Wilderness Road*, 342.

53. *New York Herald*, Sept. 12, 1909. "Just as Lincoln Studied" Clipping in O. O. Howard files, UA-LMU. The curriculum based on "Lincoln principles" is discussed in Peterson, *Lincoln in American Memory*, 197–98; 388.

54. "Will You Help Me?" LMU Endowment Association postcard (1909), Oliver Otis Howard Papers, Abraham Lincoln Museum, LMU.

55. Commendation by U.S. Sen. Robert L. Taylor, in *Catalog of LMU, 1908–1909*, 68; in UA-LMU. John A. Carpenter, *Sword and Olive Branch*, 295–98, traces Howard's LMU fundraising projects.

56. William G. Frost, "New England in Kentucky," *Advance* 29 (June 6, 1895): 1285. On Anglo-Saxonism, see Silber, *Romance of Reunion*, 136–37 and 142–49; Higham, *Strangers in the Land*, 32–34; and David Whisnant, *All That Is Native and Fine: The Politics of Culture in an American Region* (Chapel Hill: Univ. of North Carolina Press, 1983), 91–92 and 237–42. Drew Gilpin Faust, *The Creation of Confederate Nationalism: Ideology and Identity in the Civil War South* (Baton Rouge: Louisiana State Univ. Press, 1988), 10–11, notes the sectional contrast between "Saxon" northerners and "Norman" southerners.

57. Taylor, in *Catalog of LMU, 1908–1909*, 68.

58. "Living Tribute to Lincoln" (1908), O. O. Howard Papers, Abraham Lincoln Museum, LMU.

59. William G. Frost to "Brother Field," Jan. 18, 1898, Frost Papers, BCA.

60. William E. Barton to O. O. Howard, Mar. 13, 1897, Howard Papers, Bowdoin College. Despite the disagreement, Howard endorsed Barton's *A Hero in Homespun* later the same year. Barton to Howard, Nov. 13, 1897. Howard Papers, Bowdoin College.

61. William G. Frost to O. O. Howard, Feb. 4, 1897. Howard Papers, Bowdoin College. The emphasis is Frost's.

62. Ibid.

63. O. O. Howard to Charles Eager, Oct. 6, 1899. O. O. Howard Papers, Abraham Lincoln Museum, LMU.

64. William G. Frost to O. O. Howard, May 5, 1900. Frost Papers, BCA.

65. Wilson, "Window on the Mountains," 387–89; Burnside, "Philanthropists and Politicians," 170–74.

66. Board of Trustees, LMU to Board of Trustees, Berea College, May 15, 1900, in Frost Papers, BCA. Charles Eager observed later, "I hear that our letter to the members of their board had a good effect." Charles F. Eager to O. O. Howard, June 14, 1900, in Howard Papers, Bowdoin College.

67. William G. Frost to R. A. Beard, Apr. 13, 1906, in Frost Papers, BCA.

68. A. D. Mayo to William Frost, Dec. 3, 1896, in Frost Papers, BCA.

69. Booker T. Washington to William Frost, Feb. 12, 1903; A. D. Mayo to William Frost, Mar. 7, 1904; both in Frost Papers, BCA. Washington objected particularly to Frost's statement, "If we can make the mountain white right, he will make the South right."

70. Silber, *Romance of Reunion*, 141–47; Shapiro, *Appalachia on Our Mind*, 122–26.

Suggestions for Further Reading

Books

Bailey, Fred Arthur. *Class and Tennessee's Confederate Generation.* Chapel Hill: Univ. of North Carolina Press, 1987.

Carpenter, John A. *Sword and Oliver Branch: Oliver Otis Howard.* Pittsburgh, Pa.: Univ. of Pittsburgh Press, 1964.

Castel, Albert. *Decision in the West: The Atlanta Campaign of 1864.* Lawrence: Univ. Press of Kansas, 1992.

Clark, Willene B., ed. *Valleys of the Shadow: The Memoir of Confederate Captain Reuben G. Clark.* Knoxville: Univ. of Tennessee Press, 1994.

Cozzens, Peter. *The Shipwreck of Their Hopes: The Battles for Chattanooga.* Urbana: Univ. of Illinois Press, 1994.

———. *This Terrible Sound: The Battle of Chickamauga.* Urbana: Univ. of Illinois Press, 1992.

Crofts, Daniel W. *Reluctant Confederates: Upper South Unionists in the Secession Crisis.* Chapel Hill: Univ. of North Carolina Press, 1989.

Current, Richard Nelson. *Lincoln's Loyalists: Union Soldiers from the Confederacy.* Boston: Northeastern Univ. Press, 1992.

Curry, Richard O. *A House Divided: A Study of Statehood Politics and the Copperhead Movement in West Virginia.* Pittsburgh, Pa.: Univ. of Pittsburgh Press, 1964.

Davis, William C. *The Battle of New Market.* Garden City, N.J.: Doubleday, 1975.

Dew, Charles B. *Bond of Iron: Master and Slave at Buffalo Forge.* New York: Norton, 1994.

Dunn, Durwood. *Cades Cove: The Life and Death of a Southern Mountain Community, 1818–1937.* Knoxville: Univ. of Tennessee Press, 1988.

Eller, Ronald D. *Miners, Millhands, and Mountaineers: Industrialization of the Appalachian South, 1880–1930.* Knoxville: Univ. of Tennessee Press, 1982.

Godbold, E. Stanley, Jr., and Mattie U. Russell. *Confederate Colonel and Cherokee Chief: The Life of William Holland Thomas.* Knoxville: Univ. of Tennessee Press, 1990.

Inscoe, John C. *Mountain Masters: Slavery and the Sectional Crisis in Western North Carolina.* Knoxville: Univ. of Tennessee Press, 1989.

Lucas, Marion B. *A History of Blacks in Kentucky: From Slavery to Segregation, 1790–1891.* Frankfort: Kentucky Historical Society, 1992.

Marvel, William. *Southwest Virginia in the Civil War: The Battles for Saltville.* Lynchburg, Va.: H. E. Howard, 1992.

McKenzie, Robert Tracy. *One South or Many? Plantation Belt and Upcountry in Civil War–Era Tennessee.* New York: Cambridge Univ. Press, 1994.

McKinney, Gordon B. *Southern Mountain Republicans, 1865–1900: Politics and the Appalachian Community.* Chapel Hill: Univ. of North Carolina Press, 1978.

McManus, Howard Rollins. *The Battle for Cloyd's Mountain: The Virginia and Tennessee Railroad Raid, April 29–May 19, 1864.* Lynchburg, Va.: H. E. Howard, 1989.

Moore, George Ellis. *A Banner in the Hills: West Virginia's Statehood.* New York: Appleton-Century-Crofts, 1963.

Noe, Kenneth W. *Southwest Virginia's Railroad: Modernization and the Sectional Crisis.* Urbana: Univ. of Illinois Press, 1994.

Paludan, Phillip Shaw. *Victims: A True Story of the Civil War.* Knoxville: Univ. of Tennessee Press, 1981.

Peck, Elisabeth, and Emily Ann Smith. *Berea's First One Hundred and Twenty-Five Years.* Lexington: Univ. of Kentucky Press, 1980.

Pudup, Mary Beth, Dwight Billings, and Altina L. Waller, eds. *Appalachia in the Making: The Mountain South in the Nineteenth Century.* Chapel Hill: Univ. of North Carolina Press, 1995.

Salstrom. Paul. *Appalachia's Path to Dependency: Rethinking a Region's Economic History, 1730–1940.* Lexington: Univ. Press of Kentucky, 1994.

Sears, Richard D. *The Day of Small Things: Abolitionism in the Midst of Slavery, Berea, Kentucky, 1854–1864.* Lanham, Md.: Univ. Press of America, 1986.

Seymour, Digby Gordon. *Divided Loyalties: Fort Sanders and the Civil War in East Tennessee.* Knoxville: Univ. of Tennessee Press, 1963.

Silber, Nina. *The Romance of Reunion: Northerners and the South, 1865–1900.* Chapel Hill: Univ. of North Carolina Press, 1993.

Stackpole, Edward J. *Sheridan in the Shenandoah: Jubal Early's Nemesis.* Harrisburg, Pa.: Stackpole, 1961.

Stealey, John E., III. *The Antebellum Kanawha Salt Business and Western Markets.* Lexington: Univ. Press of Kentucky, 1993.

Tanner, Robert G. *Stonewall in the Valley: Thomas J. "Stonewall" Jackson's Shenandoah Valley Campaign, Spring 1862.* Garden City, N.J.: Doubleday, 1976.

Vandiver, Frank. *Jubal's Raid: General Early's Famous Attack on Washington in 1864.* New York: McGraw-Hill, 1960.

Waller, Altina L. *Feud: Hatfields, McCoys, and Social Change in Appalachia, 1860–1900.* Chapel Hill: Univ. of North Carolina Press, 1988.

Articles

Auman, William T., and David D. Scarboro. "The Heroes of America in Civil War North Carolina." *North Carolina Historical Review* 58 (Oct. 1981): 327–63.

———. "Neighbor Against Neighbor: The Inner Civil War in the Randolph County Area of Confederate North Carolina." *North Carolina Historical Review* 61 (Jan. 1984): 59–92.

Bates, Walter Lynn. "Southern Unionists: A Socio-Economic Examination of the Third East Tennessee Volunteer Infantry Regiment, U.S.A., 1862–1865." *Tennessee Historical Quarterly* 50 (Winter 1991): 226–39.

Bryan, Charles Faulkner, Jr. "'Tories' Amidst Rebels: Confederate Occupation of East Tennessee, 1861–1863." *East Tennessee Historical Society's Publications* 60 (1988): 3–22.

Burt, Jesse. "East Tennessee, Lincoln, and Sherman." Part 1, *East Tennessee Historical Society's Publications* 34 (1962): 3–25. Part 2, *East Tennessee Historical Society's Publications* 35 (1963): 54–75.

Campbell, James B. "East Tennessee during Federal Occupation, 1863–1865." *East Tennessee Historical Society's Publications* 19 (1947): 65–80.

Crawford, Martin. "Confederate Volunteering and Enlistment in Ashe County, North Carolina." *Civil War History* 37 (Mar. 1991): 29–50.

———. "Political Society in a Southern Mountain Community: Ashe County, North Carolina, 1850–1861." *Journal of Southern History* 55 (Aug. 1989): 373–90.

Drake, Richard B. "Slavery and Antislavery in Appalachia." *Appalachian Heritage* 14 (Winter 1986): 25–33.

Fink, Harold S. "The East Tennessee Campaign and the Battle of Knoxville in 1863." *East Tennessee Historical Society's Publications* 29 (1957): 79–117.

Harris, William C. "The East Tennessee Relief Movement of 1864–1865." *Tennessee Historical Quarterly* 48 (1989): 86–96.

Hesseltine, William B. "The Underground Railroad from Confederate Prisons to East Tennessee." *East Tennessee Historical Society's Publications* 2 (1930): 55–69.

Inscoe, John C. "Coping in Confederate Appalachia: Portrait of a Mountain Woman and Her Community at War." *North Carolina Historical Review* 69 (Oct. 1992): 388–413.

———. "Mountain Unionism, Secession, and Regional Self-Image: The Contrasting Cases of Western North Carolina and East Tennessee." In *Looking South: Chapters in the Story of an American Region.* Edited by Winfred B. Moore, Jr., and Joseph F. Tripp, 115–32. Westport, Conn.: Greenwood, 1989.

———. "Thomas Clingman, Mountain Whiggery, and the Southern Cause." *Civil War History* 33 (Mar. 1987): 42–62.

Klotter, James C. "The Black South and White Appalachia." *Journal of American History* 66 (1980): 832–49.

Madden, David. "Unionist Resistance to Confederate Occupation: the Bridge Burners of East Tennessee." *East Tennessee Historical Society's Publications* 52–53 (1980–81): 22–39.

Mann, Ralph. "Family Group, Family Migration, and the Civil War in the Sandy Basin of Virginia." *Appalachian Journal* 19 (Summer 1992): 374–93.

———. "Guerrilla Warfare and Gender Roles: Sandy Basin, Virginia, as a Test Case." *Journal of the Appalachian Studies Association* 5 (1993): 59–66.

Martin, James B. "Black Flag Over the Bluegrass: Guerrilla Warfare in Kentucky, 1863–1865." *Register of the Kentucky Historical Society* 86 (Autumn 1986): 352–75.

McKinney, Gordon B. "Women's Role in Civil War Western North Carolina." *North Carolina Historical Review* 69 (Jan. 1992): 37–56.

Murphy, James B. "Slavery and Freedom in Appalachia: Kentucky as a Demographic Case Study." *Register of the Kentucky Historical Society* 80 (Spring 1992): 151–69.

Nelson, Paul David. "Experiment in Interracial Education at Berea College." *Journal of Negro History* 59 (1974): 13–27.

Noe, Kenneth W. "'Appalachia's' Civil War Genesis: Southwest Virginia as Depicted by Northern and European Writers, 1825–1865." *West Virginia History* 50 (1991): 91–108.

———. "Red String Scare: Civil War Southwest Virginia and the Heroes of America." *North Carolina Historical Review* 69 (July 1992): 301–22.

———. "Toward the Myth of Unionist Appalachia, 1865–1883." *Journal of the Appalachian Studies Association* 6 (1994): 73–80.

Richardson, Hila Appleton. "Raleigh County, West Virginia, in the Civil War." *West Virginia History* 10 (Apr. 1949): 213–98.

Sarris, Jonathan D. "Anatomy of an Atrocity: The Madden Branch Massacre and Guerrilla Warfare in North Georgia, 1861–1865." *Georgia Historical Quarterly* 77 (Winter 1993): 679–710.

Shanks, Henry T. "Disloyalty to the Confederacy in Southwestern Virginia, 1861–1865." *North Carolina Historical Review* 21 (Apr. 1944): 118–35.

Sprague, Stuart Seely. "From Slavery to Freedom: African Americans in Eastern Kentucky, 1860–1884." *Journal of the Appalachian Studies Association* 5 (1993): 67–74.

———. "Slavery's Death Knell: Mourners and Revelers." *Filson Club History Quarterly* 65 (Oct. 1991): 441–73.

Tolbert, Noble J. "Daniel Worth: Tar-Heel Abolitionist." *North Carolina Historical Review* 39 (July 1962): 284–304.

Wallenstein, Peter. "South vs. South." *Now and Then: The Appalachian Magazine* 10 (Summer 1993): 5–7.

———. "Which Side Are You On? The Social Origins of White Union Troops from Civil War Tennessee." *Journal of East Tennessee History* 63 (1991): 72–103.

Wilson, Shannon H. "Window on the Mountains: Berea's Appalachia, 1870–1930." *Filson Club History Quarterly* 64 (July 1990): 384–400.

Woodson, Carter G. "Slavery and Freedom in Appalachian America." *Journal of Negro History* 1 (Apr. 1916): 132–50.

Dissertations and Theses

Bryan, Charles Faulkner, Jr. "The Civil War in East Tennessee: A Social, Political, and Economic Study." Ph.D. diss., Univ. of Tennessee, Knoxville, 1978.

Burnside, Jacqueline G. "Philanthropists and Politicians: A Sociological Profile of Berea College, 1855–1905." Ph.D. diss., Yale Univ., 1988.

Fisher, Noel C. "'War at Every Man's Door': The Struggle for East Tennessee, 1860–1869." Ph.D. diss., Ohio State Univ., 1993.

Groce, W. Todd. "Mountain Rebels: East Tennessee Confederates and the Civil War." Ph.D. diss., Univ. of Tennessee, Knoxville, 1993.

Hsiung, David C. "Isolation and Integration in Upper East Tennessee, 1780–1960: The Historical Origins of Appalachian Characterizations." Ph.D. diss., Univ. of Michigan, Ann Arbor, 1991.

McGehee, C. Stuart. "Wake of the Flood: A Southern City in the Civil War: Chattanooga, 1838–1878." Ph.D. diss., Univ. of Virginia, 1985.

Contributors

MARTIN CRAWFORD is reader in American history at Keele University, Staffordshire, England. He is author of *The Anglo-American Crisis of the Nineteenth Century* and the forthcoming *Passages of War: Ashe County, North Carolina, from the 1850s to the 1870s,* as well as many articles. He edited *William Howard Russell's Civil War: Private Diary and Letters, 1861–1862.*

JAN FURMAN is associate professor of English at the University of Michigan, Flint. She is the author of *Toni Morrison's Fiction,* as well as several articles on African-American literature. She also is editor of a forthcoming edition of John McCline's memoirs.

W. TODD GROCE is executive director of the Georgia Historical Society and the author of several articles and papers on Civil War East Tennessee. He currently is writing a history of East Tennessee Confederates, to be called *Mountain Rebels: East Tennessee Confederates and the Civil War, 1860–1870.*

JOHN C. INSCOE is associate professor of history at the University of Georgia and editor of the *Georgia Historical Quarterly.* He is the author of several books and articles, among them the award-winning *Mountain Masters: Slavery and the Sectional Crisis in Western North Carolina.* With John

David Smith, he coedited *Ulrich Bonnell Phillips: A Southern Historian and His Critics*. He currently is co-authoring with Gordon McKinney a book on the Civil War in western North Carolina.

RALPH MANN is associate professor of history at the University of Colorado. He is the author of *After the Gold Rush: Society in Grass Valley and Nevada City, California, 1849–1870*, as well as many articles. His current research involves the Civil War in Appalachian Virginia.

ROBERT TRACY MCKENZIE is associate professor of history at the University of Washington. A specialist on nineteenth-century southern history, he is the author of several articles, as well as *One South or Many? Plantation Belt and Upcountry in Civil War–Era Tennessee*.

GORDON B. MCKINNEY is director of the Appalachian Center, Berea College. In addition to many articles, he is author of *Southern Mountain Republicans, 1865–1900: Politics and the Appalachian Community*. Currently he is researching both Civil War North Carolina and the life of reform politician Henry W. Blair.

KENNETH W. NOE is associate professor of history at the State University of West Georgia. He is the author of *Southwest Virginia's Railroad: Modernization and the Sectional Crisis*, as well as editor of *A Southern Boy in Blue: The Civil War Memoir of Marcus Woodcock, 9th Kentucky Infantry (U.S.A.)*. His current research involves the Battle of Perryville.

JONATHAN D. SARRIS is a doctoral student at the University of Georgia. He is most recently the author of "Anatomy of an Atrocity: The Madden Branch Massacre and the Civil War in North Georgia," which appeared in the *Georgia Historical Quarterly*.

PETER WALLENSTEIN, associate professor of history at Virginia Polytechnic Institute and State University, is author of *From Slave South to New South: Public Policy in Nineteenth-Century Georgia* and many essays.

SHANNON H. WILSON is the archivist of Berea College and most recently the author of an article on the evolution of Berea's image during the nineteenth century. His current research centers around Civil War veterans' organizations in eastern Kentucky.

Index

Acuff, Joel A., 19
African-Americans, as allies of escaped
  Union prisoners, 165–66; and Appalachia, xxv, 165; attitudes of escaped
  prisoners, 168–70; at Berea College, 245,
  251; described in prison narratives, xxv,
  165–71; displacement from philanthropic interests, 256, 259; employment
  at Asheville Armory, xxvii, 232;
  exclusion by Lincoln Memorial
  University, 258, 259; historiography,
  xxv–xxvi; and influence of prison
  narratives, 171; intolerance, 177;
  narratives, 187–98; needs of linked with
  mountain people, 248, 249; in North
  Carolina, 167, 168, 170; as slaves, 1, 167–
  68; as soldiers, 3, 15, 192–93; in South
  Carolina, 166; in Virginia, 170
Alexander, Charles McClung, 42
Alexander, Jacob, 37
Allegheny County, N.C., 57
American Missionary Association, 243, 248,
  258; and support of Berea College, 245
Anderson, Archer, 91

Anderson, Jeff, 140
Andrews, Ebenezer B., 116, 120
Anglo-Saxonism, 248, 258; and Berea
  College, 258; and Lincoln Memorial
  University, 258
Antietam, battle of, xiv, xxi
Appalachia, and African-Americans, xxv,
  165; and Civil War, xi, 158, 252;
  contribution to Confederate defeat, 18,
  20, 21n3; contrast with Deep South, 20;
  definition, xi, xxviii n1; as depicted by
  Berea College, 244; as depicted by
  Lincoln Memorial University, 244; as
  depicted by local colorists, 158; as
  depicted by philanthropic interests, 179;
  as depicted in documentary literature,
  158; as depicted in travel accounts, 158;
  "Holy Appalachia," 179, 243; industrialization, xxvi, 237; interpretation of, xiv–
  xv; xii–xiii (map); military campaigns, xiv,
  xxi, xxii–xxiii; "myth of Savage
  Appalachia," xiv, xxv; "myth of Unionist
  Appalachia," xiv, xvi, xxv, 260; and "new
  social history," xvi; "otherness," 243; as

The Civil War in Appalachia was designed and typeset on a Macintosh computer system using PageMaker software. The text and titles are set in StempelGaramond. This book was designed and composed by Sheila Hart and was printed and bound by Thomson-Shore, Inc. The recycled paper used in this book is designed for an effective life of at least three hundred years.